Praise for *Winn*

"*Winning on Appeal* is a resource that every professor and practitioner of appellate advocacy should keep within arm's reach. What makes this book so important is that it covers not only the mechanics of appeals—the *what* and the *how*—but also the theory and psychology of persuasion—the *why* of successful arguments. This third edition brings new insights and advice from appellate lawyers and judges, including a foreword by Supreme Court Justice Samuel A. Alito, on each aspect of appellate practice, from choosing the issues to making the oral arguments. I use this book constantly in my teaching and in my practice, and I consider it required reading for all appellate advocates."

Julie A. Baker
Professor of Legal Skills
University of Massachusetts School of Law
Appeals and Post-Conviction Panel Attorney
Committee for Public Counsel Services

"Judge Aldisert's classic *Winning on Appeal* has received the update that it needed and deserved. It's the rare practice guide that offers something of tremendous value to all, regardless of your level of experience and sophistication. Reflecting on my own career of more than twenty-five years as an appellate advocate, this is one of the few books that has enabled me again and again to hone my appellate brief-writing and oral advocacy skills. It was indispensable then and continues to be indispensable now."

Howard J. Bashman
Law Offices of Howard J. Bashman
Author, "How Appealing" blog

"Professor Dysart and Judge Southwick have taken what was already the gold standard in appellate advocacy treatises and given it a long-awaited and much-needed update. They have stayed true to Judge Aldisert's perfect formula of mixing practical skills instruction with reflections and tips from appellate judges and practitioners, but they have breathed new life into his work. As practice moves into the smartphone age, Professor Dysart and Judge Southwick have given appellate lawyers an elegantly designed set of tools to craft better briefs and arguments. There is no better guide to appellate advocacy than this one. An absolute must-have."

Jeffrey C. Brooks
Preis PLC Director of Advocacy and Professional Practice
Assistant Professor of Professional Practice
Louisiana State University Paul M. Herbert Law Center

"*Winning on Appeal* is an incredible resource for litigators and law students wishing to become excellent appellate advocates. Presenting the material from the perspective of the intended audience is brilliant, and I have found the instruction to be true in my years as an appellate advocate and as an appellate court attorney. Like Tessa Dysart, I have taught from the previous editions of *Winning on Appeal*, and I agree that much of the advice is timeless. As the practice has evolved, however, an update needed to be made, and Judge Leslie Southwick and Professor Dysart have honored Judge Aldisert's legacy with this latest revision. This edition of *Winning on Appeal* maintains its timelessness in providing concrete steps to writing a brief and presenting an oral argument that is persuasive to appellate judges and their law clerks, and creates a fresh perspective taking into account the current technological climate. *Winning on Appeal* is a must-read for anyone engaged in or considering a career in appellate advocacy."

Jennifer R. Franklin
Professor of the Practice
William & Mary Law School

"*Winning on Appeal* has always been my classic go-to book on how to write and argue, but this new edition really brings it into the modern era. It combines the time-tested wisdom of the original with the latest research on persuasion, and also addresses the effect of the increasingly electronic appellate environment on brief writing and arguments. New attorneys looking to improve their skills and experienced attorneys looking to refresh their own will both benefit from this book."

Jeffrey D. Jackson
Director of the Center for Excellence in Advocacy
Washburn University School of Law

"*Winning on Appeal* parallels what Judge Aldisert asks of the competent appellate practitioner: conciseness, persuasion, and compelling legal rationale. Insights from appellate law clerks, seasoned appellate lawyers, and appellate judges provide practical guidance. The checklists and bullet points are evaluative tools for both the oral argument and the appellate brief. *Winning on Appeal* is a mandatory reference for both the untested and skilled appellate lawyer. From a trial judge's perspective, *Winning on Appeal* also provides powerful instruction for successful motion practice."

Judge William G. Meyer
Denver District Court (ret.)
Judicial Arbiter Group

WINNING ON APPEAL

Better Briefs and Oral Argument

THIRD EDITION

WINNING ON APPEAL

Better Briefs and Oral Argument

THIRD EDITION

Tessa L. Dysart

Assistant Director of Legal Writing
Associate Clinical Professor of Law
The University of Arizona
James E. Rogers College of Law

Hon. Leslie H. Southwick

United States Circuit Judge
United States Court of Appeals
for the Fifth Circuit

FOREWORD BY
Justice Samuel A. Alito, Jr.

Associate Justice
Supreme Court of the United States

PREVIOUS EDITIONS BY
Hon. Ruggero J. Aldisert

Senior United States Circuit Judge
United States Court of Appeals
for the Third Circuit

NATIONAL INSTITUTE FOR TRIAL ADVOCACY

Address inquiries to:

Reprint Permission
National Institute for Trial Advocacy
1685 38th Street, Suite 200
Boulder, CO 80301-2735
Phone: (800) 225-6482
Fax: (720) 890-7069
Email: permissions@nita.org

ISBN 978-1-60156-724-6
eISBN 978-1-60156-725-3
FBA 1724

Library of Congress Cataloging-in-Publication Data

Dysart, Tessa L. author. | Southwick, Leslie H., 1950- author.

Winning on appeal: better briefs and oral argument / Tessa L. Dysart, Assistant Director of Legal Writing, Associate Clinical Professor of Law, The University of Arizona, James E. Rogers College of Law; Hon. Leslie H. Southwick, United States Circuit Judge, United States Court of Appeals for the Fifth Circuit.

Third edition. | Boulder, CO: National Institute for Trial Advocacy, [2017] | Series: NITA practical guide series | Includes bibliographical references and index.

LCCN 2017029071| ISBN 9781601567246 | ISBN 9781601567253 (eISBN)

LCSH: Appellate procedure—United States. | Legal briefs—United States. | Trial practice—United States. | Forensic oratory.

LCC KF9050.A935 2017 | DDC 347.73/8--dc23 LC record available at https://lccn.loc.gov/2017029071

Printed in the United States.

CONTENTS

PART ONE: THE THEORY AND CRITICISMS OF WRITTEN AND ORAL APPELLATE ADVOCACY

CHAPTER ONE: APPELLATE REVIEW: A PANORAMA

CHAPTER TWO: THE PURPOSE OF BRIEF WRITING

CHAPTER THREE: THE PURPOSE OF ORAL ARGUMENT

PART TWO: TECHNICAL REQUIREMENTS FOR BRIEFS

CHAPTER FOUR: JURISDICTION

CHAPTER FIVE: ISSUE PRESERVATION AND STANDARDS OF REVIEW

Part Three: The Nuts and Bolts of Brief Writing

Chapter Six: The Brief: Selecting Issues and Finding a Winning Argument

Chapter Seven: The Brief: Research and Use of Authorities

CHAPTER EIGHT: THE BRIEF: STATING THE ISSUE(S) AND POINT HEADINGS

CHAPTER NINE: WRITING TO WIN: CLEAR WRITING, EDITING, AND CITATION FORM

CHAPTER FOURTEEN: THE BRIEF: FINALIZING AND FILING THE BRIEF, RESPONSIVE STATEMENTS

CHAPTER FIFTEEN: THE BRIEF: A COMPENDIUM OF ADVICE

PART FOUR: THE NUTS AND BOLTS OF PREPARING
AND DELIVERING ORAL ARGUMENT

CHAPTER SIXTEEN: PREPARING FOR ORAL ARGUMENT

CHAPTER SEVENTEEN: HOW APPELLATE LAWYERS PREPARE

CHAPTER EIGHTEEN: DELIVERING THE ARGUMENT

PART FIVE: CHECKLISTS

CHAPTER NINETEEN: TWO IMPORTANT CHECKLISTS: BRIEF WRITING AND ORAL ARGUMENT PREPARATION

Contents

Foreword to the Third Edition

Winning is the immediate objective of every appellate advocate. So what does an advocate need to know in order to win on appeal? The answer is the sort of argument that will convince at least a majority of the appellate panel. And who is in the best position to tell advocates what will do the trick? Successful appellate attorneys? They can certainly provide helpful guidance. They know what has seemed to work for them and for fellow practitioners. But attorneys have a limited perspective. An attorney may write a great brief, present a great argument and nevertheless lose. Why? Was the case hopeless from the beginning? What went wrong? The attorney can never be sure. Conversely, an attorney who writes a bad brief and presents a dreadful argument may prevail. Believe me. I have seen it happen time and again.

The sort of person who is in the best position to know what *really* works on appeal is someone who has a wealth of experience behind the scene. Someone who has read many, many briefs, and heard many, many oral arguments in all kinds of cases. Someone who has experienced the kind of argument that changes minds (for better or for worse) in those cases in which a decision one way or the other is possible. Someone who has first-hand knowledge about the thinking of a broad array of judges (because, needless to say, all judges do not think alike and are not moved by the same types of arguments). Someone who has heard judges say, "I came into this case or I came into the oral argument thinking we should decide the case one way, but the briefs or the oral argument changed my mind."

The author of this book, the late Judge Ruggero Aldisert, was that someone. He was a distinguished litigator in his native Pittsburgh and served as a trial judge for seven years on the Court of Common Pleas of Allegheny County, Pennsylvania. In 1968, President Johnson appointed Judge Aldisert to the United States Court of Appeals for the Third Circuit, where he served with great distinction for the next forty-six years. He was widely recognized as one of the leading circuit judges of his time—and his time spanned many generations of judges and attorneys. When Judge Aldisert joined the Third Circuit, his oldest colleagues had been born before the Wright brothers made the first airplane flight. They included famous judges appointed by Presidents Roosevelt and Truman—John Biggs, Jr., a college roommate of F. Scott Fitzgerald, and William Hastie, the first African American appointed to the federal bench, to name just two. When Judge Aldisert finally retired from the Third Circuit in the summer of 2014, his youngest colleague, appointed by President Obama, had been born just two weeks before his appointment to the federal bench. It goes without saying that over the years, he saw a lot.

Judge Aldisert served as chief judge of the Third Circuit until 1986, when his health forced him to move from his beloved Pittsburgh to the gentler climate of southern California. But neither his health nor the move slowed him down. While continuing to sit on the Third Circuit, he was invited by other circuits to join them as a visiting judge, and this gave him the opportunity to work with judges from around the country. In earlier editions to this book, he shared the views of many of the judges he came to know.

It is mind-boggling to think of the number of briefs that Judge Aldisert read over the years. I am sure they included briefs that should be honored in an appellate hall of fame—and others on the opposite end of the spectrum. He heard oral arguments by the best appellate advocates in the country and by new attorneys nervously making their first appearance in an appeals court. He read briefs and heard arguments by attorneys with eye-popping hourly fees and by others who were paid a pittance. He sat on some of the most important cases of his time, as well as many that were routine.

Judge Aldisert not only knew what works on appeal; he knew how to teach. For twenty years, he was an adjunct professor at his alma mater, the University of Pittsburgh School of Law, and he was a regular participant in the Senior Appellate Judges Seminar at New York University School of Law. He taught seminars in the United States and abroad and imparted his knowledge to generations of attorneys and judges through his books. A prodigious writer, he authored, in addition to this volume, *The Judicial Process, Logic for Lawyers: A Guide to Clear Legal Thinking,* and *A Judge's Advice: 50 Years on the Bench,* as well as an autobiography, *Road to the Robes,* and a novel, *Almost the Truth,* which was published shortly before his death at the age of ninety-eight.

I argued before Judge Aldisert as a young attorney, and I learned from the experience of trying to hold my own in front of the former Marine. I will certainly never forget those occasions. Arguing before Judge Aldisert was the best (and therefore the most demanding) Socratic experience imaginable. Woe to the lawyer who was unprepared or, worse yet, tried to pull something on the court! But to paraphrase that famous Sinatra song, if you could make it arguing in front of Judge Aldisert, you could make it anywhere.

Years later, I had the honor of serving for fifteen years with "Rugi," as we called him, on the Third Circuit, and once again it was a formative experience. Rugi was a great judge and a great teacher. The best teachers love the subject they teach, and Rugi truly loved the law.

I am very pleased that Rugi's teaching will live on after him in this new edition of *Winning on Appeal.* For new appellate advocates, this volume should be required reading. I wish that it had been available when I argued my first case. For more experienced attorneys, the book contains advanced tips and reminders that may serve as a corrective against the bad habits that are easy to acquire. For any attorney who wants to know how to win on appeal, this is where to look.

Samuel A. Alito, Jr.
Associate Justice
Supreme Court of the United States
Washington, D.C.

June 2017

FOREWORD TO THE SECOND EDITION

For thirty-one years, Ruggero J. Aldisert—"Rugi," as he is affectionately known by his many friends, in high places and low, all around the world—has served with distinction as a judge. He had seven years as a state trial judge in Allegheny County and since 1968 has been judge, then chief judge, and now senior judge of the United States Court of Appeals for the Third Circuit. As a senior judge, he is anything but retired. He sits regularly with federal appellate courts around the country and finds time to write books such as this one.

In a Foreword to one of the earlier books, Justice Harry A. Blackmun of the Supreme Court of the United States said about Judge Aldisert:

> He loves the law. He yearns to know its history and its character or, to use the word he has employed effectively in this volume, its anatomy. He has a persistent but most refreshing curiosity about the law. He wants to know what it is, why it is, and how all of us who labor in its vineyards use or misuse it.

It is not enough, however, for him to learn about the law. Like Chaucer's Clerk, "gladly he would lerne and gladly teche." He has been a fine judge, but not very well-hidden behind the austere judicial robes is the heart and the mind of a teacher. For more than twenty of the years he was serving on the state and federal bench, he was also an adjunct professor at the University of Pittsburgh Law School. He has taught antitrust law at the University of Augsburg (Bavaria), and he came and taught for a summer at the University of Texas Law School, to the great benefit of our students and to the delight of our faculty. For years, he played an active part in the Senior Appellate Judges Seminar at New York University School of Law, and time out of mind he has been a speaker or on a panel at a judicial conference, a law school, or a seminar for newly appointed judges.

This is his fourth book. It follows *The Judicial Process* (1976), *Logic for Lawyers: A Guide to Clear Legal Thinking* (1988), and *Opinion Writing* (1990). The titles of those books, and this, show he has distilled the lessons he has learned from his service as a judge and set them out for the instruction of his colleagues on the bench and of the lawyers who appear before the judges. He is trying to teach us the things his experience tells him we ought to do.

This is a wonderfully instructive book. The writing is clear and vigorous. Comments from state chief justices, federal chief justices, and from law clerks add a broader perspective to what Judge Aldisert has himself observed. Although the instruction this book provides will be particularly valuable to the neophyte at the bar, even the most experienced veteran will find things here worth pondering.

Does this mean I agree with every piece of advice Judge Aldisert offers? Of course not—any more than I agree on all aspects of constitutional law with my four faculty colleagues who also offer the basic course in that subject. In § [16.8], for example, Judge Aldisert writes about "the mandatory rehearsal" before oral argument. I would not dream of rehearsing an argument. Indeed, I refuse even to discuss a case in the period leading up to when I am going to argue it. At least for my style of argument, freshness and spontaneity are vitally important. I think long and hard about what may be said at oral argument, but I do not put words on paper nor do I discuss the case with others.

This is only to say that there is more than one way to write a brief and prepare for oral argument. With most of the advice Judge Aldisert offers here, I agree. And even when, as with rehearsing an argument, I do not agree, I recognize that his recommendations have much force and that many lawyers will benefit from following the methods he suggests.

There is a sense in which appellate advocacy cannot be taught. Ultimately, it is the lawyer, all alone at the lectern, who must count on his or her instinct and sense of the situation—perhaps even genius—to carry the day. But that lawyer is far more likely to succeed if he or she is well schooled in the fundamentals. These are splendidly taught here by Judge Aldisert. The wise lawyer will master the methods recommended in this book before striking out on a different and individual path.

Charles Alan Wright
William B. Bates Chair for
the Administration of Justice
University of Texas Law School
Austin, Texas

November 1992

A Postscript from Judge Aldisert: *Professor Charles Alan Wright died in Austin, Texas on July 7, 2000. He was a dear friend. At the American Law Institute's Memorial Tributes to him in London, England, on July 17, 2000, Professor Gareth Jones described him as I knew him so well:*

> *Charlie was a big man in every sense of that adjective, a formidable frame, a powerful intellect. His legal memory, constant recall, never ceased to astonish me. He was a courageous parent and citizen who believed passionately in a United States which should be free of ethnic discrimination. It was typical of the man that he took away his daughter from a school which refused to admit black students.*

National Institute for Trial Advocacy

What are my personal memories of Charlie? He was first and foremost a companion whom one always looked forward to meeting, constantly challenging, never aggressively so, a correct but not pedantic grammarian who respected the proper use of the English language, a person who enjoyed material comfort, had an engaged sense of humor, and was a most hospitable host.

PREFACE TO THE THIRD EDITION

Since its First Edition was published in 1992, Judge Ruggero Aldisert's *Winning on Appeal* has become a standard reference for appellate advocates. It also has been used at many law schools as a demonstrably useful text to prepare students for the rigors of appellate work. Comprehensive, but written in a lively style, with the author's opinions complemented by advice from federal and state appellate judges around the country, practicing attorneys, and law school professors, the book brings together the best guidance available on how to write a persuasive brief and present a winning oral argument.

Admittedly, sometimes the case cannot be won (absent egregious error on the part of the appellate court), so the silent goal of some arguments may be simply to limit the damage. The advice in this book can assist in this venture as well.

The book was updated in 1996 and 2003. Judge Aldisert died at the end of 2014, three days after experiencing his ninety-sixth Christmas and three days before completing twenty-eight years as a judge on the United States Courts of Appeals for the Third Circuit. His book has remained in print. Much of the advice is timeless, but a fresh look at how the advice matches the changes to rules and technology seemed worthwhile.

Professor Tessa L. Dysart, who has taught for many years from Judge Aldisert's book, approached the National Institute for Trial Advocacy in Fall 2015 about updating the book. NITA graciously agreed that an update was in order, and Professor Dysart suggested partnering with Judge Leslie H. Southwick, who has served as both a state and federal appellate judge. The rest, as they say, is history.

Our approach was to use as light a touch as possible. We sought to retain the energy and confidence with which Judge Aldisert wrote but to revise and supplement in light of our own experiences. Technology has changed how attorneys approach brief writing and oral argument and their obligations on appeal from the time Judge Aldisert last revised his book. In many respects, technology has made brief writing and oral advocacy easier. The ease of access to the entire record, both as an attorney writes a brief and as a judge reads that same brief, has led to such innovations as the transformation of citations in briefs of the electronic record into hyperlinks that the reading judge can use. Computers and computerized research have replaced typewriters and books, and e-filing has largely replaced couriers and commercial printing of briefs. But these same technological advances present their own difficulties and can lead to the proliferation of appeals, something Judge Aldisert was certainly concerned about. The Third Edition strives to explore both the benefits and challenges of the blending of technology with appellate advocacy.

In addition to recognizing the role of technology in appellate advocacy, we have reorganized and streamlined the chapters to reflect the brief writing process. We have also highlighted lawyers' ethical obligations in the brief writing process.

Following in the footsteps of Judge Aldisert, we have obtained written insights from judges and attorneys from around the country. How each prepares to write a brief and then writes, and prepares to argue in court and then argues, are a marvelous commentary on the variable approaches that can lead to success. We also have retained many of the comments from previous editions, removing some in order to keep those sections from becoming overly lengthy. At the center of all the advice is the need for integrity. An unfairly slanted description of what a precedent holds, or misstating crucial but problematic parts of the factual record, will upon discovery make the judge distrust everything else in the brief or oral argument.

We wish to thank all of the judges and attorneys who contributed so meaningfully to this edition by responding to our requests. We would also like to thank friends and colleagues who helped review portions of this manuscript, including Michael Cantrell, Caleb Dalton, James Duane, Bill Magee, Tristen Small, and Maxwell Thelen. Thank you as well to Leah Achor, Adam Burton, Noah DiPasquale, Haley Holik, and Sharla Mylar for their research and editing assistance. A special thanks to Audrey Lynn for her help on the logic materials. We would also like to thank the National Institute for Trial Advocacy for their support and assistance throughout this project, and our families. We give very special thanks to our spouses, Sharon Southwick and Andrew Dysart, for their long-suffering support.

In closing, we return to the very First Edition of this book, published a quarter century ago. University of Texas Law School Professor Charles Alan Wright, now deceased, wrote that it may be fair to conclude that "appellate advocacy cannot be taught. Ultimately, it is the lawyer, all alone at the lectern [now there is an image to bring fear to the new advocate, and experienced ones too], who must count on his or her instinct and sense of the situation," as no colleague, mentor, or writer of books can take over at that point.

Without being able to step up to the lectern with the lawyer, the original author provided through this book a reservoir of best preparation and argument practices that can be drawn upon throughout the work of an appellate advocate. Our goal with this revised edition is to continue to be that virtual colleague who has gotten the advocate as well prepared as he or she can be to perform the work that has to be done on appeal. It is then the attorney's task to apply that guidance to the case at hand and persuade those who will decide the appeal.

Leslie H. Southwick
Jackson, Mississippi

Tessa L. Dysart
Virginia Beach, Virginia

April 2017

PREFACE TO THE SECOND EDITION

Although we call this book the Second Edition, it is really the third version. In 1996, we called the second version the "Revised First Edition" because the only changes were statistical updates—reversals on appeals in the federal courts, the frequency of oral argument and the granting of certiorari petitions in the United States Supreme Court.

With over a decade experience subsequent to the original text, we know now that, in addition to being adopted by many law schools as the text for appellate advocacy courses, the book has become a popular desk reference on how to write an effective brief and deliver a persuasive oral argument. Because it has evolved into a "how-to" manual, I have made the text more reader-friendly by overhauling the format for maximum efficiency.

This edition is a fundamental makeover. For the most part, it is more a new book, than a tweaking of the earlier versions. Without lengthening it, we now have twenty-five chapters, in place of the previous seventeen.

Part One, "The Theory and Criticisms of Written and Oral Appellate Advocacy," retains the same format, except that the tables of statistics represent the most up-to-date information available, instead of 1990 or 1995. The book continues to be unique in consolidating current empirical data on the odds of prevailing on appeal, or having a case orally argued. The tables reveal a trend of fewer published opinions, fewer reversals, and less oral argument in the appellate courts. References to appellate rules have been updated to track amendments since 1990.

Major revisions appear in Part Three, "Nuts and Bolts of Brief Writing" and Part Four, "Nuts and Bolts of Preparing and Delivering Oral Argument." Chapters have been designed to identify discrete requirements for an effective brief or argument, and to advise how to meet these prerequisites. To be sure, most of the suggestions, from personal judicial experience of more than forty years, first as a Pennsylvania state trial judge beginning in 1961, and then as a United States circuit judge since 1968. From the time the first version of this book appeared, I have continued to regularly sit with my own Third Circuit, both on merits panels as well as panels considering motions and pro se cases. In addition, I have sat with the Fifth, Seventh, Ninth, Tenth, and Eleventh Circuits, and still continue to visit with some of them. These travels have given me a unique experience of reading briefs and hearing arguments of lawyers from Atlanta, Georgia to Seattle, Washington.

As in the previous editions, however, there is more than one judge offering advice in these pages. Nineteen current chief justices of state courts, nine chief judges of United States courts of appeals, more than a score of other United States circuit judges and other state appellate judges have graciously offered excellent suggestions which I set forth to improve your appellate advocacy. On many issues—too numerous to detail here—the views of these distinguished appellate judges totally corroborate my advice. Thus, the success of this book has been that what we say here reflects not merely "one man's opinion," but rather a broad-based consensus that exclaims, "This is what you should not do," and "This is what we judges look for when reading your brief and listening to your argument."

A great new dimension also appears in this edition. It is one thing for us judges to tell you what we desire from oral argument; it is quite another to tell you how to prepare for us. This advice must come from the great lawyers. For this reason, I turned to a number of the nation's outstanding appellate lawyers, true masters in oral advocacy, and I have devoted the whole of Chapter Twenty-Three to set forth their advice. Three lawyers are from Philadelphia, two from Washington, D.C. (one a former United States Solicitor General), two from Illinois, and one each from St. Petersburg [Florida], Pittsburgh, and Los Angeles. This new chapter augments suggestions from other appellate lawyers interspersed in previous chapters on various subjects.

I am gratified that this book has been so well received by both the practicing bar and law students, and I am grateful to the many judges, scholars, and practitioners who have contributed to the present edition. In the text of pages that follow, I attribute law review sources for many references. I now thank the following authors for quoted material that appears in the tables on various subject areas: David O. Boehm, *Clarity and Candor are Vital in Appellate Advocacy*, N.Y. St. B.J., Sept./Oct. 1999, at 52; Joel F. Dubina, *How to Litigate Successfully in the United States Court of Appeals for the Eleventh Circuit*, 29 Cumb. L. Rev. 1 (1998); Henry D. Gabriel, *Preparation and Delivery of Oral Argument in Appellate Courts*, 22 Am. J. Trial Advoc. 571 (1999); Thomas R. Haggard, *Writing the Reply Brief*, Scrivener, Mar./Apr. 2001; Mark R. Kravitz, *Oral Argument Before the Second Circuit*, 71 Conn. B.J. 204 (1997); Marcia L. McCormick, *Selecting and Framing the Issues on Appeal: A Powerful Persuasive Tool*, 90 Ill. B.J. 203 (2002); Gary L. Sasso, *Anatomy of the Written Argument*, 15 Litig. 30 (1989); *Appellate Oral Argument*, 20 Litig. 27 (1994); Jacques Weiner, Jr., *Ruminations From the Bench: Brief Writing and Oral Argument in the Fifth Circuit*, 70 Tul. L. Rev. 187 (1995); Karen Williams, *Help Us Help You: A Fourth Circuit Primer on Effective Appellate Oral Arguments*, 50. S.C.L. Rev. 591 (1999); Patricia M. Wald, *Tips from 19 Years on the Appellate Bench*, 1 J. App. Prac. & Proc. 7 (1999).

I also thank the many state appellate judges and the judges of the United States courts of appeals who graciously responded to my requests for their advice. I thank all lawyers who have written briefs and argued before me over the years; those judges of the U.S. Court of Appeals for the Third and Tenth Circuits who responded to my specific request on how lawyers may more effectively persuade appellate judges; the various state court administrators who answered my request for specific court statistics; and Professor J. Thomas Sullivan, of William H. Bowen School of Law, University of Arkansas at Little Rock, for supplying me with all back issues of his excellent new publication, *The Journal of Appellate Practice and Procedure.*

I want to thank the folks at the National Institute of Trial Advocacy (NITA), my publisher. They are an exceptionally talented cadre of dedicated and efficient professionals. It is an honor to be associated with them.

I extend my appreciation to Mimi Hildbrand for her loyalty and devotion to this project. I am especially indebted to Michael A. Mugmon, Esq. and Robert K. Simonds, Esq. for profound editorial, analytical, and research assistance.

But most of all, I thank my wife of over fifty years, Agatha, who patiently endured many weekends while I was closeted in the den preparing this new edition and infringing upon our personal time. I publicly acknowledge her constant inspiration and loving support, and the many acts of kindness and assistance, including the authorship of its title, as I wrote the several editions of this book.

Ruggero J. Aldisert
Santa Barbara, California

July 2003

PREFACE TO THE REVISED FIRST EDITION

This book on appellate advocacy is more than a style manual on how to write for and speak to an appellate tribunal. It is a practical guide about how to avoid pitfalls that often prevent your written or oral argument from being considered on the merits. In particular, we emphasize that success in preserving arguments on the merits comes only through a complete understanding of conditions precedent to being heard by the court.

We explain the importance of demonstrating that the appellate court has jurisdiction to hear your appeal. We underscore the necessity of preserving the points for review; this means presenting for consideration at the trial level those arguments which you intend to present to the appellate court. We emphasize the distinctions among the various standards of review, critical factors that determine the power of the magnifying lens adjusted by appellate courts to examine your various arguments.

But much more emerges from these pages. We discuss the theory and criticisms of written and oral advocacy, the technical requirements for briefs, the nuts and bolts of brief writing as well as preparing for the delivering of oral argument. We have created practical checklists to be used in every case. All of this reflects my firm conviction (and that espoused by the many appellate judges who contributed to these pages) that preparation for appellate advocacy begins at trial. Appellate strategy is an important aspect of trial advocacy. A sure approach for getting nowhere on appeal is to wait until the adverse verdict or ruling has been made and then attempt to flyspeck the record to fashion points for appeal. It is therefore most fitting that this edition be published under the auspices of the National Institute for Trial Advocacy (NITA), because effective appellate performance begins with good trial advocacy. I am proud to be associated with NITA, universally recognized by lawyers and law schools as the premier force in advocacy training.

I am gratified that this book has been extremely well received by judges and lawyers since it first appeared in the hardcover edition. One of my favorite comments came from Senior Circuit Judge John C. Godbold of Montgomery, Alabama, who served variously as chief judge of the United States Court of Appeals for both the Fifth and Eleventh Circuits, as well as Director of the Federal Judicial Center:

If you know a young lawyer who wants to be a litigator, give him a copy of this book for Christmas. If you know an old lawyer who engages in litigation and fancies himself an expert, give him a copy without waiting for Christmas.

Ruggero J. Aldisert
Santa Barbara, California

May 1996

National Institute for Trial Advocacy

PREFACE TO THE FIRST EDITION

I wrote this book for one purpose: to suggest methods of improving appellate written and oral advocacy.

I wrote it from the perspective of one who has been reading briefs and listening to arguments since 1961, both in a state trial court and in many federal appellate courts. I wrote it also from the perspective of one who has long been active in state and federal judicial education programs; in programs where the quality of written and oral presentations by lawyers constantly commanded our attention.

The book is for lawyers. I call it *Winning on Appeal*, because that is what lawyers want to do and should want to do. But we cannot promise that what follows in these pages will do just that. More often than not, hefty, hearty precedents and facts embedded in concrete will control the outcome. But in a certain percentage of cases—in which the rule of law, and therefore, the decision, could go either way—how and where the axe will fall may depend upon the quality of appellate advocacy.

It is here where what is said in these pages may produce a difference. And it is here where I will make a guarantee: if you follow the advice contained in these pages, you will create the maximum impression on the judges who will hear your case; your written and oral presentation will generate maximum effectiveness in convincing the court to your point of view. Certainly, you will not always prevail; only one party wins on appeal. Factual findings, controlling legal precepts, or previously stated policy concerns of the court often run counter to propositions that you advance. But if you follow the proffered advice, you will be discharging the high responsibility of an officer of the court: to assist judges in achieving a completely informed, totally rational and probably correct decision.

I am a senior United States circuit judge now living in California, although my home court is still the Court of Appeals for the Third Circuit in Philadelphia. One of the privileges of senior judge status is the opportunity to sit by designation in other United States Courts of Appeals. Thus, I have had the unique experience of working with judges and lawyers in a wide geographic area. I have become a circuit rider. No saddlebags or horse here, just a jet plane.

In my own Third Circuit, lawyers from Pennsylvania, New Jersey, Delaware, and the Virgin Islands have appeared before me by brief or oral argument for many years. I have learned that the phrase, "a Philadelphia lawyer," may indeed mean the best, but alas, less often than not. I have been designated to sit on the Eleventh Circuit and learned to respect members of the bar from Florida, Alabama, and Georgia; and the fine professionals from Texas, Louisiana, and Mississippi when I sat with the Fifth Circuit in New Orleans. When sitting on the Tenth Circuit on many occasions, I learned something about some very competent lawyers from Wyoming, Utah, Kansas, Colorado, New Mexico, and Oklahoma. Because I now am a California resident, I regularly sit on the Ninth Circuit and have a fair exposure to some excellent advocates from Montana, Idaho, Nevada, Arizona, Washington, Oregon, California, Alaska, Hawaii, Guam, and the Marianas Islands.

I have heard the best, "in every clime and place," as in the Marines' Hymn, and I probably have heard the worst. After all these years, however, I have not become jaded. The juices still run swiftly when a brief truly inspires and oral argument "ceases to be an episode in the affairs of a client and becomes a stone in the edifice of the law," as once described by Supreme Court Justice Robert H. Jackson:

> To participate as advocate in supplying the basis for decisional law-making calls for the vision of the prophet, as well as a profound appreciation of the continuity between the law of today and that of the past. He will be sharing the task of reworking decisional law by which every generation seeks to preserve its essential character and at the same time to adapt it to contemporary needs. At such a moment the lawyer's case ceases to be an episode in the affairs of a client and becomes a stone in the edifice of the law.

Now a few words about the book. It is designed to be a desk reference, not as an essay to be read from cover to cover (although it would not be a bad idea for neophytes to the appellate process to do just this). Read Part One (Chapters [One through Three]) to learn what judges expect from lawyers; learn also to avoid the stated criticisms of written and oral arguments. Part Three (Chapters [Six through Twenty-One]) and Part Four (Chapters [Twenty-Two through Twenty-Four]) are required reading; they address the nuts and bolts on how to improve your written and oral skills.

The Table of Contents is all-important. It is your roadmap to this book. Totally familiarize yourself with it. Immerse yourself in it so you will know exactly where to go when you need particular assistance. Although placed near the rear of the book, check lists for briefs and oral argument, contained in Chapter [Twenty-Five], are all-important. Photocopy them. Keep them handy as you prepare and implement your appellate strategy.

I am indebted to many. Over thirty chiefs of our states' highest courts (as well as a number of their colleagues) responded to my request for advice on how to improve briefs and arguments. Their wise counsel appears throughout the text as well as in tables set forth in sections [9.7.1, 21.2, 22.3]. The chief judges of the United States courts of appeals kindly offered suggestions to a difficult situation that often faces lawyers at argument when a single judge embarks on an irrelevant, intellectual frolic. Their guidance has been summarized and appears in tables at sections [9.7.2, 21.3, 22.4, 24.6.3.2].

I am grateful for the insights received from many United States circuit judges and state supreme court justices who attended the Senior Appellate Judges Seminars of the Institute of Judicial Administration in New York during the many years when I served as a faculty discussion leader and associate director. I acknowledge the contributions contained in many articles written by judges to which references are made with appreciation.

An appellate judge soon learns that the quality of the judicial process is often commensurate with the quality of appellate advocacy, and though we judges may tell lawyers what improvements we want and why we want them, it is for successful appellate lawyers to tell us how they do it. I have researched many thoughtful articles and make generous references and attributions to them, especially Stephen M. Shapiro, of Mayer, Brown & Platt, Chicago, and Jordan B. Cherrick of [Thompson Coburn], St. Louis.

I acknowledge the contributions of Kenneth Starr, the [former] United States Solicitor General; James D. Crawford of Schnader, Harrison, Segal & Lewis, and Edward F. Mannino, Philadelphia; John H. Bingler, Jr., of Thorp, Reed & Armstrong, Pittsburgh; and Bobby R. Burchfield of Covington and Burling, Washington, D.C.; Michael T. Reagan of Ottawa, Illinois, and Nancy J. Arnold of Chicago graciously invited me to present some of this material at 1991 and 1992 workshops of the Appellate Lawyers Association of Illinois, which I found stimulating and most helpful.

Several knowledgeable colleagues in appellate advocacy read the manuscript, or parts thereof, and provided thoughtful commentary that greatly enhanced the finished text. These reviewers included Senior Judges Max Rosenn, Joseph F. Weis, Jr., and Leonard I. Garth, my longtime colleagues on the Third Circuit; also three distinguished former law clerks, United States District Judge Robert J. Cindrich of the Western District of Pennsylvania (Pittsburgh), and [Dean] David W. Burcham of Loyola of Los Angeles Law School, and Margaret D. McGaughey, Assistant United States Attorney for the District of Maine. They expended much valuable time in this endeavor and I thank them for many perceptive observations. I thank Anne Marie Finch, Susan Simmons Seemiller, Linda Schneider, Glenn J. Dickinson, and Kathleen M. Vanderziel for research and editorial assistance.

There now have been three generations of Aldiserts in the law (I do not exclude my father John S. Aldisert, who, though not formally trained, became a self-taught medico-legal specialist in his thirty-three years as Chief Deputy Coroner of Allegheny County [Pittsburgh], Pennsylvania, supervising investigations and presiding at inquests). In preparing this book, I turned to the third generation for advice and counsel. An appreciative father is gratified to have available the wisdom of his sons, Robert L. Aldisert, of Perkins Coie, Portland, Oregon, and Gregory J. Aldisert of Kinsella, Boesch, Fujikawa and Towle, Los Angeles.

Most of all, I am profoundly grateful to my wife, Agatha, for her understanding, inspiration, and love, and for graciously permitting so many intrusions into our "retirement" time.

Ruggero J. Aldisert
Santa Barbara, California

November 1992

PART ONE

THE THEORY AND CRITICISMS OF WRITTEN AND ORAL APPELLATE ADVOCACY

CHAPTER ONE

APPELLATE REVIEW: A PANORAMA

1.1 Overview

This book is for lawyers. It is for a special breed of lawyers—those who write briefs and argue appeals before state and federal appellate courts. It is also for individuals who aspire to be appellate lawyers, either as members of the bar or as law students.

Moreover, this book looks in one direction—from the bench to the bar. It is a perspective that perceives written and oral argument from the viewpoint of those to whom arguments are addressed. In 1940, John W. Davis, one of the nation's great appellate advocates, drew an interesting analogy:

> [S]upposing fishes had the gift of speech, who would listen to a fisherman's weary discourse on flycasting, the shape and color of the fly, the size of the tackle, the length of the line, the merit of different rod makers and all the other tiresome stuff that fisherman talk about, if the fish himself could be induced to give his views on the most effective methods of approach[?] For after all it is the fish that the angler is after and all his recondite learning is but the hopeful means to that end.[1]

In this book, the fish are giving the advice. Judicial fish are explaining to lawyer anglers how to catch them.

This book recognizes that there are different types of skilled anglers. Many are great trial lawyers, but their well-honed skills that are effective in familiar lakes do not necessarily translate to unpredictable, swift-moving rivers.

Appellate advocacy is specialized work. It draws upon talents and skills that are far different from those utilized in other facets of practicing law. Being a good trial lawyer does not mean that you are also a qualified appellate advocate. The consummate trial lawyer knows how to open to a jury, examine witnesses, protect the trial record with objections and motions, and close during summation. A good trial

---

1. John W. Davis, *The Argument of an Appeal*, 26 A.B.A.J. 895, 895 (1940). Davis also presented, in effect, an argument to the American people in 1924 as the Democratic nominee for President. He lost that appeal. Perhaps it was because—to use his analogy—this marvelous attorney was a fish out of water as a politician.

lawyer knows how to prepare a succinct trial memorandum that has the capacity to persuade the harried trial judge who is chained to the bench, a prisoner to an overloaded calendar.

The successful trial lawyer is really a successful salesperson—successful in the sense of persuading the fact-finder to select from the mass of testimony and evidence those adjudicative facts that favor the lawyer's client. To persuade is to sell effectively. Many good trial lawyers, however, would eschew this salesman label. There comes to mind the rebuke flung in the face of Willy Loman in the play, *Death of a Salesman*: "The only thing you got in this world is what you can sell. The funny thing is that you're a salesman, and you don't know that."[2]

But salespersons have different customers, dissimilar audiences, disparate objectives, and diverse time frames. At trial, the major objective is to persuade the fact-finder, often a panel of lay jurors, that credibility lays on the side of your witnesses, and to show that the evidence, although disputed, favors your client.

For the most part, trial lawyers work within a framework of existing legal precepts. Out of a pile of conflicting evidence, they seek but one objective: to persuade the fact-finder to accept a version of the dispute favoring their client. Trial lawyers ascertain the factual strengths and weaknesses of both sides of their cases and then sift, select, and evaluate the evidence to be presented.

The best of this stellar breed carve a convincing argument from an amorphous mass of testimony and create an aura of moral justification around the client and the cause. This is not to say that trial lawyers need only know how to manage the facts. They must also know and be prepared to argue the legal precepts that will control the precise shade of fact-finding that is sought in order to protect the record and to guard against both improper and unfavorable rulings.

The trial courtroom is where the great stars of the legal galaxy shine. But trial courts and appellate courts are constellations far apart in that galaxy. The two settings demand different skills, knowledge, and tools. Those lawyers who perform as both trial and appellate advocates must learn to adjust their techniques to match the demands of each court. The appellate lawyer deals primarily with law, not facts, and only with professional judges, not lay juries.

A trial lawyer may take days, or even weeks, to persuade a trial judge or jury; an appellate lawyer, on the other hand, has time dribbled out in minutes. In the United States Courts of Appeals (and other "hot" courts where the judges have studied the briefs prior to oral argument), much of the time is devoted to answering questions from members of the bench.

---

2. Arthur Miller, Death of a Salesman 71 (Dramatists Play Service, 1981).

The trial environment honors the oral tradition. Persuasion takes place by speech, rather than by written word. Rhetorical skills, in the effective use of words to influence or persuade, may properly shape the argument before a lay body, and yet be totally unacceptable when arguing points of law to a court. Although arguments of distraction are fair tactics to sway or arouse the jurors in a trial court, they are not acceptable in an appellate court.

The trial advocate is not limited to reasoned argument, but rather may speak of many things, including irrelevant, somewhat irrational, or shamelessly emotional matters. These are ploys, but ploys that are used everywhere, every day. They are used in advertising and political campaigns, and by essay writers, columnists, editorial writers, and television commentators. They are of such ancient lineage that many bear Latin names: *argumentum ad misericordiam* (appeal to pity), *ad verecundiam* (appeal to prestige), *ad hominem* (appeal to ridicule), *ad populum* (appeal to the masses/popular opinion), *ad antiquitam* (appeal to the ages/tradition), *ad terrorem* (appeal to fear), *ad superbium* (appeal to snobbery or pride), *ad superstitionem* (appeal to credulity). And if the wind is right and the sail is full, the trial advocate can hoist a little *dicto simpliciter* (applying the general rule to exceptional circumstances) or some hasty generalization, or tie on a *non sequitur* or *post hoc ergo propter hoc* (fallacy of false cause) or *ignoratio elenchi* (fallacy of irrelevance, an argument that has nothing to do with the point at issue).[3]

But do not carry this stuff upstairs to the appellate court. Check this baggage after you finish your closing summation. You are still a salesperson when you appear before the multi-judge court, but it is a different audience, requiring different rhetorical skills. The oral tradition of the trial court gives way to a mixture of writing and speaking, but the proportions are not equal. Being a salesman at the appellate level is heavily weighted toward writing as opposed to oral presentation, perhaps as much as three to one. The oral tradition in which trials are often measured in weeks gives way to ever-shrinking enforced page or word limits in briefs. Furthermore, *if* oral argument is granted, lawyers in the United States Courts of Appeals normally have a mere fifteen or twenty minutes per side to argue their case.

The appellate lawyer is still a salesperson, but the lawyer carries a different sample case. Principally, the law is argued, and the tools of argument—the rhetoric, if you please—must be adjusted accordingly. Too many lawyers fail to make this adjustment. Indeed, too many lawyers do not even realize that an adjustment is required.

All of which leads to the question: "What is the quality of appellate advocacy today?" There is no quick answer. Certainly, most advocacy by brief or by oral argument cannot be rated as "good," let alone "excellent." A substantial amount

---

3. *See* Ruggero J. Aldisert, Logic for Lawyers: A Guide to Clear Legal Thinking 144, 169–206 (3d Ed. 1997) (describing many of these types of logically irrelevant arguments, and providing examples of cases where the judges called attention to an advocate's attempt to use such arguments).

of "poor" advocacy hangs out there, too much for judges to be lackadaisical about, and too pervasive for the American Bar Association or state bars to do much about. While it would be difficult to assign percentages in the form of a general evaluation, it suffices to say that there is a vast wasteland of mediocrity in the appellate field. At the very least, the quality quotient is not commensurate with the fees being charged for appellate brief writing and oral argument. The problem was extensive enough to prompt Judge Ruggero J. Aldisert to first write this book in 1992, and the problem remains significant enough to warrant an update more than twenty years later.

These critiques of modern advocacy are not a result of judicial crankiness or fatigue from reading too many briefs. The comments from state and federal appellate judges presented in this book demonstrate the pervasiveness of the problem. Likewise included in this book are reactions from law clerks who have come to clerk for judges as top students from our great law schools. When working on their assignments in chambers, many have immediately noted the poor quality of briefs, even those from prestigious law firms with which they had summered or interviewed. Law clerks are equally surprised at the poor quality of some of the oral advocacy they hear in this country's most prestigious appellate courts.

In a 1982 law review article, after witnessing the civil law systems in force on the European continent, Judge Aldisert expressed these concerns:

> Because I trust the American system and its reliance on pragmatic, strident, and vigorous advocate lawyers more than I trust a system of relying on judges ensconced in ivory towers with their law clerk acolytes, I believe that professional competence of lawyers is essential. Because I see so many dangerously incompetent appellate lawyers, I would like to see an immediate emphasis on improving professional competence so that we do not slip by default into an ivory-tower law system . . . . I believe that the thrust and parry of opposing appellate briefs is the best instrument to refine the law and to achieve justice.[4]

This book seeks to provide that emphasis on improving professional competence by giving appellate lawyers the inside perspective on how to persuade appellate judges.

1.2 The Avalanche of Appeals

Look for a moment at the paper storm that has descended on the West Publishing Company. The 27,527 published opinions that West received in 1929 represented

---

4. Ruggero J. Aldisert, *The Appellate Bar: Professional Responsibility and Professional Competence— A View from the Jaundiced Eye of One Appellate Judge*, 11 CAP. U.L. REV. 445, 455 (1982) (footnote omitted).

approximately the same number it received in 1964—some thirty-five years later. Yet by 1981, the volume had almost doubled to 54,104. By 1991, the number of published opinions peaked at 65,333. Although the number of published opinions has progressively dropped since then to 47,295 in 2015, this reduction is deceptive. With the rise in unpublished opinions over that same time, the total number of opinions—published and unpublished—was roughly 62,000 in 2015.[5]

Is case law churning and developing at the rate reflected by the increasing number of published and unpublished opinions? Of course not. Our common law tradition requires unity of law throughout a jurisdiction and requires also the flexibility to incorporate legal precepts as they develop. Within this tradition is the concept of gradual change, with case law that creeps from point to point, testing each step, in a system built by accretion from the resolution of specific problems. Nevertheless, no one, not even the most fervent supporter of publication in every case, can seriously suggest that every one of these cases submitted for publication refines or defines the law or has precedential or institutional value. The reason for the avalanche is not only the expansion of trial and appellate litigation, but also because today there is no institutional inhibition against the paper storm.

Reasons for this deluge of appeals are easily identifiable. First, there is the general litigation increase attributed to the growth of population, commerce, industry, civil rights laws, environmental and securities regulation, products liability, and the expanded concepts of torts. But there are other reasons. The advent of the personal computer, the Internet, and e-filing has made it possible and affordable for any attorney to write and file a brief. Furthermore, although there is a specialized Supreme Court bar, an increasingly specialized federal appellate bar, as well as state solicitor general offices and appellate divisions in U.S. Attorney offices, most lawyers now believe that they are competent to pursue and to win an appeal. However, even though good trial lawyers know the rocky terrain of trial courtrooms, their expertise does not guarantee successfully scaling the slippery slopes of appellate advocacy. Experienced appellate judges despair when they examine the superficial preparation by some lawyers whose cases unreasonably crowd their dockets.

Moreover, we have also seen a profound change in the lawyer-client relationship. Many lawyers are no longer able to control, or even to moderate, the demands of emotion-laden clients. Often, professional advice and wisdom are insufficient to curb the excesses of losing parties in lawsuits. Persons who would never dare to instruct a cardiovascular specialist on heart surgery have no qualms about instructing their lawyers when and how to prosecute appeals of highly technical cases. Most people think cases are retried on appeal *de novo*. They simply cannot recognize that courts of appeals have limited review powers.

---

5. Letter from Kate MacEachern, Attorney Editor, Westlaw, to Tessa L. Dysart (Mar. 10, 2016).

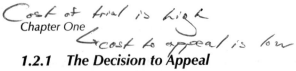

Cost of trial is high
cost to appeal is low

1.2.1 The Decision to Appeal

Lawyers are also to blame for the deluge of appeals. Some lawyers accede to their client's demands to appeal because they fear they may lose clients and earn reputations as "no-guts" lawyers. Others resort to a self-interested, protective maneuver, taking appeals as calculated defenses against possible malpractice suits by clients for failure to exhaust all remedies. Others, unfortunately, take appeals to keep the fee meter running.[6]

Another very important factor is economics. The high cost of delivering legal services at trial also has a direct bearing on the increase of appeals. Once a litigant has invested a substantial amount of money at trial, the additional expenses of taking an appeal do not appear extremely formidable. Unlike trial costs, where additional witnesses and depositions and prolonged court days make the legal costs an open-ended affair, there are discrete steps of processing an appeal that can be calculated with specificity in advance.

Even in the most borderline case, if the losing party has already invested significant funds to present or defend a claim at trial, the costs of taking an appeal, by comparison, do not appear prohibitive. For a relatively small investment, a respectable appeal may often be lodged and carried to fruition.[7] Comparatively speaking, the appeal expenses are not high because counsel can take the trial brief, cut and paste it for appellate court consumption, examine the record already prepared for post-trial argument, select parts for inclusion in the appendix or excerpts of record, and e-file the brief. Counsel can then take a few hours to prepare for oral argument, travel to the city (coach class) where the appellate court sits, deliver the fifteen-minute argument, and return home.

To be sure, these shortcuts do not produce the most desirable or effective advocacy—as is suggested in the chapters that immediately follow—but taking an appeal today is relatively cost-effective when compared to massive trial expenses. And if the appeal is lost—unless the case involves a fee-shifting statute—the client, or perhaps the attorney, only has to pay the minimal court costs and expenses. Thus, the sheer cost-effectiveness at the appeal level when compared to the astronomical costs at trial is probably a major factor causing the dramatic recent increase of appellate filings. It is the exact opposite of the old adage, "In for a penny, in for a pound."[8]

Surprisingly, though, the increase of appeals has not been directly related to the increase of trial court filings. Proportionately, the increase in appeals has been much

---

6. Roger J. Miner, *Professional Responsibility in Appellate Practice: A View from the Bench*, 19 Pace L. Rev. 323, 326 (1999).

7. For example, a 2013 study by the National Center for State Courts found that the appeal stage of a typical civil case often consists of only 7 to 9 percent of an attorney's total billable hours for all stages of the litigation. Paula Hannaford-Agor & Nicole L. Waters, *Estimating the Cost of Civil Litigation*, 20 Caseload Highlights 1, 2, 6 (2013).

8. Terry Freedman & David Freedman, The Wordsworth Dictionary of Cliché 192 (1996).

higher. When Judge Aldisert first became a United States circuit judge, in the fiscal year ending in 1969, the district courts terminated 73,354 cases.[9] By 2015, this figure had increased to 353,480 or an increase of 482 percent.[10] By comparison, the appeals terminated in 1969 numbered 9,014; in 2015, there were 52,881 appeals, or an increase of 586 percent.[11] Although the raw numbers are smaller, the rate of appeals increased much more drastically.

1.3   The Odds of Winning an Appeal

Despite the relative ease of taking an appeal, the chances of winning an appeal are not good. For example, for a direct appeal as of right to the United States Court of Appeals, the odds of a reversal are as follows.

United States Court of Appeals—National Average of Reversals (%)[12]

Nature of Proceeding	1998	2002	2010	2015
All Appeals	10.4%	9.5%	8.4%	8.6%
Criminal	6.5%	5.6%	5.6%	6.9%
U.S. Prisoner Petitions	10.3%	9.5%	10.2%	4.2%
Other U.S. Civil Cases	11.0%	11.0%	13.0%	15.0%
Private Prisoner Petitions	7.5%	9.9%	8.5%	4.8%
Other Private Civil Cases	12.7%	12.2%	12.1%	14.2%
Bankruptcy	14.4%	13.9%	16.0%	24.4%
Administrative Appeals	6.6%	12.3%	7.1%	7.8%

---

9. Statistics on federal court filings and dispositions are published biannually each June and December by the Administrative Office of the United States Courts. To access all figures, visit the Administrative Office's comprehensive website at www.uscourts.gov. Admin. Office of the U.S. Courts, *Statistical Tables for the Federal Judiciary,* U.S. Courts, http://www.uscourts.gov/statistics-reports/analysis-reports/statistical-tables-federal-judiciary (last visited Feb. 16, 2017).

10. Admin. Office of the U.S. Courts, Table C-1. U.S. District Courts—Civil Cases Commenced, Terminated, and Pending During the 12-Month Period Ending December 31, 2015 (2016); Admin. Office of the U.S. Courts, Table D-1. U.S. District Courts—Criminal Defendants Commenced, Terminated, and Pending (Including Transfers) During the 12-Month Period Ending December 31, 2015 (2016).

11. Admin. Office of the U.S. Courts, Table B-1. U.S. Courts of Appeals—Cases Commenced, Terminated, and Pending, by Circuit and Nature of Proceeding, During the 12-Month Period Ending December 31, 2015 (2016).

12. *Admin. Office of the U.S. Courts, Statistical Tables for the Federal Judiciary,* U.S. Courts, http://www. uscourts.gov/statistics-reports/analysis-reports/statistical-tables-federal-judiciary (last visited Feb. 16, 2017). Choose appropriate year, and then choose Table B-5: Decisions in Cases Terminated on the Merits, by Nature of Proceeding.

From this, we conclude that the reversal rates from 1998 to 2015 for all appeals averaged 9.23 percent. Expressed otherwise, here are the odds of reversing the district court:

- All appeals: 1 in 10

- Criminal cases: 1 in 14

- Private civil actions: 1 in 8

What are the odds of reversal in the state appellate court? The numbers are not much better. The next table reflects activity in the intermediate courts of some jurisdictions.

State Intermediate Appellate Courts[13]

State	Total Number of Cases Decided on Merits	Reversal Percentage of Cases Decided on Merits
Alaska	135	16%
Colorado	1,805	18%
Florida	17,566	21%
Illinois	4,765	22%
Kansas	1,339	26%
New York	1,061	38%
Pennsylvania	5,315	15%
Texas	5,863	22%

1.3.1 Certiorari Appellate Courts

When the highest court of the jurisdiction grants a petition for review (also known as a petition for writ of certiorari), the odds of prevailing generally increase. The real trick is to get the court to grant your petition. During the 2013–2014 court term, the United States Supreme Court granted only 117, or 2.4 percent, of the 4,943 petitions it received from litigants attempting to appeal from judgments of the various United States Courts of Appeals.[14]

---

13. The state court statistics in this section were obtained from the National Center for State Courts. Court Statistics Project DataViewer, COURT STATISTICS PROJECT, www.courtstatistics.org (last updated Feb. 12, 2015) (follow "Launch Dataviewer" hyperlink, choose "Appellate Court Overview" tab, select the Date Year "2013," and then select "Case Outcome by Court Type" table to view the data for the above listed states).

14. ADMIN. OFFICE OF THE U.S. COURTS, TABLE B-2–U.S. COURTS OF APPEALS JUDICIAL BUSINESS (SEPTEMBER 30, 2014), U.S. COURTS (SEPT. 30, 2014), http://www.uscourts.gov/statistics/table/b-2/judicial-business/2014/09/30 (last visited Mar. 20, 2017).

The following table reflects the chances of having an appeal as a matter of permission granted by the highest courts of several representative states, if applicable, as well as the odds for obtaining a reversal. The statistics represent figures from 2013:

State Highest Courts[15]

State	Total Dispositions	Percentage Disposed Prior to Decision	Percentage Permission Denied	Percentage Decided on Merits	Percentage Reversed on Merits
Alaska	399	24%	33%	43%	41%
Kansas	1,521	5%	81%	14%	40%
Michigan	1,789	4%	88%	8%	—
Missouri	819	24%	64%	12%	24%
Montana	848	31%	16%	54%	—
South Carolina	1,561	73%	16%	11%	—
Tennessee	1,159	13%	77%	10%	24%
Texas (Supreme Court)	1,059	8%	82%	10%	63%
Texas (Court of Criminal Appeals)	7,740	40%	54%	6%	28%
Washington	1,506	72%	20%	7%	—
West Virginia	1,767	14%	8%	78%	—
Wyoming	268	22%	17%	61%	29%

1.4   The Odds of Being Granted Oral Argument

When Judge Aldisert was appointed to the United States Court of Appeals for the Third Circuit in 1968, the court permitted oral argument in every case. When, later in the year, the judges reduced the length of argument from forty-five minutes a side to thirty minutes, the Philadelphia bar moaned and wailed as if it would be the end of the advocacy world. Nearly fifty years later, the customary allotted time allowance is between fifteen and twenty minutes, and oral argument is now the exception, not

---

15. Court Statistics Project DataViewer, COURT STATISTICS PROJECT, www.courtstatistics.org (last updated Feb. 12, 2015) (follow "Launch Dataviewer" hyperlink, choose "Appellate Court Overview" tab, select the Date Year "2013," and then select "Case Outcome by Court Type" table and "Manner of Disposition by Court Type" table to view the data for the above listed states) (last visited Mar. 20, 2017).

the rule.[16] In the United States Courts of Appeals, the advocate's major tool is the written brief, not oral presentation.

1.4.1 Federal Appellate Courts

Generally, if an appeal presents an issue of institutional or precedential significance, oral argument will be granted by the court. Various courts have different procedures through which this decision is reached, but by and large, the judges seem to err on the side of granting oral argument in unworthy cases, rather than denying the opportunity in deserving cases. Some circuits, such as the Fifth Circuit, require the parties to provide a statement explaining the need for oral argument (or lack thereof).[17]

What then are the odds that the judges will grant oral argument in your case? The following records of the United States Courts of Appeals provide some indication.[18]

Circuit	Percentage Argued in 1990	Percentage Argued in 2002	Percentage Argued in 2015
All Circuits	44.8%	33.5%	18.6%
D.C.	56.5%	49.1%	34.4%
First	66.8%	64.0%	27.8%
Second	76.4%	59.6%	27.8%
Third	25.8%	24.5%	9.5%
Fourth	31.9%	18.2%	8.3%
Fifth	27.9%	25.4%	15.9%
Sixth	48.1%	36.9%	15.9%
Seventh	56.2%	50.8%	34.8%
Eighth	44.1%	34.5%	18.4%
Ninth	51.6%	38.5%	21.8%
Tenth	41.1%	30.0%	26.2%
Eleventh	45.7%	21.3%	10.5%

16. *See* 1ST CIR. R. 34.0(c)(1) (allowing "no more than 15 minutes per side for oral argument"); 4TH CIR. R. 34(d) (providing that "[e]ach side is normally allowed 20 minutes," but restricting the time to 15 minutes in certain types of cases); 5TH CIR. R. 34.11 ("Most cases are allowed 20 minutes to the side.").

17. 5TH CIR. R. 28.2.3.

18. Office of the U.S. Courts, *Statistical Tables for the Federal Judiciary*, U.S. COURTS, http://www.uscourts.gov/statistics-reports/analysis-reports/statistical-tables-federal-judiciary (last visited Mar. 20, 2017) (select appropriate year, then select Table B-1: Cases Filed, Terminated, and Pending, by Nature of Proceeding. The percentage of cases argued can be calculated by dividing the number of cases terminated on the merits "After Oral Hearing" from the total number of cases terminated on the merits).

The comparison of these three years illustrates a significant development in the judicial process during the span of a decade: a nationwide decline of 26.2 percent in cases being argued. Fewer than one appeal in five—18.6 percent to be precise—will be listed for argument. These statistics do not take into account the many appellants who fail to ask for oral argument in circuits that require such a request. While the judges can still order oral argument if it is not requested, judges generally will no longer vote for oral argument where the law is clear and the application of facts to the law equally plain. Another facet of this phenomenon is the increase of non-precedential opinions being written in cases that have no precedential or institutional value in lieu of opinions to be published in the *Federal Reporter.*

This should be a signal to lawyers that today, more than ever, the appellant's brief takes on a vital and decisive role. You must not only write to persuade the court to reverse the judgment of the district court, but you must meet a threshold burden of demonstrating that, on the basis of the proper standard of review, a serious reversible error was committed in the trial court. A serious and arguable question of law must be presented.

1.4.2 State Appellate Courts

The chances of obtaining oral argument in the state appellate courts vary widely from state to state. For example, the Oklahoma Supreme Court very rarely grants oral argument.[19] Because most states do not maintain published statistics on the percentage of oral arguments granted, it is difficult to determine if there is a national trend in the states favoring or disfavoring oral argument. Recent statistics from the highest courts of several representative states suggest that oral argument is frequently allowed in those cases submitted on the merits. The statistics represent percentages from 2014 or 2015.

State	Percentage Argued[20]
Indiana	62%
Iowa	65%
Mississippi	15.3%
Michigan	82%
Nebraska	83.6%
New York	81.7%
North Carolina	57%
Oregon	90.6%
Vermont	66%

---

19. *See* Joseph T. Thai & Andrew M. Coats, *The Case for Oral Argument in the Supreme Court of Oklahoma*, 61 OKLA. L. REV. 695, 698 (2008) ("[I]n the last decade, the [Oklahoma Supreme Court] heard barely more than a dozen oral arguments out of more than a thousand published cases.").

20. This information was collected from each court and is on file with Tessa L. Dysart.

1.5 Summary

The reality is that a large majority of cases stand or fall at the intermediate appellate level. As shown above in section 1.3, the chances of winning are small. Why then are more cases appealed than ever before? The cause, at least in part, can be found in the forces described above: the litigious temperament of our American society and the attitudes of many lawyers. It should be noted that this thesis does not apply to the many advocates of ability and integrity who practice before the appellate courts of this country—attorneys distinguished not only by the appeals they present, but also by those they do not.

This book will not devote much space to the process of deciding which cases to appeal. But a basic premise underlying the entire discussion is that altogether too many cases are sent up, or rather dragged up willy-nilly, before appellate courts. Honing cases along the lines suggested in the pages that follow will cause some to disappear entirely. What will remain, hopefully, will be a solid core of substantial questions, adequately explored and clearly presented. The judicial system would benefit from this result, certainly, and lawyers could conserve their resources and use their time more effectively.

This is a book about bringing effective appeals. It is a book for lawyers—and lawyers like to win. It does not guarantee to the reader greater successes than the merits of the cases warrant. However, it will help lawyers bring their cases with merit into the minds of the deciding judges.

Over the years, many judges and state chief justices have graciously furnished advice for appellate lawyers for inclusion in this book. In his remarks, one federal appellate judge pointed to a quote by the late Judge Alvin B. Rubin, who served for over twenty years as a judge on the United States Court of Appeals for the Fifth Circuit. In a law review article on appellate advocacy, Judge Rubin wrote, "The best brief is like a good song. It plays a melody the judge will remember and hum when he writes the opinion. Never be satisfied with the first draft. Rewrite it until it is the best you can do."[21]

Judge Rubin recognized a distinction here. Appellate justice at its best is a cooperative effort between the court and counsel. Excellence on either side is infectious. We should hold each other, and ourselves, to the highest standards. We hope this book will serve that important and honorable endeavor.

---

21. Alvin B. Rubin, *The Admiralty Case on Appeal in the Fifth Circuit*, 43 La. L. Rev. 869, 874 (1983).

Chapter Two

The Purpose of Brief Writing

2.1 Overview

An appellate brief may be defined as a written, reasoned elaboration that justifies a conclusion. It is a demonstration of written, reflective thinking expressed in a logical argument designed to educate and to persuade. In a practical sense, it is a written statement of reasons explaining why an appellate court should reverse, vacate, or affirm the judgment or final order of the tribunal from which the appeal is taken.

Briefs are written for one audience and one audience only: judges and their law clerks. They have the most limited readership of any professional writing. You write to persuade a court, not to impress a client. You write to persuade a court to your point of view; at a minimum, you write to convince the court to grant oral argument in your case. The key word is "persuasion." If a brief does not persuade, it fails. Every brief writer must understand this and never forget it. As you write, prop a sign, literally or figuratively, on your desk that asks, "Will this brief persuade the reader?"

Persuasion is the only test that counts. Literary style, massive displays of scholarship, citations that thunder from the ages, and catchy phrases are uniformly pointless if the writing does not persuade.

Authorities may differ as to a precise definition of "persuasion." Kenneth Andersen describes it as "a communication process in which the communicator seeks to elicit a desired response from his receiver."[1] Erwin Bettinghaus is more specific: "As a minimal condition, to be labeled as persuasive, a communication situation must involve a conscious attempt by one individual to change the attitudes, beliefs, or behavior of another individual or group of individuals through the transmission of some message."[2]

Although both of these definitions effectively express a general concept, what Bettinghaus says has a special relevance to counsel for the appellant, who has the

---

1. KENNETH E. ANDERSEN, PERSUASION: THEORY AND PRACTICE 6 (1971).
2. ERWIN P. BETTINGHAUS, PERSUASIVE COMMUNICATION 4 (3d ed. 1980).

burden of persuading the appellate court that the trial judge committed reversible error. Although not usually stated as a traditional burden of proof, in actual practice, the presumption of correctness lies with the trial tribunal. Evidence of this presumption is the jurisprudential axiom: when an appellate court is equally divided, the judgment of the trial court must be affirmed.

The appellant is required to rebut this presumption of correctness. To do this, the appellant must challenge the attitudes or beliefs expressed by the trial court and presumably endorsed by the appellate court; the appellee's task is to reinforce these attitudes or beliefs.

When considering persuasion in the abstract, however, Professor Nicholas M. Cripe reminds us that persuasion in an appellate court "differs from the common persuasive [writing or] speaking situation such as political speeches, protest rallies, legislative debates, revival meetings, jury trials, and especially commercial advertising and selling."[3] Appellate advocates must tackle rhetorical problems rarely encountered by other persuasive writers or speakers. They are limited to a small number of available relevant arguments. They must carefully select and present these contentions in a setting where the atmosphere and traditions render ineffectual or inappropriate many techniques commonly used in other types of persuasive writing and speaking.

The audience is a concise grouping of "highly trained, intelligent, frequently articulate judges who likely will react unfavorably" to anything but the formal style of authoritative persuasion.[4] Moreover, unlike most literature of scholarly persuasion, appellate briefs are not read at a leisurely pace and their contents savored and digested in a contemplative environment. Rather, briefs must compete with other demands on an appellate judge's time and attention, as described in section 2.4, "The Brief-Reading Environment." For now, it is enough to say that astronomical caseloads require judges to read large numbers of briefs while simultaneously performing other judicial functions demanding equal priority.

2.2   Gaining and Maintaining Attention

Pioneer psychologist William James once said, "What holds attention determines action."[5] To the brief writer, this means two things: 1) you must gain the attention of the reading judge, and 2) you must maintain it. Attention is a necessary condition for persuasion.

When you start to plan your brief, place yourself in the judge's shoes. The judge will either take a set of briefs from the shelf, or, increasingly, read those same briefs in digital form on a tablet or computer. The judge will then open the briefs and

---

3. Nicholas M. Cripe, *Fundamentals of Persuasive Oral Argument*, 20 FORUM 342, 345 (1985).
4. *Id.*
5. WILLIAM JAMES, PSYCHOLOGY: THE BRIEFER COURSE 315 (1892).

National Institute for Trial Advocacy

ask, "Now, what is the excuse for this appeal?" This is not an indication that the judge is prejudging the merits; it is only the presumption of trial court correctness at work.

The appellant must always be conscious of this presumption and remember that the odds of prevailing on appeal favor the appellee. Keep in mind the track records set forth in Chapter One: between 1998 and 2015, the appellant's odds of prevailing were one in ten in the United States Courts of Appeals.

Whether representing the appellant or appellee, lawyers must plan their briefs to gain the immediate attention of the judge. This can be done by:

- Leading from strength; hitting the reader between the eyes with the strongest argument.

- Expressing a message that the reader will understand.

- Structuring a presentation within the framework of the reader's knowledge, beliefs, and attitude.

Noted lawyer and politician, John W. Davis, who argued over 130 times before the Supreme Court including successfully in the famous case *Youngstown Sheet & Tube Co. v. Sawyer*,[6] once wrote:

> [Judges] are anxiously waiting to be supplied with what Mr. Justice Holmes called the "implements of decision." These by your presence you profess yourself ready to furnish. If the places were reversed and you sat where they do, think what it is you would want first to know about the case. How and in what order would you want the story told? How would you want the skein unraveled? What would make easier your approach to the true solution?[7]

To gain the attention of the judge, the writing must be simple and clear. Here you may benefit from the advice of speech and debate professors at the undergraduate level. Robert Huber at the University of Vermont taught his debate students a simple argument pattern designed to keep the argument clear,[8] which brief writers can adopt to gain and maintain the judges' attention. The schematic is N-E-P-C: NAME IT, EXPLAIN IT, PROVE IT, CONCLUDE IT. Although devised for oral argument, this design works equally well for written briefs. Professor Cripe explains how this schematic can be adapted to written form: "If outlined, NAME IT would be a Roman numeral, EXPLAIN IT the capital letters, PROVE IT the

---

6. 343 U.S. 579 (1952). He also argued unsuccessfully in *Brown v. Board of Education*, 347 U.S. 483 (1954). That he was an advocate in both of those landmark cases is an indication of his prominence.

7. John W. Davis, *The Argument of an Appeal*, 26 A.B.A.J. 895, 896 (1940).

8. *See* Cripe, *supra* note 3, at 350.

Arabic numbers and small letters under the EXPLAIN IT sections, CONCLUDE IT probably a capital *D* or *E* tying up the point."[9]

The first principle of gaining and maintaining attention is to write for the person who will read your brief. You do not write for publication. You do not write to show your colleagues how smart you are, how well you know the subject matter, or how stupid you believe the judges to be. All this may well be true. But the name of the game is "persuade the judge." You don't score points for anything else.

The second principle is subsumed in the first. To gain the judge's attention, you must immediately establish your credibility as a brief writer. Without credibility you may possibly gain the judge's attention, but you will never maintain it. Unless the judge's attention is maintained, the judge will never be induced to accept your conclusion. And unless the judge is persuaded to accept the conclusion, the brief is not worth the paper (real or electronic) it is written on. Getting the judge to accept the conclusion is to appellate advocacy what the bottom line is to business.

Gaining and maintaining the attention of judges who read briefs in an electronic format poses even greater challenges. Robert Dubose, a partner at Alexander Dubose & Townsend LLP, has written and presented on the topic of legal writing in the digital era.[10] Dubose argues that the increasing use of technology has changed how lawyers work and communicate.[11] This new environment has "rewired" our brains and "change[s] the way we read" and possibly even "think."[12] For example, while reading a brief on a computer or tablet provides increased mobility, it also provides an array of distractions, which are just one click away.[13]

Technology is also changing how we gather information. Millennials have grown up in an environment where an endless amount of information is available through Internet search engines by just typing or saying a few words into their phone or electronic tablet. Dubose notes that computerized legal research may cause "rewired" lawyers to begin to view the law "as a series of quick answers obtained through a quick and easy Google-like search," which could result in losing the understanding of law as an "interrelated web of principles and rules that require hard work to untangle."[14]

Drawing from research on web usability, Dubose argues that lawyers must adapt to this new style of reading and information gathering to be successful

---

9. *Id.*

10. Robert B. DuBose, Legal Writing For the Re-wired Brain: Persuading Readers in a Paperless World (2010).

11. *Id.* at 1.

12. *Id.* at 1–2.

13. *Id.* at 21–23.

14. *See id.* at 32.

communicators.[15] He outlines several usability tools that can help legal writers reach their digital readership, including:

- Make it easy for your reader to skim by using headers, topic sentences, and a structure that a reader can easily grasp, such as bullet points or number lists.[16]

- Keep your documents brief.[17]

- Keep your documents simple in design, language, and logic.[18]

- Use "white space" to give the reader's eyes a break.[19]

In surveying state and federal appellate judges for this book, we found that judges are increasingly using electronic tablets to read briefs. Therefore, Dubose's techniques are important to consider when brief writing in the twenty-first century.

2.3 Criticisms of Briefs

Before addressing the criticisms of briefs that judges lodge against lawyers, certain things must be said. First, writing an appellate brief is not easy. It may be the most difficult task of advocacy. What you write, in most cases, is your client's last and only opportunity to address the appellate court.

On a scale of difficulty, writing a brief is much more arduous, calls for much more research, and requires much more intellectual choice and judgment than writing a judicial opinion. It is easier for a judge to write an opinion than for a lawyer to write a brief from scratch; the judge has the advantage of both parties' work product. The brief writer has to narrow the issues, select the precedents, and supply the authorities. The judge examines the precedents and authorities, confirms their authenticity and, via independent research, ascertains their continued vitality. In so doing, the opinion writer has a distinct advantage over the brief writer, because it can be assumed that the cited authorities already have been cross-checked by opposing counsel in answering briefs.

Second, many of the criticisms leveled against briefs may also be directed against judicial opinions.[20] Both the bench and the bar have much room for improvement. A litigant, however, does not lose a case because a judge's opinion fails to convince. Judges' tenures seldom are affected if their work product is sloppy, turgid, rambling, repetitious, or, at times, incomprehensible. But the quality of professional legal

---

15. *Id.* at 50–51.
16. *Id.* at 58–62, 71.
17. *Id.* at 99.
18. *Id.* at 103–15.
19. *Id.* at 117.
20. Ruggero J. Aldisert, Opinion Writing 6–7 (1990).

writing directly affects the persuasive powers of briefs, and, indirectly, the reputation of the lawyer in the professional community and personal standing in the law firm.

Examine the following criticisms and decide if you are guilty of any of the practices. Remember the bottom line—this is about winning your case, or losing it. It is that simple.

2.3.1 *General Criticisms*

What then are the criticisms generally expressed by judges against lawyers' briefs today? Here are some.

- Too long. Too long. Too long.
- Too many issues or points.
- Repetitive.
- Rudderless; no central theme(s).
- Failure to disclose the equitable heart of the appeal and the legal problem involved.
- Absence of organization.
- Too many acronyms.
- Excessive footnotes.
- Misrepresented facts and case holdings.
- Failure to mention or properly cite cases against you.
- Failure to come to terms with weaknesses in your case.
- Failure to apply the standard of review properly.
- Misrepresenting or exaggerating the adversary's arguments.
- Attacking opposing counsel or the lower court.
- Inaccurate or incomplete citations.
- Citing cases that have been overruled.
- Discussing unnecessary details of precedents and compared cases.
- Failure to show similarity or dissimilarity of material facts in compared cases.
- Failure to cite to the record when necessary.
- Citing to a record not contained in the appendix or excerpts of record.
- Failure to support the brief with a sufficient appendix or excerpts of record.
- Failure to state the relief requested.

- Typos, misspellings, and grammatical mistakes.

- Failure to observe the court's appellate rules.

2.3.2 *The Law Clerks Speak*

Having listed the complaints expressed by veteran judges, it is important to also consider observations generally shared by law clerks. Where a judge may have spent hours examining the briefs and records, the law clerks have spent days studying and analyzing the briefs in depth and performing original research on the legal issues involved. Their comments reflect many of the same criticisms offered by judges:

- Too long and wordy.

- Rearguing the case rather than explaining how the lower court's decision was wrong.

- Excessive use of adjectives and adverbs.

- Misrepresenting the law.

- Lack of organization. Making it difficult to identify the key issues.

- Disparaging the lower court or opposing counsel.

- Failure to apply the appropriate standard of review.

- Substituting "strong language" for "strong reasoning."

- Failing to proofread the brief.

- Forgetting about style and presentation with respect to font, formatting, cover, and tables.

- Excessive quotations from cases without explaining how the cases and quotes supported one's argument.

2.4 The Brief-Reading Environment

Lawyers should understand the environment in which briefs are read. The general public and the legal profession generally are familiar with the working environment of trial judges—the courtroom and the chambers. But they are typically unfamiliar with where and when appellate judges complete their work. Briefs are sometimes, but not very often, read in a cloistered setting—a quiet, library-like room. Usually, however, briefs must compete with a number of other demands on the judge's time and attention. The telephone rings. Motions and petitions for rehearing arrive electronically and clamor for immediate review. The chamber's email account pings with an urgent message or another judge's draft opinion, the reviewing of which is given a higher priority than drafting your own opinions. The Clerk's office emails an emergency motion. The courier arrives with an overnight delivery. The law clerks email or appear at the door because they have hit a snag in a case. So the death-less prose that the judge has been reading in a brief must wait another moment. Or another hour. Or another day.

This means the electronic tablet is taken home, so briefs can continue to be read when there is time around other family needs and personal interests. For some, the nightly news or an evening television show may interrupt the work. For many, a spouse wants to talk, or the kids clamor for attention, or friends telephone. The briefs may be set aside for another time. Or they are read waiting at an airport gate, or aboard a plane with the person in the next seat glancing across and specu-lating, "Gee, I suppose you're a lawyer. Let me ask you about this lawsuit I want to bring." Or the briefs are read late at night in hotel rooms.

One of the more unusual venues for brief-reading was used by Justice John Paul Stevens for a large portion of each Supreme Court term, namely, a Florida beach.

> [Justice Stevens] and his wife have a condominium in Fort Lauderdale, Fla., and they spend two weeks a month there from November through April . . . . "I do much more work in Florida than I do here," Stevens told [a reporter], looking contented. He sometimes reads briefs on the beach. "One of my favorite memories is the time I was sitting" on the Supreme Court bench in Washington just after returning from Florida, he recalled. "I shook the sand out of the brief!"[21]

A brief needs to be written with sufficient clarity as to maintain the beach-read-er's attention (most of the time), and the attention of other judges no matter their peculiarities of study. Obviously, then, an appellate brief cannot be a quick cut-and-paste production from various trial-court documents.

Look at the numbers. When Judge Aldisert first became an appellate judge in 1968, each active judge on the court was required to hear ninety appeals a year, which amounted to six sittings a year and fifteen sets of briefs per sitting. Each active judge on the court now has to decide approximately 550 appeals a year,[22] partici-pate in standing panels for *pro se* cases and motions, and sit in approximately seven scheduled sittings a year. This means that each judge must read, at least, approxi-mately 1,000 briefs a year and frequently many reply briefs. In many of the state intermediate courts, the caseload is even more formidable.

It is important to understand the brief-reading environment, because it explains why the written brief can be an effective instrument of persuasion only if it is con-cise, clear, accurate, and logical.

---

21. Jeffrey Rosen, *The Dissenter, Justice John Paul Stevens*, N.Y. TIMES MAG. (Sept. 23, 2007), http://www.nytimes.com/2007/09/23/magazine/23stevens-t.html?_r=0 (last visited Mar. 20, 2017).

22. Admin. Office of the United States Courts, *U.S. Court of Appeals—Judicial Caseload Profile*, U.S. COURTS, http://www.uscourts.gov/statistics-reports/federal-judicial-caseload-statistics-2015 (last visited Mar. 20, 2017).

CHAPTER THREE

THE PURPOSE OF ORAL ARGUMENT

3.1   Overview

We have said that the purpose of the written brief is to educate the court and to persuade it to accept a conclusion. Many, if not most, appellate courts today are "hot" in the sense that prior to oral argument, the judges have read the briefs and key precedents. An exception that at least suggests the need for the rule is that of a legendary, long-serving, and superb former judge of the United States Court of Appeals for the Fifth Circuit, famously remembered by his still-living colleagues for, at least at some point in his career, not reading the briefs before argument. Instead, this judge relied on his numerous questions at the beginning of each advocate's argument to inform him of relevant case details. Other than informing judges who take that approach, what is the purpose of oral argument? Why is it necessary? These are good questions, and lawyers who understand the proper answers are well on their way to becoming effective appellate advocates.

The late former chief justice of the United States Supreme Court, William H. Rehnquist, once suggested that the brief may be compared to the entire motion picture show, and the oral argument to the previews. "[T]he preview selects the dramatic and interesting scenes that are apt to catch the interest of the viewer and make [the viewer] want to see the entire movie."[1] On the other hand, the late Judge Frank Coffin of the First Circuit, who served for over forty years as a federal appellate judge, described the relationship differently:

> The challenge in planning and making an oral argument differs significantly from that in writing a brief. In constructing an effective brief, the writer may rely on felicity and grace to ease the burden of reading, but his purpose remains to convince the reader through what must largely be an intellectual effort. The purpose of oral argument, on the other hand, is to appeal to all the springs of motivation, to persuade.[2]

---

1. William H. Rehnquist, *Oral Advocacy*, 27 S. Tex. L. Rev. 289, 299 (1986).
2. Frank M. Coffin, The Ways of a Judge: Reflections from the Federal Appellate Bench 109 (1980).

While there may be some instances where the oral argument is but a preview, such as in the U.S. Supreme Court or with unique judges like the one mentioned at the beginning of this chapter, these situations are the exception to the "hot" court practice. Nearly all U.S. circuit judges and most judges of the states' highest courts have a comprehensive understanding of the written briefs before listening to the argument. In the cold courts, however, where the drill is to hear arguments first and to read briefs later, the oral argument can be considered the "preview." But in the vast majority of appellate courts today, the differences in the purposes of written and oral argument are far more pervasive.

The written brief is designed to educate and inform. Ostensibly, the brief has been written by a specialist in a particular field of law—one who has become thoroughly familiar with the issues and law over a long period of time and who has spent more than a year narrowing the legal issues. Ideally, this specialist has proceeded through the pretrial motion skirmishes and a possible trial or hearing, decided upon a strategy to upset the trial court's determination, and performed detailed legal research for appellate consumption. The specialist then summarizes the relevant law for presentation before a group of judicial generalists—appellate judges who are regularly exposed to the entire gamut of legal issues. The specialist lawyer then prepares for the benefit of the generalist judge a detailed segment of a small portion (or what purports to be a detailed segment of a small portion) of the grand mosaic of the law. The brief is a comprehensive presentation of relevant law concerning a tiny corner of the legal world.

By the time oral argument comes around, the generalist judge, having examined and studied the briefs, is no longer a stranger to the relevant substantive law. The court has been furnished with a lens through which to examine the intricate pattern of that tiny portion of the grand legal mosaic. Oral argument gives the lawyer an opportunity to furnish the court with a magnifying power to the lens, to focus on how the relevant segments of the grand mosaic fit together. Oral argument must not be considered as the first glimpse of the scene, or a reconnaissance, or even an exploration of the territory to be covered. The brief is designed to do this. Oral argument is neither preparatory artillery nor a preliminary probe to determine soft or hard spots. Oral argument takes judges by the hand and directs them through the maps previously supplied them. It merely supplements and reinforces what has gone before and directs the judges to a desired objective in the forensic battle by opening wide the pathways that were previously identified as possible routes in the written brief.

The judges already know your battle plan. They have read the brief. At oral argument, this plan is put to the test; as Holmes would say, it will be washed in cynical acid.

3.2 The Judges' View

Reduced to its essence, the purpose of oral argument is to clarify and emphasize what has been written. Lawyers must understand that the clarification process must be viewed not only from the perspective of the lawyer, but also from that of the judge.

Consider what judges expect oral argument to accomplish:

To question legal and factual positions. Perhaps what you must be the most prepared to handle are challenges to the legal and factual contentions that were made in the briefs, and for an appellant, the difficulties of the trial court ruling. A well-prepared judge, who has studied relevant parts of the record and read the important case precedents, will be as aware of the weaknesses as is opposing counsel, but it is a judge who gets to require oral responses to those weaknesses. The judges may ask you to substantiate factual claims by referring to the record. They may ask you to bring into better focus important record facts, details of pleadings, findings of the tribunal, and evidentiary support. They may ask you to clarify confusing legal contentions by referring to precise quotations in the precedents cited. They may ask for information as to the party's specific position in the trial court. They may ask what steps were taken at trial to preserve points for review.

To clarify issues. The judges want you to help them isolate the issues they must decide and to assist them in resolving any collateral issues—such as jurisdiction, standing, or mootness—that might not have been briefed but now stand in the way of reaching the merits of the stated argument. The judges may insist on a further explanation of the claims or defenses asserted in the briefs. Notwithstanding the best efforts of writers, ambiguity does exist. The judges use oral argument to ask what counsel is actually contending.

To examine the practical impact of claims or defenses. The judges are always interested in knowing how far the requested legal precept will carry. This is where hypothetical questions come into play, and lawyers must be ready for them. The answer "that is not this case," which is frequently heard, should be left unspoken. The judge is fully aware in using hypotheticals that the case differs from the example. Because every holding is a potential precedent, the judges must know how wide a swath in the law is being cut and what type of limiting principle can be crafted to address the judges' concerns. Judges may also inquire as to the potential burdens imposed on the individual or on society, such as the effects on employer-employee relations, the implications as to freedoms of private citizens and effective law enforcement, and possible hindrances on commercial transactions or on the use of private property. That is, the judges want to know whether acceptance of an argument will produce impractical or nonsensical results.

To lobby other judges for or against particular positions. Having read the briefs, and having some intimate knowledge of their colleagues' inclinations, judges may use oral argument as a form of internal advocacy. They may stake out tentative positions in advance of the decision conference. The problem for the lawyer, however, is that he often does not know if the judge is staking out a position or playing devil's advocate. What is stated as a question might actually be a message for other judges on the panel, particularly if the "question" is a long statement of a position which is closed by something like, "do you agree?" or "is that so?"

To assist the advocate in presenting the case. Somewhat similar to the preceding point, if a judge agrees with the advocate and thinks a point needs to be made or at least made more clearly, what is known in the trade as a "friendly question" may be asked. Be careful, though, as questions may not be as friendly as they appear. Or, another judge on the panel may answer a question before the advocate does. Not having to answer may seem helpful, but be alert. The answer may not be a friendly one, and the lawyer may need to disagree, respectfully. One respectful way, which serves also when the lawyer is unclear of the import of the judge's answer, is to express appreciation and then give a separate answer. In one argument in the Fifth Circuit, one judge answered three questions posed by another judge to the same lawyer, each of which supported that lawyer's position. On the fourth question, with only silence from the other judge, the stumped advocate finally turned to his helper: "Well, what are we going to say now?" The answer was: "You are on your own." The moral: do not depend on such help.

3.3 The Lawyers' View

Lawyers have different goals in the oral argument process:

To face the decision makers eye to eye. Oral argument is one of two occasions when the judges get together to consider a case (the other is the decision conference), but it is the only opportunity for the lawyer to face the court eyeball to eyeball without "filtering" by the law clerks who figure greatly in the brief-reading and bench memorandum-writing process. Here, the lawyer has the opportunity of conveying to the court that quality that Aristotle called ethos—the personal character of the speaker.[3] Other aspects of Aristotle's *The Rhetoric* may emerge from the written brief: pathos (the proper attitude in the recipient of the argument) and logos (arguments that demonstrate the truth, real, or apparent).[4] But oral argument is the only opportunity the lawyer has to personally motivate the judges by the force of his or her personality, and to convey what Bettinghaus described as three factors that people use in judging a speaker's credibility: trustworthiness, qualifications, and personal characteristics.[5]

To emphasize and simplify the pivotal or gut issues of the brief. Here, the lawyer distills from usually a fifty-page brief two or three pivotal issues (no more, please) that will make or break the case. The lawyer truly must strike for the jugular and give the court what Holmes called the "implements of decision."[6]

---

3. ARISTOTLE, RHETORIC 8 (W. Rhys Roberts trans., 1954).

4. Nicholas M. Cripe, *Fundamentals of Persuasive Oral Argument*, 20 THE FORUM 342, 357 (1985).

5. ERWIN P. BETTINGHAUS, PERSUASIVE COMMUNICATION 95 (3d ed. 1980).

6. John W. Davis, *The Argument of an Appeal*, 26 A.B.A. J. 895, 896 (1940).

To come to grips with real questions that trouble the court. Early in the argument, you will learn from the judges' questions any misgivings, concerns, or doubts about the arguments presented in the brief. This is the only opportunity to lay these to rest. Put aside any prepared remarks and immediately respond to the court's invitation to dispel the uncertainty. Essentially, this is counsel's opportunity to participate in the judges' decision conference.[7]

To correct misimpressions of fact or law. Be alert to any misimpressions the judges may have about the case. Be alert to any signs that the judges are proceeding on erroneous assumptions of fact or law, and take the opportunity to correct such errors in a respectful manner.

To demonstrate the logical soundness of your position. Show the court that your argument hangs together under fire. Stephen M. Shapiro—a former Deputy Solicitor General and an appellate specialist with Mayer Brown—offers this perspective:

> Oral argument is the anvil on which a solid position is hammered out and confirmed—or shattered entirely by repeated blows. Effective advocates use oral argument to dramatically demonstrate that [their] position is sound. Thus, despite difficult questions and criticisms, there always is a logical response and the argument hangs together in a coherent way. There are, in short, no hidden defects, gaps in reasoning, or unanticipated consequences. Some arguments fall apart entirely under the pressure of argument. Other arguments, which have been carefully honed in advance, are strengthened and confirmed by the process of debate.[8]

Arguing a case before an appellate court is not easy today. Judges know this and lawyers must understand this. As discussed in Chapter One, the tactics and style that win at trial do not translate to victory at the appellate level.

Therefore, attorneys who infrequently handle appeals fail 1) to understand what is expected, 2) to distill the trial loss into what is important on appeal, and 3) to avoid being jittery, high-strung, agitated, and tense during the presentation. Appearing before an appellate court is to revisit whatever ogre of a professor you had in law school. In the "hot" courts, the Socratic method comes storming back at you with a ferocity that you have not experienced in years. The snide remarks and sarcasm of trial judges in evidence rulings are love taps by comparison.

But here, in the majesty of the huge appellate courtroom, you suddenly are faced with an unrelenting attack on your brief. You are bombarded with hypotheticals of which you never dreamed. You may find yourself the target of an unyielding, obdurate, and

---

7. Stephen M. Shapiro, *Oral Argument in the Supreme Court of the United States*, 33 Cath. U. L. Rev. 529, 531–32 (1984).
    8. *Id.* at 532.

unrelenting line of questioning from a judge inexorably committed to an idiosyncratic frolic, or you may find yourself caught in the crossfire among the various members of the bench totally immersed in intracourt judicial advocacy. In such circumstances, how do you perform as a competent, persuasive appellate advocate?

The short answer is that you must prepare, prepare, prepare. You must master the subject matter of your case—the subject matter of which your case is only a part, not merely the limited factual and legal perimeters of your case itself—so that you will know as much as possible about the ramifications of a decision and its capacity to expand or contract the law. You must master the record completely and devise means to effect instant entry to particular passages when requested by the judges. Justice Robert H. Jackson supplied appellate advocates with these inspiring words: "If the day of one's making an oral argument is not one of the great days in a lawyer's life, he should not make the argument."[9] Justice William O. Douglas's experience suggests that many lawyers were not moved by this spirit: "Few truly good advocates appeared before the Court. In my time 40 percent were incompetent. Only a few were excellent."[10] More recently, Judge Laurence H. Silberman, a senior federal appellate judge, noted that, while his court "reputedly hears the best appellate advocates in the nation . . . it is astonishing how many cases are presented by lawyers who are simply not up to the task."[11]

3.4 Criticisms of Oral Argument

To be adequately prepared for an appellate argument, you must learn to avoid the following litany of complaints judges lodge against the quality of oral argument today.

3.4.1 General Criticisms

- Inadequate preparation.

  — Failure to master the facts.

  — Failure to master the record.

  — Failure to master the relevant law.

- Ineptitude in answering the court's questions (*see* section 3.4.2).

- Repeating excerpts from the written brief instead of designing a hard-hitting oral presentation.

---

9. Myron H. Bright, *The Ten Commandments of Oral Argument*, 67 A.B.A. J. 1136, 1136 (1981) (citation omitted).

10. *Id.*

11. Laurence H. Silberman, *Plain Talk on Appellate Advocacy*, 20 LITIGATION 3 (1994).

- Reading a prepared speech, or even worse, reading the brief.

- Talking too much.

  — If you have made your point, sit down. Do not exhaust every minute of allotted time. You might open a door and get into trouble.

  — If it is obvious that the court understands your argument on a point, then stop and move to another.

  — Rebut, do not repeat.

- Getting sidetracked on minor, not controlling, points.

- Not knowing when to concede a point.

- Making disparaging comments about opposing counsel or the lower court.

- Leading off the argument with a weak point or an unnecessarily provocative contention that generates friction on the bench at the outset.

- Mangling the facts.

  — Do not reargue evidentiary matters that have been resolved adversely by the fact-finder.

  — Do not use hyperbole, overstatement, or exaggeration in describing record facts.

- Failing to communicate effectively.

  — Do not mumble and mutter. All is lost unless the judges can hear you. As Fifth Circuit Chief Judge Carl Stewart will say when necessary, "Counsel, use your theater voice."

  — Do not use emotional rhetoric, high-flown oratory, or irrelevant lines of argument intended to incite emotional responses instead of logical conclusions. Leave the jury tone at home.

  — Do not speak in monotone, too fast, or to yourself.

  — Do not lose eye contact with the judges by reading at length from the text of an oral argument script or from legislative history, opinions, statutes, regulations, or the trial record.

- Failing to relate the appropriate standard of review to the particular issue.

- Failing to come to grips with the plain language of case holdings or statutory or constitutional provisions.

- Failing to marshal valuable time allotted you.

— Do not waste time on trivial matters or on issues already discussed adequately. Recognize when everything has been said and move on.

— Do not continue to talk after the red light has flashed on or the presiding judge has called time, unless the court wishes argument to continue.

• Failing to accept or acknowledge helpful observations or reformulations of argument suggested by a judge.

3.4.2   Inept Handling of Questions

Many of the criticisms of oral argument lodged by judges concern the manner with which lawyers answer questions from the bench. Whatever had been the custom of judges in yesteryear, most appellate arguments today take the form of a colloquy between the bench and the bar. Avoid these faults:[12]

• Failing to listen carefully to a question from the bench and answering some other question that the judge has not asked.

• Evading hypothetical questions by stating "That's a different case. . . ."

• Failing to give a direct, simple, and comprehensible answer.

• Refusing to give a "yes" or "no" answer when the judge requests one and when it is possible to do so.

• Attempting to postpone answers to questions, or promising to cover matters that are never covered adequately later.

• Giving long-winded, multiple-paragraph answers to straightforward questions, or relying on complex and incomprehensible factual descriptions in responding to questions.

• Giving timorous responses to questions that seem overbearing, or displaying disappointment when questioning is hostile. Or, in the reverse, getting angry with the judges when a seemingly hostile question is asked.

• Attempting to answer questions by propounding other questions back to the court.

3.4.3   The Law Clerks Speak

Just as with briefs, it is important to also consider observations generally shared by law clerks, who witness oral argument after having done important preparatory

---

12. *See generally* Shapiro, *supra* note 7.

work. Law clerks know enough about the issues and the record to follow the oral argument precisely. Their comments, as follow, reflect many of the same criticisms offered by judges and lawyers.

- Attorneys too often do not answer the questions put to them. They dodge questions or try to bluff when they do not know the answer. They often show a defensive attitude to questions.

- They spend too much time repeating what has already been said in the brief, instead of letting the brief speak for itself.

- They do not know when to sit down. ("If you have said all you planned to say, ask the judges if they have any questions. If they don't, sit down. The best oral advocates do.")

- They attempt to retry the evidence in the case before the appellate court. Attorneys often fail to recognize the difference between effective trial advocacy before a jury and effective appellate advocacy before an appellate court.

- They become too attached to one argument, instead of listening to the judges' concerns and moving to other points.

- Attorneys often are not adequately prepared. They do not know the record, the facts, or the law.

- Attorneys display poor manners. They argue with judges.

- They adopt a style or rhetoric aimed at convincing a jury, without having the substance mastered to convince the panel.

3.5   The Purpose of Oral Argument: A Summary

Chapters Sixteen through Eighteen, on preparing for and delivering the argument, will contain detailed suggestions on how to avoid pitfalls that have led to these criticisms.

We conclude our discussion on the purpose of oral argument at this juncture by emphasizing again that because most judges in most appellate courts read briefs prior to argument, the oral argument should not be a cut-and-paste job of excerpts from the written brief. Extensive preparation is necessary, and it must range far from that required for writing the brief. You must be prepared for an onslaught of questions from the bench that not only test the logical premises of the written submission, but may extend to outer perimeters of the subject matter of which your case is but an isolated part. The questions often take the form of hypotheticals seeking assistance from you as to where the lines should be drawn to expand or contract the specific legal precept you are urging upon the court. To argue effectively, familiarity with your brief is not enough. You must know the extensive perimeters of the law and know precisely where your case fits in that larger landscape. Demonstrate a comprehensive familiarity with the entire subject matter of substantive law of which your case is but a part.

What Justice Robert H. Jackson once said of his experiences as solicitor general summarizes the joys and pitfalls of any lawyer arguing before any court:

> The order and progression of an argument are important to its ready comprehension, but in the Supreme Court these are not wholly within the lawyer's control. It is difficult to please nine different minds, and it is a common experience that questions upset the plan of argument before the lawyer has fairly started. I used to say that, as Solicitor General, I made three arguments of every case. First came the one that I planned—as I thought, logical, coherent, complete. Second was the one actually presented—interrupted, incoherent, disjointed, disappointing. The third was the utterly devastating argument that I thought of after going to bed that night.[13]

Your goal to achieve the purpose of the oral presentation is to make "the utterly devastating argument" that Solicitor General Jackson thought of after going to bed on the night following his court appearance.

Every appellate lawyer must recognize the fundamentals of persuasion—how the case, with all its warts and blemishes, looks to the court. What do the judges know about the case? How do the judges feel about what they know or do not know? Your strategy will determine how to order your arguments, how much time to allow each part, and how to word and support your arguments. You must be satisfied that the arguments you select are the arguments the court will most likely accept.

Cicero summarized it well when he advised would-be orators centuries ago:

> Be clear, so the audience understands what is being said.

> Be interesting, so the audience will want to listen to what is being said.

> Be persuasive, so the audience will agree with what is being said.[14]

---

13. Robert H. Jackson, *Advocacy Before the United States Supreme Court*, 37 Cornell L. Rev. 1, 6 (1951).

14. Cripe, *supra* note 4, at 357 (quoting Cicero).

PART TWO

TECHNICAL REQUIREMENTS FOR BRIEFS

CHAPTER FOUR

JURISDICTION

4.1   Overview

In a previous edition of this book, Judge Aldisert told the story of a senior partner in one of the nation's prestigious law firms who was arguing a case before a panel of judges in the United States Courthouse in Philadelphia. After he announced his name as attorney for the appellant, Judge John J. Gibbons interrupted: "Counsel, I don't think this court has jurisdiction. This looks like a Rule 54(b) situation because certain claims are still open below."

The urbane practitioner, who for years had played a dominant role in the American Bar Association, paused for a moment, folded up his notes, and said, "I apologize for taking up the court's time. There is no jurisdiction. May I have the court's permission to withdraw the appeal?" His embarrassment was equaled by the chagrin of partners in the two opposing law firms, equally renowned, who likewise had failed to consider the question of appellate jurisdiction and had failed to raise the issue in their briefs.

Is there jurisdiction to bring the appeal? Not a word in an appellate brief should be written on the substantive merits of a case until this question is answered in the affirmative. Indeed, even though time constraints may require you to file a notice of appeal before jurisdiction can be ascertained with certainty, no serious discussions with your client as to the advisability of pursuing the appeal should go forward until you are absolutely confident that the appellate court has jurisdiction *at this time*. Likewise, the appellee's first chore is to determine whether the appellant has the right to file the appeal *at this time*.

An appellate lawyer in federal court has an additional burden to determine whether the federal district court had jurisdiction to entertain the case. The jurisdiction of federal courts is more limited than that of their state counterparts. The federal courts may hear cases based only on diversity of citizenship (with the requisite amount in controversy); federal questions, statutory or constitutional; and cases in which the United States is a party.[1] Unlike other

---

1. 28 U.S.C. §§ 1331, 1332, 1345, 1346.

appellate issues placed in contention, which must be preserved by objection unless they are subject to review under the plain error doctrine, the question of jurisdiction may be raised at any time on any appellate level either by the court *sua sponte* or by one of the parties.[2]

The Federal Rules of Appellate Procedure now require the appellant's brief to include a jurisdictional statement.[3] This statement should include:

(A) the basis for the district court's or agency's subject-matter jurisdiction, with citations to applicable statutory provisions and stating relevant facts establishing jurisdiction;

(B) the basis for the court of appeals' jurisdiction, with citations to applicable statutory provisions and stating relevant facts establishing jurisdiction;

(C) the filing dates establishing the timeliness of the appeal or petition for review; and

(D) an assertion that the appeal is from a final order or judgment that disposes of all parties' claims, or information establishing the court of appeals' jurisdiction on some other basis.[4]

A word of caution is warranted: you must make sure that you understand the pertinent state or federal jurisdictional rules where you practice. This book is not intended to be an authority on these important rules. Rules change, as do the ways that the courts interpret them, so you must stay informed in this crucial area.

It is also important to remember that a federal district court's lack of subject-matter jurisdiction does not affect the jurisdiction of a circuit court of appeals to review all jurisdictional issues. If the appeals court determines the district court had no jurisdiction, any merits decisions by the district court become invalid and are not in any way reviewable.[5]

4.2 Appealability in the Federal System

Rule 12(h)(3) of the Federal Rules of Civil Procedure provides that "[i]f the court determines at any time that it lacks subject-matter jurisdiction, the court must dismiss the action."[6] The lawyer, and the court before which an appeal is brought, have a duty to inquire into jurisdiction—both jurisdiction as to the appeal and jurisdiction as to the original action. The Supreme Court has stated that "every federal

---

2. Erwin Chemerinsky, Federal Jurisdiction § 5.1 (6th ed. 2012).

3. Fed. R. App. Proc. 28(a)(4).

4. *Id.*

5. *See, e.g.,* Am. Fire & Cas. Co. v. Finn, 341 U.S. 6 (1951); Bell v. Hood, 327 U.S. 678 (1946) (reviewing on appeal the district court's dismissal of an action for lack of jurisdiction); Switchmen's Union of N. Am. v. Nat'l Mediation Bd., 320 U.S. 297, 300 (1943).

6. Fed. R. Civ. P. 12(h)(3).

appellate court has a special obligation to satisfy itself not only of its own jurisdiction, but also that of the lower courts in a cause under review."[7] The advocate also must do as much.

To begin the examination of federal appellate jurisdiction, consider that every appeal from a district court presents at least three jurisdictional issues: 1) whether the district court order or judgment is appealable immediately, either under the final judgment rule or a recognized exception; 2) whether the notice of appeal is sufficient; and 3) whether the notice of appeal was timely filed.

4.2.1 *Final Orders*

Is the decision final? Under 28 U.S.C. § 1291, "[t]he courts of appeals . . . shall have jurisdiction of appeals from all final decisions of the district courts . . . except where a direct review may be had in the Supreme Court."[8] Parties may appeal certain interlocutory orders by right,[9] and others by permission,[10] but generally, the courts of appeals have the power to review only final decisions.[11]

A final decision is "one which ends the litigation on the merits and leaves nothing for the court to do but execute the judgment."[12] The finality requirement of 28 U.S.C. § 1291 is to be given its practical rather than its technical construction.[13] A court will consider the balance between "the inconvenience and costs of piecemeal review" and "the danger of denying justice by delay."[14] A lawyer arguing against finality focuses on the justice issue, while a lawyer arguing for finality emphasizes the inconvenience and costs of piecemeal review.[15]

---

7. Grupo Dataflux v. Atlas Global Grp., L.P., 541 U.S. 567, 593 (2004) (citing Bender v. Williamsport Area Sch. Dist., 475 U.S. 534, 541 (1986) (quoting *Mitchell*, 293 U.S. at 244)).

8. 28 U.S.C. § 1291. Cases of direct review to the Supreme Court are very rare and are specifically delineated by statute. 28 U.S.C. §§ 1253, 2101; *see, e.g.*, 47 U.S.C. § 555(c)(2) (Cable Act).

9. 28 U.S.C. § 1292(a).

10. 28 U.S.C. § 1292(b).

11. Swint v. Chambers Cty. Com'n, 514 U.S. 35, 41–42 (1995).

12. Riley v. Kennedy, 553 U.S. 406, 419 (2008) (quoting Catlin v. United States, 324 U.S. 229, 233 (1945)).

13. Florida v. Thomas, 532 U.S. 774, 777–78 (2001) (citing Cox Broad. Corp. v. Cohn, 420 U.S. 469 (1975)); Brown Shoe Co. v. United States, 370 U.S. 294, 306 (1962) (collecting cases through which the Supreme Court "adopted essentially practical tests for identifying" final judgments).

14. Johnson v. Jones, 515 U.S. 304, 315 (1995) (citing Dickinson v. Petroleum Conversion Corp., 338 U.S. 507, 511 (1950)); *see* FED. R. CIV. P. 54(b).

15. *See also* Cobbledick v. United States, 309 U.S. 323, 324–25 (1940) ("Finality as a condition of review is an historic characteristic of federal appellate procedure. It was written into the first Judiciary Act and has been departed from only when observance of it would practically defeat the right to any review at all . . . . To be effective, judicial administration must not be leaden-footed.") (footnote omitted).

The final judgment rule furthers four goals: 1) deference to the district courts,[16] 2) efficient use of judicial resources,[17] 3) the prevention of harassment and the avoidance of a costly appeal,[18] and 4) dilatory succession of separate appeals.[19] The result is that some erroneous trial court rulings go uncorrected until the appeal of the final decision, but this is preferable to a rule that would permit piecemeal appellate review to disrupt litigation in the trial court. The rule can either help or hinder you depending upon which side of the courtroom you stand.

a) Examples of appealable "final orders":

1) Grant of a motion to dismiss.[20]

2) Grant of a motion for summary judgment that resolves all issues regarding all parties.

3) Entry of judgment after a bench or jury trial.[21]

4) Imposition of sentence in a criminal case.[22]

5) Ordering immediate change in possession of property to a private party but continuing with related proceedings.[23] There may be no right of appeal if possession is to be delivered to a governmental body or the court.[24]

b) Examples of orders that are not "final" and are not immediately appealable:

1) Denial of a motion to dismiss.[25]

2) Denial of a motion to disqualify counsel in a civil trial.[26]

3) Denial of a motion for judgment on the pleadings.[27]

4) Denial of summary judgment.[28]

---

16. Flanagan v. United States, 465 U.S. 259, 263–64 (1984); *see also* Cunningham v. Hamilton Cty., Oh., 527 U.S. 198, 203–04 (1999) (quoting Firestone Tire & Rubber Co. v. Risjord, 449 U.S. 368, 374 (1981)).

17. Cunningham v. Hamilton Cty., Oh., 527 U.S. 198, 203–04 (1999) (quoting Firestone Tire & Rubber Co. v. Risjord, 449 U.S. 368, 374 (1981)).

18. *Id.*

19. *Cobbledick*, 309 U.S. at 324–25.

20. Montes v. United States, 37 F.3d 1347, 1350 (9th Cir. 1994).

21. *See, e.g.*, Sell v. United States, 539 U.S. 166, 176 (2003); United States v. River Rouge Improvement Co., 269 U.S. 411, 413–14 (1926).

22. Flynt v. Ohio, 451 U.S. 619, 620 (1981) (per curiam); Berman v. United States, 302 U.S. 211, 212–13 (1937).

23. Radio Station WOW, Inc. v. Johnson, 326 U.S. 120 (1945); United States v. Davenport, 106 F.3d 1333, 1335 (7th Cir. 1997).

24. United States v. Beasley, 558 F.2d 1200, 1201 (5th Cir. 1977).

25. Catlin v. United States, 324 U.S. 229, 232 (1945).

26. *Firestone Tire*, 449 U.S. at 369–70.

27. Sinclair Ref. Co. v. Stevens, 123 F.2d 186 (8th Cir. 1941).

28. Pacific Union Conference of Seventh Day Adventists v. Marshall, 434 U.S. 1305 (1977) (Rehnquist, Circuit Justice).

5) Grant of partial summary judgment.[29]

6) Rulings on discovery motions.[30]

7) The granting of a motion for a new trial after the verdict.[31]

Some of these non-final matters, however, may be reviewable under exceptions to the final judgment rule established by statute, rule, or case law.

To be clear, orders that were not final and, therefore, not immediately appealable may nonetheless be reviewed on appeal once a final order has been entered.[32]

4.2.2 *Finality on Cases Involving Multiple Claims or Parties*

What should you do in a case involving multiple claims and parties when you want to appeal from a decision resolving fewer than all of the claims against all of the defendants? Federal Rule of Civil Procedure 54(b) governs the entry of final judgment in civil cases involving multiple claims and parties. If an order or decision adjudicates fewer than all claims or determines the claims of fewer than all parties, Rule 54 provides that such order or decision "does not end the action as to any of the claims or parties and may be revised at any time before the entry of a judgment adjudicating all the claims and all the parties' rights and liabilities"; such an order is, therefore, not appealable until the entire action is decided.[33] However, you may request that the district court enter final judgment under Rule 54(b) as to fewer than all the claims or parties after an express determination that there is no just reason for delay.[34]

The purpose of Rule 54(b) is to avoid the possible injustice of a delay in entering judgment (and thus delay of appeal) on distinctly separate claims and to reduce the risk that a litigant will inadvertently forfeit his or her right to appeal.[35] The decision whether to certify an order for immediate appeal is within the district court's discretion.[36]

To qualify for certification under Rule 54(b), the order must be final as defined by 28 U.S.C. § 1291,[37] it must involve multiple claims or parties,[38] and there must

---

29. Brooks v. Fitch, 642 F.2d 46, 48 (3d Cir. 1981).

30. Barrick Grp., Inc. v. Mosse, 849 F.2d 70, 72 (2d Cir. 1988) ("Generally, orders denying or compelling discover are non-appealable . . . .").

31. Allied Chemical Corp. v. Daiflon, Inc., 449 U.S. 33, 34–35 (1980).

32. "The general rule is that a party is entitled to a single appeal, to be deferred until final disposition of the case." Franklin v. Dist. of Columbia, 163 F.3d 625, 629 (D.C. Cir. 1998).

33. FED. R. CIV. P. 54(b).

34. *Id.*

35. Gelboim v. Bank of Am. Corp., 135 S. Ct. 897, 902 (2015) (citing Dickinson v. Petroleum Conversion Corp., 338 U.S. 507, 511 (1950)).

36. Curtiss-Wright Corp. v. Gen. Elec. Corp., 446 U.S. 1, 8 (1980).

37. 28 U.S.C. § 1291; Sears Roebuck & Co. v. Mackey, 351 U.S. 427, 435 (1956).

38. FED. R. CIV. P. 54(b); *see, e.g.,* Liberty Mutual Ins. Co. v. Wetzel, 424 U.S. 737, 742–44 (1976) (concerning a single claim appeal).

be an express determination that there is "no just reason for delay."[39] In addition, some courts of appeals require that the district court's certification should be accompanied by a reasoned explanation, however brief, of its conclusion.[40]

4.2.3   Collateral Orders

The absence of a final order does not eliminate all chances for appeal. In some circumstances, an order may qualify as a "final decision" under § 1291 absent an entry of final judgment. The Supreme Court created this common-law exception to the final judgment rule in *Cohen v. Beneficial Industrial Loan Corporation*.[41] "To come within the 'small class' of decisions excepted from the final-judgment rule by *Cohen*, the order must conclusively determine the disputed question, resolve an important issue completely separate from the merits of the action, and be effectively unreviewable on appeal from a final judgment."[42]

Under the *Cohen* doctrine, where rights will "be irretrievably lost in the absence of immediate appeal," collateral review is available.[43] The Supreme Court has strictly construed this requirement and refused to convert the limited exception carved out in *Cohen* into a license for broad disregard of the finality rule imposed by Congress in § 1291.[44]

Examples of appealable collateral orders:

1) Denial of alleged requirement to provide security before proceeding with litigation, which was the issue in *Cohen*.[45]

2) Denial of a motion to dismiss on the basis of qualified immunity from suit.[46]

3) Denial of bail.[47]

---

39. FED. R. CIV. P. 54(b).

40. *See, e.g.,* O'Bert *ex rel.* Estate of O'Bert v. Vargo, 331 F.3d 29, 41 (2d Cir. 2003) (noting the Second Circuit's "frequent[ ] dismiss[al of] appeals where no reasoned explanation for the Rule 54(b) judgment was given"); Ebrahimi v. City of Huntsville Bd. of Educ., 114 F.3d 162, 166 (11th Cir. 1997) (providing an exception to the Eleventh Circuit's explanation requirement). However, the failure to provide this information does not, under the "prevailing rule," pose a jurisdictional defect. *See* Carter v. City of Philadelphia, 181 F.3d 339, 343–45 (3d Cir. 1999) (choosing to follow the "prevailing rule" in holding that "a district court's failure to state the reasons for its Rule 54(b) certification does not pose a jurisdictional barrier to appeal") (citing Bank of Lincolnwood v. Federal Leasing, Inc., 622 F.2d 944, 948–49 (7th Cir. 1980)).

41. 337 U.S. 541 (1949).

42. Coopers & Lybrand v. Livesay, 437 U.S. 463, 468 (1978) (footnote and citations omitted); *see also* Mohawk Indus., Inc. v. Carpenter, 558 U.S. 100, 106 (2009); Swint v. Chambers Cnty. Comm., 514 U.S. 35, 42 (1995).

43. Richardson-Merrell, Inc. v. Koller, 472 U.S. 424, 430–31 (1985).

44. *Firestone Tire*, 449 U.S. at 374–75.

45. *Cohen*, 337 U.S. at 546–47.

46. Mitchell v. Forsyth, 472 U.S. 511, 528–30 (1985).

47. Stack v. Boyle, 342 U.S. 1 (1951) (codified in 18 U.S.C. §§ 3145(c) and 3731).

National Institute for Trial Advocacy

4) Denial of motion to dismiss brought on the basis that the suit is intended to chill First Amendment rights when a state has adopted a statute barring "strategic lawsuits against public participation," or an "anti-SLAPP" statute.[48]

5) Order requiring defendants to pay ninety percent of the costs of notice to prospective class members in class action.[49]

6) Denial of dismissal based on double jeopardy.[50]

7) Denial of dismissal of a criminal case against a person entitled to protection under the speech or debate clause of Article I of the Constitution.[51]

Examples of orders that are not appealable:

1) Denial of motion to dismiss on grounds of forum non conveniens.[52]

2) Discovery orders.[53]

3) Denial of a petition to disqualify an attorney.[54]

4) Denial of a motion to dismiss based on vindictive prosecution.[55]

5) Denial of a motion to apply the judgment bar of the Federal Tort Claims Act.[56]

6) An order under Federal Rule of Civil Procedure 37(a)(4) imposing sanctions on an attorney.[57]

Generally, a federal district court's order remanding a case to state court on the basis that it was improperly removed is not reviewable on appeal.[58] By statute, though, a remand to state court of a suit against federal officers or agencies under 28 U.S.C. § 1442 or a civil rights case under 28 U.S.C. § 1443 may be appealed.[59] In addition, if a case is removed under the terms of the Class Action Fairness Act, the court of appeals "may accept an appeal" in its discretion from the grant or denial of a motion to remand.[60]

---

48. *See, e.g.*, Liberty Synergistics Inc. v. Microflo Ltd., 718 F.3d 138, 150–51 (2d Cir. 2013); Henry v. Lake Charles American Press, L.L.C., 566 F.3d 164, 181 (5th Cir. 2009); Batzel v. Smith, 333 F.3d 1018, 1024–26 (9th Cir. 2003).

49. Eisen v. Carlisle & Jacquelin, 417 U.S. 156 (1974).

50. Abney v. United States, 431 U.S. 651, 662 (1977).

51. Helstoski v. Meanor, 442 U.S. 500, 508 (1979).

52. Van Cauwenberghe v. Biard, 486 U.S. 517 (1988).

53. Mohawk Indus., Inc. v. Carpenter, 558 U.S. 100, 108 (2009).

54. *Firestone Tire*, 449 U.S. at 370.

55. United States v. Hollywood Motor Car Co., 458 U.S. 263 (1982).

56. Will v. Hallock, 546 U.S. 345, 347 (2006).

57. Cunningham v. Hamilton County, Ohio, 527 U.S. 198, 200 (1999).

58. Quackenbush v. Allstate Ins. Co., 517 U.S. 706, 714 (1996).

59. 28 U.S.C. § 1447(d).

60. 28 U.S.C. § 1453(c)(1). There are special rules, including deadlines for the court of appeals to act, under this provision.

If you can demonstrate irreparable harm from one of these usually non-appealable orders, you might be entitled to seek certification under 28 U.S.C. § 1292(b) or relief by mandamus.

4.2.4 *Nonfinal Appealable Orders*

4.2.4.1 Interlocutory Appealable Orders under 28 U.S.C. § 1292(a)

Appeal may be permitted by rule or statute, *e.g.*, 28 U.S.C. § 1292(a), which permits appeal from:

- "[i]nterlocutory orders of the district courts . . . granting, continuing, modifying, refusing or dissolving injunctions, or refusing to dissolve or modify injunctions . . . ."[61]

- "Interlocutory orders appointing receivers, or refusing orders to wind up receiverships . . . ."[62]

- "Interlocutory decrees of... district courts . . . determining the rights and liabilities of the parties to admiralty cases . . . ."[63]

Under § 1292(a)(1), you may confront the situation where a district court enters an order not technically granting or denying an injunction, but having the same effect.[64] When a district court order does not expressly deny an injunction, but has that ultimate effect, you must "show that [the] interlocutory order of the district court might have a 'serious, perhaps irreparable consequence,' and that the order can be 'effectively challenged' only by immediate appeal."[65]

4.2.4.2 Certification under 28 U.S.C. § 1292(b)

Sometimes, in the midst of litigation, the district court decides an important and reasonably disputed issue of law prior to trial that does not finally dispose of any claim or party, but that has substantial consequences for the outcome of the case. In this circumstance, you may wish to seek certification under § 1292(b) so that the order is immediately appealable.[66] Unlike a Rule 54(b) certification, however, the court of appeals may decline jurisdiction under § 1292(b) and, thereby, deny

---

61. 28 U.S.C. § 1292(a)(1).

62. 28 U.S.C. § 1292(a)(2).

63. 28 U.S.C. § 1292(a)(3).

64. Gulfstream Aerospace Corp. v. Mayacamas Corp., 485 U.S. 271 (1988); Stringfellow v. Concerned Neighbors in Action, 480 U.S. 370, 378–79 (1987); Carson v. American Brands, Inc., 450 U.S. 79, 83–84 (1981). *But see* Hershey Foods Corp. v. Hershey Creamery Co., 945 F.2d 1272, 1278–79 (3d Cir. 1991). In *Connecticut Nat. Bank v. Germain*, the Supreme Court also held that § 1292(b) grants appellate courts jurisdiction over district courts' interlocutory orders in bankruptcy cases. 503 U.S. 249, 251–52 (1992).

65. Carson v. Am. Brands, Inc., 450 U.S. 79, 84 (1981).

66. 28 U.S.C. § 1292(b).

National Institute for Trial Advocacy

the certification of the interlocutory appeal.[67] The scope of appellate jurisdiction extends to the order certified by the district court.[68]

How do you get an appeal under § 1292(b)? First, the district court must certify the order for appeal. Under § 1292(b), the district court will certify the order for appeal only on a showing that 1) the order raises a controlling question of law; 2) there is a substantial ground for difference of opinion on the question; 3) the interlocutory appeal may materially advance the ultimate termination of the litigation; and 4) the order involves an actual, not hypothetical, question of law.[69] Certification is not easy to obtain, but if the issue has a serious impact on the case or even on trial strategy, do not disregard it as an option.

How does one know if "a substantial ground for difference of opinion exists regarding the correctness of the decision"? Look at the relevant case law. For example, the Sixth Circuit has said that it means:

> (1) the question is difficult, novel and either a question on which there is little precedent or one whose correct resolution is not substantially guided by previous decisions; (2) the question is difficult and of first impression; (3) a difference of opinion exists within the controlling circuit; or (4) the circuits are split on the question.[70]

4.3 Appealability in State Systems

States range across the board in their treatment of appealability. At least forty state court systems offer both intermediate appellate courts and a court of last resort.[71] The structure of these courts varies greatly, with the scope of jurisdiction set out in statute or the state constitution.[72] Depending on the state, these courts can exercise

---

67. *Id.* ("The Court of Appeals which would have jurisdiction of an appeal of such action may thereupon, in its discretion, permit an appeal to be taken from such order, if application is made to it . . . .").

68. United States v. Stanley, 483 U.S. 669, 677 (1987); 16 Charles Alan Wright & Arthur R. Miller, et al., Federal Practice & Procedure § 3929 (3d ed. April 2016 Update) ("Even more clearly the court of appeals will not consider matters not yet ruled upon by the district court. The court may, however, consider any question reasonably bound up with the certified order, whether it is antecedent to, broader or narrower than, or different from the question specified by the district court. Jurisdiction extends to the order, not the question alone, and includes cross-petitions if they be deemed necessary.") (footnotes omitted).

69. 28 U.S.C. § 1292(b); Yamaha Motor Corp., U.S.A. v. Calhoun, 516 U.S. 199, 204–05 (1996).

70. *In re* Miedzianowski, 735 F.3d 383, 384 (6th Cir. 2013) (quoting City of Dearborn v. Comcast of Mich. III, Inc., No. 08–10156, 2008 WL 5084203, at *3 (E.D.Mich. Nov. 24, 2008)).

71. Ron Malega & Thomas H. Cohen, Bureau of Justice Statistics, U.S. Dep't of Justice, State Court Organization, 2011, 3 (2013) [hereinafter BJS State Court Organization Report], *available at* http://www.bjs.gov/content/pub/pdf/sco11.pdf (last visited Mar. 20, 2017).

72. Council of Chief Judges of the State Courts of Appeal, The Role of State Intermediate Appellate Courts, 4 (2012) [hereinafter Council of Chief Justices Report], *available at* http://www.sji.gov/wp/wp-content/uploads/Report_5_CCJSCA_Report.pdf (last visited Mar. 20, 2017).

mandatory or discretionary review, or both.[73] In most states, the intermediate appellate courts review, in the first instance, most administrative decisions and appeals from trial courts.[74] However, in most states a small subset of cases—usually at least death penalty cases—are appealed directly to the court of last resort.[75]

4.4   The Notice of Appeal

On a more basic level, an appellate case begins with the notice of appeal.[76] In most states and in the federal system, the notice of appeal is filed with the clerk of the trial court, not the appellate court.[77] Federal Rule of Appellate Procedure 3(c) sets of the basic rules for what must be included in the notice of appeal:

- "the party or parties taking the appeal by naming each one in the caption or body of the notice, but an attorney representing more than one party may describe those parties with such terms as 'all plaintiffs,' 'the defendants,' 'the plaintiffs A, B, et al.,' or 'all defendants except X';"

- "designate the judgment, order, or part thereof being appealed;"

- "name the court to which the appeal is taken."[78]

The courts tend to be generous in ruling on the adequacy of the document itself. Federal Rule of Appellate Procedure 3(c), for example, provides that an appeal "must not be dismissed for informality of form or title of the notice of appeal."[79]

4.5   Mandatory Timely Filing

The notice of appeal must be filed within the period prescribed. The jurisdiction of the appellate court depends on it. If you fail to comply with this requirement, the court must dismiss the appeal.[80] This can be a potent litigation tool for the appellee and something to be carefully watched and adhered to by counsel representing the appellant.

---

73. BJS State Court Organization Report, *supra* note 71, at 2.

74. Council of Chief Justices Report, *supra* note 72, at 4.

75. *Id.* at 4 n. 6.

76. The one exception is for a mandamus petition, which is filed in the court of appeals. Fed. R. App. P. 21.

77. *See* Carey v. Saffold, 536 U.S. 214, 219 (2002) (outlining states' general collateral review and appeal procedures); Fed. R. App. P. 4(a)(1)(A). *But see* Fed. R. App. P. 4(d) (requiring the court of appeals clerk to note the date on which it receives a mistakenly filed appeal notice and forward it to the district court clerk for entry as if properly filed on the date noted).

78. Fed. R. App. P. 3(c)(1).

79. A document intended to serve as an appellate brief may qualify as the notice of appeal required by Rule 3. Smith v. Barry, 502 U.S. 244, 254 (1992); Fed. R. App. P. 3(c)(4).

80. Bowles v. Russell, 551 U.S. 205, 210 (2007) (noting the Supreme Court's "longstanding treatment of statutory time limits for taking an appeal as jurisdictional" but distinguishing time limits in civil cases from those in criminal cases); Browder v. Dir., Dep't of Corr. of Ill., 434 U.S. 257, 264 (1978).

Federal Rule of Appellate Procedure 4(a) sets out the time limits for an appeal of right in a civil case. The notice of appeal must be filed with the district court within thirty days after the entry of the judgment or order appealed.[81] A cross-appeal is timely if filed within fourteen days of the filing of the notice of appeal or within the original appeal period, whichever period ends later.[82] If the United States or its officers or agencies is a party, however, any appellant has sixty days in which to appeal.[83]

A criminal defendant has fourteen days from the entry of judgment or order appealed from to file a notice of appeal with the district court.[84] The government may file an appeal within thirty days.[85] If the government files a notice of appeal, the defendant then has fourteen days to file an appeal.[86]

The time period begins to run under Rule 4(a)(1) from the date of entry of judgment or order appealed from, not from the date of the order.[87] This may give the lawyer some extra time, should the district court delay entering judgment until several days or even weeks after it has issued an order. Always remember the "separate document rule." As required by Rule 58, the time period begins to run from the date on which a judgment has been set forth in a separate document or 150 days from the entry in the civil docket.[88] The purpose of this requirement is to avoid "uncertainties as to the date on which the appeal period begins."[89] However, a separate document is neither a jurisdictional requirement nor cast in stone; an appeal may be allowed in its absence.[90]

The computation of time for the filing of a notice of appeal is governed by Federal Rule of Appellate Procedure 26(a). The basic rules are:

---

81. FED. R. APP. P. 4(a)(1)(A).

82. FED. R. APP. P. 4(a)(3).

83. FED. R. APP. P. 4(a)(1)(B).

84. FED. R. APP. P. 4(b)(1)(A).

85. 18 U.S.C. § 3731; FED. R. APP. P. 4(b)(1)(B).

86. FED. R. APP. P. 4(b)(1)(A)(ii).

87. FED. R. APP. P. 4(a)(1)(A). *But see* FirsTier Mortg. Co. v. Investors Mortg. Ins. Co., 498 U.S. 269 (1991) (holding that a notice of appeal filed after order but before judgment is effective if the order would have been appealable had the entry of judgment immediately followed).

88. FED. R. CIV. P. 58; FED. R. APP. P. 4(a)(7)(A)(ii). "The rules were changed in 2002 . . . precisely to address the problem that a failure to comply with the separate document rule meant that the time to appeal never expired because it never began to run." Outlaw v. Airtech Air Conditioning & Heating, Inc., 412 F.3d 156, 163 (D.C. Cir. 2005) (considering the situation when the clerk does not docket the judgment). Rule 58(b) includes the update that a party has 150 days after the notice of judgment to file an appeal. FED. R. CIV. P. 58(b).

89. Bankers Trust Co. v. Mallis, 435 U.S. 381, 385 (1978) (per curiam). *Mallis* was decided before the addition of Rule 58(b), which should serve to eliminate any remaining uncertainties. *See* FED. R. CIV. P. 58(b).

90. *Mallis*, 435 U.S. at 385 ("Certainty as to timeliness . . . is not advanced by holding that appellate jurisdiction does not exist absent a separate judgment. If, by error, a separate judgment is not filed before a party appeals, nothing but delay would flow from requiring the court of appeals to dismiss the appeal.").

1) Do not include the day of entry of judgment or order in the computation.[91]

2) If Saturday, Sunday, or a legal holiday is the last day of the period, the period ends on the next day which is not a Saturday, Sunday, or legal holiday.[92]

3) The notice of appeal is filed when it is received by the clerk of the district court.[93]

Courts give extra consideration to the difficulty encountered by pro se prisoners in filing a notice of appeal. Under Federal Rule of Appellate Procedure 4(c), a prisoner's notice of appeal is considered "timely if it is deposited in the institution's internal mail system on or before the last day for filing."[94]

If you fail to file a timely notice of appeal, there are two ways in which you can extend the time for taking an appeal: the tolling doctrine and a motion under Rule 4(a)(5) for extension due to excusable neglect. Wise attorneys avoid relying on these remedies by filing timely notices of appeal.

4.5.1 *Tolling*

Under Federal Rule of Appellate Procedure 4(a), the appeal period is tolled for all parties if one of these motions under the Federal Rules of Civil Procedure is timely filed:

1) A motion for judgment as a matter of law under Rule 50(b).

2) A motion to amend or make additional findings of fact under Rule 52(b).

3) A motion to alter or amend the judgment under Rule 59.

4) A motion for a new trial under Rule 59.

5) A motion for relief under Rule 60 if the motion is filed no later than twenty-eight days after the judgment is entered.[95]

In accordance with each of the rules under which these motions are filed, the motions must either be filed or served within twenty-eight days of the district court's entry of judgment.[96]

Frequently, a party will file a post-judgment motion within twenty-eight days of the entry of judgment without indicating which rule is being invoked.[97] The court

---

91. FED. R. APP. P. 26(a)(1)(A).
92. FED. R. APP. P. 26(a)(1)(C).
93. *Cf.* FED. R. APP. P. 4(d).
94. FED. R. APP. P. 4(c).
95. Fed. R. App. P. 4(a)(4)(A).
96. Fed. R. Civ. P. 50(b), 52(b), 59(b), 59(e), 60(b).
97. *See id.*

must then construe the motion to determine whether it tolls the time for taking an appeal. The court usually must choose between Rules 52(b) or 59 and 60(b), which all cover post-judgment requests for relief from judgment.[98] A motion can be construed differently than its styling.[99]

Under Rule 4(a)(4), once the district court has decided the motion that tolls the appeal period, the appeal period begins again from the date of entry of the decision on the motion.

4.5.2 Extension of Time under Rule 4(a)(5)

A second way you can enlarge the appeal period is by obtaining an extension from the district court. The court of appeals is without power to waive the time requirement for appeal,[100] but the district court may extend the time for appeal under Rule 4(a)(5).[101] In a civil case, if a lawyer files a motion before the expiration of the appeal period provided in Rule 4(a), the district court, on a showing of excusable neglect or good cause, can extend the period to file for up to thirty days past the prescribed time or fourteen days from the date of the order granting the motion, whichever occurs later.[102] These limits, however, are strictly enforced and, as the Supreme Court has recently clarified, jurisdictional in nature.[103]

---

98. *See* Fed. R. App. P. 4(a)(4)(A). *Cf.* Buchanan v. Stanships, Inc., 485 U.S. 265, 268–69 (1988) (holding that a post-judgment motion, though styled as a Rule 59 motion, was properly considered a Rule 54(d) motion).

99. *See, e.g.*, *Buchanan*, 485 U.S. at 268–69 (choosing between characterizations of a post-judgment motion based on the 1988 Rules of Federal Civil Procedure); Harcon Barge Co. v. D & G Boat Rentals, Inc., 784 F.2d 665, 668, 670 (5th Cir. 1986) (holding that a late Rule 59(e) motion was properly construed as a Rule 60(b) motion); Skagerberg v. Oklahoma, 797 F.2d 881, 882 (10th Cir. 1986); *see also* Lucas v. Fl. Power & Light Co., 729 F.2d 1300, 1301–02 (11th Cir. 1984) (construing an intended Rule 59 motion as a notice of appeal); Miller v. Transamerican Press, Inc., 709 F.2d 524, 527 (9th Cir. 1983) (construing an intended Rule 59(e) motion as a Rule 60(a) motion).

100. "[T]he timely filing of a notice of appeal in a civil case is a jurisdictional requirement." *Bowles*, 551 U.S. at 214; *see* FED. R. CIV. P. 6(b)(2) ("A court must not extend time to act under Rules 50(b) and (d), 52(b), 59(b), (d), and (e), and 60(b).").

101. FED. R. APP. P. 4(a)(5); *see* 28 U.S.C. § 2107(c). Note, however, that eleven circuits have held that "a notice of appeal cannot be treated as a motion for extension of time." Hickey v. Scott, 987 F. Supp. 2d 85, 89 (D.D.C. 2013) (citing United States *ex rel.* Green v. Serv. Contract Educ. & Training Trust Fund, 863 F. Supp. 2d 18, 20–21 (D.D.C. 2012) (collecting cases)).

102. FED. R. APP. P. 4(a)(5)(C).

103. *Bowles*, 551 U.S. 205.

CHAPTER FIVE

ISSUE PRESERVATION AND STANDARDS OF REVIEW

5.1 Issue Preservation for Review

A mainstay of the common law tradition is that the trial court must decide all matters in the first instance. Questions and objections must be presented at the trial level, and the opposing party must be allowed to respond. This process ensures that issues appealed have actually been decided by the trial court.

For an appellate court to find reversible error, three interrelated circumstances must be present:

- Specific rulings, acts, or omissions by the trial tribunal constituting trial error;

- An objection by counsel or the grant or denial of an oral or written motion or submission; and

- A proper and appropriate course of action recommended by the appellant that was rejected by the tribunal.

When all three elements are present, the issue has been properly preserved for review. Exceptions to preservation will be discussed below, but reliance on them in lieu of proper preservation is foolhardy.

The necessity of issue preservation is the short answer to the question, when does one start to prepare for an appeal? The textbook response is, the earlier the better. A competent football coach would not dare go into a contest without a game plan. Likewise, no competent trial lawyer will participate in a trial or hearing without a definite theory or strategy supporting the contention or defense. The coach prepares for the entire game, for all four quarters. Most lawyers do not. They prepare only for the first half, the trial itself. If an appeal is necessary, they will wing it.

Most trial lawyers hope to win on the facts. The bulk of trial work is fact-specific, both in discovery and at trial. In the event that the fact-finder finds against them, in many cases, too many lawyers immediately file a notice of appeal without really considering on what grounds to base it. Once the notice is filed, if the trial lawyer belongs to a large firm, some junior associates are called in and given their marching orders: "Get a transcript and help me find some trial error. I am very busy with this next case. You will note that I made some objections to evidence rulings, and I submitted some points for charge that were rejected. Look over the transcript and then get back to me." Then the junior associates start to write the brief. This is the first time they consider the issues in the case from the perspective of an appeal—although the horse may have escaped from the barn long ago. To be sure, this is one extreme. But it happens frequently enough to cause concern.

At the other extreme is the ideal scenario. The lawyer starts preparing for the appeal with the filing of a complaint or indictment, keeping one eye focused on the appellate process, knowing that without careful planning and monitoring a possible trial error may not be preserved and trial strategy not directed toward ultimate protection on appeal.

At a minimum, before the last pretrial conference, when you decide upon your *trial* strategy, you should also lay plans for the *appeal*. This will take some work, but this action is what sets real lawyers apart from paralegals collecting facts. The full-game strategy requires you to develop alternative tactics based on the different possible approaches that the fact-finder could take in the course of the trial.

Objections to evidence at trial are often casually made—perhaps, too casually. This results in several problems. First, you deprive yourself of a strategic advantage at trial by not having the evidence admitted or rejected. Second, casual objections fail to lay the proper groundwork for success on appeal. Often, upon reflection and study, appellate judges may conclude that the trial court was wrong on an evidentiary ruling, but will not disturb it because the reasons asserted on appeal were not given to the trial court in the heat of battle. It is one thing to say, "Objection, the evidence is inadmissible." It is something else to say, "I am objecting under Rule 403, and I am requesting to be heard with the appropriate cases." In preparing for trial, you must be prepared with the appropriate law of evidence, including case citations, that covers the expected trial testimony.

Preserve the issue at all costs. Unless the trial transcript discloses it or a pretrial or post-trial colloquy or ruling has been transcribed or appears in a filed motion and order, appellate review will not be available—or, at best, it will only be available under strict plain error restrictions. A lawyer cannot be content with "informal" rulings made at sidebar or in chambers with no court reporter present. Always request that the trial court's ruling and the objection be entered on the record immediately after the "informal" ruling is made, no matter how inconsequential it may appear at the time. Do not depend on "resurrecting" or "reconstructing" the record on appeal. Your adversary invariably will have a different recollection of what was said in chambers or in other off-the-record discussions, and you cannot depend upon the trial judge's memory for assistance.

Generally speaking, if the issue was not first presented to the trial judge or administrative agency, the reviewing court will not consider it. There are, of course, exceptional cases in particular circumstances that will prompt a reviewing appellate court to consider questions of law, even though these questions were not pressed upon the court or administrative agency below. A ruling by the appellate court in the first instance may be appropriate where blatant injustice might otherwise result.[1] Such cases, however, are very rare and come under the category of "plain error" or the notion of basic and fundamental error.[2] As Justice Blackmun explained, "It is the general rule, of course, that a federal appellate court does not consider an issue not passed upon below."[3]

Argue plain error if you must—if your jurisdiction allows it—but do not in the trial court rely on it as a means to contest the issue on appeal.

The bottom line: the broad contours of your appellate theory should be sketched out, replete with alternatives, at the same time your trial tactics and strategy are developed. There is time to do it. Instead of spending thousands, if not hundreds of thousands, of dollars in discovery in search of a theory of claim or defense, decide first upon a long-range theory for the trial and appellate courts. As part of that theory, you must preserve issues for appeal by making the proper contemporaneous objections or motions at pretrial, trial, or post-trial stages, and must be certain that the record reflects that the objections or motions were made and that the trial court adversely ruled on them.

5.2   Introduction to Standards of Review

Standards of review used by the appellate court are critically important in effective advocacy. In large part, they determine the power of the lens through which the appellate court may examine a particular issue in a case. The error that may be grounds for reversal under one standard of review may be insignificant under another. It does not matter what the court is asked to do on appeal if the court cannot jump the hurdle posed by the standard of review. You must craft your brief on appeal to reflect the proper standard and to show why, under that standard, your client deserves to win. If your appeal raises more than one issue, then you should state the applicable standard of review for each issue raised.

The appellate process generally reduces to limited types of review: fact-finding by judges under the clearly erroneous rule or by the administrative agency under

---

1. Singleton v. Wulff, 428 U.S. 106, 121 (1976) ("Certainly there are circumstances in which a federal appellate court is justified in resolving an issue not passed on below, as where the proper resolution is beyond any doubt, . . . or where 'injustice might otherwise result.'") (citing Turner v. City of Memphis, 369 U.S. 350, 353–54 (1962), and quoting Hormel v. Helvering, 312 U.S. 552, 557 (1941)).

2. Fed. R. Evid. 103(e); *see also* Glen Weissenberger & James J. Duane, Federal Rules of Evidence: Rules, Legislative History, Commentary and Authority 42–44 (7th ed. 2015) (explaining the plain error doctrine).

3. *Singleton*, 428 U.S. at 120.

the substantial evidence standard;[4] review of the trial court's exercise of discretion; and *de novo*[5] review of the choice, interpretation, and application of the controlling legal precepts.[6] Thus, where the controversy is one of *fact*, findings ordinarily are permanent. Practical and philosophical impediments prevent an appellate court from displacing the fact-finder's resolution of conflicting evidence. When a *legal* determination is challenged, a popular misconception is that reversal may be easily obtainable given the *de novo* standard. Although reviewable, a legal ruling, even if shown to be erroneous, may occasionally not be sufficient grounds for reversing. Some appellate judges may, consciously or subconsciously, require a little more to overturn a lower court's legal ruling than the standard of review implies. There can be a type of informal deference to what a judge has already decided, particularly if the trial court judge has earned the respect of the appellate court. When the trial court has the clear right to exercise discretion, the appellate court may not properly substitute its views for those of the trial court. Here, the appellate court's function is limited to discovering and defining the parameters of allowable discretion and interfering only when convinced that the use of discretion below has exceeded those limitations. The reviewing court calls such a transgression an "abuse," or more accurately, a "misuse" of the exercise of proper discretion. The competent advocate will have a clear understanding of the standard of review pertaining to each point in the brief. The Federal Rules of Appellate Procedure require a statement of the review standard for each issue presented in the briefs, "which may appear in the discussion of the issue or under a separate heading placed before the discussion of the issues."[7]

The ability to correctly state the standard of review is a question of minimum professional competence. A psychological block seems to crush lawyers who refuse to recognize that trial tribunals' fact-finding processes can fast-freeze evidence into rigid and nearly unchangeable facts. Applying standards of review to the argument is, in fact, one of the most significant distinctions between trial and appellate briefs. It makes no sense for lawyers to take a closing argument to a jury and dress it up as a brief to an appellate court. The closing summarizes the litigant's best *evidence*; appellate courts address findings of *fact*. This is a key distinction.

"A defendant is entitled to a fair trial but not a perfect one."[8] Although the trial court may err in some of its rulings, the determination as to whether the judgment should be reversed turns on whether the error is "reversible." To recognize these

---

4. 5 U.S.C. § 706(2)(E); *see also* 2 Am. Jur. 2d Administrative Law § 479 (2016) (describing the substantial evidence standard of review for an administrative agency's findings of fact).

5. *De novo* review is sometimes also called "plenary" review. *See, e.g.*, Chad Oldfather, *Universal De Novo Review*, 77 Geo. Wash. L. Rev. 308, 313 (2009) ("'De novo review' . . . [a]lso occasionally referred to as 'plenary,' 'independent,' or 'free' review.").

6. *See* Amanda Peters, *The Meaning, Measure, and Misuses of Standards of Review*, 13 Lewis & Clark L. Rev. 233, 243–46 (2009) (describing abuse of discretion review, clearly erroneous review, the substantial evidence standard, and *de novo* review).

7. Fed. R. App. P. 28(a)(8)(B).

8. Lutwak v. United States, 344 U.S. 604, 619 (1953).

distinctions and to accommodate this precise awareness to the cause at hand is the hallmark of an expert appellate advocate.

For a proper understanding of standards of review, it is necessary to separate the distinct concepts involved in the review of judicial findings. The difference in these concepts—especially with respect to fact-finding—is fundamental in the review process.

5.3 Three Categories of Facts

Fact-finding is the province of the trial tribunal, be it a court or administrative agency. The skill of a trial advocate is measured by an ability to persuade the fact-finder to convert a mass of testimony and evidence into adjudicative facts. The fact-finder may be a jury, a judge, an arbitrator, a hearing examiner or an administrative law judge, or the board to which the examiner or administrative judge reports.

The fact-finder is the sole judge of credibility and is free to accept or reject even uncontradicted oral testimony.[9] Without regard to the number of rungs an appellant may climb up the appellate ladder, the American tradition—in most cases—does not permit a reviewing court to disturb findings of credibility.[10]

For a proper understanding of appellate fact-finding review, it is necessary to segregate three distinct and fundamental concepts: basic facts, inferred facts, and mixed facts. The importance of distinguishing these three types is reflected in the various standards of judicial review. When the trial court, sitting as fact-finder, identifies the basic facts and facts permissibly inferred from the basic facts, neither may be disturbed on review unless they are deemed clearly erroneous.[11] Mixed facts or questions, on the other hand, "require the consideration of legal concepts and the exercise of judgment about the values underlying legal principles," and are reviewed under a *de novo* standard of review.[12]

5.3.1 Basic and Inferred Facts

Although writers and judges are not uniform in the labels placed on various types of facts, "basic facts" are best understood as historical and narrative accounts elicited

---

9. Borough of Nanty Glo v. Am. Surety Co. of N.Y., 309 Pa. 236, 238 (1932) (quoting Reel v. Elder, 62 Pa. 308, 316 (1869)); *see also* Sartor v. Ark. Nat. Gas Corp., 321 U.S. 620, 627–28 (1944) (quoting The Conqueror, 166 U.S. 110, 131 (1897)); Rhoades, Inc. v. United Air Lines, Inc., 340 F.2d 481, 486 (3d Cir. 1965) (citing Wooley v. Great Atlantic & Pacific Tea Co., 281 F.2d 78, 80 (3d Cir. 1960)).

10. *See* section 5.4.1.

11. Fed. R. Civ. P. 52(a); *see* United States v. U.S. Gypsum Co., 333 U.S. 364, 394 (1948).

12. Cooper Tire & Rubber Co. v. St. Paul Fire and Marine Ins. Co., 48 F.3d 365, 369 (8th Cir. 1995); *see also* Universal Minerals, Inc. v. C.A. Hughes & Co., 669 F.2d 98, 102–103 (3d Cir. 1981) (discussing the distinction between the review of basic and inferred facts on the one hand and of ultimate facts, or mixed questions, on the other).

from the evidence presented by witnesses at trial, or admitted by stipulation, or asserted in the pleadings and not denied in responsive pleadings.

Evidence that is inferred from witness testimony or documentary evidence, rather than being direct, is often called circumstantial. These inferences of facts are permissible when logic and human experience indicate a probability that basic events or conditions will result in certain consequences.[13] No legal precept is implicated in drawing permissible factual inferences.

The inferences that the court permits the jury to adduce in a courtroom do not differ significantly from the inferences that people reach daily in informally accepting a probability or arriving at a conclusion when presented with some basic evidence. A court permits the jury to draw the inference because of shared experiences in human endeavors. Perhaps the only distinction between extracting these factual conclusions from daily life and from the courtroom is that a jury's act of drawing or not drawing an inference is preceded by a judge's instruction. The instruction serves to guide the jury through some process of ordered consideration. The court informs the jury that it must weigh the narrative or historical evidence presented, make credibility findings when appropriate, and then draw only those inferences that are reasonable in reaching a verdict.

The difference between basic and inferred facts can be seen in the following example. Assume a bench trial involving an automobile accident. The judge does several things during the trial. The judge may hear evidence and find that the defendant was going twenty miles per hour over the speed limit and ran a red light. These are findings of basic fact. The judge may also hear evidence that there were no skid marks at the scene or that the wear on the tires suggest that the defendant did not hit his brakes. From these basic facts, the judge draws an inference that, in fact, the defendant did not hit his brakes. This is an inferred fact.

5.3.2   *Mixed Questions of Law and Fact*

We usually express mixed questions[14] in the language of a standard enunciated by case law or by statute. For example, we say that an actor's conduct was negligent, or the injury occurred in the course of employment, or the rate is reasonable, or the company has refused to bargain collectively. Mixed questions are "questions in which the historical facts are admitted or established, the rule of law is undisputed,

---

13. *See, e.g.*, Edward J. Sweeney & Sons, Inc. v. Texaco, Inc., 637 F.2d 105, 116 (3d Cir. 1980), *cert. denied*, 451 U.S. 911 (1981).

14. Mixed questions are also sometimes referred to as "ultimate facts." We will use the term "mixed question" here, since the term "ultimate facts" often harkens back to the complex pleading requirements that existed prior to the adoption of the Federal Rules of Civil Procedure. *See* RICHARD D. FREER, CIVIL PROCEDURE § 7.3.2 (3d ed. 2012).

and the issue is whether the facts satisfy the statutory standard, or to put it another way, whether the rule of law as applied to the established facts is or is not violated."[15]

It is always the responsibility of the fact-finder—jury, judge, or administrative agency—to find the narrative or historical facts and to draw proper inferences from those facts. Often, the fact-finder must go further and determine the mixed questions as well, based on the court's instructions in a jury case or on a proper application of a legal precept in a nonjury trial or agency hearing.

Consider again the automobile accident hypothetical. After the judge has found the basic facts of speed and the running of the red light, and the inferred fact that the defendant did not hit his brakes, the judge rules on what the applicable negligence standards are in this particular jurisdiction and what defenses might be available. These are rulings of law. The judge then rules that the defendant in this case was negligent. This is a mixed question of law and facts—applying the applicable law in the jurisdiction to the facts of this particular case.

5.4   Determining the Standard of Review

The first inquiry in reviewing findings of fact is whether the facts were found by a judge, jury, or administrative agency. The nature of the fact-finder will determine the scope of the appellate court's scrutiny and guide the launching of the lawyer's attack.

5.4.1   *Fact-Finding: Judicial Proceedings*

The Seventh Amendment has controlling force in federal jury cases: "In Suits at common law, where the value in controversy shall exceed twenty dollars, the right of trial by jury shall be preserved, and no fact tried by a jury shall be otherwise re-examined in any Court of the United States, than according to the rules of the common law."[16] State constitutions also protect the right to a jury trial.[17] So long as there is some evidence from which the jury could arrive at the finding by a process of reasoning, the jury's findings of fact, especially those resolving conflicts in testimony, will not be disturbed. As the United States Court of Appeals for the Seventh Circuit has stated:

> Insufficiency arguments based on a witness's purported lack of credibility are "wasted on an appellate court" because "the jury . . . is the only entity entitled to make such credibility determinations." In fact, we have held that a conviction for conspiracy may be supported by

---

15. Pullman-Standard v. Swint, 456 U.S. 273, 289 n.19 (1982).

16. U.S. CONST. amend. VII.

17. *See, e.g.*, CAL. CONST. art. I, § 16; DEL. CONST. art. I, § 4; N.J. CONST. art. I, § 9; PA. CONST. art. I, § 6; TEX. CONST. art. I, § 15.

testimony that is "totally uncorroborated and comes from an admitted liar, convicted felon, large scale drug-dealing, paid government informant."[18]

Review of found facts and credibility, of course, is a different issue than the quantum of evidence necessary to sustain the various burdens of proof in civil and criminal cases.[19]

Facts found by a judge alone need a stronger evidentiary base. The findings, under the federal rules and in those states adhering to the substance of Federal Rule of Civil Procedure 52(a) shall not be set aside "unless clearly erroneous, and due regard shall be given to the opportunity of the trial court to judge of the credibility of the witnesses." "Clearly erroneous" has been interpreted to mean that a reviewing court can upset a finding of fact, even when supported by some evidence, but only if the court has "the definite and firm conviction that a mistake has been committed."[20] The Supreme Court has explained that the "clearly erroneous" standard "does not entitle a reviewing court to reverse the finding of the trier of fact simply because it is convinced that it would have decided the case differently."[21] Rather:

> If the district court's account of the evidence is plausible in light of the record viewed in its entirety, the court of appeals may not reverse it even though convinced that had it been sitting as the trier of fact, it would have weighed the evidence differently. Where there are two permissible views of the evidence, the factfinder's choice between them cannot be clearly erroneous.[22]

The "clearly erroneous" standard has been construed by one United States Court of Appeals to mean that the appellate court must accept the factual determination of the fact-finder unless that determination "either (1) is completely devoid of minimum evidentiary support displaying some hue of credibility, or (2) bears no rational relationship to the supportive evidentiary data."[23]

Because only the fact-finder has an opportunity to observe the demeanor of witnesses, it is generally the rule "that a fact finder's determination of credibility is not subject to appellate review."[24] This is true even if the evidence is not oral. Under Federal Rule of Civil Procedure 52(a)(6), "Findings of fact, whether based on oral or other evidence, must not be set aside unless clearly erroneous, and the reviewing

---

18. United States v. Pulido, 69 F.3d 192, 206 (7th Cir. 1995) (citations omitted).

19. *See, e.g.,* Jackson v. Virginia, 443 U.S. 307, 318–19 (1979).

20. United States v. U.S. Gypsum Co., 333 U.S. 364, 395 (1948).

21. Anderson v. City of Bessemer City, 470 U.S. 564, 573 (1985) (citing United States v. Yellow Cab Co., 338 U.S. 338, 342 (1949)).

22. *Id.* at 573–74.

23. Krasnov v. Dinan, 465 F.2d 1298, 1302 (3d Cir. 1972).

24. Government of the Virgin Islands v. Gereau, 502 F.2d 914, 921 (3d Cir. 1974), *cert. denied,* 424 U.S. 917 (1976).

court must give due regard to the trial court's opportunity to judge the witnesses' credibility."

In some state systems, it is necessary to inquire about and understand the stability given to facts found by a chancellor in equity. Historically, these facts were subject to a broad review in equity, but some jurisdictions, like Pennsylvania, give the same effect to a chancellor's findings as to a jury verdict when considering a post-trial motion.[25]

5.4.2   Fact-Finding: Administrative Agencies

The reviewing court may not set aside the findings of administrative agency hearings unless they are "unsupported by substantial evidence" in light of the whole record.[26] What, however, is substantial evidence? For some time recourse has been made to a Supreme Court statement by Chief Justice Hughes: "Substantial evidence is more than a mere scintilla. It means such relevant evidence as a reasonable mind might accept as adequate to support a conclusion."[27] Justice Stone gave further clarification:

> [Substantial evidence] means evidence which is substantial, that is, affording a substantial basis of fact from which the fact in issue can be reasonably inferred . . . . [I]t must be enough to justify, if the trial were to a jury, a refusal to direct a verdict when the conclusion sought to be drawn from it is one of fact for the jury.[28]

By 1988, the Supreme Court was prepared to state:

> Judicial review of agency action . . . regularly proceeds under the rubric of "substantial evidence" set forth in the Administrative Procedure Act . . . . That phrase does not mean a large or considerable amount of evidence, but rather "such relevant evidence as a reasonable mind might accept as adequate to support a conclusion."[29]

In the review of administrative agency proceedings, as in the review of judicial fact-finding, the question of credibility is for the administrative law judge to

---

25. Schwartz v. Urban Redevelopment Auth., 206 A.2d 789 (Pa. 1965).

26. 5 U.S.C. § 706(2)(E); *see* Beth Israel Hospital v. NLRB, 437 U.S. 483 (1978); Universal Camera Corp. v. NLRB, 340 U.S. 474 (1951); 4 K. DAVIS, ADMINISTRATIVE LAW chs. 29–30 (1958 & Supp. 1970).

27. Consol. Edison Co. v. NLRB, 305 U.S. 197, 229 (1938).

28. NLRB v. Columbian Enameling & Stamping Co., 306 U.S. 292, 299–300 (1939).

29. Pierce v. Underwood, 487 U.S. 552, 564–65 (1988) (quoting *Consol. Edison Co.*, 305 U.S. at 229).

determine.[30] When the agency does not accept the administrative law judge's findings, substantial evidence is not found so readily.[31]

5.4.3 Fact-Finding: Legislative Bodies

Legislative facts—facts that have been authoritatively found by an extralegal body—also figure in the judicial process at both levels, trial and appellate. Use of such facts is not only permissible, but extremely helpful in deciding the interpretation or applicability of a given legal precept. When a court arrogates to itself the role of the legislative fact-finder, without supporting data in the record, its action is at best, questionable.

5.4.4 Fact-Finding: Mixed Questions of Law and Fact

When dealing with mixed questions of law and fact, the reviewing court may not disturb, except for clear error, the basic fact component, but the appellate court is free to review the "law" component *de novo*.[32] This means that review is available

---

30. Thus, in NLRB v. Lewisburg Chair & Furniture Co., 230 F.2d 155, 157 (3d Cir. 1956), the Third Circuit stated, "Questions of credibility of witnesses have to be resolved in litigation but in labor cases this court is not the place where such resolving takes place." Under the substantial evidence standard, a reviewing court does not reweigh the evidence, resolve testimonial conflicts or "displace the Board's choice between two fairly conflicting views, even though the court would justifiably have made a different choice had the matter been before it *de novo*." Universal Camera Corp., 340 U.S. at 488. The Court does not pass on the credibility of the witnesses, reweigh the evidence or reject reasonable Board inferences simply because other inferences might also reasonably be drawn. *See* NLRB v. Walton Mfg. Co., 369 U.S. 404, 405 (1962).

31. Eastern Engineering & Elevator Co. v. NLRB, 637 F.2d 191, 197 (3d Cir. 1980):

> In our review of the Board's order, the statute furnishes our basic direction: the reviewing court treats as conclusive the factual determinations in a Board decision if they are "supported by substantial evidence on the record considered as a whole." 29 U.S.C. § 160(f). That the responsibility of fact finding is placed on the Board and not on the hearing judge, however, does not end our inquiry. The Supreme Court has directed us to recognize that an [administrative law judge's] findings of fact constitute a vital part of the whole record that the court must review. These findings "are to be considered along with the consistency and inherent probability of testimony. The significance of his report . . . depends largely on the importance of credibility in the particular case." *Universal Camera Corp. v. NLRB*, 340 U.S. 474, 496 (1951). We must "recognize that evidence supporting a conclusion may be less substantial when an impartial, experienced examiner who has observed the witnesses and lived with the case has drawn conclusions different from the Board's than when he has reached the same conclusion."

32. *But see* Adam Hoffman, Note, *Corralling Constitutional Fact: De Novo Fact Review in the Federal Appellate Courts*, 50 DUKE L.J. 1427 (2001) (discussing possible conflicts in the circuits as to what portion of a mixed question should be subject to plenary review); Evan Tsen Lee, *Principled Decision Making and the Proper Role of Federal Appellate Courts: The Mixed Questions Conflict*, 64 S. CAL. L. REV. 235 (1991) (same); Chad M. Oldfather, *Universal De Novo Review*, 77 GEO. WASH. L. REV. 308, 315, 315 n.33 (2009) (stating that "mixed questions of law and fact . . . are often subject to de novo review," but noting that "[s]tandards of review relating to mixed questions differ from one jurisdiction to the next, and not for any apparent philosophical or jurisprudential reasoning").

when there is insufficient evidence to sustain the requirements of the legal precept upon which the mixed question is premised.[33]

Consider *Universal Minerals, Inc. v. C.A. Hughes & Company*,[34] which presented the question of whether there had been an "abandonment" of a pile of culm (refuse from a coal mine). The court explained that "abandonment" is not a question of narrative or historical fact, but a legal concept with a factual component, making it a mixed question of law and fact. Therefore, in reviewing the trial court decision, the appellate court

> must accept the trial court's findings of historical or narrative facts unless they are clearly erroneous, but [it] must exercise a plenary review of the trial court's choice and interpretation of legal precepts and its application of those precepts to the historical facts . . . . Thus [the appellate court] separate[s] the distinct factual and legal elements of the trial court's determination . . . and appl[ies] the appropriate standard to each component.[35]

An appellate court uses the same approach when it reviews a jury's findings on a mixed question, but the distinction is more apparent due to the requirements of the Seventh Amendment and the strict allocation of power between the jury and the trial court. If, for example, a jury finds that a party has abandoned an interest in property, the appellate court will review the trial court's jury instructions to determine whether the court erred in its explanation of the law. If the appellate court does not find an error, then it will look at the record to see if there is sufficient evidence to justify a reasonable person drawing the factual inferences underlying the conclusion.[36] As the Seventh Circuit has noted, a criminal defendant challenging the sufficiency of the evidence faces "a nearly insurmountable hurdle."[37]

5.5 Discretion

Lawyers must be very cautious and aware of raising an issue on appeal that implicates the lower tribunal's discretion. To try to beguile the appellate court to review discretionary actions *de novo* is simply a waste of the lawyer's abilities, the client's money, and the court's time. Minimal competence demands at least a recognition that certain decisions are committed to lower tribunal discretion and will not be set aside absent a showing of abuse—more properly, misuse—of that discretion.

---

33. 1 Steven Alan Childress & Martha S. Davis, Federal Standards of Review § 2.18 (4th ed. 2010) ("When the court's error goes to the heart of the legal conclusion, the finding, though similar to one of fact, should not be protected . . . . [T]here is a point where objective facts shade into legal reasoning.").

34. 669 F.2d 98 (3d Cir. 1981).

35. *Id.* at 103.

36. *Id.*

37. United States v. Teague, 956 F.2d 1427, 1433 (7th Cir. 1992).

Bouvier's Law Dictionary defines "discretion," in part, as:

> [T]he judgment of a person making a decision, as well as the scope of office or responsibility within which the person is responsible for making such a decision. To act with discretion is not to act on a whim. Discretion requires the person acting to consider all of the evidence that might be relevant to the decision, all of the possible decisions that might be made in a circumstance, the reasons for deciding in one or another manner, and then to seek an outcome that will best fit with the purposes for which the person has the discretion to make such a decision.[38]

Hart and Sacks define "discretion" as "the power to choose between two or more courses of action each of which is thought of as permissible."[39] Finally, *Black's Law Dictionary* defines "judicial discretion" as "The exercise of judgment by a judge or court based on what is fair under the circumstances and guided by the rules and principles of law; a court's power to act or not act when a litigant is not entitled to demand the act as a matter of right."[40]

As a legal concept, discretion admits of some lack of precision, and formal definitions of the concept mark only the beginning of understanding. Professor Ronald Dworkin noted that discretion, like the hole in the doughnut, does not exist except as an area left open by a ring of restriction.[41] Legislative or judicial authorities should guide both the exerciser and the reviewer by defining with some specificity the outer limits of the discretion. The Third Circuit has noted:

> The mere statement that a decision lies within the discretion of the trial court does little to shed light on its reviewability. It means merely that the decision is uncontrolled by fixed principles or rules of law . . . . In our judicial system, a wide variety of decisions covering a broad range of subject matters, both procedural and substantive, is left to the discretion of the trial court. The justifications for committing decisions to the discretion of the court are not uniform, and may vary with the specific type of decisions. Although the standard of review in such instances is generally framed as "abuse of discretion," in fact the scope of review will be directly related to the reason why that category or type of decision is committed to the trial court's discretion in the first instance.[42]

---

38. *Discretion*, THE WOLTERS KLUWER BOUVIER LAW DICTIONARY DESK EDITION (2011 2012 ed.).
39. HENRY M. HART & ALBERT SACKS, THE LEGAL PROCESS 144 (1994).
40. *Discretion*, BLACK'S LAW DICTIONARY (10th ed. 2014).
41. RONALD DWORKIN, TAKING RIGHTS SERIOUSLY 31 (1977).
42. United States v. Criden, 648 F.2d 814, 817 (3d Cir. 1981) (footnote omitted).

Therefore, knowing simply that one is invested with discretion does not tell much. The crucial inquiry is the extent of the discretionary power conferred.

Dworkin delineates two "weak" senses of discretion and one "stronger sense."[43] At one end of the scale is discretion conferred because "for some reason the standards an official must apply cannot be applied mechanically but demand use of judgment."[44] At the same end is discretion conferred because "some official has final authority to make a decision and cannot be reviewed and reversed by any other official."[45] Dworkin calls both of these senses "weak" and distinguished them from a discretion in which the official "is simply not bound by standards set by the authority in question."[46]

Professor Maurice Rosenberg has explained that:

> probably the most pointed and helpful [reason] for bestowing discretion on the trial judge as to many matters is, paradoxically, the superiority of his nether position. It is not that he knows more than his loftier brothers; rather, he sees more and senses more. In the dialogue between the appellate judges and the trial judge, the former often seem to be saying: "You were there. We do not think we would have done what you did, but we were not present and we may be unaware of significant matters, for the record does not adequately convey to us all that went on at the trial. Therefore, we defer to you."[47]

If one starts with an understanding of discretion as encompassing the power of choice among several courses of action, each of which is considered permissible, it would seem difficult, if not conceptually impossible, to disturb discretionary choice on review. Nonetheless, appellate courts continue to do so, couching their actions in language that disclaims a substitution of choices for those of the trial courts. This type of review generates tension between trial and appellate courts.

Consider the differences among the following: 1) The sergeant is to pick his five best people to go on foot patrol. 2) The sergeant is told to pick his five fastest runners to go on patrol. 3) The sergeant is told to pick any five people to go on patrol. Can you see the difference in the degree of discretion granted? The exercise of discretion depends upon the discretionary power:

---

43. Ronald Dworkin, *The Model of Rules*, 35 U. CHI. L. REV. 14, 32–33 (1967).
44. *Id.* at 32.
45. *Id.*
46. *Id.* at 33.
47. Maurice Rosenberg, *Judicial Discretion of the Trial Court, Viewed from Above*, 22 SYRACUSE L. REV. 635, 663 (1971).

Conferred Power	*Discretionary Extent*
Pick any five persons.	Very broad, totally unfettered.
Pick any five men.	Broad, but constrained by gender.
Pick the five best.	Somewhat constrained: What is meant by "best"?
Pick the five fastest runners.	Moderate, constrained by running ability.
Pick the five strongest.	Moderate, constrained by muscle strength.
Pick the five youngest or oldest.	Very limited.
Pick the five tallest or shortest.	Very limited.

How do we convert these illustrations to appellate review of trial court discretion? Professor Rosenberg has given us some excellent examples showing a range of gradations beginning with what he calls Grade *A*, where discretion is extremely broad and virtually impervious to appellate assault, and running to Grade *E*, where discretion is almost certainly reviewable.[48]

The lesson from this is that there are degrees of discretion. An able appellate lawyer will analyze the extent of the discretionary power available and the policy behind it, and then demonstrate whether the lower tribunal was endowed with broad, limited, or very little prerogative.

Review of discretion is somewhat broader than the very narrow range that governs fact-finding, but its scope has stated limitations. Appellate lawyers must understand that the exercise of discretion by the trial court has its limits and they must be able to articulate those limits. The competent lawyer carefully sets forth the boundaries of a permissible exercise of discretion and then demonstrates how those boundaries were transgressed. The outstanding appellate lawyer persuades the court to expand or narrow its review of discretion on the basis of the policies underlying the grant of discretion.

5.6 Questions of Law

When it comes to the review of the trial court's determination of the law, the appellate courts are given free rein. The review of fact-finding is the nadir of the appellate function; the examination of the trial court selection, interpretation, and application of legal precepts is the zenith. Generally speaking, the appellate court is free to examine *de novo* all aspects of legal precepts: the choice by the tribunal of the controlling legal precept, the interpretation of it, and the application of the precept as chosen and interpreted to the findings of fact.

---

48. Maurice Rosenberg, Appellate Review of Trial Court Discretion, http://www.fjc.gov/public/pdf.nsf/lookup/review.pdf/$file/review.pdf (last visited Mar. 20, 2017).

A reviewing court's function is to determine whether a trial court committed a mistake of law of sufficient magnitude to require that its judgment be reversed or vacated. Putting aside those jurisdictions in which appellate courts must search the record for error, the reviewing court's role is inexorably entwined with the performance of the advocates. An appellate court may, under circumstances, consider matters *sua sponte* but, generally, when an appellate court considers questions raised by an appeal alleging error of law, it relies upon the issues and legal arguments set forth by the advocate. Although the doctrine of plain error allows courts to consider some matters not initially brought before it, generally "substantial rights" must be implicated for the plain error doctrine to apply.[49] In the criminal law context, the Supreme Court has explained that appellate courts are not required to correct plain error, but should do so "'if the error seriously affects the fairness, integrity or public reputation of judicial proceedings.'"[50]

In 1877, a reviewing court stated: "The court erred in some of the legal propositions announced to the jury; but all the errors were harmless. Wrong directions which do not put the traveler out of his way furnish no reasons for repeating the journey."[51] The difficult question is to decide whether the trial error becomes reversible error. Working under the assumption that one is not entitled to a perfect trial, but only to a fair one, it becomes necessary to fashion a method of ascertaining the circumstances under which the results of an admittedly imperfect trial will be disturbed. Under the doctrine of harmless error, "courts should exercise judgment regarding errors . . . and should ignore errors that do not affect the essential fairness of the trial."[52]

It is impossible to draw any line in the sand to determine when run-of-the-mill trial mistakes transform themselves into reversible error. The line to reversible error is crossed when the mistake seriously infected the truth finding process, or when the final judgment has been rendered on uncontroverted facts and the party against whom the ruling was made could possibly have been entitled to relief.

5.7   Examples of Standards of Review

See Appendix A.

5.8   Summary

Identifying, understanding, and applying the standard of review are critical aspects of appellate advocacy. In talking to appellate judges about this book, several

---

49. Fed. R. Civ. P. 52(b); Fed. R. Civ. P. 51 (d)(2).
50. 3B Charles A. Wright et al., Federal Practice. & Procedure § 856 (4th ed. 2016).
51. Cherry v. Davis, 59 Ga. 454, 455 (1877).
52. James Wm. Moore et al., Moore's Manual: Federal Practice and Procedure § 24.100 (2016).

judges said that the standard of review should guide attorneys in their selection of issue to appeal. Several judges also cited the failure to utilize the standard of review as one of their biggest critiques on brief writing today. As one judge put it, "Some briefs look upon the standard of review as a mere box to be checked at the outset of the brief, and miss the opportunity to use the standard of review as the lens through which the judge will view the facts and law."

So how do you use the standard of review effectively on appeal? First, the standard of review section should be written persuasively, with the standard clearly stated along with explanatory material from cases that explains the standard in detail. Second, each argument in the brief should be tailored to the applicable standard of review for that issue. One way to do this is by including language identifying the relevant standard of review in major point headings, as discussed in Chapter Eight. Third, the standard of review should weave through the entire brief and infiltrate the entire brief writing process. All of the sections of the brief, from the Issues Presented and the Statement of Facts to the Argument Section should be written with an eye to the standard of review. Harnessed effectively, the standard of review can be a powerful tool of persuasion. Accordingly, a proper understanding of the concepts explained in this chapter will carry an advocate a long way toward winning on appeal.

PART THREE

THE NUTS AND BOLTS OF BRIEF WRITING

Chapter Six

The Brief: Selecting Issues and Finding a Winning Argument

6.1 Overview

You are now ready to research and write your brief. But before you start, you should get a couple of things straight: 1) what is the purpose of your brief? and 2) why are you writing it?

Think about these questions for a moment and you will realize that you are doing it for one reason. If you are the appellant, you want the judges to starting thinking of a two-syllable word—"reverse." If you are the appellee, it is spelled another way—"affirm."

Your brief's only purpose is to convince the appellate court to reverse or to affirm. Forget about how you spotted and discussed all those issues on your law school exams. Forget about how you wrote that law review article setting a new world record for footnotes per paragraph. And forget the memo you wrote to the firm's senior partner outlining your brilliance with regard to some tiny corner of the law. You are not writing to get tenure on the law school faculty or to persuade the American Law Institute to accept your view in a new Restatement.

If you are the appellant, you know that the statistics are against you. You know you have to beat the odds. In the United States Courts of Appeals, you want to be that one appeal in ten that reverses the trial court—or if it is a criminal appeal, you want to be that one case in fourteen.

To do this you have to grab the judges' interest immediately and never let go. You have to tell the judges what the trial court did, why it found in appellee's favor, and why such a finding constituted *reversible* error. Not only a run-of-the-mill error, mind you, but such a departure from propriety that it is highly probable that the breach affected the outcome of the case. Note the nicety here: "highly probable," not "more probable than not." Remember, you were not entitled to a perfect trial, only a fair one. Not every mistake is reversible error. Many of the trial judge's decisions were within the realm of his discretion, and to argue an abuse of this discretion is a daunting task.

So, before you write one word, sit down and ask yourself this: what's the overriding message I want to send to the appellate court? How do I convince the appellate judges that this case merits reversal?

When you are thinking of the message you want to send, do not start to write your argument unless you have already mastered the record. Do not play the "have-theory-need-facts" game—picking and choosing tiny tidbits of evidence from the transcript that favor your case but are contrary to those facts found by the fact-finder. You tried that before a judge or jury and *it did not work*. Once the appellate judge examines the district court opinion—and most of us read these before we read your argument—we will see the gaping hole in your argument through which the appellee will drive his big rig.

The cornerstone of your argument on appeal is anchored on the facts found by the fact-finder, and here we follow the common law tradition.[1]

What you must do is construct your argument from these facts. As you select issues to appeal, you must keep the concepts learned so far in mind.

6.2 Overview of the Brief-Writing Process

We have done housekeeping thus far: jurisdiction, issue preservation, and standards of review. We must now decide what to say, and the first step is to flush out the specific issues of appeal and research those issues.[2]

Your brief-writing process should be informed by a detailed strategy. Attorney Jordan B. Cherrick, now senior litigation counsel at Sidley Austin LLP, is credited with the acronym "PASS"—Preparation, Anticipation, Selectivity, and Style.[3] He fashions these elements as the keys to successful appellate advocacy:

> *Preparation*: An attorney's mastery of the record, the law, and the rules of the appellate court.
>
> *Anticipation*: A brief writer's effort to determine how to frame the issues and develop appellate strategy in a way that will best influence the judges who decide the case.
>
> *Selectivity*: Choosing the facts, events, and legal arguments likely to control the outcome.
>
> *Style*: The ability to persuade by writing and thinking well.[4]

The previous chapters, and the following chapter on research, deal with preparation. We now come to *Anticipation*: deciding what issues or points the brief will discuss. This requires an intelligent, extremely careful consideration of both the

---

1. See Chapter Five for a discussion of how factual findings are reviewed.
2. See Chapter Seven for a discussion of how to start your research.
3. Jordan B. Cherrick, *Issues, Facts, and Appellate Strategy*, LITIG. Spring 1990, at 15.
4. *Id.* at 15.

quantity and *quality* of the issues. Considerations of *quantity* will determine the size of the brief, and the determination of *quality* will give you the all-important theme or focus for the argument. At the very beginning, therefore, before you write or type any of the issues, focus on these objectives.

6.3   Choosing the Issues: The Lawyer's Decision and the Ethical Dilemma

Your first chore is to decide what issues you want to discuss. An issue is a separate and discrete question of law or fact, or a combination of the two, set forth in the brief as a reason for reversing or affirming the trial court or agency. Craft a succinct description of the alleged error committed by the judge below.

It is the lawyer, not the client, who has the ultimate responsibility for deciding what issues will be discussed on appeal. Remember, it is your name on the brief, and your reputation with the court that is potentially at issue. In fact, there are ethical responsibilities that guide the lawyer's choice. The American Bar Association's Model Rule of Professional Conduct 3.1 states:

> A lawyer shall not bring or defend a proceeding, or assert or controvert an issue therein, unless there is a basis in law and fact for doing so that is not frivolous, which includes a good faith argument for an extension, modification or reversal of existing law. A lawyer for the defendant in a criminal proceeding, or the respondent in a proceeding that could result in incarceration, may nevertheless so defend the proceeding as to require that every element of the case be established.[5]

What does this mean for you as you select your issues for appeal? It means that you should not raise a frivolous appeal.[6] Unfortunately, there is not a clear definition of what "frivolous" means. From the Model Rules, it is clear that arguing in good faith to extend, modify, or reverse existing law is not frivolous. Under the Model Rules, the test under Rule 3.1 is an objective, rather than subjective, test.[7]

The restriction on raising frivolous claims can be especially difficult in the case of a criminal appeal. While that lawyer must, at trial, make sure that "every element of the case [is] established," once the relevant facts are found by the fact-finder, there might not be meritorious issues to raise on appeal. What then does the lawyer do in the direct or post-conviction criminal appeal when the client insists on presenting improvident, unreasonable, or even downright outrageous contentions?

---

5. MODEL RULES OF PROF'L CONDUCT r. 3.1 (AM. BAR ASS'N 1983).
6. *See* United States v. Patridge, 507 F.3d 1092, 1093–95 (7th Cir. 2007).
7. RONALD D. ROTUNDA & JOHN S. DZIENKOWSKI, LEGAL ETHICS, THE LAWYER'S DESKBOOK ON PROFESSIONAL RESPONSIBILITY § 3.1-1 (2016).

In *Anders v. California*,[8] the Supreme Court provided lawyers with an option that is now used in the federal system and in many state court systems.[9] If a lawyer seeks to withdraw from a case on the grounds that the appeal is frivolous, the lawyer first must "certify she has carefully reviewed the entire record and then [] file a brief identifying the legal issues counsel has deemed frivolous but that might be deemed nonfrivolous by the appellate court."[10] This brief is known as an *Anders* brief. In a later case, the Supreme Court made clear that while the procedure in *Anders* is a "prophylactic framework" aimed at "vindicat[ing] the constitutional right to appellate counsel," it is not the "*only* prophylactic framework that could adequately vindicate this right."[11] In fact, some states have taken approaches that are more, and less, strict than the *Anders* approach.[12]

If there are meritorious issues to appeal, but the criminal defendant also wants you to raise frivolous issues, you can suggest that your client file a *pro se* brief raising the additional issues.[13]

6.3.1　Narrowing Down the Issues: Step One

The first step in deciding what issues to raise on appeal is to make an informal list of the issues that possibly may be presented. Do not worry about writing style. This listing is only an inventory. You merely want to know what issues are available, so do not start winnowing out the losers yet through in-depth legal research. This stage occurs before researching. Catalog every conceivable argument, and set out the complete case in all its unrefined potentiality. University of Texas English Department Professor Emeritus Betty Flowers devised a method that dramatizes the writing process. She suggests that each of us possesses "a character" or personality that we all have within us.[14] Variously, these are the madman, the architect, the carpenter, and the judge.[15] The madman "is full of ideas, writes crazily, and perhaps rather sloppily, gets carried away by enthusiasm and desires, and if really let loose, could turn out ten pages an hour."[16]

In step one, the brief writer should let the madman takeover. List *every* possible legal point that you can conjure up. This list is only the beginning point, and it

---

8. 386 U.S. 738 (1967).

9. *Frivolous Appeals: No Rush in Most States for Alternatives to* Anders *Briefs Despite Implicit Invitation*, 16 No. 18 Crim. Prac. Rep. 3 (2002).

10. Brent E. Newton, Almendarez-Torres *and the Anders Ethical Dilemma*, 45 Hous. L. Rev. 747, 756 (2008).

11. Smith v. Robbins, 528 U.S. 259, 273 (2000) (emphasis original).

12. *Frivolous Appeals: No Rush in Most States for Alternatives to Anders Briefs Despite Implicit Invitation*, 16 No. 18 Crim. Prac. Rep. 3 (2002).

13. Alan DuBois & Brett G. Sweitzer, Winning Strategies Seminar: Anders Briefs & Other Issues for Appeal 6, https://www.fd.org/docs/select-topics---appeals/anders_briefs.pdf (last visited Mar. 20, 2017; paywall).

14. Betty S. Flowers, *Madman, Architect, Carpenter, Judge: Roles and the Writing Process*, 58 Language Arts 834, 834 (1981).

15. *Id.*

16. *Id.*

will be over-inclusive. Unfortunately, too many brief writers consider it the ending point as well. They dump this gross listing on the laps of appellate judges instead of performing the crucial next step: making a critical judgment as to which issues will probably influence the court.

6.3.2 Narrowing Down the Issues: Step Two

The second step is weeding out those issues that do not have a reasonable probability of prevailing in the appellate court. This may be the most difficult decision you make. It is certainly the most important one, because what you exclude is as important as what you include.

Here, you must trade places with the judge, the person you seek to persuade. You must be dispassionate, detached, and imperturbable. You also must be intellectually objective, in the sense that you must put aside emotions and passions that you certainly possess as a result of having lost a case before the trial tribunal.

Having lost, you are understandably disturbed. Not only are you disappointed, but you are angry—a normal reaction. You want to vent your feelings by throwing in not only the kitchen sink, but the plumbing, and street sewers as well. If you do this, and many lawyers do, you make a devastating mistake. Cool it. Calm down. Act like a lawyer, not like a client. Analyze carefully to ascertain where there is an arguable question of trial court error, not simply an imaginable one.

Appellate judges are not law professors. They have different responsibilities. They do not give high grades to lawyers who can spot all the issues. More is not better in appellate advocacy. Judges are interested only in arguable points. The key here is selectivity, not fertility. You should be interested only in case-dispositive issues and arguments that may carry the day.

You cannot afford to dilute, or shall I say, pollute, your brief with superfluous contentions—such futile arguments infect your advocacy. Transfer yourself figuratively to the environment in which your brief will be read by the court, which was discussed in Chapter Two. Judges spend hours or maybe days with a brief that took weeks, even months, for you and your colleagues to prepare. Active United States circuit judges were swamped with an average annual caseload of 550 cases per judge during the 2015 court year.[17] Briefs must be read within a period of five or six weeks, while judges simultaneously write opinions from previous sittings, examine *pro se* briefs and counseled responses, wade through hundreds of motions, keep abreast of contemporary opinions, and attend a host of judicial conferences and committee meetings. This brief-reading cycle is repeated approximately seven

---

17. Administrative Office of the United States Courts, *U.S. Court of Appeals—Judicial Caseload Profile*, UNITED STATES COURTS, http://www.uscourts.gov/statistics-reports/federal-judicial-caseload-statistics-2015 (for the year ending June 2015) (last visited Mar. 20, 2017).

to nine times a year.[18] In many state appellate courts, the cycle is even more onerous. "Given such a demanding work load," writes Senior Judge Harry Pregerson of the Ninth Circuit, "it is not difficult to imagine our frustration when we are required to trudge through a fifty-page brief that could have presented its points effectively in fewer than twenty-five pages."[19]

James L. Robertson, a former Justice on the Mississippi Supreme Court, wrote:

> Before putting the first words on paper, try to think like a judge. But not just any judge. Crawl into the minds of the judges who will hear and decide your appeal. Ted Williams always got into the pitcher's mind, not just hours, but days before the game; you must do the same with your judge. Ask yourself, "If I were Judges Nasty, Brutish, and Short, of the Court of Appeals, how would I view these facts and this law?"[20]

When you change places, you should realize at least three things: 1) in the judge's day, many matters other than your brief compete for attention; 2) you never get a second chance to make an initial good impression; and 3) on the appellate court, you do not have the luxury of time that you had in the trial tribunal.

6.4 Arranging the Issues

Your most important point should be presented first. Always lead from a position of strength. Picking this point requires you to come up with an intelligent answer to the following question:

> *What argument, objectively considered, based on precedent and previously stated policy concerns of the court, is most calculated to persuade the court to your point of view?*

You cannot make this decision in a casual manner. It cannot be based on a hunch or a guess, even an educated one. It must be based on careful study of and

---

18. The practices vary a little among the United States Courts of Appeals, but the annual caseload per judge is about the same. Judge Jane Roth offers this perspective from the United States Court of Appeals for the Third Circuit:

> The main goal when writing a brief is to persuade the judge that the advocate's argument is the correct one to resolve the parties' dispute. This persuasion must be done quickly because judges read mountains of briefs every year. For instance, each year an appellate judge on the Third Circuit will participate in six court sittings. For each sitting, the Third Circuit judge will have, at most, two months to study all the briefs. For the twelve-month period ending on September 30, 2009, almost 58,000 appeals were filed in the thirteen federal courts of appeals. In the Third Circuit alone, 3750 appeals were filed, adding up to about 300,000 pages of briefs. Indeed, Chief Judge Alex Kozinski of the Ninth Circuit estimates that he reads 3,500 pages of briefs per month. Simply put, the appellate judge reads, writes, reads—and then repeats the cycle.

Jane R. Roth & Mani S. Walia, *Persuading Quickly: Tips for Writing an Effective Appellate Brief,* 11 J. App. Prac. & Process 443, 443–44 (2010).

19. *Id.* at 434.

20. James L. Robertson, *From the Bench: Reality on Appeal,* 17 Litig. 3, 5 (1990).

research into the possible issues that could be raised in the appeal, a careful review of the decisions of the court, and an understanding of factors that trigger judicial decision-making.

The most important point is the one that has a reasonable probability to persuade. We define "probability" as being more likely than not and distinguish it from a mere "possibility," something that may or may not succeed, or something that lies between probable and impossible.

You lead with your strongest suit in this judicial card game because you are in the persuasion business. You cannot save the best argument until last. This is not a drama of the theater or a Pulitzer Prize novel. Make a favorable impression on the decision-maker as soon as possible. Listen to Senior Judge Clyde Hamilton of the Fourth Circuit:

> Undeniably, of the hundreds of appellate briefs I have read, the most persuasively written argument components were those written with the precision of a neurosurgeon—not a millisecond of time was wasted getting in, doing precisely what needed to be done, and getting out. In the bulk of these briefs, the parties . . . led with their best argument . . . .[21]

If we ranked the metaphysical factors that go into decision-making, the initial impression received by the judge who reads your brief may be more important than any other aspect of the art of persuading.

There is one exception to this rule. Prior to reaching the main issue of the merits you may be required to address a threshold matter, like jurisdiction or some procedural question. In that case, the preliminary housekeeping matters must be addressed.

With respect to jurisdiction, you may have addressed the issue in papers filed with the court prior to filing the brief. Non-action by the court indicates that the question is still open. The appellant and the appellee should repeat the jurisdiction arguments in the briefs—*do not* rely on the previously filed papers. Making the judge rummage through preliminary briefings when considering the briefs-in-chief does not make your position more acceptable.

Having decided on the lead issue, in what order do you set forth the others? You will often find that several issues rise in logical order, with some issues subordinate to others. You have already determined the major thrust of the brief and decided what points will support the dominant theme. We offer these suggestions for issue arrangement:

- The issues should be listed in order of importance. If you cannot resist including a throwaway issue, save it until last.

---

21. Clyde H. Hamilton, *Effective Appellate Brief Writing*, 50 S.C. L. Rev. 581, 587 (1999); *see also* Roth & Walia, *supra* note 18, at 453.

- At times, the arguments must be listed in logical order. Often, a series of syllogisms is linked, with conclusions of previous ones forming the premises of those which follow. Where one point follows the other in logical order, the statement of issues takes the form of an inverted pyramid. If you lose the top, or fattest issue, you lose the entire argument, for each subsequent point is dependent on the acceptability of the previous one.

- If at all possible, then, construct your brief with points that are independent of each other. In this manner, you give the court an alternative basis for decision, so that if the judges reject your major point and those subsequent to and dependent on it, you may be entirely successful on an independent, alternative ground. Here, your statement of issues more resembles an egg carton with self-contained supports than a single inverted pyramid.

One way to ensure that your issues flow logically and that your strongest issues are raised first, is to carefully outline your argument before starting to write. Outlining also serves as a useful way to organize your research and the relevant facts from the record. It is important to write persuasively, even with the outline. In the outline, list all of the main points and subpoints that you plan on briefing. For each point, identify the relevant legal rules that pertain to the point. Identify material facts in analogous cases that apply the rules, and compare these cases and facts to the facts in your case. Reviewing the strength of each argument in your outline will help you decide what issues are worth keeping.

6.5   The Appellee's Issues

The appellee has a choice to make on the arrangement of issues. One theory is to always place your issues in the same sequence as the appellant. Another viewpoint is that an appellee, like the appellant, should lead with her strongest issues. Indeed, it may be that an affirmative defense is key to a defendant-appellee's case, but the appellant-plaintiff placed that issue last. As appellee, if that issue resolves the case, you would certainly want to lead with it. Regardless of what approach you take, clarity is the indispensable requirement. An appellee must indicate in the statement of issues exactly where the response to specific points raised by the appellant may be found.

The appellee's phrasing of the issue need not be an exact copy of the appellant's. Often, the wording cannot be duplicated because the appellant's choice of terms is inappropriate and not persuasive for your purposes, or just plain incorrect. Paramount in setting forth the responding issues is giving clear directions to where the response is located. Appellate lawyers must understand the brief reading environment. It is hard to predict how appellate judges will read the briefs. Some judges will read one brief all the way through and then read the other. Others will read the discussion in each brief of one issue, then move on to the next one. Often interspersed in this process is a rereading of relevant portions of the trial court's opinion.

In a consolidated appeal from multiple appellants—often in a criminal case—we generally have a single appellee's brief. Most United States Attorney's offices, but not all, handle this very well by succinctly and accurately cross-indexing the rejoinder to those questions that have been duplicated in the several briefs.

The bottom line: the framework of the appellee's statement of issues should provide a roadmap for the judge who reads your brief.

6.6   How Many Issues?

The most important decision you make in writing a brief is usually to limit the issues to no more than three. Judges react differently to the stimuli of advocacy. While our initial impressions vary, many judges, when faced with a brief that raises no more than three points, breathe a sigh of satisfaction and conclude that the brief writer may have something to say.

Some judges may react in the same manner, or perhaps to a slightly lesser degree, when four or five points are presented. Beyond this point, an appellant is really pressing his luck. Even when we reverse a trial court, rarely does a brief establish more than one or two reversible errors. When an appellant's brief contains more than six points, a presumption arises in the mind of some judges that there is no merit to *any* of them. This is not an irrebuttable presumption, but it is nevertheless a presumption that reduces the effectiveness of the writer's brief.[22]

Senior Fifth Circuit Judge W. Eugene Davis has noted:

> I see very few cases with more than two or three issues that are truly dispositive of the appeal. Most of the briefs I see that raise eight or ten issues include issues that make no difference in the outcome of the appeal. This sends a signal that the losing party or losing lawyer has a badly bruised ego but not much of an appeal. When some of counsel's multiple points of error are obviously weak or insubstantial, counsel loses credibility. With this loss in credibility, the judge becomes less receptive to the notion that the trial judge erred in any respect.[23]

As the comments at the end of this chapter demonstrate, many judges share a dislike for "shotgun"-style briefs that raise too many issues. Although appellate attorneys frustrated by this perspective can claim that they don't know what will attract the attention of the court or that the court will consider important, the

---

22. Just as James Russell Lowell wrote to Charles Eliot Norton, "In general those who have nothing to say, contrive to spend the longest time in doing it." An Oriental Apologue, Stanza 15, The Poetical Works of James Russell Lowell, 1848.

23. Bryan A. Garner, *Judges on Briefing: A National Survey*, 8 SCRIBES J. LEGAL WRITING 1, 7 (2001–2002).

truth is that they should know what will interest the court. With the availability of computer-assisted legal research and the wealth of fine law libraries in the states, counties, cities, and law schools, any reasonably competent researcher should be able to determine which aspects of a given subject have commanded the interest of a given court and, therefore, which ones will do so in the present case. But this presupposes that the reasonably competent researcher has actually done the research. Judges expect as much.

How many issues then should be raised? It depends. Certainly in a criminal case the question of the Sixth Amendment right to competent counsel makes even the most expert appellate advocates lean on the side of too many, rather than too few. In an earlier edition of this book, Judge Aldisert provided, what he termed "purely subjective guidelines," for civil cases, all of which are subject to the caveat that they do not apply in unusual and extraordinary circumstances.

Litmus Test: Number of Issues in the Brief

Number of Issues	*Judge's Reaction*
Three	Presumably arguable points. The lawyer is primo.
Four	Probably arguable points. The lawyer is primo minus.
Five	Perhaps arguable points. The lawyer is no longer primo.
Six	Probably no arguable points. The lawyer has not made a favorable initial impression.
Seven	Presumably, no arguable points. The lawyer is at an extreme disadvantage, with an uphill battle all the way.
Eight or more	Strong presumption that no point is worthwhile.

This litmus test is arbitrary, to be sure, but veteran appellate judges are virtually unanimous in complaining that today's briefs are too long.[24]

As described in Chapters One and Two, the reality of a judge's workload and the brief reading environment also play a role in the need to keep a brief precisely that: brief.

---

24. *See generally* Garner, *Judges on Briefing: A National Survey*, 8 SCRIBES J. LEGAL WRITING 1 (2001–2002) (collecting comments from several judges describing their preferences for briefs). But the late former Missouri Supreme Court Chief Justice Charles B. Blackmar (nationally known for his co-authorship of Federal Jury Practice and Instructions), offered this caveat in an earlier edition of this book:

> It is easy for me to say that counsel should limit the number of issues presented. But there are problems about generalizing. I remember from my practice, many years ago, that a younger lawyer was working with me on a brief. He suggested an additional point and I tried to argue him out of it because we had too many but he persisted and I included it in the brief. We got a favorable opinion which led off with his point, after which it said: "This point is dispositive, and so we do not have to consider the other interesting issues presented and arguments made."

6.7 Perspectives From The Bench: Selecting Issues

Much of what has been said emanates from Judge Aldisert's and Judge Southwick's personal experiences as state and federal judges. It also comes from friends and colleagues on the state and federal benches who have shared their experiences and perspectives for this book.

6.7.1 Current and Former State Court Justices

Below are perspectives shared by current and former state court justices.

Charles E. Jones *Former Chief Justice, Arizona Supreme Court*	Omit weak arguments that are largely, if not completely irrelevant, and focus exclusively on the most persuasive, authoritative arguments that will lead to the disposition of issues. State the strongest and best arguments first. Try to anticipate the difficult questions and provide answers. The latter point is also valid in preparing for oral argument.
Chase T. Rogers *Chief Justice, Connecticut Supreme Court*	More than three issues is suspect (the "spaghetti thrown against the wall" problem).
Sabrina McKenna *Associate Justice, Supreme Court of Hawai'i*	Focus on fewer than five strong points. Three is good.
Rita B. Garman *Justice, Illinois Supreme Court*	Make a decision tree. If there is a threshold issue, deal with it first. Beyond that, the "kitchen sink" approach is not effective. Including several clearly losing arguments only weakens the credibility of the stronger issues.
Bill Cunningham *Justice, Supreme Court of Kentucky*	Pick strongest points. And keep the issues to a limited few.
Leigh Ingalls Saufley *Chief Justice, Maine Supreme Judicial Court*	Always provide a brief, nontechnical summary of issues presented at the beginning of the brief and a clear and explicit indication of the relief requested at the end of the brief.
Stephen N. Limbaugh, Jr. *Judge, U.S. District Court for the Eastern District of Missouri, formerly Chief Justice, Supreme Court of Missouri*	Do not be repetitive. The persistent recapitulation of arguments—as if that is necessary to beat the arguments into the judges' heads—is often counterproductive because judges will find it irritating rather than enlightening.
Michael G. Heavican *Chief Justice, Nebraska Supreme Court*	It will always depend, but a lawyer should think twice about including issues that obviously lack merit, particularly where other, more meritorious, arguments are also made. Lawyers should also not include issues unless they are prepared to fully brief/argue that issue.

Thomas G. Saylor
Chief Justice, Supreme Court of Pennsylvania

While appreciating how difficult this may be to do, lawyers do need to exercise good judgment in screening and selecting issues so that their best arguments may resonate.

David Gilbertson
Chief Justice, South Dakota Supreme Court

Lead with your best punch. Go with one or two of your best issues that will really decide the case. A brief with fifteen or twenty assignments of error tells me the attorney is desperate and really is grasping at straws. No trial judge I ever knew was so bad as to make that many errors. As far as oral argument, do the same. Some of the best presentations I have seen discussed only one crucial issue, which usually decides the case. The attorney went directly to that issue, spoke for seven minutes and waived the rest of his time.

Sharon Keller
Presiding Judge, Texas Court of Criminal Appeals

Step back and honestly consider what might win. Ditch arguments that are personally appealing to you, but you know in your heart are unlikely to get traction.

Nathan L. Hecht
Chief Justice, Supreme Court of Texas

Lawyers often "moot" their oral argument—present it before a panel of lawyers not involved in the case, acting as judges, asking questions, and evaluating the presentation.

6.7.2 Circuit Court Judges

Below are perspectives from federal circuit court judges.

Bruce M. Selya
Judge, First Circuit

Use common sense, only those issues that have a (fighting) chance should be briefed.

John M. Walker, Jr.
Senior Judge, Second Circuit

The poorest, least persuasive briefs are all too often those that the lawyer has not taken the time to reduce to its essence. Be highly selective in choosing the few points that have the best chance of prevailing. How often has the fourth or fifth point raised ever resulted in a victory for the appellant?

Thomas L. Ambro
Judge, Third Circuit

A lawyer should choose which are the most credible issues, which have the best chance to succeed, and what is the best way to achieve success. On the last point, counsel should ask whether, for example, it is best to emphasize the text of a statute or regulation, the structure of an enactment (e.g., if the same words appear in three places and the first two are understood to mean X, should not the third place also mean X), the consequences of a decision for or against counsel, or the fairness of what counsel or his/her opponent proposes. In some cases, all four principles may be in play.

Kent Jordan
Judge, Third Circuit

Good lawyers do not dilute their position by including marginal arguments. Having the good judgment to decide what is "marginal" is what separates good lawyers from the rest of the pack.

Anthony J. Scirica *Senior Judge, Third Circuit*	You must focus on the dispositive issue or issues only.
Albert Diaz *Judge, Fourth Circuit*	Choose only the issues that matter, and brief only the ones that really matter. We have a system that (rightly) gives trial judges (and juries) the benefit of the doubt. A good appellate advocate accepts that reality and tailors his brief accordingly.
Diana Gribbon Motz *Judge, Fourth Circuit*	Generally, there should be no more than four questions; do not repeat the same question in different ways. Often a case presents only one or two questions. Very occasionally, a case presents many questions. It is, however, almost impossible to treat adequately more than four issues in a thirty-five- to fifty-page brief.
Gregg J. Costa *Judge, Fifth Circuit*	Even in an appeal from a complicated trial, I think counsel should rarely raise more than three points of error. Raising weaker arguments undermines credibility and takes focus away from your stronger arguments (especially in an era of page limits). As far as which ones make that cut, it comes down to that most important qualities a lawyer can possess: good judgment. And there are some issues that the standard of review or a review of recent case law will demonstrate face long odds.
Carolyn Dineen King *Senior Judge, Fifth Circuit*	Pick the most important issues, deal with them thoroughly, and omit the others. Be concise.
Edward C. Prado *Judge, Fifth Circuit*	Would you be willing to spend your entire oral argument on that issue? If so, include it.
Richard Clifton *Senior Judge, Ninth Circuit*	Try to limit the brief to plausible arguments. An argument that seems silly to a judge may undermine the credibility of other arguments made in the same brief. Hail Mary passes connect once in a while, and so do Hail Mary arguments, but there is something to lose in making a Hail Mary argument. That kind of argument is rarely worth the cost. If there is an issue controlled by binding precedent to the contrary that the brief is simply trying to preserve, say as much.
Carolyn B. McHugh *Judge, Tenth Circuit*	Lawyers should realistically assess the likelihood of success based on the applicable standard of review, and be cognizant of the fact that weak arguments distract the reader from more meritorious claims.
Harris L. Hartz *Judge, Tenth Circuit*	I do not envy the difficulty facing the advocate. It is essential to avoid raising too many issues, because judicial fatigue can make all of them losers. But as a practitioner, I recall winning in the Tenth Circuit on a ground that I thought was so weak that I omitted it from the brief. And I have written opinions deciding the case on a ground that received perfunctory attention in the

prevailing brief. The only thing that I might suggest, which is probably a minority view among judges, is that it is sometimes useful to include a marginal (even a clearly losing) argument that tees up a better argument. For example, the court may be more likely to reverse because of an error on an evidentiary issue if the brief raises a sufficiency-of-the-evidence issue that has no chance of succeeding but indicates how important the credibility of a witness was. The weakness of the evidence can, of course, be addressed when discussing the evidentiary issue, but that discussion may be more effective rhetorically in a separate section.

Deanell Reece Tacha
Former Judge, Tenth Circuit

It seems to me that before ever writing a brief, and certainly before oral argument, counsel should have a very candid discussion with himself or herself about what precisely the issues are that will result in a favorable decision on appeal. By that, I mean in the typical case there are usually only one or two outcome-determinative issues. Whether one is appellant or appellee, the question to be answered precisely is: "What is it that the court must decide to decide in my favor?" If counsel honestly and analytically answers this question, the brief and the oral argument are very clearly targeted to reaching that answer. For example, the appellant must answer in a focused manner: What issue or issues will require the appellate court to reverse the judgment of the court below, and what cases and/or facts precisely address that issue? For appellee, the question is perhaps even more straightforward: What issue requires that the appellate court affirm the district court, and what facts or cases support that result? As I have worked with advocacy classes, I have been struck by the difficulty that advocates have in answering those questions precisely. Either because of a lack of focus or the difficulty of honing a case to that particularity, lawyers seem to have an exceedingly difficult time answering directly these pivotal questions.

Haldane Robert Mayer
Senior Judge, Federal Circuit

Be clear and concise—write and rewrite until the issue and answer can be identified in one short sentence. This will also aid the practitioner in culling out the real issues for appeal.

Patricia M. Wald
Former Chief Judge, D.C. Circuit

Visualize the whole before you begin. What overriding message is the document going to convey? What facts are essential to the argument? How does the argument take off from the facts? How do different arguments blend together? Better still, visualize how the judge's opinion should read if it goes your way. (Too many briefs read as if the paralegal summed up all conceivable relevant facts, and then the lawyer took over with the legal arguments, and never the twain doth meet.)

CHAPTER SEVEN

THE BRIEF: RESEARCH AND USE OF AUTHORITIES

7.1   Preparing to Research

Insofar as legal research on appeal is concerned, you do not start from scratch. You have already had a trial or pretrial proceeding. You have preserved the point by making an objection or filing the appropriate motion and receiving an adverse ruling either on the record or by written order. You have asserted some legal propositions in the form of cases, statutes, constitutional provisions, or rules that support your position. Ideally, you or the lawyer who appeared before the trial court already had prepared and submitted a pretrial memorandum, trial brief, or memorandum in support of any post-trial motion. Now that the case has been lost at the trial level and a notice of appeal has been filed, it is time for additional research.

If you were the trial lawyer, you should update research to find out if there is anything new. Ask yourself whether there is anything else you can look for that may be more convincing than what you already have found. You must cite-check the authorities to ascertain their present vitality. Online subscription-based research systems, such as WestlawNext, Lexis Advance, and Bloomberg, are particularly helpful here, as are the websites of some courts, which post recent decisions.

If you are brought in as fresh counsel for the appeal, the research should be started from the beginning. You should not rely solely on the efforts of the attorney below. In either event, the research should be complete and current at the time the brief is written. Although court rules typically allow parties to file supplemental authorities, this process should only be used to bring to the court's attention cases that have been handed down since the brief was filed. Under Federal Rule of Appellate Procedure 28(j), if a party becomes aware of "pertinent and significant authorities," either after the brief has been filed or after oral argument but before the court's decision, the party can inform the circuit clerk and other parties by submitting a letter. According to the Rule, the letter "must not exceed 350 words" and "must state the reasons for the supplemental citations, referring either to the page of the brief or to a point argued orally."[1] When a judge receives "supplemental authorities" right before oral

---

1. FED. R. APP. P. 28(j).

argument that predate the filing of the brief, the reaction can be to consider the lawyer's initial work on the case sloppy.

An important aspect of preparing to research and write a brief is reviewing the trial record, including all documents and exhibits. You must carefully study the entire record, not just the portions that favor your arguments. It is important to examine the record impartially, as Oliver Cromwell would say, with its "warts and all." This advice holds true for attorneys who were trial counsel.

For attorneys who were not trial counsel, the process of the reviewing the record is even more important. Minimum levels of professional competence require you to be familiar with every page of the record. Judges too often hear at oral argument, "I'm sorry, your honors, I can't answer that question. I was not trial counsel." Keep in mind that when you assume an appeal, you are taking over from a lawyer who has lost the case. Ask yourself: "Should I independently review everything carefully or start by receiving advice from someone who already has lost? Can I trust the loser's memory?" Indeed, even if you were trial counsel, you cannot trust your own memory. Recollections of what took place do not matter; what does matter is what appears in the record in black and white.

The importance of the record does not end with this detailed review. During the brief writing process, you should decide, after consulting the court rules, what portions of the record to include in the appendix or excerpts of record accompanying the brief. Though many, if not most, courts have the record available to the judges electronically, and some even require hyperlinks in the briefs to the record pages, many judges still use the record excerpts while reading the paper briefs or while on the bench during oral argument. Record excerpts are also used in some courts to decide whether oral argument should be granted. You should consider excerpting limited, but critical, portions of the record to include in the appendix. Often, an excerpt from the record covering testimony of a witness under questioning may be the most effective and dramatic way of getting a point across.

The trial court's opinion (or that of the administrative agency or intermediate appellate court) is a crucial part of this record. Appellate judges study these opinions very carefully, often before reading the briefs. The lawyers for both parties must read the trial court's opinion and understand it thoroughly. The appellant's brief should carefully address both the trial court's rulings on the points presented for appeal and also the reasoning given by the court for each ruling. Even if the appellee disagrees with the reasoning in the trial court opinion, the better practice is for the appellee at least to set it forth in the brief and then proceed to offer an alternative basis for support.

7.2   Researching and Compiling Research

How should you start research on an appellate brief, especially if you were not counsel below? Most attorneys have a host of research tools at their fingertips, from subscription-based services like Lexis Advance or WestlawNext, to law books, to asking their smartphone for the answer. While each of these research tools has its use, it is important for you to develop a research strategy that uses your time, and your client's money, most efficiently and effectively.

The first step in researching a brief is identifying the pertinent legal and factual issues that are at the heart of the dispute.[2] If you are unfamiliar with the area of law at issue in an appeal, you should first read secondary materials, such as a treatise, to ensure that you understand the relevant legal principles.[3] You cannot identify the key issues in the case, or the right search terms to use, if you do not understand the area of law.[4] Secondary materials also often provide citations to important cases in the particular area of law.[5] Once you understand the law, you can start thinking about the specific legal and factual issues in the case.[6]

Identifying the relevant legal issues and material facts in the appeal allows you to evaluate the usefulness of the sources identified in research.[7] Professor Kent Olson has identified several important aspects of the case to consider when trying to identify the material facts and legal issues in the case:

- Consider the parties the case and any relationship they may have to each other that could be relevant, such as employer/employee.[8]

- Consider the "objects or places" involved in the case, including the relevant jurisdiction.[9]

- Consider the "acts or omissions giving rise to a cause of action," such as malpractice by a doctor or discrimination by an employer.[10]

- Consider the relief sought.[11]

- Consider any possible defenses that may be at issue, such as sovereign immunity or statute of limitations.[12]

- Consider the procedural posture of the case.[13]

---

2. Kent Olson, Principles of Legal Research 21 (2d ed. 2015).
3. *Id.* at 22.
4. *Id.*
5. *Id.*
6. *See* Chapter Six for a more detailed discussion of selecting the issues for appeal.
7. *Id.* at 21.
8. *Id.*
9. *Id.*; *see also* Amy Sloan, Basic Legal Research 28 (2012).
10. Olson, *supra* note 2, at 21.
11. *Id.*
12. *Id.*
13. *Id.*

Examining these aspects of the case can help you craft search terms that will be important in finding cases.[14]

Once you understand the area of law and have put together a list of issues and material facts, you can start looking for the relevant primary source materials, such as cases or statutes.[15] Most case law and statutory research is now done online. In law school, students are given subscriptions through their school's law library to the large subscription-based legal research tools, like WestlawNext, Lexis Advance, and Bloomberg. Once these students enter practice, however, they may not have access to these services, or the subscription might be more limited in scope. Some states, such as Virginia, offer bar members free access to lesser-known subscription legal research services, such as Fastcase.[16] In addition to these more well-known sources, there are several newer, and perhaps more affordable, subscription-based legal research tools, such as Ravel, Casetext, and ROSS, that are using computer technologies to identify the most relevant search results.[17] Subscription-based legal research services are not the only sources available. There are also free legal research tools available, including Google Scholar and the Cornell University Legal Information Institute. The newer and free services, however, might not carry as many sources or be as easy to use. Some of the sources are weak on statutory materials and may not contain annotated statutes.

Once you identify the relevant sources for your brief, you must ensure that these sources are current.[18] Some of the legal research services offer ways of checking the currency of case law or statutes, such as "Shepardizing" a case using Lexis Advance. In some instances, you can even set email alerts to notify you if your authorities are cited in subsequent cases.

As Professor Olson insightfully notes, "Knowing when to stop researching can be just as difficult as knowing where to begin."[19] He suggests that when you have used "several research approaches that lead to the same answers," that is a good sign that you have found the necessary sources.[20]

Once you have found all the relevant sources, you must find a way to organize the research. Some subscription-based legal research programs offer software that can

---

14. Sloan, *supra* note 11, at 27–30.

15. Olson, *supra* note 2, at 23.

16. *Bar Association Subscribers*, Fastcase, http://www.fastcase.com/barmembers/ (last visited Mar. 20, 2017).

17. Michele R. Pistone & Michael B. Horn, *Disrupting Law School: How Disrupting Innovation Will Revolutionize the Legal World* 7 (2016), at http://christenseninstitute.org/wp-content/uploads/2016/03/Disrupting-law-school.pdf (last visited Mar. 20, 2017).

18. Olson, *supra* note 2 at 23–24.

19. *Id.* at 24.

20. *Id.*

help organize research, such as Westlaw's Case Notebook software.[21] Spreadsheets or outlines can also help organize research.[22]

Attorney James D. Crawford of Philadelphia[23] offers this useful brief writing advice to the junior partners and associates in his firm:

- Organize your research before you write. A major brief may involve days or even weeks of research, usually done by more than one person. If the accumulated research is to be used effectively in the brief, you must have some way to find the right cases or statutes to support each point you wish to make when you want to make it.

- It does not matter what technique you choose. Some lawyers find file cards useful. Others make photocopies of cases, mark important passages with a highlighter, and make notes at the head of each case of the propositions for which it stands or the ways in which it can be used. Still others scribble notes meaningful only to themselves on scraps of yellow pads. None, on the other hand, relies primarily on memoranda prepared by others. An author of a brief based on secondary sources alone is not an author or even an editor; he or she is at best a compiler, and appellate practice has a great ability to expose compilers.

- What is important is that you find some way of retrieving the cases you have found in the course of your research. Few things are more frustrating than knowing you have read a controlling case directly on point but cannot find it.

- Know and follow the rules of court. Once you have mastered the facts and the law and are ready to write the brief you have outlined, it is time to turn to the applicable rules of court. These rules will answer many of your questions concerning the form and content of your brief, and failure to follow them—in their current version— invites hostility or even literal rejection by the court. Only a good lawyer can write a really fine brief. But any competent lawyer can write a brief that complies with the applicable rules. What is more, whereas a court will not reject a brief for lack of brilliance, it has the right—exercised with increasing frequency—to reject a brief that

---

21. *Case Notebook*, Thomas Reuters, http://legalsolutions.thomsonreuters.com/law-products/solutions/case-notebook/ (last visited Mar. 20, 2017).

22. *See, e.g., The Art and Craft of Strategic Legal Research*, The Writing Center at Georgetown University Law Center (2004), https://www.law.georgetown.edu/academics/academic-programs/legal-writing-scholarship/writing-center/upload/strategicresearch.pdf (providing examples of charts and outlines) (last visited Mar. 20, 2017).

23. Mr. Crawford, retired partner at Schnader, Harrison, Segal & Lewis, is a longtime leading appellate lawyer. He was chief appellate counsel in the Philadelphia District Attorney's office during the late 1960s and early 1970s, a period when federal courts were developing new concepts of Fourteenth Amendment protections. He served as chief assistant to then District Attorney Arlen Specter.

does not comport with the rules and will, almost inevitably, think less of arguments presented in a non-complying brief. At oral argument it may take counsel to task for his noncompliance, to his discomfort and at a time when he would like to be arguing his case.

7.3   Evaluating Your Authorities

When it comes to verifying or authenticating statements in your brief, be aware that you can earn a helpful or a destructive reputation by the level of accuracy and honesty found in your brief. Attorneys should fear the reader's first reaction upon reading the brief being, "I don't trust you. I won't take your word for any statement. Your credibility level is in the negative numbers, and your reputation for veracity is even lower." These are harsh statements, to be sure, but too many judges have been burned too many times not to recognize that statements in a brief must be checked and double-checked. When you authenticate a statement with a citation, the strongest bite of authority is a short verbatim quote with a pinpoint page cite. This gives your argument the greatest credibility, negating the suspicion that you are putting a special interpretation on the citation or are crafting an impermissible paraphrase.

To be sure, all authorities are not currency of equal value. At one extreme is precedent of the sharpest bite—a decision of the jurisdiction's highest court in which the material facts are identical to those in your case, or if you are before an intermediate court, a similar decision of that court. At the other extreme is the least persuasive authority—a conclusory statement contained in a student law review note.

The mix most often seen in briefs is somewhere in between, usually at the higher end of the scale, consisting of decisions of the appellate court that hears the appeal or a decision of the jurisdiction's highest court in which the material facts, although not identical, are similar. Here you must apply the rules of logical analogy.[24] The mix also includes analogous decisions from courts of coordinate authority, or courts lower in the judicial hierarchy or from other jurisdictions; plurality or concurring opinions of the highest court; and treatises, law review articles, the Restatements, and similar sources.

What authorities should you use? The best answer is, "Anything that will help." But keep in mind that all authorities do not have equal weight. An excellent authority sometimes overlooked by the appellee is a reference to the trial court's opinion. Another effective authority often overlooked in appeals to the jurisdiction's highest court is a persuasive dissenting opinion of an intermediate appellate court judge.

---

24. Ruggero J. Aldisert, Logic for Lawyers: A Guide to Clear Legal Thinking 93–115, 232 (3d ed. 1997); *see also* Chapter Eleven.

An informal checklist could be used by appellate lawyers:

- Statutes. Always examine the legislature's website or, if you are using a paper version of the code, the pocket parts for any amendments to a statute. Use an annotated code to understand how the statute has been interpreted by the courts. Be alert and imaginative in your research. For example, a legislative recodification of the state code may have changed the section number for the relevant statute without changing its language. A court opinion interpreting an earlier, differently numbered codification may be right on point, but current web-based research services overlook the precedent. One example of such an omission may have caused an attorney for the challenger to be unaware of a deadline for contesting an election. The relevant precedent was not shown as authority on Westlaw or Lexis, but counsel for the election winner searched the annotations in the older Codes and found the opinion.[25]

- Cases. Always update your research electronically such that your brief has the latest relevant case law.

- Relevant agency decisions. If your case concerns a regulatory matter, you should refer to the decisions of the relevant regulatory agency. You might also need to look at the regulations that provide the framework for that agency.

- Furnish the court with the text of all difficult-to-access authorities.

- Always cite-check authorities.

- Go directly to the cases, and read as much of the case as you can find the time to do. Context matters for the judicial statements you want to use. Do not rely on digests, the syllabus, headnotes, or secondary sources that refer you to the case.

- Use citation forms recommended by the *Bluebook*, or other controlling citation formats used in the jurisdiction.

When citing cases and other authorities, you must understand the difference between mandatory and persuasive authorities. Mandatory authorities are those the court must follow as recognized precedent. They include cases from the court's highest jurisdiction that are directly on point, as well as unambiguous statutory language. Persuasive authorities, on the other hand, do not bind the court; they are cited for their persuasive value only. A good example of persuasive authority is

---

25. *See* McDaniel v. Cochran, 158 So.3d 992, 997–98 (Miss. 2014) (applying Kellum v. Johnson, 115 So. 2d 147 (Miss. 1959), which had explained why the directly relevant statute, which had no deadline for filing an election contest, and another which did, should be read *in pari materia*). Judge Southwick talked about the case with one of the counsel and was told of the approach taken to research the Code.

a case from another jurisdiction that is directly on point.[26] Your task is to convince the court to adopt the case holding and the reasons supporting it.

7.4 Citation Evaluation Chart

Here is a helpful chart to evaluate the persuasive weight and usefulness of common legal research materials:

Authority	*Persuasive Value*
Applicable statutes	Strongest possible authority if statutory provision is invoked. Annotations after statute can assist in finding cases.
Direct quote from a case from the highest court in the jurisdiction with identical material facts	Strongest possible authority. Royal straight flush.
Paraphrased holding from a case from the highest court in the jurisdiction with identical material facts	Strongest possible authority without a direct quote.
Case from the court hearing your appeal with identical material facts	Almost as strong as above.
Legislative history, if applicable	Can be dreadfully overworked, but persuasive if the statutory language is ambiguous. Committee and conference committee reports reflect more consensus than isolated statements of individual legislators. Be aware of the fallacy of hasty generalization. (But beware—some judges despise legislative history and consider it irrelevant.)
Case from the highest court in the jurisdiction with similar material facts	Must analogize to prove that the material facts are similar.
Case from the court in which you appear with similar material facts	Must prove that the material facts are similar.

---

26. Another example would be an unpublished opinion, which, according to the Federal Rules of Appellate Procedure, cannot be barred for its persuasive value of for another reason and cannot be "discouraged, nor may a court forbid parties to cite unpublished opinions." 32.1(a). Justice Stevens noted that "the fact that the Court of Appeals' opinion is unpublished is irrelevant. Nonpublication must not be a convenient means to prevent review. An unpublished opinion may have a lingering effect in the Circuit and surely is as important to the parties concerned as is a published opinion." Smith v. United States, 502 U.S. 1017, 1020 (1991).

Case from the highest court in the jurisdiction or the court hearing the appeal with identical or similar facts but with a strong dissent	Precedential value slightly weakened.
Plurality opinion from the highest court in the jurisdiction or the court hearing the appeal	Persuasive argument, but reasoning is not controlling precedent.
Case from a coordinate jurisdiction completely supporting your position	Must show that it is good law and demonstrate, with good reasons, it is in accordance with the weight of authority. Must also show why this majority rule should be adopted. Multiple citations may be impressive.
Citing and quoting directly from the trial court opinion in your case	Very persuasive, as evidenced by the frequency with which trial court opinions are quoted in appellate opinions.
If the question is an open one in your jurisdiction, a case from the jurisdiction's trial court completely supporting your position	Must show that it is good law and demonstrate, with good reasons, that it is in accordance with the weight of authority.
If the question is an open one in your jurisdiction, cases from coordinate jurisdictions that recognize a split with a pronounced majority view	Numbers help, but the bottom line is the soundness of the reasons supporting the view. Multiple citations probably are necessary.
Case from the highest court in the jurisdiction or the court in which you appear where the material facts are not identical or similar	Admit the flaw or lack of completeness, but argue that the facts in your case are nevertheless sufficient to support the same holding.
Controlling (mandatory) authorities are against your position (note that the rules of professional responsibility of many jurisdictions require parties to disclose controlling authorities against their position)	This is a problem. You must try to distinguish the case. If you cannot distinguish the case, you can ask the court to overrule it. Just be aware that at the federal court of appeals level, it takes an en banc court to overrule circuit precedent. You may request initial consideration of a case by the *en banc* federal court of appeals, pointing out the futility of the appeal otherwise. Do not expect the request to be honored, though it happens. Furthermore, a court of appeals cannot overrule the United States Supreme Court.
Restatements and Comments	Controlling only if the jurisdiction has adopted a particular section. Otherwise, simply very persuasive authority.
Treatises and texts	Persuasive, with degree of persuasion depending upon the reputation of author and the degree of technical sophistication of the subject.

Legal encyclopedias, such as Corpus Juris Secundum *and* American Jurisprudence	Secondary sources only.
Law review articles	May be excellent research tools for finding primary authorities. Conclusions may be persuasive in furnishing reasons to support a proposition. The article should stand on its substance and not on the reputation of the law school.

7.5   Understanding What Is Precedent

"A judicial precedent attaches a specific legal consequence to a detailed set of facts in an adjudged case or judicial decision, which is then considered as furnishing the rule for the determination of a subsequent case involving identical or similar material facts and arising in the same court or a lower court in the judicial hierarchy."[27]

The definition seems simple enough. And you will probably have no problem in deciding what are "identical" facts; but what delivers the real drama on appeal is the fight over which facts are materially similar. It is now that the process of analogy comes center stage. Analogy does not seek proof of identity of one thing with another, but only a comparison of resemblances. In analogies, the degree of similarity is always the crucial inquiry.

This analytical process involves several steps: 1) you establish the holding of your chosen case to understand the legal consequences attached to the specific set of facts; 2) you exclude any dictum from the decision; and 3) you determine whether the holding is a binding precedent for a succeeding case containing prima facie similar facts. This last step then involves a double analysis. First, you must state the material facts in the putative precedent and then attempt to find those that are material in the compared case. If the facts are identical or materially similar, then the first case is binding precedent for the second and the court's conclusions should be the same. If the first case lacks any fact deemed material in the second case, or contains any material fact not found in the second, then it is not a bulletproof precedent. Here, the skill of the advocate will often be the determining factor. The plaintiff's lawyer may argue that the historical event or entity in the putative precedent bears many resemblances to the case at bar, whereas the opponent will argue that, although the facts are similar in some respects, those similarities are not material.[28]

The art of advocacy resolves itself into convincing the court which facts in previous cases are indeed positive analogies and which are not. The judge is required to draw this distinction. The successful lawyer is one who is able to convince the judge

---

27. Allegheny Cty. Gen. Hosp. v. NLRB, 608 F. 2d 865, 969–70 (3d Cir. 1979).
28. *See* Aldisert, *supra* note 24; *see also* Chapter Eleven.

National Institute for Trial Advocacy

to draw the distinction in the manner most favorable to her client. The problem, however, is that there are seldom perfectly identical experiences in human affairs.

The judges know this. What we look for is a reasonable comparison. What is "reasonable" in determining analogies may permit endless differences of opinion. The existence of varying views in multi-judge courts is one of the most vitalizing traditions animating the growth of the common law.

7.5.1   What Facts Are Material?

No individual test of materiality may succeed unless there is first a complete understanding of the relevant substantive law precepts and why they came to be.

While it is impossible to set out an ironclad test as to what facts are material, below are some tests that present some possibilities as to identifying material facts.

- All facts that the court specifically stated to be material must be considered material.

- All facts that the court specifically stated to be immaterial must be considered immaterial.

- All facts that the court impliedly treats as immaterial must be considered immaterial.

- All facts of person, place, time, kind, and amount are immaterial unless stated to be material.

- If the opinion omits a fact that appears in the record this may be due to a) oversight or b) an implied finding that the fact is immaterial. (Option "b") will be assumed to be the case in the absence of other evidence.)

- If the opinion does not distinguish between material and immaterial facts, then all the facts set forth must be considered material.

- A conclusion based on a hypothetical set of facts is dictum.

This is not to say that these are the only tests of what facts are material—and, therefore, important—and what facts are merely interesting. There are, no doubt, others. Whatever the test, the process requires patience, care, and thoroughness.

Ultimately, law is reduced, in the case of the judge, to the art of drawing distinctions, and, in the case of the lawyer, to the art of anticipating the distinctions the judge is likely to draw. To be sure, "[i]n a system bound by precedent such distinctions may often be in the nature of hair-splitting, this being the only instrument to hand for avoiding the consequences of an earlier decision which the court considers unreasonable, or as laying down a principle which is 'not to be extended.'"[29] As an

---

29. Dennis Lloyd, *Reason and Logic in the Common Law*, 64 LAW Q. REV. 468, 482 (1948).

art, both the study and practice of law consist of problem solving. Because of the doctrine of *stare decisis*, however, problem solving must not be performed on an ad hoc basis. We must respect the overarching consideration that like cases be decided alike. The real question, as you now understand, is deciding what is a "like case."

7.6   How to Cite and Discuss Cases, Yet Be Concise

If one message has come clear from these pages, with virtually uniform support from the judges surveyed, it is that lawyers should shorten their briefs. The tightening process must cover all components of the brief. Condense your procedural history to a minimum, reduce the number of issues, limit the statement of facts to those that are material and adjudicative and give the judges a short summary of your argument. This is especially important as the newest amendments to the Federal Rules of Appellate Procedure go into effect, which reduce the word length of some briefs by as much as 1,000 words in the federal circuits that have not opted out of the changes.[30]

One of the most difficult aspects of tightening up the brief is concisely explaining the holdings of relevant case authority, replete with facts and reasoning. At times it is not enough merely to give a citation, because you feel that this puts an additional burden on the judge to look up the case. At other times, especially in appellee and reply briefs, you want to expose why certain cases relied upon by your adversary are irrelevant.

The key to citing cases concisely is to understand that appellate judges are interested only in the material facts and the legal consequences attached to them. It often becomes necessary to condense the material facts in discussing a particular case. Limit the fact recitation in the cited cases to critical facts. These are the adjudicative facts. Decide which facts were important to the ruling and which were not. For example, do the names of the parties in the cited case matter, or is it only important that the case involved a teacher, student, and parent? What you say in your brief depends on why you are citing the case. First, you may be citing the case for the purpose of analogy, for the purpose of comparing the material facts here with those of the compared case. Second, you may be citing the case only for the reasons stated in the compared case; you cite the case because you like the reasons; you like the reasons because they support your theory. But if the compared case is fact-specific, then the reasons may not be too critical. Third, you may be interested only in the conclusion of the case and are citing it only to support the public policy argument asserted to support your brief's conclusion.

---

30. Lee Peifer, *New Federal Rules of Appellate Procedure Take Effect*, 11TH CIRCUIT BUSINESS BLOG, http://www.11thcircuitbusinessblog.com/2016/12/new-federal-rules-of-appellate-procedure-take-effect/ (last visited Mar. 20, 2017).

The dimensions of your discussion of the case you cite, therefore, are determined by why you have cited it—for the facts, for the reasons, or for the conclusion, or for any combination of the three. You must balance the desire to present something that is tightly written with the necessity of furnishing the court with sufficient tools to accept your argument. The question is always: why have I cited the case? The answer to this depends upon the overarching question: where does this case fit into the theme or focus of the brief?

When you answer this question, you recognize that a case should not be cited, in former Loyola Law Dean David W. Burcham's words, "in the nude"[31]—that is, without any explanation for it. The historical purpose and function of citing cases is to record the holding. It is to validate the statement of a legal rule. Consider, for example, how Chief Justice Roberts used past precedent in the Supreme Court's 2014 decision in *Riley v. California,* concerning whether police may search the cell phone of an arrested individual without a warrant.[32] Writing for the Court, Chief Justice Roberts explained the Court's three prior decisions regarding warrantless searches by citing the relevant facts and legal conclusions underlying those decisions.[33] He then applied this reasoning to the question of cell phones to determine that the rule should not be extended to cell phones.[34]

7.6.1 Use the Parenthetical

In recent years, the parenthetical has become very popular, and some judges recommend its use. A caveat about parentheticals appears below, as the temptation can be to put in parentheses important material from a precedent that should be in the text of your brief. If a case is cited to show resemblances or differences in the facts, a parenthetical disclosing the material facts of the cited case will be very effective. A parenthetical can also be used to state the reasons that supported the conclusion of the cited case or to state the legal rule that constitutes the holding. Consider these examples from recent Supreme Court cases:

- See, e.g., Bridgeport Music, Inc. v. WB Music Corp., 520 F. 3d 588, 593–595 (CA6 2008) (awarding fees against a copyright holder who filed hundreds of suits on an overbroad legal theory, including in a subset of cases in which it was objectively reasonable).[35]

---

31. Judge Ruggero J. Aldisert, *Perspective from the Bench on the Value of Clinical Appellate Training of Law Students,* 75 MISS. L.J. 645, 658 (2006) (citing a series of informal telephone discussions on an unspecified date with David W. Burcham, Dean of Loyola Law School).
32. Riley v. California, 134 S. Ct. 2473 (2014).
33. *Id.* at 2483–85.
34. *Id.* at 2486–89, 2493–94.
35. Kirstsaeng v. John Wiley & Sons, Inc., No. 15-375 (S. Ct., June 16, 2016), available at http://www.supremecourt.gov/ opinions/15pdf/15-375_4f57.pdf (last visited Mar. 20, 2017).

- See also Knowles v. Iowa, 525 U.S. 113, 119 (1998) (declining to extend Robinson to the issuance of citations, "a situation where the concern for officer safety is not present to the same extent and the concern for destruction or loss of evidence is not present at all").[36]

- See, e.g., Smith, 494 U.S. at 890 . . . ('[A] society that believes in the negative protection accorded to religious belief can be expected to be solicitous of that value in its legislation . . . . ').[37]

- [S]ee FCC v. AT&T Inc., 131 S. Ct. 1177, 1182–83 ("We have no doubt that 'person,' in a legal setting, often refers to artificial entities. The Dictionary Act makes that clear").[38]

- Cf. *Loving*, supra, at 12 . . . ("[T]he freedom to marry, or not marry, a person of another race resides with the individual and cannot be infringed by the state").[39]

Accompanying a citation with a parenthetical serves three important purposes: 1) it tells the brief reader why you are citing the case; 2) it shows where the case fits into the theme or focus of your brief; and 3) it achieves the objective of concise brief writing.

The use of parentheticals comes with a warning. What brief and opinion writers often slip into is a default of putting into parenthetical whatever is found in a precedent, particularly case law that seems secondary to that which supports the main point. The problem is that parentheticals interspersed in lists of citations lose their force, thus their persuasiveness. Much like readers do for case citations that appear in a text, the reader may skim past the parenthetical to find the beginning of the next sentence. Indeed, the mere fact that the explanation is closeted in parentheses is an implicit statement that the writer does not believe the information needs to be out front in the argument. So think before potentially hiding an explanation—is this something important to my argument that I want to urge a judge to read carefully?

7.7 String Citations and Other "Don'ts"

Do not use string citations. They are generally irritating and useless. Former California Supreme Court Chief Justice Malcolm Lucas emphasized, "Do not use string cites: explain the application of each case or other authority to your argument. Back up your arguments with direct, analogous, or otherwise persuasive authority."[40]

---

36. Riley v. California, 134 S. Ct. 2473, 2485 (2014).
37. Cutter v. Wilkinson, 544 U.S. 709, 719 (2005).
38. Burwell v. Hobby Lobby, 134 S. Ct. 2751, 2768 (2014).
39. Obergefell v. Hodges, 135 S. Ct. 2584, 2599 (2015).
40. L. RONALD JORGENSEN, MOTION PRACTICE AND PERSUASION xv (2006).

What is a string citation? String citations typically set forth a list of authorities from the same jurisdiction supporting a single, sometimes well-accepted, proposition. Not only are such citations unnecessary, but they also tend to distract the reader from the thrust of the argument. It is far more effective to cite to the single, most recent or prominent case supporting the proposition.

Multiple citations, however, are very helpful when used to support a proposition that has not been addressed by the court hearing your appeal. In such an instance, you may properly set forth a list of multiple authorities demonstrating the proposition's acceptance in coordinate jurisdictions. This will give the court the opportunity to consider how other jurisdictions have handled the same issue.

Do not "trampl[e] on graves" of precedents. This phrase was coined by Judge William H. Hastie of the Third Circuit to describe a citation that fails to support the proposition as represented.[41] There is no quicker way to lose credibility with an appellate court than to employ this form of citation. If you cannot find an authority to support your proposition, you must reject the proposition or acknowledge that it is presently unsupported. Do not attempt to twist an available authority to suit your needs; the court will not buy it. You may, however, analogize. It is entirely proper—indeed, it is effective advocacy—to explain to the court that although a compared case is not precisely on point, there are sufficient resemblances to employ the process of analogy.

You can avoid "trampling on graves" by using full quotations from cases.[42] By full quotation, we do not mean setting forth large portions of the text in order to fill up your brief or to avoid having to select the critical text. We mean taking a significant sentence or short paragraph and inserting it as a direct quote to inform the court exactly what the case stands for. This will help lend authoritative quality to your argument. Another highly effective tool, if not overused, is using parentheticals, as discussed above.

Do not use long quotations. It is a strong judge who can resist the temptation to skip all or a part of a long, unindented quotation.

Do not quote phrases or sentences out of context. This is the fallacy of vicious abstraction. Your credibility suffers. Judges do not like it, and opponents can discover it and pounce on you.

7.8   Ethical Responsibilities in Citing Precedent

While the mechanics of citing a case are important, it is more important that you understand your ethical responsibilities in citing precedent. Under the ABA Model

---

41. United States v. Gibbs, 813 F.2d 596, 605 (3d Cir. 1987) (Aldisert, J., dissenting).

42. This is not to say that judges, and some of our most outstanding ones, do not indulge in the grave-trampling process. They do. And, if they are on the highest courts, they can get away with it.

Rules of Professional Conduct, which have been adopted in nearly every state,[43] "A lawyer shall not knowingly . . . fail to disclose to the tribunal legal authority in the controlling jurisdiction known to the lawyer to be directly adverse to the position of the client and not disclosed by opposing counsel."[44] This rule, however, raises two questions. First, what is "the controlling jurisdiction?" As Judge Elaine Bucklo has explained, the rule does not require you to disclose a decision from the Supreme Court of Alaska, if your case is in Illinois and is controlled by Texas law.[45] Determining "the controlling jurisdiction" will come down to whether the issues that you raise are state or federal law issues and what court you are appearing before.[46] If you are unsure of whether a particular case is controlling, you should err on the side of caution and include it. The Georgetown University Law Center's Writing Center has put together a nice chart to help you understand what courts decisions are binding authority and what are persuasive, based on the issue raised the court that you are appearing before.[47]

The second question raised by this rule is what does "directly adverse" mean? Does it require you to disclose a case that can be distinguished?[48]

A 1949 American Bar Association opinion offered this test for "directly adverse":

> Is the decision which opposing counsel has overlooked one which the court should clearly consider in deciding the case? Would a reasonable judge properly feel that a lawyer who advanced, as the law, a proposition adverse to the undisclosed decision, was lacking in candor and fairness to him? Might the judge consider himself misled by an implied representation that the lawyer knew of no adverse authority?[49]

Full candor to the court and good appellate strategy call for erring on the side of disclosure. Failing to disclose an adverse case that a judge deems controlling and directly adverse can destroy your credibility before the court. It is not as if your opponent will overlook it. Furthermore, by taking the first stab at discussing an adverse case can allow you to frame the discussion of that case, by pointing out how it is distinguishable or why it should not be followed in your case.[50]

---

43. *State Adoption of the ABA Model Rules of Professional Conduct*, AMERICAN BAR ASSOCIATION, http://www.americanbar.org/groups/professional_responsibility/publications/model_rules_of_professional_conduct/alpha_list_state_adopting_model_rules.html (last visited Mar. 20, 2017).

44. RULE 3.3(a)(2).

45. Hon. Elaine Bucklo, *The Temptation Not to Disclose Adverse Authority*, LITIGATION 2 (Winter 2014), http://www.americanbar.org/publications/litigation_journal/2013-14/winter/the_temptation_not_disclose_adverse_authority.html (last visited Mar. 20, 2017).

46. Robyn Painter & Kate Mayer, *Which Court is Binding?*, WRITING CTR. GEO. U. L. CTR. 1, http://www.law.georgetown.edu/academics/academic-programs/legal-writing-scholarship/writing-center/upload/which_court_is_binding_painter-and-mayer-final.pdf (last visited Mar. 20, 2017).

47. *Id.* at 5.

48. Bucklo, *supra* note 45.

49. *Id.* (quoting ABA Comm. On Prof'l Ethics & Grievances, Formal Op. 280 (1949)).

50. NANCY L. SCHULTZ & LOUIS J. SIRICO, FIVE PITFALLS IN PERSUASIVE WRITING 165–67 (2001).

7.9 The Use of Cases to Persuade the Court to Extend or Compress the Law

What if you have a case from another jurisdiction that helps you, but it is different than the case law in your jurisdiction, or not directly on point with your case? So the case is hanging out there. You do not think you can "tame" it in order to show that your facts are "similar material facts." You want the chosen case to support your theory, but you also want to be candid with the court. Therefore, you must tell the court that to agree with you might require the formation of new law. Is it possible to convince the court to agree? It depends.

7.9.1 Jurisprudential Temperament

It is here where the lawyer must become familiar with the members of the court before the brief is written. You have to examine the opinions the judges have written in the area of the law where your case fits.

You examine these cases not only for the holding and reasoning, but also for insight into the opinion writer's jurisprudential temperament. This temperament is a major determinant of whether the case is controlled by precedent or settled law, or whether judges must, in certain cases, resort to penumbral areas.

Some judges have lower thresholds than others and are more inclined to find solace in shades and fringes rather than the black letter law. But when they so function, it means that they have exhausted the guidance that hefty, hearty precedents can give and they feel that they must turn to other resources. These resources are found in the body of first or super-eminent principles, legal or moral, concepts of desirable public policy that form the body of legal philosophy.

But to understand jurisprudential temperament is to recognize that the judge's initial reaction as to whether a case is controlled by precedent (or by unambiguous statutory language) or comes within what some might call the penumbral area is, itself, a gauge of that temperament. We judges have different thresholds, or, as Ralph Waldo Emerson said, "We boil at different degrees."[51] What makes a case controversial or difficult at times is precisely this judicial difference. These judicial reactions are not mechanical, as the label tossers of "liberal" and "conservative" would have us believe; nor are they entirely unpredictable. Our legal system is both a system and a history of reasons—reasons that judges have given for past determinations and reasons that embody many conceptions of human nature. The judge's matured decision is informed by this history. His or her own determination of benefit and harm will be informed by consulting the justifications offered by other judges in other relevant opinions.

---

51. 7 RALPH WALDO EMERSON, *Society and Solitude, in* THE COLLECTED WORKS OF RALPH WALDO EMERSON 30 (2007).

This inflow from the cumulative experience of the judiciary also mixes with what is already in the judge's mind. What is already there is an accumulation of personal experience including tendencies, prejudices, and maybe even biases. Not conscious biases, but the unconscious ones that any person may have and which the judge cannot eradicate because he does not know they exist. One of these may be a bias in favor of the judge's notion of the justice or equity of the particular case and against any precedent or law that seems to deny it. This is an example of temperament. When such a feeling dominates, the judge's mental notes may emphasize those facts that he deems to be significant; the insignificant, being omitted, will disappear from memory. The facts will be molded to fit the judge's notion of the justice of the case, and the law will be stretched. Meanwhile, another judge may possess the same intensity of justice for the case, but will refuse to stretch the law and instead state, "We are constrained to hold." In these two circumstances, the feelings of justice are the same, but disparate jurisprudential temperaments command different results. In some cases, the judges may disagree as to what constitutes the justice of the case.

So, get to know the court. You want to learn what Walter Schaefer, a great Illinois common law judge, once wrote:

> If I were to attempt to generalize, as indeed I should not, I should say that most depends upon the judge's unspoken notion as to the function of his court. If he views the role of the court as a passive one, he will be willing to delegate the responsibility for change, and he will not greatly care whether the delegated authority is exercised or not. If he views the court as an instrument of society designed to reflect in its decisions the morality of the community, he will be more likely to look precedent in the teeth and to measure it against the ideals and the aspirations of his time.[52]

But that is only for openers. You have to be conscious of the limitations of changing the law, even if the judge is inclined to do so.

7.9.2 *How Far a Judge May Go*

To be sure, Roscoe Pound, Oliver Wendell Holmes, and Benjamin Cardozo were instrumental in changing our approach to decision-making and rejecting what the Maryland Court of Appeals said in 1895: "Obviously a principle, if sound, ought to be applied wherever it logically leads, without reference to ulterior results."[53] To Cardozo, filling in the gaps of the law in addressing novel legal questions law was the social welfare, defined as "public policy, the good of the collective body" or "the social gain that

---

52. Walter v. Schaefer, *Precedent and Policy*, 34 U. CHI. L. REV. 3, 23 (1966).
53. Gluck v. City of Baltimore, 32 A. 515, 517 (Md. 1895).

National Institute for Trial Advocacy

is wrought by adherence to the standard of right conduct, which find expression in the mores of the community."[54]

Also to be sure, this enthusiasm for filling in the gaps in the law with ideas of social welfare has led to counter-arguments about the proper role of judges. For now, we are examining the views expressed by the original author of this book, Judge Aldisert.

In *The Path of the Law*, Holmes gently admonished:

> I think that the judges themselves have failed adequately to recognize their duty of weighing considerations of social advantage. The duty is inevitable, and the result of the often proclaimed judicial aversion to deal with such considerations is simply to leave the very ground and foundation of judgments inarticulate, and often unconscious.[55]

Within a decade, Roscoe Pound was trumpeting the same theme: "The most important and most constant cause of dissatisfaction with all law at all times is to be found in the necessarily mechanical operation of legal rules."[56] Critics labeled this blind adherence to precedents, or to the rules and principles derived therefrom, "mechanical jurisprudence" and "slot machine justice."[57] Pound called for a new look at what he described as "pragmatism as a philosophy of law," and stated vigorously: "The nadir of mechanical jurisprudence is reached when conceptions are used, not as premises from which to reason, but as ultimate solutions. So used, they cease to be conceptions and become empty words."[58] He is famous for the epigram: "The law must be stable, and yet it cannot stand still."[59]

This historical recital is important for two reasons. First, it demonstrates that public policy justifications can be legitimate reasons for supporting an appellate argument. As Justice Schaefer put it, "I suppose that whether a precedent will be modified depends on whether the policies which underlie the proposed rule are

---

54. Benjamin Cardozo, The Nature of the Judicial Process 71–72 (1921).

55. Oliver Wendell Holmes, *The Path of the Law*, 10 Harv. L. Rev. 457, 467 (1897).

56. Roscoe Pound, *The Causes of Popular Dissatisfaction with the Administration of Justice*, in The Pound Conference: Perspectives on Justice in the Future 337, 339 (A. Leo Levin & Russell R. Wheeler, eds. 1979).

57. Lee Anne Fennell, *Between Monster and Machine: Rethinking the Judicial Function*, 51 S.C. L. Rev.183, 196, 198 (1999).

58. Roscoe Pound, *Mechanical Jurisprudence*, 8 Colum. L. Rev. 605, 620 (1908).

59. Roscoe Pound, Interpretations of Legal History 1 (1923). Lord Denning, a British cousin, tells us exactly where his temperament stands on the gauge:

> What is the argument on the other side? Only this, that no case has been found in which it has been done before. That argument does not appeal to me in the least. If we never do anything which is not done before, we shall never get anywhere. The law will stand still whilst the rest of the world goes on, and that will be bad for both.

Packer v. Packer, 2 All E.R. 127, 129 (1953).

strong enough to outweigh both the policies which support the existing rule and the disadvantages of making a change."[60]

Second, these masters of the American legal tradition emphasized that there are limitations to judicial lawmaking. There are and should be limits. In 1917, Holmes counseled:

> I recognize without hesitation that judges do and must legislate, but they can do so only interstitially; they are confined from molar to molecular motions. A common law judge could not say I think the doctrine of consideration an act of historical nonsense and shall not enforce it in my court. No more could a judge exercising the limited jurisdiction of admiralty say I think well of the common law rules of master and servant and propose to introduce them here en bloc.[61]

Cardozo limited judicial lawmaking to gap-filling. Although the precise limits of judicial lawmaking have not been staked out, do not expect any court to make radical changes in a single case. To be sure, judicial lawmaking often has exceeded the function of "filling interstices"—the judicially created doctrine of products liability comes to mind in the state courts, and students of federal constitutional law can debate over other examples—but these are rare, pushing-the-envelope cases. You will have better luck remembering that changing the law in the common law tradition is based on gradualness.

Judge Aldisert, the original author of this book, believed that the test of judge-made law, as with any law, is its effect on social welfare and its acceptance by society. It behooves the judge who makes law, therefore, to focus openly on policy considerations as she seeks to keep the law in tune with changing societal values. It may be argued that this approach pays mere lip service to the doctrine of separation of powers. The response of Judge Aldisert was that the federal and state constitutions must be read against the backdrop of the common law tradition—a tradition which has given to the courts the authority to interpret rules enacted by the legislature, and to fashion the aggregate of legal precepts that govern society. Further, if legislative authority disagrees with the judicial action, it can overrule that action by statute. So the question is, how can a lawyer persuade the court to overrule a precedent?

An excellent and early expression by one of the more recent objectors to some of what Judge Aldisert wrote here is found in the late Justice Antonin Scalia's *A Matter of Interpretation* (1997). We will not attempt to review Justice Scalia's premises about the role of a judge. What is important to the brief writer is to know the appellate court to which the brief is being directed. Consider what judicial role seems to fit best

---

60. Schaefer, *supra* note 52.
61. S. Pac. Co. v. Jensen, 244 U.S. 205, 211 (1917) (Holmes, J., dissenting).

with the view of a majority of those judges and write accordingly, or write knowing you must overcome those predilections.

7.9.3 Precedential Vitality

Stare decisis is the policy of the courts to stand by precedent.[62] The expression "stare decisis" is but an abbreviation of *stare decisis et non quieta movere* (to stand by or adhere to decisions and not disturb that which is settled).[63] *Decisis* means literally and legally: "the decision."[64] A case is important only for what it decides, for the detailed legal consequence following a detailed set of facts. *Stare decisis* serves to preserve what the court *did*, not what it *said*. There are two basic forms of *stare decisis*: "vertical stare decisis, a court's obligation to follow the precedent of a superior court, and horizontal stare decisis, a court's obligation to follow its own precedent."[65]

While vertical *stare decisis* tends to be strict, exceptionless doctrine, horizontal *stare decisis* is not.[66] The Supreme Court has noted that *stare decisis* is not an "inexorable command."[67] In fact, the strength to which *stare decisis* is applied at the Supreme Court may depend on the subject matter of the case, with the strongest form being applied to statutory precedents and the weakest in constitutional law cases.[68]

Why do we adhere to precedent? To a considerable extent, rules are grounded in factors of habit, tradition, historical accident, and sheer intellectual inertia. We can also go back to the predictability factor in law, recalling Holmes's definition, "[t]he prophecies of what the courts will do in fact, and nothing more pretentious, are what I mean by the law."[69]

As Justice Harlan has explained, there are strong policy reasons for adhering to precedent:

> Very weighty considerations underlie the principle that courts should not lightly overrule past decisions. Among these are the desirability that the law furnish a clear guide for the conduct of individuals, to enable them to plan their affairs with assurance against untoward surprise; the importance of furthering fair and expeditious adjudication by eliminating the

---

62. For a more thorough discussion of Judge Aldisert's views on this subject, see Ruggero J. Aldisert, *Precedent: What It Is and What It Isn't; When Do We Kiss It and When Do We Kill It?*, 17 PEPP. L. REV. 605, 607 (1990).

63. *Id.*

64. *Id.*

65. Amy Coney Barrett, *Precedent and Jurisprudential Disagreement*, 91 TEXAS L. REV. 1711, 1712 (2013).

66. *Id.*

67. Payne v. Tennessee, 501 U.S. 808, 827–28 (1991).

68. Barrett, *supra* note 65, at 1713.

69. Holmes, *supra* note 55, at 461.

need to relitigate every relevant proposition in every case; and the necessity of maintaining public faith in the judiciary as a source of impersonal and reasoned judgments. The reasons for rejecting any established rule must always be weighed against these factors.[70]

When do we overrule? No black letter guidelines determine when to follow precedent. In the state courts, the place for relief, of course, is in the state supreme court. But in the federal courts, where the courts of appeals have internal operating procedures preventing a panel from overruling a previous panel's decision, the avenue of relief lies in the petition for en banc rehearing. It is perfectly legitimate to argue to the panel that a given case is ripe for overruling, and urge the panel to so recommend to the full court. Although the foregoing weighty considerations underlie the precept that courts should not lightly overrule past decisions, the Supreme Court has set forth a body of concepts that should give a lawyer some guidance when making the frontal assault on the viability of a precedent.

In *Planned Parenthood of Southeastern Pennsylvania v. Casey*, a plurality of the Court set out several factors that the Court considers when determining whether to overrule past precedent:

> [W]hen this Court reexamines a prior holding, its judgment is customarily informed by a series of prudential and pragmatic considerations designed to test the consistency of overruling a prior decision with the ideal of the rule of law, and to gauge the respective costs of reaffirming and overruling a prior case. Thus, for example, we may ask whether the rule has proven to be intolerable simply in defying practical workability, whether the rule is subject to a kind of reliance that would lend a special hardship to the consequences of overruling and add inequity to the cost of repudiation, whether related principles of law have so far developed as to have left the old rule no more than a remnant of abandoned doctrine, or whether facts have so changed, or come to be seen so differently, as to have robbed the old rule of significant application or justification.[71]

Here are some of the current Supreme Court's observations on *stare decisis* culled from the cases.

- "When neither party defends the reasoning of a precedent, the principle of adhering to that precedent through *stare decisis* is diminished."[72]

- "*Stare decisis* is . . . a 'principle of policy.' When considering whether to reexamine a prior erroneous holding, we must balance the importance of

---

70. Moragne v. States Marine Lines, 398 U.S. 375, 403 (1970).

71. Planned Parenthood of Se. Pennsylvania v. Casey, 505 U.S. 833, 854–55 (1992) (citations omitted).

72. Citizens United v. Fed. Election Comm'n, 558 U.S. 310, 364 (2010).

National Institute for Trial Advocacy

having constitutional questions decided against the importance of having them *decided right*."[73]

- "Although it is a vital rule of judicial self-government, *stare decisis* does not matter for its own sake. It matters because it 'promotes the evenhanded, predictable, and consistent development of legal principles.'"[74]

- "Although the doctrine of *stare decisis* is of fundamental importance to the rule of law[,] . . . [o]ur precedents are not sacrosanct . . . . [W]e have overruled prior decisions where the necessity and propriety of doing so has been established."[75]

- "While *stare decisis* is not an inexorable command, it is a basic self-governing principle within the Judicial Branch, which is entrusted with the sensitive and difficult task of fashioning and preserving a jurisprudential system that is not based upon 'an arbitrary discretion. We generally adhere to our prior decisions, even if we question their soundness, because doing so promotes the evenhanded, predictable, and consistent development of legal principles, fosters reliance on judicial decisions, and contributes to the actual and perceived integrity of the judicial process."[76]

- "[W]e require a special justification when departing from precedent . . . . [W]hen procedural rules are at issue that do not govern primary conduct and do not implicate the reliance interests of private parties, the force of *stare decisis* is reduced."[77]

- "*[S]tare decisis* carries enhanced force when a decision . . . interprets a statute . . . . Indeed, we apply statutory stare decisis even when a decision has announced a 'judicially created doctrine' designed to implement a federal statute."[78]

- In "cases involving property and contract rights—considerations favoring *stare decisis* are at their acme."[79]

---

73. *Id.* at 378 (2010) (Roberts, C.J., concurring opinion) (citations omitted) (emphasis added).

74. Johnson v. United States, 135 S. Ct. 2551, 2563 (2015) (citations omitted).

75. Hurst v. Florida, 136 S. Ct. 616, 623 (2016) (citations omitted) (internal quotations omitted) (alterations in the original).

76. Alleyne v. United States, 133 S. Ct. 2151, 2164 (2013) (Sotomayor, J., concurring opinion) (citations omitted) (internal quotations omitted).

77. *Id.*

78. Kimble v. Marvel Entm't, LLC, 135 S. Ct. 2401, 2409 (2015) (citations omitted).

79. *Id.* at 2410 (2015) (citations omitted) (internal quotations omitted).

- "*Stare decisis* has added force, we have held, when overturning a precedent would require States to reexamine [and amend] their statutes."[80]

- "We have never relied on stare decisis to justify the continuance of an unconstitutional police practice."[81]

As you can see from these quotes, *stare decisis* can play an important role in cases. But, it is also not an "inexorable command." If the factors discussed in *Planned Parenthood v. Casey* are present in your case, feel free to argue that the court should reconsider precedent. But try to have another argument that allows you to win without requiring the court to overrule precedent.

---

80. Harris v. Quinn, 134 S. Ct. 2618, 2652 (2014) (Kagan, J., dissenting opinion) (citations omitted) (internal quotations omitted) (alterations in the original).
81. Arizona v. Gant, 556 U.S. 332, 348 (2009).

CHAPTER EIGHT

THE BRIEF: STATING THE ISSUE(S) AND POINT HEADINGS

8.1 How to State an Issue: Overview

You are a judge sitting in your office, or on a plane, about to read a brief. Which of the following issue statements immediately informs you of the point the lawyer intended to make?

- The appellant was denied due process.

- The defendant was denied due process when the court denied him the right to counsel in his trial for bank robbery.

Properly stating the issues is your first opportunity to persuade the court. Almost all court rules call for some statement of "issues presented for review," "points," "propositions," or "questions presented." The advice in this book on drafting issues presented is, of course, qualified by the admonition to always frame the issue presented in terms of the applicable court rules. Generally, each issue presented includes one major legal issue. The issue presented will generally correspond to the first level point headings in a brief, such as the Roman numeral I, II, etc. According to the rules of the Supreme Court of the United States: "The questions [presented] should be short and should not be argumentative or repetitive. . . . The statement of any question presented is deemed to comprise every subsidiary question fairly included therein."[1]

In every issue formulation, be certain to state expressly or implicitly a legal proposition that the court will immediately accept as settled law. That proposition is the stated or implied major premise. For the court to accept a *conclusion* that you proffer, it first has to agree absolutely with your major premise.[2]

Gary L. Sasso, a Florida appellate specialist at Carlton Fields, makes the important point:

---

1. S. Ct. R. 14(1)(a) (2013).
2. The logical structure of an argument is discussed in greater detail in Chapter Eleven: *The Brief: The Required Logical Form for Each Issue.*

In constructing your affirmative case, be sure to start at the beginning—not the chronological beginning, but the logical beginning. Every argument has a predicate. You must identify it and establish it before moving on. This is a rule that is usually honored in the breach. Countless briefs just jump into the middle of a legal analysis. They start arguing a point of view before laying the groundwork. Such a brief will do little to persuade someone who does not subscribe to that point of view from the start.

Your objective in constructing an affirmative case should be to start with a proposition that the court—whatever its bent—must accept; then reason, logically, step by step, to your conclusion. If you do this well, you will arrive at your destination with the court right beside you. Your conclusion will make sense, not just because you say so, but because the court will have reasoned along with you. In a way, the technique is one familiar to cross-examiners. You nibble toward your destination with a series of points or questions that can only be answered yes. The main constraint on this approach is the page limit on your brief and the realization that judges do not have all day to read.[3]

Be absolutely certain that your statement of an issue is a rock-bound precedent, a statute with a settled interpretation, an unambiguous procedural rule. This is required no matter where the flashpoint of controversy lies between the parties—whether in the choice of competing precepts, in the interpretation of a controlling precept, or in the application of an integral precept to the found facts.[4]

While the first draft of the issue presented should be included in the initial outline of the argument, the issue presented must be refined throughout the argument drafting process. Many attorneys, however, put little thought into writing the issue presented and miss their first opportunity to persuasively frame their client's case for the court. Do not be one of those attorneys. Ponder your issue presented for days—craft something that will grab the judge's attention and not let it go!

8.1.1 Basic Form

Judge Aldisert was a longtime advocate of writing issues presented in the form of a simple declarative sentence phrased so that the court could adopt it as a topic sentence in its opinion in your favor. He advocated giving the court a simple categorical statement of the issue in a declarative sentence, fairly stated, yet psychologically inclined in your favor.

It is also perfectly acceptable to write the issue in the form of a question, worded in a manner so that a judge reading it would want to answer "yes." Again, the question

---

3. Gary L. Sasso, *Anatomy of the Written Argument*, 15 Litig. 30 (1989).
4. We will treat this subject in some detail later in Chapter Ten, *The Brief: Writing Your Argument.*

should be fairly stated and psychologically inclined in your favor. Whatever form you use, however, unless the rules require, do not be a "whetherman," phrasing the issue with "Whether . . . ." You would never use that phraseology in discussing a case with colleagues—it is simply bad grammar. So, why would you use it in writing to a judge?

Bryan Garner, a well-known legal writing expert, advocates for the "deep issue" approach to writing issues presented. According to Garner, a good issue presented consists of "separate sentences, following a premise-premise-question form."[5] It should "weave in enough facts so that the reader can truly understand the problem" and be written "in such a way that there is only one possible answer."[6] Garner advocates keeping the "deep issue" to less than seventy-five words, with between sixty and seventy-five words as the optimal length.[7]

While the "deep issue" approach has been gaining prominence and can be seen in briefs before the United States Supreme Court and the federal appellate courts, it is important to recognize that not all judges appreciate it. Remember, some judges already think that briefs are too long. A long "deep issue" format on the first page of the brief can perpetuate those feelings. Other judges might not be familiar with the formulation and be put off by seeing it in a brief. So, be sure to follow the issue-writing conventions in your jurisdiction. Also think about the nature of your appeal. The more complex or technical the question before the court, the more likely that the "deep issue" formulation will best explain the issue presented.

8.1.2 Basic Substance

Regardless of what form you use—declarative sentence, interrogative, or "deep issue"—it is critical that your issue presented be persuasive, clear, and concise, and weave in the relevant facts and legal standards.

A persuasive issue presented, in the words of attorney James D. Crawford, "inspire[s] the answers you want."[8] Thus, if your issue presented is in the form of a question, it should inspire the answer of "yes" from the court. Mr. Crawford further explains, "This is the first place you can be sure of presenting your legal contentions to the court. . . . If the court's attention and sympathy are not caught here, they may well never be caught at all."[9] You must put significant time and thought into the words that you use to craft your issue presented. Do they invoke sympathy and catch attention? Do they persuade the court, in an accurate and fair manner, to consider the issues from your client's perspective? Consider the following examples

---

5. BRYAN A. GARNER, WINNING BRIEF: 100 TIPS FOR PERSUASIVE BRIEFING IN TRIAL AND APPELLATE COURTS 79 (3d ed. 2014).
6. *Id.*
7. *Id.* at 107.
8. RUGGERO J. ALDISERT, WINNING ON APPEAL: BETTER BRIEFS AND ORAL ARGUMENT 142 (2d ed. 2003).
9. *Id.*

from the case *United States v. Nixon*,[10] in which the president sought to withhold his taped conversations from judicial proceedings. Although these examples could have benefitted from the inclusion of more facts and law, the persuasive language used by the attorneys is masterful. Even without seeing the caption of the case and knowing who appealed, it is clear that the president is respondent and the special prosecutor is petitioner.

Respondent[11]	*Point I*: This internal dispute within co-equal branches does not present a justiciable case or controversy within the meaning of Article III, Section 2 of the Constitution.
Petitioner	*Point I*: This dispute between the United States, represented by the special prosecutor, and the President—two distinct parties—presents a live, concrete, justiciable controversy.
Respondent	*Point II*: A presidential assertion of privilege is not reviewable by the courts.
Petitioner	*Point II*: The courts have both the power and the duty to determine the validity of a claim of executive privilege when it is asserted in a judicial proceeding as a ground for refusing to produce evidence.
Respondent	*Point III*: The judicial branch cannot compel production of privileged materi0al from the President.
Petitioner	*Point III*: Courts have the power to order the production of evidence from the executive when justice so requires.

Be sure to remember that being persuasive is different from being overly argumentative. Consider this example:

> Should *Enmund* be applied retroactively, or should the state be permitted one last cruel and unusual punishment before *Enmund* takes effect?[12]

While this statement of the issue highlights the importance of the question before the court, the use of the phrase "one last cruel and unusual punishment" could be seen by some judges as too argumentative. Remember, you must fairly describe the issue before the court. This is critical for several reasons. The court must get the impression that the question presented will control the decision. The judges must also be confident that the proposition stated may be affirmed or denied as a legal precept. To be sure, the value judgments required in affirming or denying the proposition of

---

10. United States v. Nixon, 418 U.S. 683 (1974).

11. These examples are from S. Eric Ottesen, *Effective Brief Writing for California Appellate Courts*, 21 *San Diego L. Rev.* 371, 377–78 (1983–1984).

12. Jones v. Thigpen, 741 F.2d 805, 811 (5th Cir. 1984), *vacated*, 475 U.S. 1003 (1986) (mem.).

necessity may differ, but the proposition itself must be fashioned so that the court can fairly accept it or reject it.

The example above also highlights the importance of including sufficient law and facts in the issue presented to inform the judge of the nature of the dispute, the legal standards that will lead to the resolution of the dispute, and the important facts in the case. In some cases, it might also be important to work the standard of review into the issue presented—particularly if the standard is something other than de novo review.

For example, a judge (or law clerk) who was unfamiliar with either *Enmund v. Florida* or the case law regarding retroactive application of the Eighth Amendment protections would be at a loss after reading that issue statement as to which legal standards to apply or how the court should review that issue. Consider, however, this example:

> Does the Supreme Court's holding that the Eighth Amendment prohibits imposing the death penalty in a felony murder case where the defendant did not kill nor have the intent to kill another person apply retroactively when that holding sets forth a substantive, rather than procedural, rule of law that is not a clear break from past cases and will not disrupt the administration of justice?

This second example sets out the importance of *Enmund* and the legal standards to apply when considering whether a new rule from the Supreme Court can be applied retroactively.

Writing an issue presented that mixes in law and facts, while still being clear and concise, can take significant time. It requires you to understand the legal issues in the case, the "equitable heart" of the appeal, and how these two aspects of the case fit together.[13] Consider this example from Jordan B. Cherrick:

> Suppose you have a case in which the jury returned a $10 million verdict for your client, the husband of the late Karen Smith. Dr. Smith, a brilliant young physician, was killed when the airplane in which she was traveling exploded over the ocean. Your problem is that the trial court granted the defendant's motion for a judgment notwithstanding the verdict. The court concluded that your case was insufficient because your expert witness was not competent to testify that the explosion was caused by defective engines manufactured by the defendant.
>
> What is your appellate strategy? You decide to concentrate on two issues: the ample evidence supporting the jury's verdict and the trial court's failure to apply the proper standard in setting aside the verdict. Argument on the first point will show that an injustice occurred. The second will identify the legal error at stake.

---

13. Jordan B. Cherrick, *Issues, Facts, and Appellate Strategy*, 16 Litig. 15, 16–17 (1990).

With this general approach, you begin to write, starting with the question presented. Here are two ways it could be done:

> Should the trial court's judgment N.O.V. be reversed because plaintiff's expert witness, an aviation mechanic with more than twenty years of experience, was competent to render an opinion "based on reasonable scientific certainty" that the explosion that killed Dr. Smith was caused by defendant's defective engines?

or

> Should the court of appeals conclude that the trial court erred in granting defendant a judgment notwithstanding the verdict?

The first version is far better. It outlines the equitable heart of the appeal and implies the legal problem involved. The second formulation just sits there, arid and lifeless. It makes the case indistinguishable from all other appeals of [judgment] N.O.V.s—most of which are affirmed. Your statement of issues must do more: It must, from the first page, acquaint the court with why your case is different.

How do you frame the case for the appeals court if you represent the appellee? Again, there are good and bad ways to do it. Compare this statement:

> Did the trial court properly enter judgment N.O.V. for the defendant because plaintiff's expert, a mechanic with no engineering training, was not competent to testify that electronically complex jet engines caused the airplane's explosion?

with this one:

> Should the trial court's judgment notwithstanding the verdict be affirmed because the court properly concluded that the plaintiff's expert was not competent to testify about the accident?

Again, the first version is better. It conveys the trial court's primary reason for entering a [judgment] N.O.V. in forceful terms. Reading it, the appeals court knows, at one glance, the essence of the appellee's argument. The second version is much inferior. It merely asks whether the [judgment] N.O.V. should be affirmed. This statement ignores the real problem in the case: Was the plaintiff's expert witness competent to opine on causation, and how did his dubious competence affect the plaintiff's case?[14]

Cherrick, however, warns against writing an issue that is too argumentative:

> Though it is wise to weave the facts through the legal question, do not go overboard. It is one thing to convey crisply what the case is about. It is another to engage in strident special pleading. In our crash case, this would *not* be good form:

>> Did the trial court's reversal of the jury's careful verdict wrongly depend on the conclusion that plaintiff's expert was incompetent to testify that a jet engine's slipshod design caused a shattering explosion that, in a searing flash, snuffed out the life of a brilliant young physician over the chilly waters of the Atlantic?[15]

In weaving the relevant law and facts into the issue presented, it is important to remain concise. Even Bryan Garner's "deep issue" format for issues presented limits the issue to no more than seventy-five words.[16]

Here is an example of an issue statement commonly used in appellate briefs:

> Whether the trial court committed reversible error by denying defendant's motion.

This formulation is useless. It might be concise, but it fails to weave in the relevant facts and legal standards so that the court understands the flashpoint of the controversy. But issues presented that are devoid of substance are not the only obstacle to understanding. Consider this one:

> The trial court erred in giving flawed essential elements instructions to the jury and thereby denied the defendant due process and fundamental fairness since it is error to give the jury, within the essential elements instructions, one statement containing more than one essential element of the crime and requiring of the jury simple and singular assent or denial of that compound proposition, fully capable of disjunctive answer, which if found pursuant to the evidence adduced would exculpate the defendant.[17]

This issue presented brings in too many facts. It fails to be clear or concise. It tells the court too much in confusing and, at times, incomprehensible, language. Although

---

14. Jordan B. Cherrick, *Issues, Facts, and Appellate Strategy*, 16 Litig. 15, 16–17 (1990).

15. *Id.*

16. Bryan A. Garner, Winning Brief: 100 Tips for Persuasive Briefing in Trial and Appellate Courts 107 (3d ed. 2014).

17. S. Eric Ottensen, *Effective Brief-Writing for California Appellate Courts*, 21 San Diego L. Rev. 371, 377 (1984).

this example might make sense to the attorney writing the brief and enmeshed in the legal issues on appeal, it is difficult for an educated outsider, such as a judge or law clerk, to understand. Your issue presented should be written in a way that an intelligent non-lawyer can pick up your brief and understand the heart of your case.

There are a few other important tips to follow in crafting the substance of the issue presented.

Citations. Do not include citations in the issue presented. The meat of your brief—the argument section—will contain all of the necessary citations that can guide the judge and clerks to the relevant statutes, administrative rules, or cases. Citations in the issue presented only detract from your point. Consider these two examples from *Enquist v. Oregon Department of Agriculture*:[18]

> Whether traditional equal protection "rational basis" analysis under *Village of Willowbrook v. Olech*, 528 U.S. 562 (2000), applies to public employers who intentionally treat similarly situated employees differently with no rational basis for arbitrary, vindictive or malicious reasons.[19]

> Whether class-of-one equal protection analysis applies to decisions made by public employers with respect to their employees? If so, how should the theory apply and should it be limited so as to avoid subjecting every state and local government employment decision to federal court review?[20]

The citation to *Olech* in the first issue adds nothing but nine words to the issue presented. The words "traditional equal protection 'rational basis' analysis" give sufficient information as to the standard that may apply in the case.

Even if it is important to include the name of a case or statute in the issue presented, there is no need to include the citation. The following example would be improved by omitting the citation:

> Whether the Military Commissions Act of 2006 (MCA), Pub. L. No. 109-366, 120 Stat. 2600, removes federal court jurisdiction over habeas petitions filed by aliens detained as enemy combatants at Guantanamo Bay, Cuba.[21]

---

18. Enquist v. Oregon Department of Agriculture, 553 U.S. 591 (2008).

19. Brief for the Petitioner, at i, Enquist v. Oregon Department of Agriculture, 553 U.S. 591 (2008), http://www.americanbar.org/content/dam/aba/publishing/preview/publiced_preview_briefs_pdfs_07_08_07_474_Petitioner.authcheckdam.pdf (last visited Mar. 20, 2017).

20. Brief of the Merits for Respondent, at i, Enquist v. Oregon Department of Agriculture, 553 U.S. 591 (2008), http://www.americanbar.org/content/dam/aba/publishing/preview/publiced_preview_briefs_pdfs_07_08_07_474_Respondent.authcheckdam.pdf (last visited Mar. 20, 2017).

21. Brief of the Merits for Respondent, at I, Boumediene v. Bush and Odah v. United States, 553 U.S. 723 (2008), http://www.americanbar.org/content/dam/aba/publishing/preview/publiced_preview_briefs_pdfs_07_08_06_1195_Respondent.authcheckdam.pdf (last visited Mar. 20, 2017).

Names. Think carefully about how you will refer to the parties in the issue presented. When the judge opens your brief and reads the issue presented, she knows very little about the case. She, perhaps, has already read the lower court opinion. But, if you refer to Smith and Jones in the issue presented, rather than employer and employee, landlord and tenant, or defendant and prosecutor, you may leave her wondering who exactly Smith and Jones are and how they fit into the appeal. Similarly, some court rules direct attorneys to use minimally the terms petitioner and respondent or appellee and appellant in writing the brief.[22] These terms should also be avoided in the issue presented.

Don't Go Too Broad. The objective of appellate advocacy is to win on appeal— to win *this* appeal. Accordingly, state the issue as narrowly as possible to achieve your objective. There is a difference between succeeding as an advocate and mounting a full-scale assault to expound a cause in which you passionately believe. The law develops incrementally; there are few sea changes. Do not expect the court to change the law drastically in a single case.

Be satisfied if the court will rule in your favor as narrowly as possible. Remember that the lawyer's primary obligation is to a *client*, not to a *cause*. To insist that the court give you a full loaf when half a loaf will do may result in nothing but crumbs for your client. Save the broader expansion of the law to another case.

8.1.3 Examples of Issue Statements

See Appendix B.

8.2 Point Headings

Much of what has been said regarding the substance of the issue presented applies to the major point headings as well. The point headings should persuade, weave in the applicable law and facts (particularly the standard of review), and state the concise premise with clarity. The accepted practice is to identify each major point with a Roman numeral that corresponds with each numbered issue presented. Under Point

---

22. FED. R. APP. P. 28(d) ("References to Parties. In briefs and at oral argument, counsel should minimize use of the terms 'appellant' and 'appellee.' To make briefs clear, counsel should use the parties' actual names or the designations used in the lower court or agency proceeding, or such descriptive terms as 'the employee,' 'the injured person,' 'the taxpayer,' 'the ship,' 'the stevedore.'"); TEX. R. APP. P. 3.2 ("Otherwise, papers should use real names for parties, and such labels as appellee, petitioner, respondent, and movant should be avoided unless necessary for clarity."), http://www.txcourts.gov/media/806639/texas-rules-of-appellate-procedure-updated-with-amendments-effective-1114-w-appendices.pdf (last visited Mar. 20, 2017); MISS. R. APP. P. 28(e) ("References in Briefs to Parties. Counsel will be expected in their briefs and oral arguments to keep to a minimum references to parties by such designations as 'appellant' and 'appellee.' It promotes clarity to use the designations used in the lower court or in the agency proceedings, or the actual names of the parties, or descriptive terms such as 'the employee,' 'the injured person,' 'the taxpayer,' or 'plaintiff.'").

Headings, subsequent subparts are identified with capital letters, followed by Arabic numerals, and then lowercase letters. If your case raises only one issue presented, you do not need to assign it a Roman numeral.

Bryan Garner came up with the following guidelines for point headings reflected in briefs he reviewed from the United States Solicitor General's Office:[23]

- Use complete, declarative sentences of fifteen to thirty-five words for all point headings.

- Do not use acronyms unless the acronym is very well known.

- Do not include citations, even if a case name is mentioned.

- Do not use all capital letters or initial capital letters for each word. These formats are difficult to read. Garner recommends using bold text. As a side note, another strategy is to use a different typeface for each level of point heading, so it is easy for the reader to scan through the brief and see the different levels of argument.

According to Garner, in briefs filed by the Solicitor General's Office the point headings generally move from major to minor premises and end with rebuttal points. He provides this template:

    I. [Full-sentence conclusion.]

        A. [Full-sentence rationale.]

        B. [Full-sentence rationale.]

        C. [Opponent's position on this point is wrong because . . . .][24]

As you can see from the example above, the point headings, which appear in the table of contents of the brief, serve as an outline of the argument. They should be crafted with enough law and facts that before reading the brief the judge can (and many do) review the table of contents and get a good grasp of your argument.

Below are good and bad examples of point headings in both single issue and multi-issue briefs. Be sure to read the comments.

8.2.1 Single-Issue Briefs

Petitioner (Government)   The Leadership Act's funding condition is a valid exercise of Congress's authority under the Spending Clause.

---

23. Bryan A. Garner, Winning Brief: 100 Tips for Persuasive Briefing in Trial and Appellate Courts 404–05 (3d ed. 2014).

24. *Id.* at 405.

A. Congress has wide latitude to attach conditions to the receipt of federal funds in order to further broad policy objectives of federal programs.

B. Section 7631(f) ensures that the Leadership Act's policy opposing prostitution and sex trafficking is effectively implemented by funding recipients.

  1. The policy condition is an appropriate step to ensure that the Act's policy opposing prostitution and sex trafficking is not distorted by recipients.

  2. Congress determined that the policy condition is an important part of the Leadership Act's comprehensive strategy.

C. Section 7631(f) is not unconstitutional on the rationale that it compels recipients to speak with respect to prostitution and sex trafficking.

D. Section 7631(f) does not aim at the suppression of disfavored viewpoints.

E. Section 7631(f) is not a direct speech regulation but a condition on the receipt of federal funds.

F. The agencies' affiliation guidelines obviate any constitutional difficulty.

G. Respondents' vagueness challenge is not presented and lacks merit in any event.[25]

Respondent

I. The Policy Requirement Imposes An Unconstitutional Condition On Government Funding.

A. The First Amendment Bars The Government From Imposing Conditions On Government Funding That Prohibit Or Compel Private Speech.

B. The Policy Requirement Is An Unconstitutional Condition.

25. Brief for the Petitioners at III–IV, Agency for Int'l Dev. v. All. for Open Soc'y Int'l, Inc., 133 S.Ct. 928 (2013) (No. 12-10), http://www.americanbar.org/content/dam/aba/publications/supreme_court_preview/briefs-v2/12-10_pet.authcheckdam.pdf (last visited Mar. 20, 2017).

1. The policy requirement unconstitutionally compels grantees to adopt the government's viewpoint and express it as their own.

2. The policy requirement unconstitutionally suppresses private speech based on the speaker's viewpoint.

II. The Policy Requirement Cannot Be Upheld Under The Government Speech Doctrine.

A. The Policy Requirement Is Not "Government Speech" And Respondents Are Not Government Speakers.

B. The Policy Requirement Is Not A Legitimate And Appropriate Means Of Protecting Any Government Message.

1. Imposing an ideological purity test is not a "legitimate and appropriate" means of protecting the integrity of any government policy.

2. The policy requirement is unnecessary to advance the government's policy of eradicating prostitution.

III. The Affiliate Regime Does Not Cure The Policy Requirement's Constitutional Defects.

A. The Possibility That An Affiliate May Remain Silent Or Express Another View Does Not Cure The Policy Requirement's Unconstitutional Compulsion Of Speech.

B. The Possibility That An Affiliate May Engage In Speech "Inconsistent" With An Opposition To Prostitution Does Not Cure The Policy Requirement's Organization-Wide, Viewpoint-Based Restriction Of Speech.

C. The Affiliate Guidelines Are Too Burdensome And Vague To Provide An Adequate Alternative Channel For Protected Speech.[26]

---

26. Brief for Respondents at iii-iv, Agency for Int'l Dev. v. All. for Open Soc'y Int'l, Inc., 133 S.Ct. 928 (2013) (No. 10-12), http://www.americanbar.org/content/dam/aba/publications/supreme_court_preview/briefs-v2/12-10_respondent.authcheckdam.pdf (last visited Mar. 20, 2017).

5

Comment: Notice how with both briefs you can easily understand the subject matter of the dispute: a condition on government funding. The various arguments raised are also easily identifiable—the Government is arguing that this is a Spending Clause issue and the nonprofits are claiming that the restriction violates the First Amendment.

The Petitioner's point headings move from affirmative arguments to rebuttal points. The point headings could be improved by calling Section 7631(f) the "Condition" instead of using the section number.

The Respondent includes too many Roman numerals (there was only one issue presented in the case). But, the point headings clearly lay out the First Amendment concerns with the act.

Petitioner

I.   AFTER AN OFFICER HAS COMPLETED THE INVESTIGATION INTO A MOTORIST'S TRAFFIC VIOLATION, CONTINUED DETENTION OF THE MOTORIST WITHOUT INDIVIDUALIZED SUSPICION OF CRIMINAL ACTIVITY VIOLATES THE FOURTH AMENDMENT.

II. THE EIGHTH CIRCUIT'S "DE MINIMIS" EXCEPTION IS BASED ON FLAWED REASONING AND A FUNDAMENTAL MISUNDERSTANDING OF THIS COURT'S FOURTH AMENDMENT JURISPRUDENCE.

   A.   The Line Marking The End Of A Traffic Stop Is Not Artificial, And Using It To Gauge The Constitutionality Of The Stop Is An Appropriate Application Of The Fourth Amendment's "Reasonableness" Standard.

   B.   The Justification For The "De Minimis" Intrusion Authorized In *Pennsylvania v. Mimms* Does Not Transfer To The "De Minimis" Extension Of A Traffic Stop.

   C.   The Fact That A Dog Sniff Is Not A Fourth Amendment "Search" Is Immaterial When The Seizure During Which It Occurs Is Itself Unlawful.

III. A BRIGHT-LINE RULE PROHIBITING THE SUSPICIONLESS EXTENSION OF A TRAFFIC STOP IS EASILY ADMINISTERED IN THE FIELD AND REFLECTS THE PROPER BALANCE BETWEEN LAW ENFORCEMENT INTERESTS AND THE INTERESTS OF INNOCENT MOTORISTS.

IV. THE POST-STOP DETENTION IS NOT INDEPENDENTLY JUSTIFIED BY REASONABLE SUSPICION OF CRIMINAL ACTIVITY.[27]

Respondent (Government) I.   A police officer may conduct a dog sniff during a traffic stop, after issuing a traffic ticket, so long as the detention is not unreasonably prolonged.

   A.   An officer may conduct a range of investigatory inquiries in a traffic stop, so long as the stop is not unreasonably prolonged.

      1.   Officers may conduct inquiries designed to resolve the traffic violation and safely conduct the stop.

      2.   Officers may perform certain investigatory actions unrelated to the traffic violation.

   B.   An officer may perform a dog sniff during a traffic stop so long as it does not unreasonably extend the stop.

      1.   *Caballes* permits a dog sniff to extend a stop, so long as the stop does not exceed the time reasonably required to resolve the traffic violation.

      2.   Courts considering dog sniffs and unrelated inquiries made before the issuance of a ticket have generally assessed the overall reasonableness of the stop

   C.   When an officer conducts a dog sniff after, rather than before, issuing a ticket, that sequencing decision should not render the reasonableness inquiry inapplicable.

      1.   When during a traffic stop the officer issues a ticket is not an event of constitutional significance.

      2.   Petitioner's proposed bright-line rule would have adverse consequences.

---

27. Brief for Petitioner at ii-iii, Rodriguez v. United States, 135 S. Ct. 43 (2014) (No. 13-9972), http://www.americanbar.org/content/dam/aba/publications/supreme_court_preview/BriefsV4/13-9972_pet.authcheckdam.pdf (last visited Mar. 20, 2017).

    D.   A post-ticket dog sniff is permissible if the officer does not unreasonably prolong the stop.

    E.   Petitioner's arguments for a bright-line prohibition on post-ticket dog sniffs are unpersuasive.

    F.   The dog sniff did not unreasonably prolong the traffic stop in this case.

  II. The dog sniff of petitioner's car was independently justified by the officer's reasonable suspicion of criminal activity.[28]

Comment: The point headings in both briefs offer a clear roadmap of the arguments that will be raised in the briefs. The petitioner's point headings would be much easier to read if they were written without all capital letters and initial capital letters. This is a single issue brief, but both briefs contain multiple Roman numerals.

Appellant

The following conclusions of law are in error and should be reversed in favor of the Findings of Fact proposed by the plaintiff:

    1.   Conclusion of Law number 4 is erroneous.

    2.   Substitute Conclusion of Law 4.

    3.   Conclusions of Law Numbers 8, 10, 11, and 12 are erroneous.

    4.   Substitute Conclusions of Law 8, 10, 11, and 12.

Appellee

The district court's determination that the plaintiff was not the victim of discrimination should be affirmed.

    A.   The disparate treatment theory.

    B.   The disparate impact theory.

    C.   The district court's evidentiary rulings were correct.

Comment: These point headings are terrible. The appellant's point headings tell you nothing about the case. From the appellee's point headings you can, at a minimum, understand the basic subject matter of the case and the desired outcome; however, there are no facts included that help a judge understand the details of the underlying dispute. Look at how the court described the case:

---

28. Brief for the United States at III–IV, Rodriguez v. United States, 135 S. Ct. 43 (2014) (No. 13-9972), https://www.justice.gov/sites/default/files/osg/briefs/2014/12/22/13-9972bsunited-states.pdf (last visited Mar. 20, 2017).

In 1986, the Forest Service rejected the plaintiff, a black woman who served as Civil Rights Director for the Food and Nutrition Services, for appointment as Equal Employment Manager in the United States Department of Agriculture's Southwest region. The position went ins. tead to a white woman who was then the Administrative Officer for the Mt. Hood National Forest and Director of the Forest Service's Equal Employment Office program. Because the plaintiff failed to satisfy her burden of persuasion under either a disparate treatment or disparate impact theory of the case, the trial court found for the Forest Service. We affirm.[29]

This description provides information that should have been included in the point headings.

8.2.2 Multi-Issue Briefs

Petitioners

I. Petitioners Have Standing To Defend Proposition 8.

II. Proposition 8's Validity Does Not Turn on the Timing of its Adoption.

    A. This Court has established that a State is not required to adhere forever to policies that exceed federal constitutional requirements.

    B. Proposition 8 is not unconstitutional under *Romer.*

III. The Equal Protection Clause Does Not Forbid California from Defining Marriage as the Union of a Man and a Woman.

    A. Proposition 8 advances society's vital interest in responsible procreation and childrearing.

        1. Responsible procreation and childrearing has been an animating purpose of marriage in virtually every society throughout history.

        2. Proposition 8 furthers society's vital interests in responsible procreation and childrearing.

        3. That Proposition 8 did not eliminate domestic partnerships does not render it irrational.

---

29. Johnson v. Yuetter, No. 89-16031, 1991 WL 3059, at *1 (9th Cir. Jan. 11, 1991).

B. Proposition 8 serves California's interest in proceeding with caution before fundamentally redefining a bedrock social institution.

C. Proposition 8 restores democratic authority over an issue of vital importance to the People of California.

D. Proposition 8 does not "dishonor" gays and lesbians.[30]

Respondents

I. Proponents Lack Standing To Appeal.

II. Proposition 8, By Denying Gay Men And Lesbians The Right To Marry, Violates Due Process.

A. The Right To Marry Is Fundamental For All People.

B. The Trial Record And Factual Findings Establish That "Responsible Procreation" Is Not The Defining Purpose Of Marriage.

III. Proposition 8, By Denying Gay Men And Lesbians The Right To Marry, Violates Equal Protection.

A. Discrimination On The Basis Of Sexual Orientation Triggers Heightened Scrutiny.

B. Laws That Prohibit Gay Men And Lesbians From Marrying Cannot Survive Rational Basis Review, Let Alone Heightened Scrutiny.

C. Proposition 8 Is Unconstitutional Because It Was Motivated By A Bare Desire To Make Gay Men And Lesbians Unequal To Everyone Else.[31]

Comment: This case raised two issues: standing and the substance of the case (which also raised two issues: due process and equal protection). While the point headings for both briefs give you a general idea of the issues raised in the case, both briefs could have benefited from providing facts to support their standing arguments. The Supreme Court, in fact, decided this case on standing grounds, holding that the petitioners raised a generalized grievance.[32]

---

30. Brief of Petitioners at iv–v, Hollingsworth v. Perry, 133 S. Ct. 786 (2012) (No. 12-144), http://www.americanbar.org/content/dam/aba/publications/supreme_court_preview/briefs-v2/12-144_pet.authcheckdam.pdf (last visited Mar. 20, 2017).

31. *Id.*

32. Hollingsworth v. Perry, 133 S. Ct. 2652, 2662 (2012).

I. AN UNWED BIOLOGICAL FATHER WHO HAS NO PARENTAL RIGHTS UNDER STATE LAW IS NOT A "PARENT" UNDER SECTION 1903(9).

A. State Law Determines the Meaning of "Parent."

B. An Unwed Biological Father Is a "Parent" Only if He Possesses Parental Rights Under State Law.

II. A PARENT MUST HAVE CUSTODY OF AN INDIAN CHILD TO INVOKE SECTIONS 1912(d) AND 1912(f).

A. The Statutory Text Precludes Application to Parents Without Custodial Rights.

1. Section 1912(d) requires measures "designed to prevent the breakup of the Indian family."

2. Section 1912(f) requires "continued custody."

B. Other Provisions of ICWA that Apply Only to Custodial Parents Confirm that the Act Does Not Create Custodial Rights.

1. Section 1914's reference to an Indian child unlawfully "removed" from the parent's "custody."

2. Section 1916's references to "return" of "custody" and "from whom such custody the child was originally removed."

3. Section 1913's reference to "return to the parent."

4. Section 1920's reference to "improperly removed the child from custody of the parent" and "return" to the parent.

C. The Creation of Custodial Rights Does Not Further ICWA's Purpose To Preserve an Indian Child's Existing Tribal Connections.

III. INTERPRETING ICWA TO CREATE NEW PARENTAL RIGHTS RAISES GRAVE CONSTITUTIONAL CONCERNS.

A. Creation of Parental Rights Based On Indian Lineage Conflicts with Principles of Equal Protection.

B. Creation of Parental Rights Based On Indian Lineage Conflicts with Principles of Substantive Due Process.

C. Creation of Parental Rights Based On Indian Lineage Conflicts With Federalism Principles.

IV. ABSENT A PREEXISTING INDIAN FAMILY, A TRIBE CANNOT INVOKE SECTION 1915(a).

A. Section 1915(a) Requires a Preexisting Indian Family.

B. At a Minimum, Section 1915(a) Applies Only When a Preferred Party Seeks Custody.[33]

Respondent

I. An undisputed biological father who has both expressly acknowledged and conclusively proved paternity of an Indian child is a "parent" under ICWA.

II. The "existing Indian family doctrine" has no basis in ICWA.

A. ICWA governs all child custody disputes involving Indian children.

B. Non-custodial parents may invoke ICWA provisions limiting the termination of parental rights.

III. The adoption also is precluded by ICWA's preferential placement provision.

IV. ICWA is in all respects constitutional.[34]

Comment: This case raised two issues: (1) whether a non-custodial parent can invoke the Indian Child Welfare Act and (2) whether the father, who is not married to the mother, falls under the definition of "parent" under the Act if he has not followed the state law rules to attain parental status.[35] Both the petitioner and respondent divided the case into more

---

33. Brief for Petitioners at iii–v, Adoptive Couple v. Baby Girl, 133 S. Ct. 2552 (2013) (No. 12-399), http://sblog.s3.amazonaws.com/wp-content/uploads/2013/02/12-399-pet-brief.pdf (last visited Mar. 20, 2017).

34. Brief for Respondent Birth Father at ii, Adoptive Couple v. Baby Girl, 133 S. Ct. 2552 (2013) (No. 12-399), http://www.americanbar.org/content/dam/aba/publications/supreme_court_preview/briefs-v2/12-399_resp_birth_father.authcheckdam.pdf (last visited Mar. 20, 2017).

35. Adoptive Couple v. Baby Girl, 133 S. Ct. 2552, 2559–61 (2013).

issues and switched the order that they addressed the issues, which makes sense since the resolution of the second issue controls the first. While the point headings give you a general grasp of the case, more facts could certainly be added to make the point headings stronger, particularly for the respondent.

8.2.3   Examples of Point Headings

See Appendix B.

Chapter Nine

Writing to Win: Clear Writing, Editing, and Citation Form

9.1 Introduction to Clear and Concise Writing

In an earlier edition of this book, Judge Aldisert estimated that he had read fifty thousand briefs—approximately two million pages—as a state and federal judge. In his estimation, probably fewer than half of these pages were necessary. The comments of the judges set forth below confirm his impressions. They send this very loud message to the appellate bar: *You write too much. Prepare better and write less.* As one federal appellate judge quipped, quoting a colleague, "[T]hey're called briefs, not longs." Think back to Chapter Two and the brief-reading environment. Active federal appellate judges read approximately 1,000 briefs a year. If these briefs average fifty pages each, then each appellate judge reads 50,000 pages a year in appellate briefs. This is, of course, on top of bench memoranda, draft opinions, and other motions that come into chambers. Therefore, appellate judges have little sympathy for lengthy briefs. Despite admonitions from the bench to emphasize the muscle of the brief and cut out the flab, most lawyers continue to ignore the uniform advice of the appellate judges who decide their cases. While judges may not heed their own advice in drafting opinions, this is a book for lawyers.

When you start to write the argument, you know by then that the court has jurisdiction. You know that the issues have been properly noticed in the trial tribunal. You know what issues you want to discuss. You are ready to take them on, one by one. It is here, in the argument portion of the brief, where the judges direct their closest attention. And it is here where you must buckle down and demonstrate superior writing skills.

In their briefs, many lawyers seem—like the poor little lambs in Yale's "Whiffenpoof Song"—to have lost their way. Many briefs are no longer instruments of persuasion or explanation. Rather, they emerge from the computers as instruments of commentary or summary, looking more like wide-blade axes than precision decision-making tools.

A stuffy style and fluffy padding shows that the legal profession suffers from a crippling case of acute and possibly terminal pedantry. We seem to forget that all lawyers and judges are naturally called upon to be professional writers. The tools of the trade consist entirely of words. Professional writers know and accept the hard truth that prose, like any other art, calls for frequent compromise among desirable aims—sound and sense, force and fluidity, clarity and precision, emphasis and nuance, wit and truth. The very need for balance rules out consistency in writing. Each word, each sentence, each paragraph is a special case.[1] Yet judges and lawyers alike stand guilty of bombastic propositions and legal dialectics in "[l]ong sentences, awkward constructions, and fuzzy-wuzzy words that seem to apologize for daring to venture an opinion."[2]

Many brief writers suffer chronic cases of literary hiccups. They insert citations as often as possible, three or four in a simple declaratory sentence, irrespective of how these interfere with the flow of the prose, the rhythm of the presentations, or the order of argument. Such static impedes easy comprehension.

Habits like this stem perhaps from a skewed view of legal writing—that it must be technical in subject, multisyllabic in form, and highly complex in sentence structure. To be sure, the writing must be technical in the sense of being supported by appropriate legal authorities. But writing works best when it is clear and to the point. Brief writers would be well served if they posted a little sign on their desks: "Why and for whom am I writing?" Remember that you are writing for appellate judges for the sole purpose of persuading them. Your briefs will be shorter and more to the point if you do so.

All this has not been emphasized to suggest that effective legal writing should be graded purely for literary style. Rather, it is stressed because the purpose of all legal writing is persuasion. Without clear writing, communication is lessened. To the extent that we complicate communication, we dilute our powers of persuasion.

Many books exist on good writing in general[3] and good legal writing in particular.[4] These books provide valuable learning tools to appellate lawyers. This chapter is not meant to replace these books. Rather, our goal is to highlight some of the key writing issues that judges see in briefs. As an initial matter, however, before starting any writing venture, there are two things that lawyers can do to improve their writing overall.

---

1. Jacques Barzun, *Behind the Blue Pencil*, 54 Am. Scholar 385, 387–88 (1985).

2. Fred Rodell, *Goodbye to Law Reviews*, 23 Va. L. Rev. 38, 39 (1936).

3. William Strunk, Jr. & E.B. White, The Elements of Style (4th ed. 1999).

4. One of the most well-known and influential books on legal writing, *Plain English for Lawyers*, was written by long time U.C. Davis School of Law Professor Richard C. Wydick. Richard C. Wydick, Plain English for Lawyers (5th ed. 2005). Professor Wydick passed away on May 11, 2016. King Hall Community Mourns Professor Richard Wydick, UC Davis School of Law (May 12, 2016), https://law.ucdavis.edu/news/news.aspx?id=5883 (last visited Mar. 20, 2017). The legal community is indebted to him for his efforts to improve legal writing. The late Supreme Court Justice Antonin Scalia and Bryan A. Garner's *Making Your Case*, is another excellent and accessible resource for appellate lawyers. Antonin Scalia & Bryan A. Garner, Making Your Case: The Art of Persuading Judges (2008).

First, to write well, you must read well. This does not mean that you should just read books on how to be a better writer, well-written judicial opinions, and excellent briefs. You should also read books written by gifted writers. Do not just focus on the old classics—feel free to delve into the new classics as well.

Second, to write well, you must think well. George Orwell is credited with saying, "If people cannot write well, they cannot think well, and if they cannot think well, others will do their thinking for them."[5] This is especially true with legal writing. A lawyer cannot effectively communicate an argument in a brief if the lawyer has not clearly thought through the structure and implications of the argument. This is why it is so important to carefully research and outline a brief before starting to write; taking time to think through the outline allows the lawyer to keep the brief-writing focused and on point. Using an outline and the writing tips below, you can make your appellate writing clear.

9.2   Omit "Lawyerisms"

In a 2015 interview with Bryan Garner, Justice Elena Kagan said that she tries to write her judicial opinions so that an educated, intelligent non-lawyer can read them.[6] She explained, "I try to write so that people who are used to reading, even if not law, would be able to follow what I'm doing."[7] You should write briefs with the same goal. An appellate brief should be a document that an intelligent non-lawyer can easily read and understand.

One way to accomplish this goal is to eliminate "lawyerisms" or "legalese" from your brief. Words like "aforementioned, whereas, res gestae, and hereinafter" have virtually no place in a brief.[8] While some Latin phrases are legal terms of art that play an important role in certain areas of the law, others are simply archaic and can be properly replaced with simple English words.[9] One great technique for omitting lawyerisms from a brief is reading the brief aloud, or using a computer program to have the brief read aloud to you. You would never, or at least *should* never, talk to your colleagues about the "said contract;" rather, you would talk about "the contract."[10] So why would you write it the first way?

The word "hereinafter" is a favorite with lawyers. It is often used with a parenthetical to inform the reader that a shorter word will be used to describe a person, place,

---

5. *See* PHYLLIS SCHLAFLY, THE POWER OF THE POSITIVE WOMAN 151 (1977).

6. Jacob Shamsian, *6 Writing Tips from a Sitting Supreme Court Justice*, BUSINESS INSIDER (Aug. 31, 2015), http://www.businessinsider.com/us-supreme-court-justice-gave-some-amazing-tips-on-how-to-be-a-better-writer-2015-8. (last visited Mar. 20, 2017).

7. *Id.*

8. WYDICK, *supra* note 4, at 58–61.

9. SCALIA & GARNER, *supra* note 4, at 114; WYDICK, *supra* note 4, at 58–59.

10. *See* WYDICK, *supra* note 4, at 59. Justice Scalia and Bryan Garner bemoan the use of "such" in a similar manner—"such action" rather than simply "that action." SCALIA & GARNER, *supra* note 4, at 113.

or thing. Consider this example from a brief opposing certiorari before the United States Supreme Court: "Alliance Capital, Inc. (hereinafter referred to as 'Alliance Capital')." In some cases, a parenthetical to introduce a short form title can be helpful, but the "hereinafter referred to as" is absolutely unnecessary. A simple parenthetical stating ("Alliance Capital") would suffice. In this particular case, however, the entire parenthetical was superfluous. The case involved only one entity known as "Alliance Capital." An intelligent reader, even without the parenthetical, would know that Alliance Capital and Alliance Capital, Inc. are the same entity. Likewise, if there is only one Act, one Secretary, or one person named Smith in your case, a parenthetical to introduce an easily understandable short form is unnecessary.[11]

Other lawyerisms worth mentioning are the uses of "petitioner," "respondent," "appellant," "appellee," "plaintiff," or "defendant" in a brief. While these distinctions certainly have meaning to the appeal, using these terms in the brief can cause confusion to the reader. As Justice Scalia and Bryan Garner explain:

> Sometimes, in reading briefs, judges will get confused about who is on the up-side and who is on the down-side—and will have to flip back to the cover to see who "Petitioner" is. Moreover, the petitioner here may have been the defendant at trial, and the respondent on the first appeal. This can make the record on appeal confusing if status-names are used in the briefing and argument at each level.[12]

Instead, proper names or descriptive terms should be used to describe the parties. John Smith should be referred to as "Smith." If the presence of several individuals on one side of the case makes proper names difficult or cumbersome to use, find a descriptive term instead, such as "employees" or "victims."[13] You can use a parenthetical to clarify for the reader that the descriptive term refers to the particular parties in the case: "Nolan Ryan, Randy Johnson, and Yu Darvish ('the pitchers') . . . ."

Despite this guidance, use the word that describes a party's relationship to the case if reminding the reader of that relationship helps make your factual or legal point.

9.3   Be Concise

One way to tackle the problem of overly long briefs is to focus on writing concisely. Strunk and White teach in *The Elements of Style* to "omit needless words."[14] This is an important lesson for appellate lawyers whose briefs must comply with strict page or word limits. Unfortunately, common idioms and archaic legal phrases work against that goal. Lawyers love to use a multi-word phrase to convey a concept

---

11. SCALIA & GARNER, supra *note* 4, at 113.
12. SCALIA & GARNER, *supra* note 4, at 121.
13. *Id.*
14. STRUNK & WHITE, *supra* note 3, at 23.

that could be explained with one or two simple words. You can use several techniques to omit needless verbiage from your brief.

First, avoid compound constructions or common idioms that are especially wordy.[15] For example, instead of writing "in the event that," simply use "if."[16] Similarly, the phrase "in spite of the fact that" can be written as "though" or "although."[17] In his book, Professor Wydick provides a list of compound constructions and common idioms and their simpler replacements. Omitting the needless words from these phrases can produce significantly shorter briefs and more clearly conveyed concepts.

Consider this example from *Plain English for Lawyers*: "The ruling by the trial judge was prejudicial error for the reason that it cut off cross-examination with respect to issues that were vital."[18] This sentence can be reduced from twenty-four words to just fifteen: "The trial judge's ruling was prejudicial error because it cut off cross-examination on vital issues."[19] The revised sentence is not only shorter, it is more persuasive because the key words in the sentence are not buried under a lot of fluff.

People use many other common idioms in oral communication that should not be used in legal writing. Rather than starting an argument with phrases like "we believe that," "in our opinion," or "appellant asserts that," the particular argument or proposition should be stated directly. Consider the following examples:

> The appellant asserts that the statute violates the First Amendment of the Constitution because it restricts speech based on the content of that speech.

> The statute violates the First Amendment as a content-based speech restriction.

The second sentence is more concise and more persuasive. Judges know briefs represent the arguments of the appellant and appellee. There is no need to state it continually in the brief.

A second technique is to replace redundant legal phrases with one word. Legal writing is full of phrases such as "give, devise, and bequeath" or "null, void, and of no effect."[20] Despite the deep historical roots of these phrases,[21] they are unnecessary today. Take the first example. According to *Black's Law Dictionary*, "give" is defined as "[t]o voluntarily transfer (property) to another without compensation."[22]

---

15. *Id.* at 23–24; WYDICK, *supra* note 4, at 11, 13–14.
16. WYDICK, *supra* note 4, at 11.
17. STRUNK & WHITE, *supra* note 3, at 24.
18. WYDICK, *supra* note 4, at 8.
19. *Id.*
20. *Id.* at 17–18.
21. For a historical explanation of why redundant legal phrases are so common, see *id.* at 17–20.
22. GIVE, BLACK'S LAW DICTIONARY (10th ed. 2014).

The terms "devise" and "bequeath" have the same meaning.[23] In fact, the *Black's Law Dictionary* entry for "give, devise, and bequeath" states "[t]his wording has long been criticized as redundant. In modern usage, *give* ordinarily suffices."[24] Do not necessarily follow this advice outside the realm of brief writing. When writing an actual will, for example, the case law of the jurisdiction may make it perilous not to have your client give, devise, and bequeath.

Third, a lawyer can write more concisely by employing the active voice. As Professor Wydick explains, "[w]hen you use a verb in the active voice, the subject of the sentence does the acting."[25] The sentence "Jane fired the gun" employs the active voice, while the sentence "The gun was fired" is a passive construction. Generally, the active voice uses fewer words, which is one reason to prefer it over the passive voice.[26] The passive voice can also cause ambiguity in writing.[27] Consider the example "The gun was fired." This passive sentence hides the identity of the actor, the person who fired the gun. Sometimes this ambiguity can be useful, particularly if a lawyer wants to deemphasize certain facts, such as the fact that her client fired the gun.[28] Normally, however, the active voice results in clearer and more concise briefs.[29]

Finally, lawyers should omit needless adjectives and adverbs. Although legal writing should be persuasive, it should not overreach. As one law clerk noted, "Too often advocates use strong language as a substitute for strong reasoning." Excessive use of adjectives and adverbs can lead to overreaching. Furthermore, some adverbs can subconsciously send a signal that an argument is weak. When a brief uses the word "clearly" or the phrase "it is clear" to introduce an argument, it sends the signal that the argument is actually not very clear, or else the adverb or phrase would not be needed. A well-written and reasoned argument stands on its own; it does not need superfluous adverbs. Overusing strong language also makes judges hesitant to attribute strength to your arguments when they actually merit strength.

9.4 Be Clear

The ability to write clearly and memorably may be innate in some and perfected by others through studious attention and constant application, much like a muscle is strengthened by proper and continuing exercise. To do the writing, editing, and rewriting required for polished text takes time. Time, unfortunately, even with

---

23. "1. The act of giving property by will." Devise, Black's Law Dictionary (10th ed. 2014) (noting that American usage is "considerably broadened" beyond application to wills). "1. To officially arrange for someone to have (something that one owns) after one's death; esp., to give property (usu. personal property or money) by will." Bequeath, Black's Law Dictionary (10th ed. 2014).

24. Give, Devise, and Bequeath, Black's Law Dictionary (10th ed. 2014).

25. Wydick, *supra* note 4, at 27.

26. *Id.*

27. *Id.* at 30.

28. *Id.* at 32.

29. *Id.*

computers, email, and laser printing, is severely rationed these days. Space is also increasingly rationed in briefs.

Unfortunately, some of the strategies lawyers employ to save space can lead to unclear writing. The most prevalent of these strategies is using acronyms. Most judges strongly disfavor the use of acronyms, especially unfamiliar ones, and they readily chastise attorneys for the overuse of acronyms in brief-writing.[30] Justice Antonin Scalia was especially known for his dislike of acronyms. In *Making Your Case: The Art of Persuading Judges*, he explained:

> Acronyms are mainly for the convenience of the writer or speaker. Don't burden your reader or listener with many of them, especially unfamiliar ones. FBI and IRS are OK, but not CPSC and FHLBB. You may be surprised how easy it is to avoid a brief of alphabet soup—and from the reader's point of view (which is the only point of view that counts) it is worth the effort. If the Consumer Product Safety Commission plays a prominent role in your case, and no other agency has any part at all, call it "the Commission" or even simply "the agency."[31]

Some jurisdictions specifically encourage lawyers to "limit the use of acronyms" and "avoid using acronyms that are not widely known."[32] Check the applicable rules in a jurisdiction before filing a brief containing acronyms. Moreover, if you have used an unfamiliar acronym but it has been several pages since it was last seen, consider explaining your short form again for clarity. You do not want to give the reader a memory test—a bad grade for the reader is a worse grade for the writer.

Likewise, using overly technical language can muddy the brief-reading waters. Remember, most appellate judges are generalists. While a lawyer writing an appellate brief has spent months—or years if she was counsel below—immersing herself in the record and applicable law, this may be the judge's first Atomic Energy Act case. Therefore, either strive to use non-technical language to describe the case or, if you must use a technical term of art, carefully explain the term's meaning.[33]

Failure to write clearly risks more than simply annoying a judge; it can lead to disciplinary action as well. A few years ago, a partner at a major law firm received

---

30. Nat'l Ass'n of Regulatory Util. Comm'rs v. U.S. Dep't of Energy, 680 F.3d 819, 820 n.1 (D.C. Cir. 2012) ("Here, both parties abandoned any attempt to write in plain English, instead abbreviating every conceivable agency and statute involved, familiar or not, and littering their briefs with references to 'SNF,' 'HLW,' 'NWF,' 'NWPA,' and 'BRC'—shorthand for 'spent nuclear fuel,' 'high-level radioactive waste,' the 'Nuclear Waste Fund,' the 'Nuclear Waste Policy Act,' and the 'Blue Ribbon Commission.'"); *see also* Mike McKee, *Judge's Footnotes Take Small Shots at Lawyers*, LEGAL PAD (September 29, 2009 5:33 PM), http://legalpad.typepad.com/my_weblog/2009/09/judges-foot-notes-take-small-shots-at-lawyers.html (last visited Mar. 20, 2017).

31. SCALIA & GARNER, *supra* note 4, at 120.

32. Nat'l Ass'n of Regulatory Util. Comm'rs, 680 F.3d at 820 n.1.

33. For more tips on dealing with a highly technical subject, see Chapter Twelve.

unwanted attention from both the Supreme Court and the media when the Court issued an order asking him to show cause why he should not be sanctioned for filing a petition for certiorari that was so full of acronyms, jargon, and technical language that it was incomprehensible.[34] While the lawyer was not ultimately sanctioned,[35] the Court's order stands as a reminder to attorneys to write clearly.

9.5   Keep It Civil (and Classy)

One criticism that judges and law clerks have of some appellate briefs is that they are, in the words of one federal judge "too nasty." A well-written appellate brief should not contain criticisms directed at other parties in the case, opposing counsel, or the judge below. Judges are, generally, a collegial bunch. While appellate judges do correct errors made by trial court judges, they still consider those judges to be colleagues and socialize with them at bench and bar functions. Therefore, they are not impressed with briefs that attack their friends and colleagues. Furthermore, at the federal level, there is a good chance that at least one judge on your panel started her judicial career as a district court judge, or a district court judge may even be sitting by designation at the circuit court level. Filling a brief with personal attacks will detract from your argument, and it could lead to disciplinary action.[36]

In the same vein, keep the brief classy. Do not try to be that lawyer who files the graphic comic book brief; it has already been done.[37] Not long ago, a lawyer filed a petition for rehearing that included the transcript of an imaginary conversation between a lawyer and client discussing the panel's original decision.[38] The panel was not amused, and in denying the motion Fifth Circuit Judge Edward Prado included a transcript of an imaginary conversation between the judges on the panel discussing the form and merits of the petition.[39]

---

34. Mark Wilson, *Details on SCOTUS' Sanction of Patent Attorney Howard Shipley*, FINDLAW (Feb. 23, 2015), http://blogs.findlaw.com/supreme_court/2015/02/details-on-scotus-sanction-of-patent-attorney-howard-shipley.html (last visited Mar. 20, 2017).

35. Lyle Denniston, *The Howard Shipley Case: A Lesson for Others*, SCOTUSBLOG (Mar. 24, 2015), http://www.scotusblog.com/2015/03/the-howard-shipley-case-a-lesson-for-others/ (last visited Mar. 20, 2017).

36. Steven Wisotsky, *Incivility and Unprofessionalism on Appeal: Impugning the Integrity of Judges*, 7 J. APP. PRAC. & PROCESS 303, 312 (citing Ramirez v. St. Bar, 28 Cal. 3d 402, 404 (Cal. 1980)); Lindsay Maleson & Joseph J. Ortego, *Under Attack: Professionalism in the Practice of Law* n. 13, 2003 EMERGING ISSUES IN MOTOR VEHICLE PRODUCT LIABILITY LITIG., Phoenix, AZ, 2003, available at http://www.nixonpeabody.com/116492 (last visited Mar. 20, 2017).

37. Debra Cassens Weiss, *Faced with a Five-Page Limit, Lawyer Files Cartoon Amicus Brief with Proper Font Size*, ABA JOURNAL (Sept. 5, 2012), http://www.abajournal.com/news/article/faced_with_a_five_page_limit_lawyer_files_cartoon_amicus_brief_with_ proper_ (describing Bob Kohn's filing of a "graphic novelette" in a complex antitrust suit involving eBooks) (last visited Mar. 20, 2017).

38. Pet. for Panel Reh'g, *Forum Subsea Rentals v. Elsharhawy et al.*, No. 14-20717 (Feb. 5, 2016).

39. Denial of Pet. for Panel Reh'g, *Forum Subsea Rentals*, On Pet. for Reh'g, No. 14-20717 (Feb. 26, 2016) ("I cannot imagine why they thought [including the hypothetical conversation in the petition] was a good idea.").

A lawyer's brief should stand out because of the excellent reasoning in the brief, not because the lawyer used a novel ploy to try and get the court's attention.

9.6   Edit Vigorously

Editing is a key step in writing clearly and concisely. Unfortunately, many lawyers (and law students) fail to leave ample time for editing their work. Before beginning the first draft of an appellate brief, develop a writing schedule that leaves sufficient time to edit your document. Justice Elena Kagan, for example, has described her opinion writing process as "very long [and] extensive."[40] While appellate lawyers may not have as much time to write their briefs as judges have to write their opinions, do not forgo the editing stage. A sloppily written brief may cause a judge to question if the reasoning is also sloppy.

While each person's editing process will be a little different, the following editing outline will assist any author.

A) Edit the work.

1) Check spelling. Run a spell check, but do not solely rely on it, as it can miss homonyms. Ensure correct spelling of all proper names. Then double-check.

2) Edit like a reader. Identify problems you encounter as a reader.

   a) Determine whether the sequence of ideas flows smoothly and logically.

   b) Determine whether the ideas are adequately supported.

   c) Recall the judges' major criticisms of briefs: they are too long. Is every point in this brief necessary? Does a weak point detract from a strong one? Have I fallen in love with my writing, or am I looking at it from the standpoint of a reading judge who will see all its warts and blemishes? If I keep the points, should I cut some of the supporting text? Have I over-discussed some of the cases? Are all the citations absolutely necessary?

   d) Look for conspicuous omissions.

   e) Look for needless repetition. Check your writing for compound constructions and redundant phrases. If necessary, make a list of phrases that you are trying to avoid.[41]

   f) Limit sentences, on average, to no more than twenty-five words, with most sentences containing no more than one thought.[42]

---

40. Shamsian, *supra* note 6.
41. *See id.* at 19–20.
42. WYDICK, *supra* note 4, at 36.

3) Edit like a writer. Assess your writing techniques and mark up the first draft as an editor would.

   a) Read certain passages aloud, if necessary, and train your ears to detect errors reliably. You might consider using a computer program to read the brief to you.

   b) Assess the "beat" of your writing. There is a difference between writing for reading and writing for speaking, even though each form has both mood and rhythm. Is the mood exaggerated? Do the words come through as a roar or as a "soft sell," soothing but nonetheless persuasive?

4) Edit to conform to page and word limitations. How long is the brief? Do I really need fifty pages to make my argument? Would the judge be impressed if I cut down the number of pages instead of presenting a forty-seven to fifty-page effort? What will sell here? A lean, mean machine or a fat, flabby one?

5) Ensure that pages are correctly numbered and properly assembled. Check to see that your appendix is paginated and contains a table of contents.

6) Ask a trusted colleague who is not mired in the technicalities of the case to edit the brief. This person can approach the brief from the perspective of a generalist judge and ensure that the facts and law are adequately explained.

7) If at all possible, leave enough time in the editing process to set the brief aside for a day or two.[43] This "cooling-off period" will allow you to approach the brief with a fresh perspective and catch mistakes that you missed in drafting.[44]

B) An appellate lawyer is a professional writer.

1) Follow the practice of all professional writers and editors. Never rely entirely upon your memory. Keep a select library of the best reference materials at your elbow: a reputable dictionary, a comprehensive thesaurus, a good book of quotations, and of course, *The Elements of Style* by Strunk and White and *Plain English for Lawyers* by Richard Wydick.

C) Read constantly.

1) Make outside reading a lifetime professional commitment. The best writing trains your ear, helping you to listen. The worst writing helps you to learn what to avoid.

---

43. Ashley Burkett, *Tips on Effective Editing*, AMERICAN BAR ASSOCIATION (May 18, 2015) http://apps.americanbar.org/litigation/committees/appellate/articles/spring2015-0515-tips-effective-editing.html (last visited Mar. 20, 2017).

44. *Id.*

2) Concentrate on masters of "the plain style," such as Mark Twain, George Orwell, James Thurber, E. B. White, Ernest Hemingway, Henry James, and Jonathan Swift, who provided models and weapons against the convoluted, lumbering style of legal prose.

D) Never become complacent with your writing.

1) Remember, effective writing is a lifetime goal, not a final accomplishment.

a) Become your best critic.

b) Write so that when you finish you can look at the result and honestly say, "I have done the very best I am capable of at this stage of my literary development."

c) Regularly review your past writing.

i) Ask yourself how it appeals to you.

ii) Assess improvement or deterioration in your writing style. Ask yourself whether your words remain as persuasive as they first seemed and whether they do a good job of expressing the thoughts you intended when you began.

d) To improve, work consciously to ensure that everything you write will be better than anything you wrote before.

e) Always keep in mind that writing is like exercising a muscle; the more you write, the easier it becomes.

9.7   Follow Proper Citation Form

Appellate judges commonly criticize lawyers' inaccurate citations to the record and to cases. By inaccurate citations, they are not criticizing failure to follow *The Bluebook* format; rather, they refer to lawyers' misrepresenting the facts and the law. As discussed in Chapter Seven, it is vital to accurately state the law and facts in an appellate brief. You should not overstate the plausible interpretation of an authority. Credibility is squandered, or never earned, when a case is cited for a proposition that it does not reasonably support.

It is also important, of course, to follow proper citation form in writing appellate briefs. Much like careful observation of proper grammar and sentence structure, attention to detail and accuracy in citation form increases the lawyer's credibility with judges. An obvious failure to invest time and diligence in properly formatting citations may cause the judges to question whether the lawyer likewise failed to invest appropriate time and diligence in research and analysis.

The purpose of a citation is to help a reader find the particular source cited. A citation does not serve this purpose if it does not provide all of the necessary information to find the source, if it contains errors, or if it causes confusion by departing from standard citation form. For better or worse,[45] most jurisdictions require legal citations to follow the format set in *The Bluebook*.[46] The good news is, proper citation formatting is the most intellectually simple part of brief writing; it requires only dedicating time to carefully look at each citation and consult the appropriate formatting rules. As tedious as it may be, it does not pay to rush this important step.

In addition to complying with citation form, it is important that lawyers avoid the epidemic of "citationitis." The infatuation with citing precedent is older than any of us. Although the citable cases are available by the thousands, few add very much to legal fundamentals. Additionally, over-citation creates the contrary impression that American law has undergone massive changes. This simply is not true. Over-citation is both a self-fulfilling prophecy and a self-inflicted wound.

The brute fact is that not all precedent represents currency of equal value. An authoritative gradation of legal precepts does exist. Some precedents are much more important than others. Recognition that a value hierarchy exists is essential if judges are to find the proper grounds of decision; if lawyers are to find the basis for predicting the course of decision; and if citizens are to obtain reasonable guidance in conducting themselves according to the demands of legal order. Even more important—much more important—is the need to bring greater order to the design of law by early and clearly identifying the family of law implicated in the case.

The time has come for lawyers to simplify, rather than complicate, current legal issues. Lawyers should identify clearly the controversy in each case and isolate the branch of the law governing it. The first step must be concentrating on the tree's trunk and its main branches, rather than fussing over the buds and blossoms that continually sprout and grow but will go when fall arrives.

We must emphasize basic legal precepts because the starting point of every judicial decision must be a recognition of controlling dogma, doctrine, and fundamental principles. Only this recognition will make our decisions consistent and coherent. To accomplish this, all judges need help from all lawyers. Simplicity and order in briefs promotes progress in the law. It creates better communication between lawyer and judge and between judge and community. It removes idiosyncrasies from judicial decisions and in their place establishes predictability and reckonability. But we are at our most persuasive when we also explain the "why" behind the legal rule. A good brief will strike the right balance between these principles.

---

45. Judge Richard Posner has, on several occasions, laid out his criticisms of *The Bluebook*. *See, e.g.*, Richard A. Posner, *The Bluebook Blues*, 120 Yale Law J. 850 (2011). For his most recent critiques, see Richard A. Posner, *What Is Obviously Wrong with the Federal Judiciary, Yet Eminently Curable*, 19 Green Bag 2D 187 (2016), available at http://www.greenbag.org/v19n2/v19n2_articles_posner. pdf (last visited Mar. 20, 2017).

46. *But see* The Greenbook: Texas Rules of Form (Texas Law Review, 13th ed. 2015).

9.8   To Footnote, or Not to Footnote

Traditionally, legal citations in court documents are provided in the text of the document, not in footnotes. Some legal writing scholars, such as Bryan Garner, have advocated for moving all legal writing citations to footnotes.[47] While this approach makes documents more aesthetically pleasing, it does not serve the intended audience: judges and their law clerks. As Justice Scalia explained in *Making Your Case*:

> You cannot make your product more readable to the careful lawyer by putting the entire citation material . . . in a footnote—because the careful lawyer wants to know, while reading along, what the authority is for what you say. So, far from enabling the reader's eyes to run smoothly across a text uninterrupted by this ugly material, you would force the eyes to bounce repeatedly from text to footnote.[48]

With respect to substantive footnotes, if it is important enough to say, say it in the text of your brief, not in a footnote. The only hard and fast rule is: "When in doubt, do not use them." But there is a caveat here. You may use footnotes to supplement or authenticate certain statements in the briefs where, if the authority were placed in the text, the additional material would detract from the argument and diminish the persuasive power of the text.

It is best not to use footnotes for the making of remarks and asides, in the manner of a character in a play sharing a private joke with the audience. These marginal comments, often with piddling objections to minor points in the opponent's brief or the lower court's opinion, add little to and subtract much from the impact of your brief.

An additional word of caution: judges know the brief writer's trick of resorting to single-spaced footnotes when the draft runs over the page limits set forth in the court rules. They also deplore the conduct of bold and foolish practice of those whose briefs are bounced back by the clerk's office for over-pagination and simply returned in smaller type. Many courts now have rules establishing a minimum type size; pay attention to them. In any event, briefs that promote eyestrain will not promote the judges' attention and inspire enthusiasm.

9.9   Writing to Persuade

The purpose of a brief is to animate the art of persuasion. The lawyer must convince the judicial reader of the rightness of his cause. A writer friend once sent Judge Aldisert a letter in which he said: "The first job for any piece of writing is to

---

47. SCALIA & GARNER, *supra* note 4, at 132–33; Bryan A. Garner, *Textual Citations Make Legal Writing Onerous, for Lawyers and Nonlawyers Alike*, ABA JOURNAL (Feb. 1, 2014), http://www.abajournal.com/magazine/article/textual_citations_make_legal_writing_onerous_for_lawyers_and_nonlawyers/ (last visited Mar. 20, 2017).

48. SCALIA & GARNER, *supra* note 4 at 133–34.

entice the reader into reading it, start to finish. That accomplished, the words must convey clearly what the writer wants them to convey. Finally, the text must perform the missionary act of persuasion, reinforcing the support of those who agree with the author and changing the minds of those who do not."

To write effectively is to sell effectively. That is why judges and lawyers can comfortably be thought of as salespeople, a function they do not always recognize and one that many would probably deny. In this sense, objections notwithstanding, being a successful lawyer or judge means selling your argument to the legal community.

Other than the suggestions set forth in these chapters, are there really any specific yet undiscovered "mechanics of persuasion" a lawyer may use to craft his or her appellate brief and argument? The comments from judges and lawyers below provide insight on both clear writing and writing to persuade.

9.10 Writing to Win: Advice from Judges and Lawyers

Below is writing advice from judges and lawyers.

John M. Walker, Jr.
Senior Judge, Second Circuit

Be concise, do not repeat arguments or facts. The poorest, least persuasive briefs are all too often those that the lawyer has not taken the time to reduce to its essence.

Thomas L. Ambro
Judge, Third Circuit

[Briefs are] [t]oo long, do not acknowledge weaknesses, and too reliant on attempting to stretch "precedent" as support for principles that do not fit.

D. Michael Fisher
Judge, Third Circuit

[Briefs are] [t]oo long, too nasty, too many issues.

Richard L. Nygaard
Senior Judge, Third Circuit

The most effective tool the lawyer has for winning on appeal is his or her brief. Long after the echoes of a brilliant argument die down in the courtroom, the Judge will still have the brief in hand. There is absolutely *no substitute* for a commanding knowledge of the record and all cases critical to the appeal. Misstating either the record or a case that either supports you or which you must distinguish *severely* weakens the lawyer's credibility in the eyes of the court.

Just as a lawyer must have a command of the record and the law, the lawyer should assume that the Judges do as well. I find it annoying when an attorney arguing on appeal states an argument or a response to a question as, "If you read the record . . .," or "If you read the district court's opinion . . .," or "If you read the case of such and such . . . ." I will usually interject, "I *have* read the record (or that case), now *you* tell *me* where it supports your argument."

National Institute for Trial Advocacy

The best way to prepare for oral argument is to prepare your own brief. Farming it out to associates or, worse still, a research or brief writing organization is a poor substitute. When you write your *own* brief, you will have performed the first test of your theories, the facts, and the law.

Dolores K. Sloviter
Senior Judge, Third Circuit

I really believe that a lawyer cannot persuade a good appellate court to adopt his or her view on the case unless the case itself is a winning case. Because we read the briefs as carefully as we do, I will go out of my way to find some basis to decide for a party if I think he, she, or it is right, unless the issue has been waived. Therefore, even the most beautifully written and argued brief cannot persuade me if I believe the facts or the law are contrary to that party's position. Furthermore, because we do not sit alone, if I miss a basis to hold for a party that has written a poor brief, usually one of my colleagues will see through the brief and find the missing piece. Therefore, the mechanics of persuasion are, in my view, limited to finding a good case with winning facts or law.

Gregg J. Costa
Judge, Fifth Circuit

[Briefs have] [t]oo many acronyms; too much extraneous factual detail (dates, names, etc. that don't matter to the issues being raised on appeal); [and lawyers spend] too much time on things the court knows (e.g., the summary judgment standard) and not enough on the question that is likely be decisive; too many footnotes and hiding weak points in the footnotes.

Jennifer Walker Elrod
Judge, Fifth Circuit

Briefs use too much sarcasm and are too critical of the district court and opposing counsel.

Richard R. Clifton
Judge, Ninth Circuit

[Briefs] are too long. Judges are human, too, and attention spans are finite. Most lawyers don't appreciate the volume of reading that judges have to do. I confess that when I was a lawyer writing briefs, I didn't think about that. But now that I'm on the other side of the bench, I have learned that a brief that is concise and to the point has more impact than briefs that seem to end only because they hit the limit. Even briefs that are well under the limit are rarely as focused as they could be. With the advent of word processing, the motivation to edit out unnecessary repetition and digressions has waned and the temptation to start writing before thinking the arguments through has grown. Both developments are unfortunate. Think first, and edit ruthlessly.

Andrew Kleinfeld
Senior Judge, Ninth Circuit

Substantially overlength briefs are a problem, because the judge cannot read them all in one sitting, so it becomes more difficult to compare the arguments.

Dorothy W. Nelson
Senior Judge, Ninth Circuit

My biggest critique against lawyers' briefs today is that they are too long, with too many issues . . . and too many citations when one or two will do.

Stephen H. Anderson
Senior Judge, Tenth Circuit

Every conceivable device should be used to promote the quick understanding, and lasting impression of that understanding, of the most important points and issues raised. Thus, in addition to law, an appeal to reasonable policy grounds supporting points and issues will go a long way toward promoting the position one wants the judge to adopt. For example, legislative history is in fact a good tool when properly used (despite Justice Scalia). Also, drawing on a parade of horribles or ultimate absurdity, unworkability, or untenability to show the fallacy of an opposing argument when carried to its logical extreme, is effective. In the same vein, comparisons to settled law with similar objectives such as comparing a line of authority under one civil rights law to an issue under another civil rights law helps.

The art of persuasion under the subheading of helping the court to "understand" should take into account that examples of this art that are all around us. We are literally drenched in Madison Avenue propaganda and enticements, in political spin doctoring, in sound bites, and so on. They are all effective in their own way, and lawyers should pay attention to the quick, colorful, slanted illustration of points in ways and embedded in compelling contexts used every day by professional persuaders. The ancient arts of parable, allegory, analogy, and so on are eminently helpful tools for helping the listener understand and for driving a point home—if short and "catchy"—anchored in the judges' common experience, and attached to a generally accepted bias of some sort.

David M. Ebel
Senior Judge, Tenth Circuit

I see three essential ingredients in a persuasive argument: (1) gaining credibility by the advocate; (2) focusing the court's attention on the dispositive matters; and (3) combining both a *reason* to rule a particular way with a roadmap as to *how* such a ruling can be fashioned. A fourth element—style—could also be added. An informal, give-and-take style, is always more persuasive than prepared remarks that are too heavily scripted and adhered to. Lawyers should trust their instinct and allow the "force" to be with them during their argument.

Harris L. Hartz
Judge, Tenth Circuit

The most important thing in a brief is clarity. If an argument makes no sense to the court, it will not prevail.

Paul J. Kelly, Jr.
Judge, Tenth Circuit

I have always thought that in addition to a good brief an advocate needs to figure out a theme for her oral argument that is perhaps different from the brief and which is designed to highlight one or two of the best points. An imaginative theme can capture a panel's interest and perhaps change initial impressions.

Deanell Reece Tacha
Former Chief Judge,
Tenth Circuit

Whether one is appellant or appellee, the question to be answered precisely is: "What is it that the court must decide to decide in my favor?" If counsel honestly and analytically answers this question, the brief and the oral argument are very clearly targeted to reaching that answer. The appellant must answer in a focused manner: What issue or issues will require the appellate court to reverse the judgment of the court below, and what cases and/or facts precisely address that issue? For appellee, the question is perhaps even more straightforward: What issue requires that the appellate court affirm the district court, and what facts or cases support that result?

As I have worked with advocacy classes, I have been struck by the difficulty that advocates have in answering those questions precisely. Either because of a lack of focus or the difficulty of honing a case to that particularity. Lawyers seem to have an exceedingly difficult time answering directly these pivotal questions.

Robin S. Rosenbaum
Judge, Eleventh Circuit

Good briefs are well organized, well researched, and clearly written. They also are true to the record and the law. Finally, they are not longer than they have to be to make their points persuasively.

Patricia M. Wald
Chief Judge Emeritus,
D.C. Circuit

The more paper you throw at us, the meaner we get, the more irritated and hostile we feel about verbosity, peripheral arguments and long footnotes. Repetition, extraneous facts, over-long arguments (by the twentieth page, we are muttering to ourselves, "I get it, I get it. No more, for God's sake.") still occur more often than capable counsel should tolerate.

Ronald T.Y. Moon
Former Chief Justice,
Supreme Court of Hawai'i

Write in a concise and direct fashion, minimizing the utilization of long, rambling footnotes.

Rita B. Garman
Justice, Supreme Court
of Illinois

Careful editing and proofreading [are attributes of a good brief]. Errors in grammar, punctuation, and spelling suggest inattention to detail, which may indicate a similar lack of attention to legal reasoning.

Bill Cunningham
Justice, Supreme Court
of Kentucky

[Briefs are] [t]oo long, which leads to them repeating themselves. They don't understand that they don't have to string it out to the maximum allowed pages.

Thomas G. Saylor
Chief Justice,
Supreme Court
of Pennsylvania

I have seen many very good briefs, but I have observed some containing excessive wordiness, unnecessary legalese, digressions into irrelevant detail, obfuscation, and occasionally even trickery. Such pitfalls obviously are to be avoided.

Nathan L. Hecht
Chief Justice,
Supreme Court of Texas

Judges read thousands of briefs. They want know from a brief as quickly as possible, this is my complaint, this how it happened, this is why I'm right, and here's the proof.

Howard J. Bashman
Law Offices of Howard J. Bashman, Willow Grove, Pennsylvania

Your brief must make sense and be persuasive to someone who knows nothing about your case and next to nothing about the areas of law involved. Pursue your strongest and most significant issues and leave the rest behind. Size matters, and quality matters too. Keep your brief as short as possible, and make sure that every cite to the record and to the law is impeccably accurate.

April L. Farris
Yetter Coleman LLP, Houston, Texas

Consider your brief as a work of craftsmanship. Draft first for accuracy and persuasion, ensuring that every argument is firmly grounded in case law or in the evidence. Next, edit for clarity and brevity, cutting a paragraph where a sentence will do. Finally, edit for enjoyment of reading. Within the confines of good judgment, exchange say-nothing verbs for better verbs, and consider a pertinent literary or cultural reference. The end result should be a polished and persuasive read, never a slog.

George W. Hicks, Jr.
Kirkland & Ellis LLP, Washington, D.C.

Judges read dozens of briefs each week. From the very first sentence of your brief, therefore, construct a narrative that will grab the judge's attention and make yours one of the few briefs that the judge wants to read a second or third time. Develop a theme that puts the judge in a frame of mind to *want* to rule for your client, with your legal arguments then providing a roadmap for reaching that result. Write vividly and in your own voice. Avoid lengthy quotes, which signal laziness; excessive string cites, which force the judge to do your work; and extensive footnotes, which are a distraction.

Lee Rudofsky
Solicitor General of Arkansas

The biggest stumbling blocks to persuasive brief writing are time and pride. Get a full draft done early enough that you can put it aside for a day or two and then spend another week revising or re-writing it. And don't get so enamored with your own voice or legal skills that you think your first draft is ever good enough. It's not, ever, regardless of the author. The best briefs I've ever written are ones I have so significantly revised two or three times that you could never link the first draft and the final product.

Lawrence VanDyke
Solicitor General of Nevada

In legal writing, no less than other types of literature, whoever tells the most compelling story captures the audience. Yet often even good legal writers fail to develop a central, compelling theme that runs throughout the briefing. After digesting and mastering the facts and law relevant to your case, deciding on your central theme should be the first thing a lawyer does—before ever putting pen to paper. The reader should have been exposed to that theme—from the question(s) presented, introduction, and factual background—before ever getting to the argument section of your brief.

Eugene Volokh
Gary T. Schwartz Distinguished Professor of Law, UCLA School of Law

To craft a persuasive argument, you need to understand the strengths and weaknesses of your case. The strengths of your case might be precedents, statutes, or constitutional provisions that support your position. They might be particular facts in the record. They might be particular details of the legal rule (whether it's a legal rule that you're relying on, or a legal rule that you're challenging).

They might be practical harms (e.g., deterrence of useful behavior) or jurisprudential harms (e.g., the creation of hard-to-administer legal rules) that would flow from your audience deciding against you. They might be practical or jurisprudential benefits that flow from your audience deciding in your favor (e.g., this sort of issue comes up very often, so if the court agrees to grant discretionary review, it can help clarify the law for thousands of cases and not just for this one).

For every case, the strongest points will be different. And for some cases, even the strongest points won't be that strong. But you must always identify those points.

And then you should stress those points at the outset of your summary of argument, starting with the strongest ones. Your readers are busy people. You need to grab them as quickly as possible, and quickly show them why they should rule in your favor.

The weaknesses of your case might likewise be precedents, statutes, constitutional provisions, facts, or practical consequences. They are the things that the readers are thinking about while reading your argument, whether because they saw the points themselves or because the other side has raised them or is sure to raise them.

You then need to frame your summary of argument in a way that shores up those weak points. For instance, say that there's an obvious precedent that cuts against your argument. Identify that weak point. Figure out how to respond to it. And then respond to it clearly and forcefully.

Beth A. Williams
Kirkland & Ellis LLP, Washington, D.C.

Your brief will be most effective if you address your opponent's strongest points head-on. A careful reader will detect evasion and attempts to side-step an issue. The strongest arguments are those that recognize opposition points and dismantle them piece by piece.

CHAPTER TEN

THE BRIEF: WRITING YOUR ARGUMENT

It is now time to start writing your argument. What is the first thing you do? That is easy: *carve out adequate time in your schedule.* Ideas need time to percolate. Crucial cases get overruled or reversed during the briefing process. Colleagues offer vital help and then get pulled away on other matters. Illness or emergency invades your schedule. Modern technology fails as deadlines approach. If you arrange to have your brief ready for filing a week, or at least two to three days early, none of these events need concern you.

If you have followed the advice in the preceding chapters and 1) limited the issues on appeal, 2) thoroughly researched those issues, 3) outlined your argument, and 4) carefully thought about your theme (which we discuss below and in Chapter Thirteen), you will be well on your way to drafting your argument. Now it is time to add the meat to your argument.

10.1   Writing the First Paragraph

The first few words can be the hardest to write. In starting your argument section, you need not recreate the wheel. You should have already been thinking about your argument theme, which should encapsulate your strongest point. This theme will appear, as discussed in Chapter Thirteen, in your summary of the argument as an orientation paragraph, or a critical opening paragraph. Repeat it, or a version of it, here. *Your strongest point is the argument, objectively considered, that is most calculated to persuade the court to your point of view.* You want to hit the judges between the eyes with it. You aim for the best possible initial impression. You do not get a second chance.

This first sentence should appear right after the argument heading in your brief and before your first main point, which is signified with a Roman numeral. Recall how your first-year college English composition instructor explained that the topic sentence sets forth a theme. Do the same thing here. The skeletal structure of a good brief may contain three or possibly four points, perhaps some independent of one another. To the extent possible, endeavor to declare and support a unifying theme that will run throughout the brief.

The theme sets the tone of your argument. It is both the focus and the thesis. It directs the judges' attention immediately to where the trial court's error took place and explains straightaway why the trial court was wrong or, when used by the appellee, why it was right. It tells the appellate court what relief you want.

The best briefs contain a unifying theme or possibly coequal themes that immediately focus the argument: the trial court's findings of fact were erroneous, and this is why; the plaintiff did not meet the burden of proof and here is the controlling law, and this is the critical element not proved; under the circumstances, the trial court's range of discretion was severely restricted as indicated by ruling case law, and here is how there was an improper exercise of that discretion; this is a case where the trial court erred as a matter of law by choosing, from competing legal precepts, the wrong one; the trial court erred in construing the relevant statute; or the trial court erred in applying settled legal precepts to the facts found by the fact-finder.

After you write the theme statement, provide a roadmap of the points that you will be arguing. This should be a roadmap of your main Roman numeral points—the major issues in the case. Later in your argument, you will roadmap your sub-points so that your reader can follow how those distinct arguments progress. This first roadmap lays out those two or three big issues that the court will be addressing on appeal.[1]

10.2   Identifying the Source of Controversy

After stating the overarching theme or focus of your brief and providing a roadmap, proceed into the argument in a highly compartmentalized, issue-by-issue format.

For each point in your argument, identify the precise flashpoint of controversy between the parties. There are three potential conflicts:

1) Where the law and its application alike are plain or, to put it another way, where the rule of law is clear and its application to the facts as found by the fact-finder is equally clear.

2) Where the rule of law is clear and the sole question is its application to the facts. In Cardozo's formulation, "[T]he rule of law is certain, and the application alone doubtful."[2]

3) Where neither the rule nor its application is clear.

The brief writer should not waste effort or unduly lengthen the brief if the point falls within Category 1, above. One or two sentences with relevant citations should suffice. If the point fits into Category 2, do not waste effort on justifying the controlling rule.

---

1. For a further discussion on how to craft a theme and for examples of themes, please see Chapter Thirteen.

2. Benjamin N. Cardozo, The Nature of the Judicial Process 164 (1921).

National Institute for Trial Advocacy

Concentrate only on the conflict, the application of the rule to the facts. If the point comes within Category 3, it is necessary first to identify the flashpoint of the conflict. Here, too, there are three subcategories:

a) *Finding the law.* Here, you must choose among competing legal precepts to determine which should control. This requires the deepest development in the brief, because after you choose among the competing precepts, you must also interpret that precept.

b) *Interpreting the law.* Here, there is no dispute about which competing precept controls, but only the question of interpreting what has been chosen. This arises most frequently in statutory construction. If the conflict falls within this category, do not discuss choice of other precepts; discuss only interpretation of the law. You then apply the facts to your interpretation.

c) *Application of the law to the facts.* Here, you need only discuss the application of the precept—as chosen and interpreted—to the facts as found by the fact-finder.

10.2.1 Examples from the Briefs

The Choice: Finding the Law

This appeal requires Pennsylvania to decide the question of whether injury to an allegedly defective product itself is compensable in tort. The majority rule, set forth in *Seeley v. White Motor Co.*, 63 Cal.2d 9, 403 P.2d 145, 45 Cal. Rptr. 17 (1965), seeks to preserve a proper role for the law of warranty by precluding tort liability if a defective product injures only itself, causing economic loss. The decision in *Santor v. A & M Kargheusian, Inc.*, 44 N.J. 52, 207 A.2d 305 (1965), embodies the minority approach. That case held that a manufacturer's duty to make nondefective products encompasses injury to the product itself, whether the defect creates an unreasonable risk of harm. For the reasons that follow we ask this court to adopt the majority rule.

———————————

This court must decide whether the captain of a merchant ship violated applicable maritime law when he buried at sea a seaman who died of a heart attack on the return trip of the vessel eight days from its next port-of-call. After seaman James Floyd died, the captain conducted a burial-at-sea ritual. Maria Floyd, the seaman's daughter, for herself, as executrix of her father's estate, and for the next-of-kin, sued the vessel's owner for improperly disposing of her father's body. The district court granted summary judgment in favor of Lykes Bros. Steamship Company. Maria Floyd has appealed. This court should affirm.

Appellant contends that state tort law has established that the spouse or next-of-kin is entitled to possession of a body for the purpose of arranging for final disposition of the remains, *see, e.g., Blanchard v. Brawley,* 75 So. 2d 891, 893 (La. Ct. App.1954), and that violation of the right of possession and burial is an actionable tort. See, e.g., *Papieves v. Lawrence,* 437 Pa. 373, 263 A.2d 118, 120 (1970). She argues that this state law tort precept should be incorporated into general maritime law. She says that currently recognized maritime authority deems burial at sea anachronistic and improper when the next-of-kin are not notified in advance.

We respond that this case is not governed by state tort concepts, but by federal maritime law. Relying on *Brambir v. Cunard White Star, Ltd.,* 37 F. Supp. 906 (S.D.N.Y. 1940), *aff'd mem.,* 119 F.2d 419 (2d Cir. 1941), we ask this court to hold that maritime law does not provide a cause of action for burial at sea.

Interpreting the Law

Appellants are two coal producing companies requesting this court to reverse the grant of summary judgment in favor of the government. This is a case of statutory construction that requires an interpretation of the expression "coal produced by surface mining" under the Surface Mining Control and Reclamation Act, 30 U.S.C. § 1201-1328.

This is not a mere semantic exercise, because your decision will determine the extent of tonnage upon which a reclamation fee of 35 cents per ton may be levied by the Secretary of the Interior. The government argued, and the district court found, that tonnage of "coal produced" includes the weight of rock, clay, dirt and other debris mined with the "coal" that was delivered by the companies to a coal washing and sizing plant. We borrow from Gertrude Stein's "a rose is a rose is a rose" and argue that coal is coal and it means a mineral that is combustible. Accordingly, we ask this court to conclude that the district court erred in determining that all the material mined by appellants was subject to the reclamation fee, and that under a proper interpretation of the statute, "coal produced" means only the mineral coal and does not include rock, clay, dirt, and other debris that was excavated with the coal.

The major question for decision is one of first impression in the United States Courts of Appeals. This court must decide whether a claim deemed filed in a chapter 11 (reorganization) proceeding remains effective when the debtor converts the chapter 11 case into one under chapter 7 (liquidation). The issue requires that the court construe relevant statutes and the rules of practice and procedure in bankruptcy. The bankruptcy judge, 43 B.R. 937, and, after appeal, the district court, 52 B.R. 960, held that listing the claim on the debtor's schedule, which was filed under chapter 11, did not preserve the claim under chapter 7. We ask this court to reverse.

The principal issue presented for decision is whether a private cause of action for damages against corporate directors is to be implied in favor of a corporate stockholder under 18 U.S.C. § 610, a criminal statute prohibiting corporations from making "a contribution or expenditure in connection with any election at which Presidential and Vice Presidential electors . . . are to be voted for." We ask this court to conclude that implication of such a federal cause of action is not suggested by the legislative context of Section 610 or required to accomplish Congress's purposes in enacting the statute. This court should hold, therefore, that it has no occasion to address the questions whether Section 610, properly construed, proscribes the expenditures alleged in this case, or whether the statute is unconstitutional as violative of the First Amendment or of the equal protection component of the Due Process Clause of the Fifth Amendment.

Applying the Law to the Facts

The major question for decision raised by these two appeals from a judgment in favor of plaintiff in a diversity action brought under Pennsylvania law is the extent to which delay damages may be awarded under Rule 238, Pa. R. Civ. P. Here, defendant obtained a directed verdict at the close of the first trial, but, after a retrial was ordered by this court, ultimately lost on the merits. Because defendant lost and because he never made a settlement offer, plaintiff was awarded Rule 238 delay damages totaling $247,500. This award included damages for the time the case was on appeal from the directed verdict, but, because of plaintiff's mathematical miscalculation, did not include damages for the 17 days immediately preceding the final verdict.

The defendant, at No. 82-5711, argues that the delay damages award was excessive. As appellant, the plaintiff below, appeals at No. 82-5836, contends that the delay damages were insufficient and we ask this court to so hold.

This appeal requires the court to decide whether Blue Shield's prepaid dental service program in Pennsylvania violates the antitrust laws. Several Pennsylvania dental associations and individual dentists appeal from a summary judgment dismissing their antitrust and state law claims brought against the Medical Service Association of Pennsylvania, doing business as Pennsylvania Blue Shield. Appellants argue that Blue Shield engaged in a price-fixing conspiracy and a group boycott in violation of § 1 of the Sherman Act, 15 U.S.C. § 1, attempted to monopolize and monopolized in violation of § 2 of the Act, 15 U.S.C. § 2, and that the district court abused its discretion in refusing to certify a subclass of cooperating dentists for treble damages purposes. This court should conclude that appellants' contentions are without merit, and affirm the judgment of the district court.

10.3   Structuring the Argument

In your first-year legal writing class, you probably learned some method for legal writing that went by an acronym such as IRAC, CRAC, or TRRAC.[3] Although these approaches differ some in the substance of what they require, they also share many common themes, including organizational approaches on how to present your argument.[4] Tracy Turner, the Director of Legal Analysis, Writing, and Skills at Southwestern Law School, has identified four core principles that the different writing acronyms have in common. Regardless of the acronym model that you employ in writing your brief, following these core principles will strengthen the persuasive quality of your brief.

"Rule-centered analysis."[5] Legal writing should be centered around a set of rules that must be explained before they are applied.[6] This makes logical sense—you cannot apply rules that you have not set out clearly. In setting out the rule you must identify the precise jurisprudential flashpoint of conflict between the parties—choice of law, interpretation of the law, or application of the precept to facts found by the fact-finder. Confine your discussion to this conflict. Do not wander or overwrite.

"Separating the analyses of discrete issues."[7] Your discussion of each issue should be separated into its own IRAC or similar analytical structure. Within a larger issue you may need further subdivision, or subheadings, with additional rules and application discussion.[8] These subdivisions are designed to support the point and they, too, should be compartmentalized. Your headings and subheadings must be full enough and clear enough so the court can understand them. If the judges cannot understand

---

3. *See* Tracy Turner, *Finding Consensus in Legal Writing Discourse Regarding Organization Structure: A Review and Analysis of the Use of IRAC and Its Progenies*, 9 LEGAL COMMUNICATION & RHETORIC 351, 353 n.6, 357–58 (2012) (IRAC stands for Issue, Rule, Application, Conclusion; CRAC stands for Conclusion, Rule, Application, Conclusion; TRRAC stands for Thesis, Rule, Rule, Application, Conclusion).
    4. *Id.* at 359.
    5. *Id.* at 356.
    6. *Id.* at 356–60.
    7. *Id.* at 360.
    8. *See id.* at 361.

National Institute for Trial Advocacy

your argument, they cannot be persuaded by it. Your headings and subheadings must be convincing enough to make the court want to accept them. Do not wander, ramble, or digress. Do not get unglued and meander. Think logically and write logically. Make your point and then move to another. In separating out the discrete issues, you must also decide whether the several issues chosen by you are independent of each other or are interrelated. You must decide whether the major premise of a subsequent issue is dependent upon the conclusion reached in the prior issue. Understand this, so you will not be surprised when a judge recognizes it at oral argument.

The ideal brief is where two or more of the issues are completely independent of each other. It is ideal because the court may completely reject one issue, but nevertheless rule in your favor on the basis of another. It is ideal because you have alternative, independent reasons supporting your submission. In other cases, you do not have the luxury of alternative choices. Instead, you have arguments that are dependent upon resolution of preceding arguments. If your brief is one that consists of interdependent points, explain that if the court accepts a preceding one, the subsequent ones must logically follow. Where one point is controlling, explain that the court need not meet the ones that follow.

Judge Aldisert once asked a lawyer who was in the process of completing his year of clerkship with another federal circuit judge to give him his "pet peeve" after reading a year of briefs. His response:

> The major flaw I've seen in the briefs submitted to this court is that the writers don't tie the issues together. Frequently, the viability of one discrete issue turns on the merits of another issue. This may require nothing more than an "if the court finds in our favor on this issue, then the remaining two issues are moot; otherwise these remaining issues must be addressed." Often, the relationship among issues is a positive point that should be explained to the appellate court: if a positive result on Issue A logically necessitates a similar result on Issue B, the advocate should point out this relationship to the appellate court. Any logical paradigm that can make the court's job easier should be highlighted by the advocate.

"Synthesis of the law."[9] A brief is not a collection of case summaries. Rather, the role of the brief-writer is to "synthesize legal principles pulled from multiple sources of law."[10] Professor Turner's review of legal writing textbooks found that many of them recommend organizing the discussion of the law into paragraphs that start with "a topic or thesis sentence that states a contention about the law rather than with a sentence that starts, 'In Case A . . . . '"[11] As Professor Turner explains, "[b]y identifying key legal principles in the topic sentences and then focusing the discussion of case examples on illustrating these principles, the writer synthesizes the case law for the

---

9. *Id.* at 362.
10. *Id.*
11. *Id.*

reader rather than present a list of case summaries that the reader must cull on her own."[12] Consider this example:

> The experience of other prisons is relevant *a fortiori* under RLUIPA's [Religious Land Use and Institutionalized Persons Act] standard of compelling interest and least restrictive means. Most courts of appeals applying RLUIPA require prison officials to explain why solutions that work in other jurisdictions would not work in theirs. Thus, in *Garner v. Kennedy*, 713 F.3d 237, 247 (5th Cir. 2013), the court found it "persuasive that prison systems that are comparable in size to Texas's—California and the Federal Bureau of Prisons—allow their inmates to grow beards, and there is no evidence of any specific incidents affecting prison safety in those systems due to beards." Similarly, in *Warsoldier v. Woodford*, 418 F.3d 989, 999 (9th Cir. 2005), where a Native American prisoner sought a religious exemption from restrictions on long hair, the court found no compelling interest, in part because "[p]risons run by the federal government, Oregon, Colorado, and Nevada all meet the same penological goals without such a policy."[13]

The first sentence sets out the topic—applying RLUIPA's compelling interest and least restrictive means standard. The rest of the paragraph gives examples from two cases, with only the necessary details related to the topic provided for comparison. The same format is seen in this example:

> Where a public employee is fired due to a supervisor's misperception of what the employee said or did, it is the supervisor's perception that matters. In *Waters v. Churchill*, 511 U.S. 661 (1994), for example, the supervisor thought the employee was "knocking the department" and saying "what a bad place [it was] to work." *Id.* at 665. The employee insisted she had said nothing of the kind, and had merely expressed an opinion about staffing policies. *Id.* at 666. The question in *Waters* was whether a court should apply the First Amendment standard "to the speech as the government employer found it to be, or should it ask the jury to determine the facts for itself?" *Id.* at 668. A plurality of four Justices held that the constitutionality of a retaliatory employment decision should be evaluated based on what the employer "really did believe," rather than on what the employee actually said. *Id.* at 679–80. Three Justices concurring in the judgment agreed that it is the employer's perception that matters; they disagreed only with the plurality's view as to the sort of investigation the employer must undertake. *Id.* at 686 (Scalia, J., concurring in the judgment).[14]

---

12. *Id.* at 363.

13. Brief for Petitioner at 22, Holt v. Hobbs, 135 S. Ct. 853 (2015) (No. 13-6827).

14. Brief for Petitioner at 14–15, Heffernan v. City of Paterson, 136 S. Ct. 1412 (2016) (No. 14-1280).

Once again, the discussion of the relevant case law is limited to what the judge needs to know to resolve the issue at hand. Rather than making the judge try and guess what is important about the *Waters* case, the brief-writer used the topic sentence and abbreviated description of the case to direct the reader to the most important parts.

"Unity." [15] The need to create a "unified document" is the final core principle that the various analytical structures share in common. Brief-writers should use transition sentences to "tie the components of the analysis together" and roadmaps to provide the reader with direction. [16]

10.4 Considering the Consequences of Your Analysis

The analysis of the law set forth in your brief does not operate in a vacuum. The immediate objective of an appellate advocate is limited—to persuade the court to accept the conclusion supported by the argument. The means you employ, however, must far transcend your immediate objective. The court has an obligation that goes far beyond considering the specific demands of the parties before the court. There must also be fidelity to what has been decided in the past as a guide to setting the course for the future. The brief-writer must realize at the outset that the submission always will be tested by judges in terms of the institutional or precedential consequences of that urged upon the court.

You must remember what your law school professor did to you after you recited the case in your first-year contracts course. The professor worked you over—exposed you in front of all your classmates. The ogre did this by offering a hypothetical in which the facts were changed somewhat (a little or a lot) and inquired whether the added or subtracted facts would make a difference in the result. Many of you breathed the proverbial sigh of relief when you received your J.D. degree and left the Socratic tyranny of the classroom. But I have news for you: the agony continues. Appellate judges pick up where the professors left off. Only this time, if you are not prepared, it is not a question of classroom embarrassment. If you are not prepared, your client is the potential loser. And if your client loses a substantial number of times, you end up losing the client. Appellate judges follow the Socratic method in evaluating every brief you write and every oral argument you present.

Judges require lawyers to evaluate resemblances and differences in the fact patterns of the compared cases, and these are constantly tossed about in a sea of analogies. They do this to decide whether the particular rationale supporting your submission can legitimately support the same result in other fact patterns, and if so, why. They do this because judges always must consider the consequences of every decision. Judges constantly inquire whether the lawyer has seriously considered the ramifications of

---

15. *Turner*, at 363.
16. *Id.*

extending or contracting the law in a given field. At work always is the jurisprudential equivalent of Immanuel Kant's categorical imperative: "Act as if the maxim of your action were to become through your will a universal law of nature."[17]

A point Judge Aldisert made, which we leave despite that there are reasons to dispute at least some of his analysis, is that modern adjudication demands more than strict adherence to the common law tradition. Because of the precise nature of today's litigation, judges must now cautiously and carefully consider—especially in the dynamic fields of criminal law, tort law, and constitutional law—exactly what social, economic, or political consequences will follow from their decision. Consider, for example, the emphasis on drinking and driving, treble damages under RICO and antitrust, employer discrimination, products liability, professional malpractice, or new concepts by which pecuniary loss or punitive damages are allocated. In the allocation of pecuniary loss, the pendulum now swings in favor of the injured and away from traditional property rights. These views, light years away from "lawyer's law" of another era, require judges to consider consequential concerns in varying degrees when evaluating an issue.

Lawyers must always recognize that for a judge, in a given case, to choose among possible competing rulings means, among other things, to choose which will best serve to create a model for human conduct in our society. For example, on the one hand, manufacturers should take reasonable care in preparing and packaging consumer goods and should be made liable for damages to anyone injured by their failure in that respect; on the other hand, the law does not require them to take such care and does not make them liable for failure to do so. To take that disjunction seriously as posing a real choice in a real society, the judge must then ask what the difference is.

The answer must be that the difference is determined, borrowing from Professor Neil MacCormick, by the three Cs: the different *consequences* that would follow from actually adopting and applying one or the other of these rival suggestions; the requirement that the choice be *consistent* with some valid and binding rule of the system; and the notion that it be *coherent* in the sense that it is a sound and sensible, just or desirable norm for the guidance of appeals.[18]

No bright-line rules are available to predict how a multi-judge court will consider the consequences of your analysis. The process is intrinsically evaluative. You must inquire about the acceptability or unacceptability of consequences, and this requires at a minimum that you have thoroughly researched the jurisprudential idiosyncrasies of the members of the court before whom you are appearing. *Know the court in general. Know the panel that will be reading your briefs.* It is not enough that you have a case written by a distinguished judge from another jurisdiction or from another circuit. It is not enough that you have a case written by a long-gone judge of the court.

---

17. Immanuel Kant, Groundwork of the Metaphysics of Morals 89 (Paton trans. 1964).
18. Sir Neil MacCormick, Legal Reasoning and Legal Theory 129, 152, 195 (1978).

Find out how the judges react to the controlling general principles involved in your case. Do your homework. Study the court and see what makes it tick. With the availability of computerized legal research, you can ascertain how individual judges react to definite and particular concepts. Read their opinions with the view of learning how they approach cases. For example, do they consider themselves bound by precedent or do they perceive the court as an instrument of social change?

To comprehend and assimilate ingredients that make up the judicial philosophies of appellate judges today does not require that you research generations of judges. For example, the active judges on the U.S. Courts of Appeals have not been in office for many years. To examine the philosophical idiosyncrasies of the majority of the judges who will decide your case does not require you to research past generations of judges on that court.

No trial lawyer worth his salt will appear before a trial judge cold. The legal profession in a given community has a "book" on every trial judge. The "book" is not always written, although some large litigating firms may have reduced comments to writing. Rather, it is the sum total of impressions by lawyers who have appeared before the judges. How does the judge rule on evidence questions or react to opening and closing statements? How far afield can I go in cross-examination? In personal injuries cases is the particular judge plaintiff-oriented or defendant-oriented? What about sidebar conferences? Suggested jury instructions? Trial memoranda (or must we sell the law clerk)? Are we chained to the counsel table or the lectern, or may we wander around the room when we ask questions?

How much an appellate lawyer can learn in advance about the panel that will decide an appeal will vary. For example, some federal circuit courts give very little notice of which judges will hear a case. In that case, at a minimum, you must still know the key case law from that jurisdiction. When there is sufficient notice, though, research the panel. Has any of the judges written a relevant law review article? In opinions on this subject do any of the judges quote any commentators? How does each judge treat precedent? Do you detect any particular approach to statutory construction? Do they like references to legislative history? Are they quick to find an abuse of discretion? How do they regard the court—as a strict tribunal for deciding narrowly only the issue before it, or as an instrument for social change?

The brief-writer must always must focus his vision on the court before which he is appearing. As the late Wisconsin Supreme Court Justice William A. Bablitch advised brief-writers: "Your vision is to your client, ours must be to how our decision will affect others in the future." For this reason, he cautioned:

> Be aware of our institutional function. Our decisions must provide predictable remedies for the rational resolution of problems that arise in

future social and economic life. We paint on a large canvas. We are concerned, first and foremost, with the effect of our decision on the state of the law, not on your client.[19]

There is no reason, however, to assume that the process of determining how the court reacts to consequences involves evaluation in terms of a single scale. Sometimes, when lawyers present the case for and against given rulings, they characteristically refer to certain criteria as "justice," "common sense," "public policy," "convenience," or "expediency." To the extent that these criteria are defined and explained in their application to the argument, they serve a useful purpose. To the extent that they are used only as buzzwords, they may not be very effective.

For a decision to be influenced by consequential factors, the brief must first respond to the rules of inductive or deductive logic, as discussed in Chapter Eleven. But not all decisions are governed by relentless rules of logic.

Set forth the rationale in your brief and explain your value-based choice, but do not dwell for long in the murky waters of subjectively defined buzzwords. Remember Humpty Dumpty, who proclaimed that any word he used "'means just what I choose it to mean—neither more nor less.'"[20] We all know what happened to that hubristic egghead.

Judges who evaluate consequences of rulings of other courts give different weight to different criteria. Not surprisingly, we do not agree as to what degree of either perceived injustice or predicted inconvenience will arise from the adoption or rejection of a given ruling. Sometimes we differ sharply and even passionately as to the acceptability of a ruling under scrutiny. At this level, there can simply be irresoluble differences of opinion—hence, the necessity of a multi-judge court as a reviewing tribunal, one that applies thorough ratiocination in its elaboration of reasons.

10.5 The Requirement of Consistency and Coherence

What institutional device do we have to keep the brakes on free-wheeling concepts of what are desirable consequences? Fortunately, the system does provide such a device. Just as fortunately, this goes to the heart of the common law tradition. Appellate decisions always should be congruent with and not antagonistic to some valid and binding rule of the system. Judges should respect at all times the notion of consistency.

We are no longer in the year 1215, when the barons forced King John to issue the Magna Carta at Runnymede, marking the start of the common law tradition in England. Our own country has a tradition that goes back more than two centuries,

---

19. William A. Bablitch, *Writing to Win*, COMPLEAT LAW., Winter 1988, at 12.

20. LEWIS CARROLL, THROUGH THE LOOKING GLASS, *reprinted in* ALICE'S ADVENTURES IN WONDERLAND & THROUGH THE LOOKING GLASS, 125, 205 (Wordsworth Classics, 1993).

originating in an era when we had already absorbed further centuries of the English common law experience with cases, recorded at least since the days of Sir Edward Coke and, later, Sir William Blackstone. Our nation's oldest appellate tribunal, the Pennsylvania Supreme Court, has been handing down recorded decisions since 1686. We have a long history of judicial experience to ensure consistency.

Justice William O. Douglas noted the reservoir of authority to aid decisions in hard cases: "There are usually plenty of precedents to go around; and with the accumulation of decisions, it is no great problem for the lawyer to find legal authority for most propositions."[21] As discussed in Chapter Seven, the tradition of *stare decisis* places the judge under an obligation to follow prior judicial decisions unless exceptional circumstances are present.[22]

Adherence to the tenet of consistency keeps the march of the law at a measured cadence. The point riders can go just so far; the outriders must keep close to the flanks; and the drags must not fall too far behind.

In his discourse on *The Seven Sins of Appellate Brief Writing and Other Transgressions*, United States Circuit Judge Harry Pregerson says that the first sin is "Long, Boring Briefs" but a close second is "Incoherent, Unfocused, and Disorganized Briefs."

> Inconsistency is an aggravated form of incoherence. In one recent case, counsel insisted that the crucial term in the statute before us had a plain and unambiguous meaning and then attempted to support that claim by citing a half-dozen cases, each of which defined the term differently.
>
> To avoid incoherence, you should ask someone unfamiliar with the matter to read your brief carefully for consistency, clarity, and logic. Such an independent reader can point out areas that are confusing and may make the difference between an intelligible brief and an incoherent one.[23]

We must also consider coherence, a concept closely related to, but in several senses somewhat different from, consistency. As Judge Pregerson formulates it, inconsistency may be considered as an aggravated form of incoherence. Yet an action may be consistent without being coherent. It may be consistent in the sense of establishing a set of norms that do not contradict one another, but at the same time, the action may pursue no just or desirable value or policy.

Thus, it can be said that "coherent" means to be connected naturally or logically as by a common principle. The child who constantly lies to his parents is certainly consistent, but there is a question as to whether the conduct follows any tenet of coherence.

---

21. William O. Douglas, *Stare Decisis*, 49 COLUM. L. REV. 735, 736 (1949).

22. In a small percentage of cases, no legal principles exist for guidance. These cases require the court to examine some justificatory principle of morality, justice, and social policy. *See* RUGGERO J. ALDISERT, THE JUDICIAL PROCESS: READINGS, MATERIALS AND CASES (2d ed. 1996).

23. Harry Pregerson, *The Seven Sins of Appellate Brief Writing and Other Transgressions*, 34 UCLA L. REV. 431, 434–35 (1986).

10.6 Standards of Review

Standards of review have already been covered in detail in Chapter Five. Keep in mind the different standards of review that apply to appeals where it is alleged that a judge or hearing tribunal 1) made findings of fact which are clearly erroneous, 2) improperly exercised discretion, or 3) committed legal error. Incorporate the proper standard of review in the topic sentence(s) introducing each point. You have already stated the various standards of review with the necessary citations, preferably from the appellate court before whom you now appear. At this point, it is not necessary to repeat the legal authority for the standard. You simply state the standard in a clear declaratory sentence: "The trial court's findings of fact are erroneous in that . . . ," "The trial court erred as a matter of law in awarding summary judgment because . . . ," or "The trial court abused its discretion in . . . ."

10.7 The Experts Speak

10.7.1 *Circuit Court Judges*

Circuit court judges express their thoughts on the makings of a good brief.

Michael Boudin *Senior Judge, First Circuit*	In brief writing, my aim was always to write a brief that was as close as to how a reasonable opinion on the issue might look while still coming out my way.
Sandra L. Lynch *Judge, First Circuit*	What I liked most was when a good brief dealt fairly with its opponents' arguments and afforded me with an outline from which I could draft an opinion; the briefs I disliked the most (other than dishonest or utterly incompetent ones, of which there are too many) were those which substituted rhetoric for reasoning.
Dennis Jacobs *Judge, Second Circuit*	The best briefs use the various sections wisely. The statement of issues should be sufficiently abstract so that a knowledge of the facts is unneeded. The preliminary material should tell the reader what needs to be known before reading the facts, so that the reader knows the issue on which the facts have bearing. The facts should omit the details that bear on principles that will be set out in the points of the argument, so that the specifically relevant frustrated by fact overload at the outset; the beginning and the conclusion should say what you want.
Gregg J. Costa *Judge, Fifth Circuit*	Good briefs acknowledge and try to counter opposing arguments and authority; for complex areas of law (bankruptcy, IP, immigration) they explain how the particular issue raised in the appeal fits into that body of the law; they also anticipate how the decision in this case could affect similar cases and providing limiting principles or a governing standard.

Jerry E. Smith
Judge, Fifth Circuit

[Good briefs] spend[] more words on the important issues; giving a detailed roadmap for exactly what relief the party seeks on appeal.

David F. Hamilton
Judge, Seventh Circuit

[Good briefs] keep in mind the applicable standard of review, both for the pending case and for the key cases being cited.

They keep in mind the perspective of the appellate court, which is responsible for the overall accuracy, fairness, and consistency of the law in the circuit, beyond the concerns of the lawyers' clients in the particular case.

Ilana Diamond Rovner
Judge, Seventh Circuit

Most briefs are unnecessarily lengthy and repetitive. Briefs often cite cases without explaining how the cases support the party's position. Brief writers sometimes misrepresent the facts, or even worse, the law. Too often, the appellant's brief and the appellee's brief read as though they are talking about entirely different cases. Brief writers who fail to come to terms with the weaknesses in their cases allow their opponent to exploit those weaknesses. Reply briefs are often repetitious of the opening brief rather than actual replies to the responsive brief.

Good briefs begin by telling a coherent story, describing the problem, and then explaining how the law supports the party's position. Good briefs are also careful to acknowledge what the district court did and did not hold and to acknowledge the degree of deference we owe to the district court's decision.

Carlos T. Bea
Judge, Ninth Circuit

A brief should start with an introduction to get the judge into the case. It should recite (1) the kind of case it is—"this is a habeas appeal of a state court murder conviction"—that (2) states the principal claim(s) on appeal—"because of race-based peremptory juror challenges" and (3) the legal grounds for the claim—"account the state court failed to perform a comparative juror analysis to show the prosecutor's purported reason for the challenge(s) were pretextual." That kind of an introduction focuses the reader to get into the historical and procedural facts.

Richard R. Clifton
Judge, Ninth Circuit

They are too long. Judges are human, too, and attention spans are finite. Most lawyers don't appreciate the volume of reading that judges have to do. I confess that when I was a lawyer writing briefs, I didn't think about that. But now that I'm on the other side of the bench, I have learned that a brief that is concise and to the point has more impact than briefs that seem to end only because they hit the limit. Even briefs that are well under the limit are rarely as focused as they could be. With the advent of word processing, the motivation to edit out unnecessary repetition and digressions has waned and the temptation to start writing before thinking the arguments through has grown. Both developments are unfortunate. Think first, and edit ruthlessly.

Bobby R. Baldock
Senior Judge, Tenth Circuit

You really are shooting yourself in the foot by not streamlining your briefs. I don't want to read *War and Peace*.

Harris L. Hartz
Judge, Tenth Circuit

The most important thing in a brief is clarity. If an argument makes no sense to the court, it will not prevail. When the case involves an area of the law that is not a staple of the appellate court's diet (search-and-seizure law is a staple; the Fair Labor Standards Act is not), the brief needs to "remind" the court of the basic principles in that area. The best briefs confront candidly the harmful evidence and law and explain why the party should nevertheless prevail.

Carlos F. Lucero
Judge, Tenth Circuit

Attorneys should avoid briefs that are too long at all costs. I detest briefs that are sixty-four pages where every word-counting rule has been bent. Avoid repetition in briefs. Avoid long string cites. And, for oral argument, I would say this: take a look at the work of typical circuit judges across America. Typically, we'll hear twenty-four cases in one week of oral argument—six cases a day for four days. If the appellant's brief is fifty pages, the response is always fifty pages, and the reply is twenty-five. That's 125 pages of reading on that case. Multiply that by six and that equals 750 pages. Multiply that by four and you are now approaching 3,000 pages of reading.

Robin S. Rosenbaum
Judge, Eleventh Circuit

To me, the worst thing that a lawyer can do in a brief is to cite cases for propositions that they simply do not support or to falsely state the record. When I see that, I conclude that I cannot rely on anything in the brief. I am similarly not a fan of briefs that do not cite controlling law.

Patricia M. Wald
Chief Judge Emeritus, D.C. Circuit

The more paper you throw at us, the meaner we get, the more irritated and hostile we feel about verbosity, peripheral arguments, and long footnotes. In my [many] years on the court we have by judicial fiat first shortened main briefs from seventy to fifty pages, then put a limit of 12,500 on the number of words that can go in the brief, and in complex, multi-party cases our staff counsel threaten and plead (we get into the act ourselves sometimes) with co-counsel to file joint or at least nonrepetitive briefs. It's my view that we can, should, and will do more to stem the paper tidal wave. Repetition, extraneous facts, over-long arguments (by the twentieth page, we are muttering to ourselves, "I get it, I get it. No more, for God's sake.") still occur more often than capable counsel should tolerate. In our court, counsel get extra points for briefs they bring in under the fifty-page limit. Many judges look first to see how long a document is before reading a word. If it is long, they automatically read fast; if short, they read slower. Figure out yourself which is better for your case. Our politicians speak often of judicial restraint; I say let it begin with the lawyers whose grist feeds our opinion mills.

10.7.2   *State Court Justices and Lawyers*

State court justices and lawyers share their thoughts on good briefs.

Rita B. Garman
Justice, Illinois Supreme Court

[The following are critiques of briefs:]
Raising issues that were not raised below, without any attempt to explain why the forfeiture rule should not apply. In criminal cases, this would include arguing plain error or ineffective assistance of counsel.

Failing to provide the standard of review for each issue and, when the standard is abuse of discretion, failure to make an effective argument that the trial court did, indeed, abuse its discretion.

Citing a case based on the content of a headnote, without actually reading the case and determining whether it supports your position.

Citing a case to argue that it is factually similar to or readily distinguishable from the present case, without providing sufficient factual detail of the cited case so that the reader can understand the comparison.

Bill Cunningham
Justice, Supreme Court of Kentucky

[Briefs are] [t]oo long, which leads to them repeating themselves. They don't understand that they don't have to string it out to the maximum allowed pages.

Sabrina McKenna
Associate Justice, Supreme Court of Hawai'i

Focus on strong arguments; don't throw in the kitchen sink, as this weakens the strong points. Get to the point. Clear, terse writing, not rambling sentences.

Michael G. Heavican
Chief Justice, Nebraska Supreme Court

Briefs that misstate either the law or the individual facts of a case [irritate]. It is one thing to frame law or facts to your advantage, but being intentionally misleading is an entirely different thing.

In an appellee's brief, not addressing all of the appellant's assignments of error/issues, or disposing on a threshold matter (jurisdiction, for example) but not also addressing the merits.

Thomas G. Saylor
Chief Justice, Supreme Court of Pennsylvania

I have seen many very good briefs, but I have observed some containing excessive wordiness, unnecessary legalese, digressions into irrelevant detail, obfuscation, and occasionally even trickery. Such pitfalls obviously are to be avoided.

Sharon Keller
Presiding Judge, Texas Court of Criminal Appeals

Good briefs let the reader know at the outset what the legal issue is and what the party's argument is. It answers arguments from the other side. It offers a logical progression to its ultimate conclusion.

Nathan L. Hecht
Chief Justice, Texas Supreme Court

Many briefs read like a murder mystery—you don't really understand what happened till the last page. If your position is not compelling enough to lead with, it may not be compelling enough to win. [Another critique of briefs is] [e]xaggeration. The-heavens-are-falling arguments are rarely taken seriously. If a party thinks he must exaggerate to win, maybe that's because he knows he shouldn't. Resist every urge to take pot shots at the other side.

Sarah B. Duncan
Chief Justice, Fourth Court of Appeals (Texas)

The secret ingredient of a good legal argument is the flow—that is, an argument which proceeds like the current of a stream naturally, uninterrupted, and logically from beginning to end. It is important that the appellate court be swept along by the current; that it understand every logical step along the way and arrive with the litigant at the ultimate point of concluding in the same frame of mind.

Howard J. Bashman, Esq.
Law Offices of Howard J. Bashman, Willow Grove, PA

Appellate judges are incredibly overworked. They are forced to read approximately one thousand pages of text to prepare for a single day of oral argument. If your brief is unnecessarily long and complicated, it may not get read completely, it may not get read carefully, or worse, it may not be understood. Moreover, most appellate judges are generalists, not specialists. They do not have an expert's understanding of every substantive area of the law. Nor, of course, do appellate law clerks, who usually arrive at that job fresh from law school.

Even the most complex factual and legal concepts can be made easy to understand if presented properly to the reader. My advice is not to avoid complexity; instead, make complicated concepts understandable to someone who may be confronting the matter for the first time.

Before I file an appellate brief that I have drafted, I ask another lawyer in my office who has had no prior involvement in the case to read it over and let me know whether he finds it understandable and persuasive. Unless someone who knows nothing about your case can understand and be persuaded by your appellate brief, the document is worthless

Chapter Eleven

The Brief: The Required Logical Form for Each Issue

11.1   Introduction to Formal Argument

What we have set forth so far in previous chapters is but prologue. You have one ultimate goal: to convince the court to accept your conclusion. The conclusion in a brief is not just the major thing; it is the only thing. The purpose of the brief's contents that precede the conclusion—statements of jurisdiction, standards of review, issues, facts, and the argument—is to set the stage for logical premises to justify the suggested conclusion. Failure to master the formalities of the preceding topics might ruin your chances of success, but mastering them is not enough to achieve your goal. We now address the most essential aspect of your brief: effective discussion of the issues.

A judge's choice, interpretation, and application of a legal precept involve value judgments justifiable only when he is convinced that the decision is *reasonable*.[1] What one judge considers "reasonable" in a given set of circumstances may differ greatly from what an outside observer, the attorneys, or even another judge believes is reasonable. Such differences of opinion may arise from differing beliefs as to whether the law should be maintained in harmony with existing precedents or considered pragmatically with respect to practical circumstances. They may arise from differing notions of what is fair, just, or sensible. The concept of what is reasonable, however, is not endlessly expansive or entirely unknowable. A reasonable conclusion is one that can be reached by *reason*—that is, by the application of rational processes to the universe of facts, rules, policies, principles, and values pertinent to the case at hand. No doubt, this allows for a plethora of possible outcomes, and judgment must come into play. Nevertheless, the broadest possible conception of what is reasonable is limited to what is *rational*.

Thus, you need to "rationalize" your conclusion so the judge can accept it as "reasonable." Therefore, the crux of your discussion of the issues will almost always consist of formal logical arguments. If the process whereby you have reached your

---

1. Aylett v. Sec'y of Hous. & Urban Dev., 54 F. 3d 1560, 1567 (10th Cir. 1995).

conclusion cannot be traced or fails to adequately support the truth of your conclusion, your argument will not be persuasive. This is where formal logic comes to the rescue. In formal logic, the word "argument" has a specific meaning. An argument is not a dispute replete with vitriol, accusations, unsupported assertions, and appeals to emotion. As used in the logical disciplines, an argument is a group of propositions in which one proposition is claimed to follow from the others and the latter are treated as furnishing grounds or support for the truth of the former. Put more simply, it is a set of statements (called propositions or premises) that are related in such a way that they support the truth of another statement, the conclusion. This is also the how the term argument is principally used in the practice of law.

The study of logic is primarily concerned with these relationships. It identifies argument structures that guarantee the truth of the conclusion given the truth of the premises (valid arguments), structures that support the likelihood of the conclusion without guaranteeing it (strong arguments), common structural errors that destroy the sought-for guarantee of the conclusion's truth (formal fallacies), other conceptual errors that purport to support the conclusion but fail to do so (material, factual, or informal fallacies), and rules whereby one statement can be transformed into a logically equivalent statement. It also provides the basis for argument by analogy, which is crucial to effective brief writing. Of course, a good discussion of a legal issue might include rhetorical devices and policy appeals that may not superficially appear to conform to a formal logical structure; however, such tools are likely to be ineffective if they do not ultimately provide logical support for the conclusion. Thus, while one trained in the law must be more than a mere logician, it is critical that she be able to formulate, recognize, and verify logical arguments with confidence.

This is not to say that the terminology and each detail of what follows here in discussing the structures of logic must be mastered by the brief writer. Indeed, many if not most brief readers will not have done so. Yet the closer the arguments come to maintaining the logical relationships between premises and conclusions, the more likely it is that judges will move through the natural flow of the reasoning to the conclusion the writer wants.

The purpose of a brief is to persuade the court to accept the conclusion you present. The *conclusion* of an argument—usually set forth in the "*therefore*" statement declaring the precise relief sought in the brief—"is the *one* proposition that is arrived at and affirmed on the basis of the *other* propositions of the argument."[2] The brief writer should carefully draft these propositions (or premises) so that they support the desired conclusion and no other.[3]

---

2. Ruggero J. Aldisert, Logic for Lawyers: A Guide to Clear Legal Thinking 28 (3d ed. 1997) [emphasis original].

3. *Id.*

National Institute for Trial Advocacy

Reasoning is the process of drawing a conclusion from a series of propositions related "in such a way as to induce belief in what is suggested on the ground of a real relation . . . between what suggests and what is suggested."[4] Propositions suggest a conclusion when they are related in specific ways. Logicians have determined that in the abstract there are only a handful of such relations.[5] Generally speaking, these are sufficient to describe and analyze the world in which we live. The most complicated argument is nothing more than a series of simple logical operations that every one of us utilizes every single day without even being aware of it. For your purposes, the ability to win your case depends upon the power to see these relationships within and between cases, as well as to recognize when such relationships do not exist.

Logical reasoning follows patterns described by *syllogisms*. Understanding syllogisms will greatly enhance your ability to discern between good and bad arguments and use rules and analogous cases effectively. Ideally, your brief should be nothing more or less than an expanded categorical syllogism. We will discuss the syllogism more in a later section, but for now you should take comfort in the fact that following a syllogistic structure will simplify your analysis and, because the correctness of the conclusion will rely solely on the correctness of the premises, produce the most persuasive argument form. You should, therefore, employ formal deductive syllogisms in your brief writing wherever possible.

Finally, it is important to note that it is possible to reach a true, correct, or desirable conclusion via a logically flawed process.[6] If you learn nothing else about formal logic, understand that *validity and validity alone preserves truth*. A valid argument based on true premises guarantees a true conclusion; such an argument is known as a sound argument. Beyond that, nothing is certain. An invalid argument can produce the desired conclusion, but the purported inference leading to that conclusion will always be faulty. A valid argument applied to untrue premises can produce a true conclusion or a false one, but again the argument will be unsatisfactory because the premises do not properly support the conclusion. Inductive arguments, in which the major premise is a generalization inferred from multiple observations, involve likelihoods that we cannot rightly say are true or false. Knowing this will

---

4. John Dewey, How We Think: A Restatement of the Relation of Reflective Thinking to the Educative Process 12 (D.C. Heath & Co. 1933) (1910).

5. This is true in particular of the relations pertinent to deductive reasoning, which logicians have described completely via a few basic syllogisms and a very manageable set of rules of logical equivalence. Inductive reasoning is less formulaic, but still has only one object (to reach a conclusion that is likely true) and one method (enumeration). Argument by analogy is a type of inductive reasoning. While difficult to describe, argument by analogy nevertheless involves a limited number of concepts discussed at the end of this chapter.

6. In law, it is usually more grammatically appropriate to refer to a legal conclusion as "correct" than "true." For instance, it would be awkward to say "the trial court's holding that specific performance should be awarded was true," although this would not be wrong. However, rudimentary formal logic treats every statement as either true or false—in fact a sentence is a statement only if one of these truth values can be assigned to it. This chapter uses the terms "true" and "correct" interchangeably with respect to the context.

help you recognize the ways in which arguments go awry, thus enabling you to discriminate between good arguments and bad. After all, if you are going to argue that a conclusion is correct and adequately supported, you must affirm both the truth of the premises and the validity of the argument (in the case of inductive logic, you must affirm the *strength* of the argument). If you are going to argue that it is wrong, you must refute either the truth of one or more premises or the logic of the argument. Or if you are refuting an inductive argument, you could show that there are additional true premises, facts, or data that should have been considered and, if considered, would change the strength of the conclusion.

11.2 The Role of Brief Writing

The written brief always has played an important role in the American appellate court system. By contrast, the English appellate system relies entirely on oral argument.[7] Oral argument in an American appellate court is a fleeting moment; a written brief is a permanent formality. The court relies on the written brief prior to oral argument, in the decision-making process afterward, and in the post-argument decision-justifying process—the preparation of the opinion. In fact, most of the federal judges who responded to our survey on brief writing noted that the brief, particularly a well-written brief, played an "important," "critical," and even sometimes "dispositive" role in a case, particularly since oral argument is not always granted (or even requested) in appeals.

Moreover, the astronomical increase in appellate court caseloads has emphasized the importance of briefs and diminished the importance of oral arguments. Crushing caseloads have imposed severe restrictions on the time available for oral argument and the length of time allotted. From 1961 to 1987, for example, the total number of filings in the United States Courts of Appeals increased from 4,204 to 35,176, or 737 percent; and from 1987 to 2015, the increase was another 51 percent resulting in a current case load of 53,266.[8]

Notwithstanding many exhortations about the importance of oral argument, in today's appellate environment you must write to win. Do not depend solely on your powers of speech, regardless of how great they may be. Your hopes hang on the written argument; the oral argument is only a safety net.

11.3 Is Logic Really Important?

Oliver Wendell Holmes is often quoted for his famous statement:

---

7. For an excellent description of the English appellate system, see ROBERT J. MARTINEAU, APPELLATE JUSTICE IN ENGLAND AND THE UNITED STATES: A COMPARATIVE ANALYSIS (1990).

8. Admin. Office of the U.S. Courts, Table B-1. U.S. Courts of Appeals—Cases Commenced, Terminated, and Pending, by Circuit and Nature of Proceeding, During the 12-Month Period Ending December 31, 2015 (2016).

The life of the law has not been logic; it has been experience. The felt necessities of the time, the prevalent moral and political theories, intuitions of public policy, avowed or unconscious, even the prejudices which judges share with their fellow-men, have had good deal more to do than the syllogism in determining the rules by which men should be governed.[9]

Holmes was speaking in 1881 of only of a type of *deductive* logic that has fixed premises.[10] *Inductive* logic is perhaps even more liable to produce the sort of skepticism about the role of rule-based reasoning in the law displayed here by Holmes, the quintessential legal realist, than deductive logic. But you should not infer from this fact that, on the one hand, deductive reasoning requires inflexible adherence to outmoded rules, nor, on the other hand, that every development in the law has resulted from a judge's failure or refusal to apply logic, inductive or deductive. Neither type of logic precludes consideration of changed circumstances or theories, and a judge's worldview or judicial philosophy can color the most logical decision. It is worth emphasizing again that logic, the *process* of reasoning, should not be confused with truthfulness, accuracy, correctness, applicability, or fairness, which are *characteristics* of the argument's components. What you write in your brief will be measured by its persuasive power, and that power will be significantly enhanced by the force of your discussion's formal logic.

Although it can be said that formal logic is not an end purpose of law, it is one of the important means to the ends of law, perhaps the most important. Logical form and logical reasoning have never been subordinated in the judicial process. After twenty-three years on the Supreme Court, Justice Felix Frankfurter recognized both the preeminent virtue of logic in the law and its realistic limitations: "Fragile as reason is and limited as law is as the expression of the institutionalized medium of reason, that's all we have standing between us and the tyranny of mere will and the cruelty of unbridled, unprincipled, undisciplined feeling."[11] Reason as a process of

---

9. OLIVER WENDELL HOLMES & G. EDWARD WHITE, *Lecture I: Early Forms of Liability, in* THE COMMON LAW 1 (Dover Publications 1991) (1881).

10. Holmes's seemingly out-of-hand dismissal of logic's pertinence in law must be considered in the context of his message: an appeal that the law adjust to changing social conditions, that we should not be bound by rigid legal precepts that were once justified by good reasons but are no longer viable in a changing society. Logic has always played an essential role and that role has largely survived Holmesian skepticism; his overarching appeal, however, did not go unnoticed. Since Holmes's time, a substantial number of legal theorists and practitioners have adopted similar views. Professor Harry W. Jones of Columbia described a "good rule" this way: "A legal rule or a legal institution is a good rule or institution when—that is, to the extent that—it contributes to the establishment and preservation of a social environment in which the quality of human life can be spirited, improving and unimpaired." Harry W. Jones, *An Invitation to Jurisprudence*, 74 COLUM. L. REV. 1023, 1025 (1974). This view, which advocates that law should be immediately adaptable to the case at hand, is prevalent in modern American jurisprudence, but has not completely supplanted the more traditional approach that judges are to interpret and apply law, not make it, and that changing a law is appropriately the exclusive responsibility of the legislative branch of government.

11. *Between Us and Tyranny*, TIME, Sept. 7, 1962, at 16.

the human mind is fragile because of human error, both with respect to the assumptions from which we reason and our frequent failure to reason correctly. Logic is not impervious to error, but insofar as our laws are fair, it does empower us to reach consistently just conclusions in a system based on the rule of law—or rather, it is the only thing that can.

Thus, the common law tradition demands respect for logical form. Without it, we are denied justification for our arguments before a court. The canons of logic are critical tools of argument; they are the implements of persuasion. When it comes to brief writing, they form the imprimatur that gives legitimacy and respect. They wash away both obscurity in your own argument and obfuscation in your opponent's. They emancipate us from impulsively jumping to conclusions, or from argument supported only by strongly felt emotions or superstitions.

An appellate brief must persuade a group of highly trained legal professionals. Any argument you make to a judge must be rigorously and intentionally well structured. This will take some practice. Typically when we have a discussion with friends, we are not terribly concerned with logical formalities. Our brains are more or less able to sort out the other person's reasoning process and articulate our own well enough to get through all but our most difficult tasks without conscious recourse to the syllogism. Furthermore, many conversations, and even much literature outside the practice of law, involve no argument at all or are merely conclusory. "Sloppy" reasoning, however, can cause problems even in ordinary situations; in a court, it is disastrous. Thus, when you present an argument to appellate judges, it must employ inductive or deductive reasoning and be free from fallacies.[12]

Trial and appellate judges appraise a specific argument from two separate, but related, analyses. First, they appraise the argument from the sole vantage of examining its reasoning to determine whether, in the language of the logician, it is valid or cogent, without at the same time troubling over the truth and falsity of its premises. Second, they appraise it from the sole vantage of the truth and falsity of its premises, without troubling over the validity or cogency of its reasoning. Again, arguments that have both valid or cogent reasoning and true premises are called sound arguments. An argument is unsound "if either a) the reasoning it employs from premises to conclusion is not acceptable, or b) one or more of its premises is false."[13]

---

12. Judge Aldisert has written a detailed text on logic in legal writing, RUGGERO J. ALDISERT, LOGIC FOR LAWYERS: A GUIDE TO CLEAR LEGAL THINKING (3d ed. 1997), in which he analyzed logical components as used in the law and illustrated concepts with excerpts from cases. This chapter is not intended to repeat those efforts, but instead synthesize certain concepts that should be followed in appellate advocacy. The reader is directed to Logic for Lawyers for a more comprehensive study.

13. *Aylett*, supra note 1, at 1567–68.

11.4   Introduction to Deductive Reasoning

Deductive reasoning is a mental operation that a student, lawyer, or judge must employ every working day of her life. In general, "deduction is reasoning in which a conclusion is *compelled* by known facts."[14] It involves moving by inference from the more general to the less general to the particular. The classic tool of deductive reasoning is the syllogism—an "argument in which a conclusion is inferred from two premises."[15]

Syllogistic argument form must appear more or less formally in almost every issue you discuss in your brief. If you only argue the superficial merits of your conclusion, be prepared to have the strength of your logical foundation tested at oral argument. An argument that is correctly reasoned may be wrong, but an argument that is incorrectly reasoned will not, or at least ought not if its audience is paying attention, be persuasive.

A syllogism is made of three main parts: the major premise, the minor premise, and the conclusion. For your purposes, the major premise of the issue will usually take the form of a rule of law, enunciated in a previous case. In a brief, the major premise usually appears as the topic sentence of the discussion of each issue and is represented as a legal precept on which all members of the court will agree is a rule of law. If the major premise is not true, your entire argument loses its persuasive force entirely. All is lost. All the facts you set forth, all the citations that follow, will not help you. The minor premise consists of the facts found by the fact-finder. The purpose is to show that these facts satisfy the conditions articulated by the major premise, i.e., that they are the very sort of circumstances that trigger the rule you are advancing as applicable. Your conclusion then will logically follow.

Consider, for example, one of the most well-known syllogisms, which illustrates these three parts of the syllogism:

Major Premise:	All men are mortal.
Minor Premise:	Socrates is a man.
Conclusion:	Therefore, Socrates is a mortal.

This type of syllogism is called a categorical syllogism.[16] It is an argument "based on the relations of classes or categories."[17] A categorical syllogism shows that "[w]hat

---

14. Ruggero J. Aldisert, Stephen Clowney & Jeremy D. Peterson, *Logic for Law Students: How to Think Like a Lawyer*, 69 U. Pitt. L. Rev. 1, 3 (2007) [emphasis original]. Another way to say this is, "A deductive argument is one whose premises are claimed to provide conclusive grounds for the truth of its conclusion." Irving M. Copi & Carl Cohen, Introduction to Logic 180 (13th ed.).

15. Copi & Cohen, *supra* note 14, at 224. In deductive reasoning, the first two propositions which imply the third proposition, the conclusion, are called *premises*.

16. The formal definition of a categorical syllogism is "a deductive argument consisting of three categorical propositions that together contain exactly three terms, each of which occurs in exactly two of the constituent propositions." There are other forms of syllogism, including the disjunctive, or alternative, syllogism and the hypothetical syllogism. Copi & Cohen, *supra* note 14, at 224, 298–99.

17. Copi & Cohen, *supra* note 14, at 224.

is true of the universal is true of the particular."[18] It may help you to recognize that the three parts of the categorical syllogism are made up of three terms—the major term, the minor term, and the middle term.

- The *major term* occurs once in the major premise and once in the conclusion. It expresses the general class or attribute with which we are concerned.

- The *minor term* occurs once in the minor premise and once in the conclusion. It identifies the particular instance that we want to include in the general class.

- The *middle term* occurs once in each premise. It is the connector we use to establish a relationship between the major term and the minor term.

Returning to our Socrates syllogism, in that example the word "mortal" is the major term, "Socrates" is the minor term, and "man" and "all men" are the middle terms.[19]

Let's look now at a more detailed syllogism from the opinion of Judge Cardozo in *MacPherson v. Buick Motor Car Company*:[20]

> *Major Premise*: Any manufacturer who negligently constructs an article that may be inherently dangerous to life and limb when so constructed is liable in damages for the injuries resulting.
>
> *Minor Premise*: A manufacturer who constructs an automobile in which the spokes on a wheel are defective creates an article that is inherently dangerous to life and limb.[21]
>
> *Conclusion*: Therefore, a manufacturer who constructs an automobile in which the spokes on a wheel are defective is liable in damages for the injuries resulting.

There are two equally good ways to think about this type of syllogism. Generally, a rule will be phrased as either a categorical statement ("All X are Y" or "Any X is Y") or a conditional statement ("If X then Y"); even if the language is complicated, you will

---

18. Aldisert et al., *supra* note 14, at 4.

19. Aldisert, *supra* note 2, at 47

20. 227 N.Y. 382, 11 N.E. 1050 (1960).

21. This premise is itself a bit conclusory. It is the product of some subtle logical gymnastics. In reality, additional premises are needed to reach the desired conclusion. The major premise provides four elements that must be met in order for liability to exist under this rule: (1) the item must be an "article" as that word is used in the rule; (2) the article must have been constructed by a "manufacturer;" (3) the manufacturer must have negligently constructed the article; and (4) the article so constructed must be inherently dangerous. The minor premise supplies three facts: (a) a manufacturer constructs wheels; (b) the wheel spokes are defective; and (c) the defective spokes are inherently dangerous. Is element (1) satisfied? The writer has assumed that wheels are an article under the rule. What about (2)? Yes, a manufacturer constructed them. Element (4) is clearly satisfied, but what about (3)? This is where the problem comes in. The writer has assumed that because the wheels are defective they were negligently constructed. That is not necessarily true, and the assumption makes this example technically conclusory. Be aware of such sleights of hand. It is easy to see how these sorts of assumptions could lead, for example, to insufficient pleading. Even if it seems simplistic, when in doubt, write it out!

　　　　　　　　　　　　　National Institute for Trial Advocacy

usually be able to transform it into either of these forms without altering its meaning.[22] The categorical approach makes sense for rules that apply to a class, a group of people, things, etc. that have a particular characteristic. Think of the class as the exact set of people, things, or events to which the rule applies. Identifying the classes to which your client (for example) belongs is intuitive and should have guided your selection of rules to start with. In the above example, the class is "manufacturers who negligently construct an article that may be inherently dangerous to life and limb when so constructed." The major term is "liable in damages for resulting injuries"—the thing that is true of the class under the rule. The minor term simply states that your client (or opponent, etc.) is a member of the class—a mechanic who negligently constructed an inherently dangerous article. Hence, the rule applies: what is true of every member of the class is true of the one you've identified as well; in this case, the mechanic is liable for damages resulting from injuries cause by the dangerous article.

The other way is to treat the major premise (again, usually your rule) as a conditional statement. Often, an event or set of circumstances triggers the application of a rule. In such instances, the conditional approach may be more intuitive. For example, consider the following rule:

> *A juror may testify about whether extraneous prejudicial information was improperly brought to the jury's attention.*

This is technically a categorical statement: "All instances in which extraneous prejudicial information may have been improperly brought to the jury's attention are instances a juror may testify about." Awkward, right? It may be more natural to think of the rule this way:

> *If it is alleged that extraneous prejudicial information was improperly brought to the jury's attention, a juror may testify about it.*[23]

Under this approach, all you need to look for in your rule is a *condition* to be met (called the *antecedent*), a description of the circumstances or events triggering

---

22. This text will not discuss rules of logical equivalence, but be aware that they exist. All categorical statements can be stated as conditional ones and vice versa. With respect to the logical equivalence of conditional and categorical statements, note that while it is true that categorical statements can be translated into conditional statements, doing so may not be as straightforward as our brief discussion suggests. Categorical statements are used in *categorical* logic, whereas conditional statements are best suited to *propositional* logic. In categorical logic, the X's and Y's are classes of things (e.g., cows, blue objects, etc.) but in propositional logic they are propositions (e.g., cows give milk, the sky is blue, etc.). The statement "Cows give milk" can be stated categorically as "All cows are milk-givers." This in turn would need to be rephrased as "If [the animal is] a cow, then [the animal is a] milk-giver." More complex sentences may be difficult to translate from one form to the other, but it is nevertheless possible to do so.

23. This also makes a common formal fallacy easier to identify. One can easily imagine a situation in which a juror improperly testified, but on appeal a party argued that "Well, a juror testified, so there must have been concern that the jury was improperly influenced" to prove that the testimony was proper. Under the conditional model, this fallacy is readily identifiable as *affirming the consequent*. We discuss this fallacy in § 11.8.2.

applicability of the rule, and a consequence (technically called the *consequent*), the result of applying the rule. The condition is the *if* part; the consequent is the *then* part. Your minor premise is the same as before: it merely points to a particular instance in which the condition held (e.g., something or someone improperly brought extraneous prejudicial information to the attention of the jury). The conclusion is simply a restatement of the consequent: A juror may testify about the information being brought to the jury's attention.[24]

These two approaches are logically equivalent and you can reach the same conclusion either way. In many cases, you can simply choose the one that seems most convenient to you for the initial analysis. You will end up refining the language of the argument in your final product, as syllogism can admittedly be a little clunky linguistically. Use caution, however, to ensure that you do not alter the meaning of the statements or the clarity and validity of the argument.

One final thought: there are certain situations in which the *if-then* formulation is likely to be the more helpful of the two. These may arise, for instance, when there are aspects of your case that do not conform neatly to existing law. Very few cases really bring about fundamental changes in the law. Most of the federal appellate cases reported each year come within the two categories suggested by Cardozo in 1921, those in which "[t]he law and its application alike are plain" and those in which "the rule of law is certain, and the application alone doubtful."[25] Generally, 90 percent of the cases appealed to the courts of appeals fall within these two categories.[26] This leaves only 10 percent of cases about which it can be

---

24. Working this example out a bit, your syllogistic argument would look something like this:
Major premise / Rule: If it is alleged that extraneous prejudicial information was improperly brought to the jury's attention, a juror may testify about it.
Minor premise / fact: It is so alleged.
Conclusion 1: A juror may testify about it.
So now you want a particular juror to be allowed to testify. Logically, Conclusion 1 becomes a new major premise and the argument looks like this:
Major premise: All jurors may testify about extraneous prejudicial information.
Minor premise: Jim is a juror.
Final Conclusion: Jim may testify about it.
Of course, in actual litigation, the syllogisms which matter (i.e., are in dispute) are going to be those about whether any particular piece of information is "extraneous prejudicial information" or whether any particular presentation of information was an "improper" presentation. This example, however, should help you get comfortable using the basic syllogism with both conditional and categorical statements.

25. Benjamin H. Cardozo, The Nature of the Judicial Process 164–65 (1921).

26. Cardozo estimated that at least nine-tenths of appellate cases in 1924 "could not, with semblance of reason, be decided in any way but one." Benjamin H. Cardozo, Growth of the Law 60 (1924). In 1961, Judge Henry Friendly wrote: "Indeed, Cardozo's nine-tenths estimate probably should be read as referring to the first category alone. Thus reading it, Professor Harry W. Jones finds it 'surprising' on the high side . . . ; so would I. If it includes both categories, I would not." Henry Friendly, *Reactions of a Lawyer—Newly Become Judge*, 71 Yale L.J. 218, 222–23 (1961) (quoting Jones, *Law and Morality in the Perspective of Legal Realism*, 61 Colum. L. Rev. 799, 803 n.17 (1961)).

said that a decision one way or the other will count for the future, will advance or retrench the development of the law. If the law and application are plain, then a categorical approach is natural (e.g., all breaches of a contract for sale of land make specific performance available as a remedy). But where the application of the law is not plain or the law needs to be advanced to address your case, you will almost certainly end up arguing that in an analogous case the rule was applied the way you advocate under similar conditions, or that similar circumstances induced another court to adopt your proposed rule, and so forth. The *if-then* formulation may be more conducive here because no categorical rule exists from which a conclusion may be drawn. The *if-then* formulation correctly frames the issues and hypothetical rules as stepping into new territory. The uncertainty should in no way discourage you from applying formal deductive logic; after all, logic helps provide certainty and maximizes your brief's persuasive power.

11.5   Introduction to Inductive Reasoning

Deductive reasoning and adherence to the "Socrates is a man" type of syllogism is only one of the major components of the common law logic tradition. Inductive reasoning is equally important. In law logic, inductive reasoning is very often used to alter either the major or the minor premise of the deductive syllogism.

In legal analysis, a statute or specific constitutional provision qualifies as the controlling major premise. It is the law of the case that will be applied to the facts (appearing in the minor premise), so as to reach a decision (conclusion). Where no clear rule of law is present, however, it is necessary, using Lord Diplock's phrase, to draw upon "the cumulative experience of the judiciary" and then fashion a proper major premise from existing legal rules—the specific holdings of other cases. This is done by inductive reasoning.

11.5.1   Inductive Generalization

Let us start with the all-men-are-mortal major premise. The premise, in general form, could be arrived at from the process of *enumeration*: it was created by the counting of millions of particulars to create a general statement. The world is inhabited by millions of men, we know all these men to be mortal, and thus we are armed with an example of *inductive generalization* that concludes: Socrates is mortal.

It should be clear that the truth of the conclusion drawn from this inductive process is not guaranteed by the form of the argument, because the inductive generalization is an *assumption* only; no matter how convinced we are that because something has held true 999 times in all 999 cases we have examined the same thing will be true the one-thousandth time, it is nevertheless *not certain* that it will be. It is, at best, *probable*. Furthermore, we always run the risk of the informal fallacy of hasty generalization if we assume something is probable based on insufficient observation. We can say, however, that the creation of a major premise in law by the technique of inductive enumeration, although not guaranteed to produce an absolute truth, does produce a proposition more likely true than not. This permits the premise to be modified as new cases are decided. Formulating a generalization—that is, enumerating a series of tight holdings of cases to create a generalized legal precept—is at best a logic of probabilities. We accept the result, not because it is an absolute truth, but because there is not an absolute truth available in our case—there is no rule, the rule does not fit the facts well, or we need the court to adopt a different one. We formulate a rule that we believe is probably applicable, probably appropriate, probably most fair; the multiplicity or authority of the cases from which we induced our rule gives it credibility.

11.5.2 Analogy

Argument by analogy is a special type of inductive reasoning whereby we infer what will happen or ought to happen in a particular situation from what happened in similar situations. It is one thing to simply enumerate the cases in which courts have applied one version of a rule, compare it to the number of cases in which they applied an alternate version, and conclude that the one which the courts more frequently applied is the one that the court in your case ought to apply. It is quite another to say that a rule that was applied in a non-identical situation should apply to yours. But the fact of the matter is no two cases are ever identical, so lawyers must use argument by analogy.

A proper analogy should identify the number of respects in which the compared cases, or fact scenarios, resemble one another (let us call these resemblances) and the number of respects in which they differ. Unlike the method of enumeration, numbers do not count in the method of analogy. Instead, what is important is *relevancy*— whether the compared facts resemble, or differ from, one another in relevant respects.

Recall Judge Cardozo's estimate that at least nine-tenths of appellate cases "could not, with semblance of reason, be decided in any way but one," because "the law and its application alike are plain," or "the rule of law is certain, and the application alone doubtful."[27]

The case most often presenting an arguable question for decision is Cardozo's second category when the law is certain but the application doubtful. Where there is an absolute right of appeal to an appellate court, this is the type of case that forms the largest number of counseled appeals. And to determine whether the application of facts found by the fact-finder apply to the rule of law, we must necessarily compare those facts to those contained in the governing rule of law. In doing this, we resort to tenets of inductive analogy.

Let us assume as the controlling rule of law: where all facts A, B, and C are present, legal consequence X follows. Assume now that in the case at bar, the facts D, E, and F were found by the fact-finder at trial. To say that the material

---

27. Cardozo, *supra* note 25, at 819.

facts are or are not analogous by merely repeating them and stating your conclusion is not enough. To persuade the court that the facts are analogous, you may need to discuss the components of the analogy doctrine. You must show that, in fact, facts *A*, *B*, and *C* are analogous to facts *D*, *E*, and *F*, therefore, the conclusion *X* also follows in your case.

In a Third Circuit opinion, Judge Aldisert discussed the process of reasoning by analogy in an important class action antitrust case where the principal argument on appeal was whether the holding in a case called *Newton* applied to the case at bar:

> The process of justifying a court's decision always requires application of a legal precept to a particular factual situation. The application may be purely mechanical, as it is in most cases. If the facts are similar to those in an earlier case announcing a rule of law, the doctrine of precedent becomes operative. Where there is no quarrel over the choice and interpretation of the legal precept, here Rule 23(b)(3), the root controversy usually is traced to a value judgment of whether there is sufficient similarity between the fact situations under comparison. Edward R. Levi amply described this kind of assessment when he stated: "the scope of a rule of law, and therefore its meaning, depends upon a determination of what facts will be considered similar . . . . The finding of similarity or difference is the key step in the legal process." To predict a court's actions in a precept-application controversy, therefore, requires a prediction of what facts in the compared cases a given court, at a given time, will deem either material or insignificant. The facts considered material are adjudicative facts, described by Hart and Sacks as "facts relevant in deciding whether a given general proposition is or is not applicable to a particular situation."
>
> For Appellants' argument to prevail, therefore, they must demonstrate that the facts in *Newton* are substantially similar to the facts in the case at bar, [using] what logicians call inductive reasoning by analogy . . . . To draw an analogy between two entities is to indicate one or more respects in which they are similar and thus argue that the legal consequence attached to one set of particular facts may apply to a different set of particular facts because of the similarities in the two sets. Because a successful analogy is drawn by demonstrating the resemblances or similarities in the facts, the degree of similarity is always the crucial element. You may not conclude that only a partial resemblance between two entities is equal to a substantial or exact correspondence.
>
> Logicians teach that one must always appraise an analogical argument very carefully. Several criteria may be used: (1) the acceptability of the analogy will vary proportionally with the number of circumstances that have been analyzed; (2) the acceptability will depend upon

the number of positive resemblances (similarities) and negative resemblances (dissimilarities); or (3) the acceptability will be influenced by the relevance of the purported analogies.[28]

For Appellants to draw a proper analogy, they had the burden in the district court, as they do here of showing that the similarities in the facts of the two cases outweigh the differences.[29]

How Judge Aldisert's panel discussed this issue here could offer some guidance to brief writers in presenting an argument based on analogy. The best analogous cases are factually similar in relevant respects, with factual dissimilarities only in irrelevant respects. The more such cases you can identify, the stronger your argument. Be sure to explain why the factual similarities matter when arguing by analogy. The similarities or resemblances in the cases must connect to the operative principle. For example, if your case concerns donkeys and you want to point the court to similar cases concerning horses and away from cases about dogs, you must show why the similarities that horses and donkeys share is more important to this case than the similarities that horses and dogs share. You could explain it this way: "This case about donkeys should be governed by this case about horses because the law is concerned with *farm animals* because of the unique absence from the public eye and commoditized market; that is also why the case cited by opposing counsel about dogs (*pets, domestic animals*) is not analogous."

11.6 Testing the Conclusion of Each Issue

Not all means of persuasion are based on reflective thinking or formal logic. For example, rhetoric is a means of persuasion. Seekers of public office, columnists, television commentators, editorial writers, advertising experts—and trial lawyers—need to be masters of persuasion. They often appeal to emotions rather than to reason. Their aim is to induce belief (perhaps by playing on the jury's own inductive reason) or a certain reaction (such as sympathy or moral revulsion), not to demonstrate a conclusion by pure logical means. These presentations may be works of art, but they do not always demonstrate the logic that must characterize legal argument in a brief or other argument to a court of law.

This is not to say that all good reasoning must be stated in the order of formal correctness. It is not the order that is critically important, but the relationship between the propositions. Furthermore, there are indefinitely many logically equivalent ways

---

28. IRVING M. COPI & KEITH BURGESS-JACKSON, INFORMAL LOGIC 166 (3d ed. 1996); Arthur L. Goodhart, *Determining the Ratio Decidendi of a Case*, 40 YALE L.J. 161, 179 (1930); JOHN H. WIGMORE, WIGMORE'S CODE OF THE RULES OF EVIDENCE IN TRIALS AT LAW 118 (3d ed. 1942); JOHN STUART MILL, A SYSTEM OF LOGIC RATIOCINATIVE AND INDUCTIVE 98–142 (8th ed. 1916). ("Two things resemble each other in one or more respects; a certain proposition is true of one; therefore it is true of the other.").

29. In re Linerboard Antitrust Litig., 305 F.3d 145, 156–57 (3d Cir. 2002).

to state the same thing. Thus, there is plenty of latitude for stylistic and rhetorical devices to be employed. Often, the conclusion is stated first, such as in a Supreme Court case where the Court reasoned that "It could hardly be denied that a tax laid specifically on the exercise of those freedoms would be unconstitutional. Yet the license tax imposed by this ordinance is, in substance, just that."[30]

Regardless of the order though, you must strive to use good reasoning in your brief. To do this you must be made aware of certain pitfalls that brief writers encounter. We have discussed the need to use logical arguments and introduced you to the basic structure you will most frequently encounter and utilize. But perhaps you feel such structure is boring, overly simplistic, lacking in rhetorical appeal. You wish to "stylize" your brief and make it capture the judge's attention. That is fine, but proceed with caution: failure to give due attention to the actual logic or syllogistic structure of your argument can give rise to fallacies. Fallacies destroy the effectiveness of your arguments.

11.7   Overview of Fallacies

Several types of fallacies rear their ugly and unwelcome heads in the law. One type of fallacy occurs when we neglect the rules of logic and fall into erroneous reasoning. Other fallacies, generally called informal fallacies, may follow logical form but suffer from improper content or emphasis. The goal of this section is to familiarize you with common errors in form and content as well as with ways of avoiding such errors.

The name comes from the Latin, *fallax*, which suggests a deliberate deception, but most fallacies are not intentional. Common fallacies abound in all writings—speeches, commentaries, legislative debates, political oratory, TV editorials, columns, articles, household and family discussions, and personal conversations. Fallacies are dangerous because they are false conclusions or interpretations resulting from processes of thinking that claim or appear to be valid but fail to conform to the requirements of logic.[31] A fallacy can be thought of as "any argument that seems conclusive to the normal mind but that proves, upon examination, not to establish the alleged conclusion,"[32] or more succinctly, a form of argument that has intuitive appeal but does not withstand rational scrutiny.

11.8   A Listing of Formal Fallacies

Formal fallacies arise when there is an error in the logical or formal structure of the argument quite apart from the content of the premises. They can be discovered without any knowledge of the subject matter with which the argument is concerned.

---

30. Murdock v. Penn., 319 U.S. 105, 108 (1943).
31. ROSENTAL J. CREIGHTON, AN INTRODUCTORY LOGIC 208 (1898).
32. RALPH MONROE EATON, GENERAL LOGIC 332 (1931).

Our inquiry into formal fallacies begins with the categorical syllogism. The rules of the categorical syllogism form guidelines upon which a deductive or inductive argument in proper logical form may be based. Conversely stated, to depart from any of these rules is to commit a logical fallacy of form; it is to commit what is known as a formal fallacy.

We furnish now only a catalog of formal fallacies without fully describing or defining them. Here again, for further study, we refer you to *Logic for Lawyers*.[33] Neal Ramee's article, "Logic and Legal Reasoning: A Guide for Law Students," which was helpful in crafting many of the examples below, also provides practical examples and further explanation, and Stephen M. Rice's 2017 book, *The Force of Logic: Using Formal Logic as a Tool in the Craft of Legal Argument*, explores the place of formal logic in evaluating legal arguments.[34]

11.8.1   Fallacies in Categorical Syllogisms

As discussed above, categorical syllogisms contain three terms, two premises, and one conclusion. Consequently, these are the characteristics of deductive arguments that contain no formal fallacies:

> *Rule 1*: A valid categorical syllogism must contain exactly three terms, each of which is used in the same sense throughout the argument.
>
> *Rule 2*: In a valid categorical syllogism, the middle term must occur in at least one premise.
>
> *Rule 3*: In a valid categorical syllogism, no term can occur in the conclusion which does not occur in a premise.
>
> *Rule 4*: No categorical syllogism is valid if it has two negative premises.
>
> *Rule 5*: If either premise of a valid categorical syllogism is negative, the conclusion must be negative.
>
> *Rule 6*: No valid categorical syllogism with a particular conclusion can have two universal premises.

Violation of any of these rules is a formal fallacy and renders the argument invalid.

11.8.2   Fallacies in Hypothetical Syllogisms

Hypothetical or conditional propositions are the darlings of law professors and of appellate judges asking questions at oral argument: "If we follow that rule, what will be the result in a case where . . . ?"

---

33. ALDISERT, *supra* note 2.

34. Neal Ramee, *Logic and Legal Reasoning: A Guide for Law Students* (2002), http://www.unc.edu/~ramckinn/Documents/NealRameeGuide.pdf (last visited Mar. 20, 2017); STEPHEN M. RICE, THE FORCE OF LOGIC: USING FORMAL LOGIC AS A TOOL IN THE CRAFT OF LEGAL ARGUMENT (2017).

The conditional proposition can be combined with other propositions to form a hypothetical argument.

- If the defendant was denied due process, the conviction is invalid.

- The defendant was denied due process.

- Therefore, the conviction is invalid.

The following moves, which constitute the two fallacies in this area, result in invalid hypothetical arguments: 1) denying the antecedent, and 2) affirming the consequent. Denying the antecedent looks like this:

- If the defendant was denied due process, the conviction is invalid.

- The defendant was *not* denied due process.

- Therefore, the conviction is valid.

This is clearly wrong. There are many other many reasons for which a conviction could be invalid. Affirming the consequent results in a similarly untenable argument:

- If the defendant was denied due process, the conviction is invalid.

- The conviction is invalid.

- Therefore, the defendant was denied due process.

Again, it should be apparent to you that something is wrong with this argument. A conviction could be invalid even though the defendant received due process, and yet your premises are true. The failure of an argument to preserve truth always indicates the presence of a fallacy.

11.9 Informal Fallacies

Informal fallacies do not result from violations of formal logic rules. They are called "informal" because they exist not in the form of an argument, but in its factual content or matter. Two basic tenets of logic provide keys to their understanding:

- Logical reasoning presupposes that the terms shall be unambiguously defined and used in a uniform manner throughout.

- The discipline of logic demands that the conclusion be derived from the premises rather than assumed.

Professors William and Mabel Sahakian describe informal fallacies as "numerous, deceptive and elusive—so elusive that a person untrained in detecting them can easily be misled into accepting them as valid."[35] Logicians differ as to the precise categorization of informal fallacies, because some resemble or relate to a type of

---

35. WILLIAM SAHAKIAN & MABEL SAHAKIAN, IDEAS OF THE GREAT PHILOSOPHERS 11 (1966).

argument rather than a type of logic, but for our purposes, we will follow in major part the classification set forth by the Sahakians.

11.9.1 Fallacies of Irrelevant Evidence

Fallacies of irrelevant evidence are arguments that miss the central point at issue and rely instead upon emotions, ignorance, and other irrelevant matters.

1) *Fallacy of irrelevance* (or irrelevant conclusions). Also commonly called a *non sequitur* (literally, "it does not follow"), this fallacy arises when the premises do not support the conclusion or instead support some other conclusion.

Example:

> "Mother wants to move somewhere without tornados and avoid high property taxes. Texas has high property taxes. She should move to Florida."[36]

The purported conclusion (Mother should move to Florida) does not follow from the premises. It is merely an assertion. The premises do not state that Florida does not have tornatos or does not have high property taxes, and even if we assume that these things are true, they may be true of other states as well. Thus, the argument does not adequately support the conclusion.[37]

Another common variety of this fallacy is the straw man argument. This arises when an argument is misstated so that it is easy to refute. Just as a straw man would be easier to knock down than a real person, so the misstated argument is easier to demolish than the actual argument.

Example:

> *Candidate A:* "We should not put a nineteen-year-old man in jail for soliciting a seventeen-year-old young woman when they've been friends since elementary school. I therefore support Romeo and Juliet laws that would lower the age of consent in such situations."

> *Candidate B:* "Do you hear that? Candidate A wants to let pedophiles run rampant on our streets! You must oppose her if you want your children to be safe."

Candidate B distorts Candidate A's argument by expanding the scope of A's proposal far beyond what A suggests, portraying A's position as one that virtually no one would support. B uses this distortion to support the conclusion that A must be opposed, thus making a straw man argument.

---

36. This example is modified from *Ramee, supra* note 34, at 4.
37. *See* Ramee, *supra* note 34, at 4.

2) *Fallacies of distraction.*

   a) *Argumentum ad misericordiam*, or the appeal to pity

   b) *Argumentum ad verecundiam*, or the appeal to prestige

   c) *Argumentum ad hominem*, or the appeal to personal ridicule

   d) *Argumentum ad populum*, or the appeal to popular opinion

   e) *Argumentum ad antiquitam*, or the appeal to tradition

   f) *Argumentum ad terrorem*, or the appeal to fearsome consequences

These fallacies are fairly self-explanatory. They seek to distract from the issue, setting forth information designed to influence the audience to form a conclusion on an inappropriate basis. In the practice of law, you may be tempted to argue that "My client should prevail because she's had a hard life and deserves a break" (an appeal to pity), or "We should not oppose this policy because the people have ratified it" (an appeal to popular opinion). You may want the judge to apply a given rule, but have not developed a better explanation for why the judge should do so than "That's always been the law throughout history" (appeal to tradition) or "The consequences will be terrible if we apply a different rule" (an appeal to fear). Your rationale will likely be inadequate because, in a rule of law society, pity, popular opinion, tradition, and fear are not permitted to form the sole basis of the judge's decision.

Ad hominem attacks—ridicule or insults directed "to the person" (i.e., concerning the person's character, appearance, habits, or similar attributes)—are fallacious because the information conveyed by the attack is usually irrelevant to the desired conclusion. In law, *ad hominem* attacks have a close parallel in the notion of character propensity evidence, which seeks to prove a specific instance of misconduct based on the defendant's bad character (e.g., "He's a drunkard and a drug addict! Of course he robbed the store."). *Ad hominem* attacks, like character evidence, usually lend little support to the desired conclusion but a have a strong tendency to bias the listener against the person at whom the attack is directed.

Finally, an appeal to prestige should not be confused with an appropriate appeal to authority. Lawyers simply must appeal to authority, but it must be the right kind of authority—authority which it is reasonable to believe. There must be a connection between the nature of the authority and the nature of the proposition you seek to support. Quoting a former Supreme Court justice's discourse on the Fourth Amendment when you are trying to prove a seizure was lawful is an appropriate appeal to authority, because the justice's knowledge in that field is substantial based on his education and experience. Quoting the same justice's opinion (not case law) on the health benefits of marijuana is an appeal to prestige. There is no reason to believe that the justice's knowledge in this area is superior to anyone else's; you quoted the justice merely because you felt his status would impress your audience or cause them apprehension about expressing a different view.

11.9.2 Miscellaneous Informal Fallacies

1) *Fallacy of accident* (or *dicto simpliciter*, applying the rule to exceptional circumstances) and *Converse fallacy of accident* (or the fallacy of selective instances or hasty generalization, deriving a general rule from an inadequate sample of instances): These fallacies occur when we misuse the process of generalization.

    Example: "I know from experience that ten workers pack up the belongings in a house ten times as fast as one worker can. Thus ten workers can do any job ten times as fast as one can. It takes one man ten minutes to change a light bulb. Therefore, it will take ten men one minute to change a light bulb."[38]

    "Ten workers can do a job ten times as fast as one" is a hasty generalization (or converse fallacy of accident) because it assumes without adequate basis that ten workers can do *any* job ten times as fast as one worker can. The speaker says the generalization is based on her experience, but is her experience relevant? She knows that ten workers can pack up the belongings in a house ten times as fast as one. But what makes the generalization hasty is that there is an important difference between changing a light bulb and packing up a house. When changing the light bulb, the workers are going to get in each other's way and thus slow down the work. Contrastingly, if each of ten workers packed a different room, they would not be in each other's way. The speaker thus commits a second fallacy, the fallacy of accident, by applying her rule to exceptional circumstances. It is not that her rule is wrong with respect to *some* jobs, but it is simply inapplicable to posthole digging. This error can be thought of as either a form of equivocation (i.e., using "job" first to mean tasks like packing up a house and then to mean all tasks) or flawed analogous reasoning in that the speaker equated two tasks that were insufficiently similar in relevant respects.

2) *False cause* (or *post hoc ergo propter hoc*, literally "after this, therefore, because of this"): concluding from the conjunction of two events that one caused the other. This fallacy results when it is wrongly assumed that event A caused event B simply because A preceded B in time.

    Example: "The crime occurred just hours before Defendant left the state. Therefore, Defendant was clearly involved in the crime."[39]

    Hopefully, the error here is clear to you: first of all, the "argument" only states a minor premise. In other words, it is no argument at all in the logical

---

38. This example is modified from *Ramee*, supra note 34, at 5–6.
39. *See Ramee*, supra note 34.

National Institute for Trial Advocacy

sense—it is a fallacy. It is merely two assertions with a deceptive "therefore" thrown in. The missing major premise, if the conclusion is to logically follow, must be that "All persons (or perhaps, all persons similarly situated as Defendant) who leave the state hours after the commission of a crime were involved in the crime." This highlights the false cause: there are many reasons a person might leave the state hours without even knowing the crime occurred. We need more information to eliminate other possible explanations.[40]

This is not to say that the minor premise (i.e., that the defendant left the state within hours of the crime) is irrelevant; it could be the sort of thing that would push the marker across the line of reasonable doubt. Combined with other facts, it might lead to quite a strong inductive argument. For example, if the defendant was at the crime scene and left home in a hurry and unexpectedly, the fact that the defendant then left the state looks more suspicious. False cause fallacies are insidious because the minor premise, the false cause, usually is relevant but is portrayed as more than that—it is portrayed as conclusive. The fallacy lies only in forming (and typically deceptively omitting) a false generalization regarding the cause of a given event and arguing deductively on that basis.

3) *Compound question* (or poisoning the well): phrasing the question so as to prefigure the answer. The desired conclusion is buried in the question.

Example: "Isn't it true that your sales increased dramatically after these misleading advertisements were published?"[41]

The hallmark of a compound question is that it seeks a "yes" or "no" answer but contains within the question an unproven assertion that makes such an answer impossible to truthfully give. The questioner here seeks the answer "yes," but if the defendant answers "yes," he's admitting not only that his sales rose dramatically, but that the advertisements were misleading. If the latter assertion has not already been established and the defendant wishes to deny that the ads were misleading, he cannot answer this question meaningfully by simply saying "yes" or "no." The solution is to divide the question into the two questions that it really poses: "Did sales increase dramatically?" and "Were the advertisements misleading?"[42]

4) *Begging the question* (or "circular argument"): assuming as true what is to be proved. The desired conclusion is buried in the premises: the conclusion has to be true in order for one of the premises to be true, instead of the other way around.

---

40. This example is modified from *Ramee*, supra note 34, at 5.
41. This example is taken from *Ramee*, supra note 34, at 7.
42. *Id.* at 7.

Example: Robber A says, "I get to keep more of the money than you do." Robber B asks, "How come?" A replies, "Because I'm the leader." "Who says you're the leader?" B retorts. "I do," answers A, "because I get the most money. Leaders always get the most money."[43]

You can imagine this will not go over well with B, and for good reason. A's argument is circular: A knows that leaders get the most money (A's major premise is "Leaders get the most money"), so he calls himself the leader (this is the minor premise).[44] From this it would follow that he should get the most money. But his minor premise is in question: B does not think A is the leader. So A justifies his self-proclaimed status by pointing to the fact that he gets the most money, which is exactly what he was trying to prove in the first place by calling himself the leader. A uses the desired conclusion to support the premise which produces the desired conclusion. In other words, the truth of A's conclusion depends on the truth of A's conclusion; this is completely unhelpful.[45]

5) *You yourself do it*: meeting criticism with the argument that the other person engages in the very conduct he or she is criticizing.

Example: "You cannot tell me slavery is immoral or that I should not support slavery. After all, many of you own slaves."[46]

This fallacy consists of justifying bad behavior by pointing to other bad behavior. To begin with, it cannot be inferred with certainty that a person does not object to something that the person permits or participates in. True, a person's continued participation in a particular practice is some evidence that he does not morally disapprove of it, but it does not come close to proving that. There are many reasons that a person might aspire to a certain moral standard and yet not attain it, including inability, lack of will or moral fortitude, self-interest, and conflicting principles. Moreover, and more importantly for our purposes, even were it possible to establish a person's moral beliefs solely on the basis of his conduct, this does little to prove that those beliefs are correct or appropriate in the present situation.

The example given here is typical of this sort of fallacy. First, the arguer points out that "You yourself do it," attempting to establish that his opponent is

---

43. This modified example is taken from *Ramee*, supra note 34, at 6.

44. *Id.* at 6.

45. *Id.*

46. This example parallels Chief Justice Roger Taney's flawed rationale in *Scott v. Sandford*, one of the most infamous Supreme Court decisions of all time. In that case, Taney reasoned in part that because many of the Framers of the Constitution owned slaves and supported the institution of slavery in their official capacity that they must have approved of it and intended for it to endure perpetually. *See* Scott v. Sandford, 60 U.S. 393 (1957).

a hypocrite, saying one thing and doing another. Then the arguer commits a fallacy, concluding that the opponent's conduct illustrates not only the opponent's personal belief but also the principle that should govern the present case. One problem is that the argument has not proved that the opponent's purported principle is right at all—in fact the accusation usually arises because the opponent claims the principle is wrong. The fact that the opponent conforms to the principle is relevant at best to whether the opponent actually believes it is wrong—it has little to do with whether it is so in the abstract. It has even less to do with whether it should be employed in any particular instance.

11.9.3 Linguistic Fallacies

These four fallacies are different types of fallacies of *ambiguity*. They arise when "[t]he meaning of words or phrases . . . shifts as a result of inattention, or [is] deliberately manipulated within the course of an argument."[47] When this happens, the conclusion no longer follows even if the argument is otherwise logical. Linguistic fallacies can produce good jokes, but must be avoided in law.

1) *Fallacy of equivocation*: using a word to mean two or more different things within the same argument. Many words have more than one meaning, and equivocation can be the source of much contention.

   Example: "The First Amendment guarantees the right to free speech. All I did was yell "Fire!" and now I'm under arrest. This is a violation of my rights."

   The problem is that "speech" in the First Amendment has a specialized meaning that does not include everything that a person might say. On the other hand, it may include things we do not normally think of as speech. Lawyers must be especially aware of the meaning of the terms they are using and need to make sure they use them consistently.

2) *Fallacy of amphiboly*: using statements whose meaning is unclear because of the syntax. This fallacy occurs when a statement which has more than one possible meaning, one of which is true and one of which is false, and a conclusion is drawn from its false meaning.[48]

   Example: An inexperienced police officer responds to a report of a shooting. A man, Joe Goodman, has been shot dead and the only other eyewitness says to the officer, "Tom Smith shot him in his own home. Joe had just gone in—right before Tom did. He broke in. They both seemed angry when I saw them a few minutes before. It's a shame. He was such a nice man. Just married, too." Outraged, the officer goes to arrest Smith without further

---

47. Copi & Cohen, *supra* note 14, at 157.
48. *Id.* at 159.

inquiry. Smith, looking annoyed, adamantly protests that it was self-defense. The officer tells him to get down on the ground. Instead of doing so, Smith says, "No, I'll show you—" and starts toward the doorway where the officer is standing. The officer shoots him. Smith dies of the injury. Smith's wife brings a wrongful death action against the officer and he pleads self-defense. The question is whether he reasonably believed Smith was assaulting him. Under applicable law of the jurisdiction where the shootings took place, in order to show this belief was reasonable, the officer needs to show that he also reasonably believed that Smith committed the crimes the officer went to arrest him for. The officer's attorney insists that the officer's belief was reasonable, arguing that "There is no other way to see it. Based on what the witness said, the officer could not have drawn any other conclusion." On a special jury form, the jury indicates that the officer's belief was not reasonable.

The witness's statement to the officer that "Tom Smith shot him in his own home" is an example of amphiboly. It is subject to two possible interpretations: either Smith shot Goodman in Goodman's home or Smith shot Goodman in Smith's home. If the former, Smith committed murder (provided all other elements were satisfied). If the latter, Smith acted in self-defense (again, all other criteria satisfied). It is impossible to tell from the statement itself which is true and which is false. The rest of the conversation sheds no light on the question. The officer drew a conclusion from the false interpretation—that Smith had entered Goodman's home and shot Goodman—when in reality Goodman had broken into Smith's home and Smith had shot him, thinking Goodman was up to no good. Thus, the officer committed the fallacy of amphiboly. It will now be a challenge for him to show that his belief that Smith committed murder was reasonable.

This example is disturbing, but not farfetched. Not only did the officer make a tragic mistake, but the officer's attorney let him down, or at least his insurer down. The officer was inexperienced; the attorney has no excuse. Had the attorney identified the amphiboly, the attorney could have tried to convince the jury that there were other reasons for the officer to believe Smith had committed murder. But because the attorney did not identify it, she relied on the theory that "there was no other way to see" what the witness had said and hence failed to make as strong an argument as possible. It is critically important that lawyers communicate clearly and be able to recognize ambiguities in statements and arguments.

3) *Fallacy of composition*: concluding that a characteristic possessed by one member of a group is also possessed by all members of the group. This fallacy is relatively easy to recognize. It comes in two forms: the first form reasons that because something is true of a part, it is true of the whole. The second reasons that because something is true of members of a collection,

the same thing is true of the entire collection. These are much the same thing, but look slightly different in practice

Example 1: Defendant Corporation builds its machines with only lightweight materials. Therefore, the machine that Plaintiff purchased from Defendant was lightweight and could not have broken Plaintiff's foot when it broke in half and fell on Plaintiff's foot.[49]

This is clearly wrong. If you put together enough lightweight parts, eventually they will be heavy enough to break someone's foot when dropped.

Example 2: A bus uses a lot more fuel than a car. Therefore, buses are more responsible for the smog in our city.[50]

It may be true that a bus burns fuel at a greater rate than a car, but there are many fewer buses than cars. Thus, while one bus would create worse pollution than one car, buses collectively might not create more pollution than cars collectively.

4) *Fallacy of division*: concluding that a characteristic possessed by the whole is also possessed by each of the parts individually. This is the opposite of the fallacy of composition.[51]

Example 1: "The machine weighed 5,000 pounds! It is obvious that if a piece fell off it and hit plaintiff's foot, the impact would have broken it."

Again, this is clearly wrong. The machine might be made up of 5,000 one-pound pieces. These would hardly be likely to break a person's foot in a short fall.

Example 2: "Buses cause only 15 percent of all pollution, whereas cars cause 50 percent. Therefore, allowing school-bus drivers to drive the buses home instead of their own cars will minimize pollution."

Buses as a collection would cause less pollution than cars in part because there are fewer of them. However, it does not follow from the fact that buses as a collection cause less pollution than cars that each bus individually causes less pollution than each car—in fact, we know this is not true (assuming both run on gasoline).

11.10   Fallacies: A Final Word

Our understanding of fallacies can be sharpened in the course of daily life. Read editorials and opinion pieces, and put the reasoning to the tests. Are the authors

---

49. Copi & Cohen, *supra* note 14, at 163.
50. *Id.*
51. *Id.* at 164.

guilty of erecting straw men and knocking them down, thus committing the fallacy of irrelevant conclusions? Do they beat their breasts over an answer expressed in a news conference by the president or governor or mayor when the question was loaded with three or four compound parts? Does the content of the piece truly follow logical form? Does it appear as a categorical or hypothetical syllogism? Do you see *ad hominem*s or other fallacies?

Pay attention to TV correspondents in their sixty-second sound bites following news accounts. Are they guilty of the fallacy of hasty generalization by prophesying broad consequences from one single event in a fast-breaking story? Do you detect any fallacies of distraction? Appeals to pity or to the masses? Are they guilty of attempting to project a general rule from that which obviously is an exception to the rule?

All of us commit fallacies every day in reaching judgments—all of us, and that includes judges, lawyers, professors, preachers, and authors of books. We do this because our thinking is not always reflective. We simply want to believe something. We are constantly influenced by emotions, beliefs, and social wants and demands.

It may not be possible to avoid such errors entirely in every aspect of our lives, but nevertheless we have an obligation when called upon to solve a problem, any problem whether at home, school, church, office, business, or in our social relations to both respect logical form and abstain from informal fallacies. Our jobs as lawyers demand that we meet this obligation.

Chapter Twelve

The Brief: Statement of the Case

12.1 Overview

Think back to writing academic legal scholarship in law school. Most students start with writing the introduction and continue from there to write the article straight through, ending with a conclusion. Writing a brief is not the same. While there is a temptation to start with the statement of the case, you cannot write this part of the brief until it is clear what persuasive facts you will need for your argument. Therefore, it is better to write the statement of the case after the first draft of the argument section. You also do not begin to write the facts until you have made the decision on the precise issues you intend to discuss. Never put the fact-writing cart before the issue-stating horse. In this manner, you limit the narrative only to those facts that are germane to the issues before the court. The judge will appreciate your uncluttered brief, devoid of facts that have no bearing on the decisional process.

The statement of the case usually contains two subsections: 1) a section laying out the facts that underlie the case before the court, and 2) the procedural history of the case. The court rules might set out the order that these sections should appear in the brief and the headings that should be used for each section. But, if it does not, it is better to set out the factual statement first, as it gives the judge a better understanding of the story leading up to the appeal.

12.2 Statement of Facts

The statement of facts is as important as any portion of the brief. Write the statement, then rewrite it, and then rewrite it again before you place it in final form. The statement is designed to inform. But a good statement does more: it engages the reader's interest, making the judge look forward to working on the case. The statement of facts tells the story of your case. This does not give you a license to embellish or to throw in irrelevant, but juicy, facts to liven up the plot. Stick to the essentials. But remember, it is not unconstitutional to be interesting.

The statement of facts must command and retain the reader's attention. Do not bore the judge. Do not make the brief difficult to read. Do not clutter the narrative. Do not, unless absolutely necessary, stray from the chronology of events.

Come closer to Ernest Hemingway, or J. K. Rowling, than Beltway bureaucratese. Noted biographer Catherine Drinker Bowen kept a sign posted above her desk to discipline herself as she wrote her books: "Will the reader turn the page?"[1] What Barbara Tuchman described in *Practicing History* as the responsibility of the historian is equally applicable to the lawyer writing the brief:

> The writer of history, I believe, has a number of duties *vis-à-vis* the reader, if he wants to keep him reading. The first is to distill. He must do the preliminary work for the reader, assemble the information, make sense of it, select the essential, discard the irrelevant—above all, discard the irrelevant—and put the rest together so that it forms a developing dramatic narrative. Narrative, it has been said, is the lifeblood of history. To offer a mass of undigested facts, of names not identified and places not located, is of no use to the reader and is simple laziness on the part of the author, or pedantry to show how much he has read.[2]

Philadelphia attorney James D. Crawford says that writing the facts in an appellate brief should not be entrusted to a junior litigator: "Many of the most effective appellate lawyers have told their junior partners and associates: 'You write the law. Let me write the statement of facts because that is where the biggest difference can be made.'"[3] Others suggest that the facts should be written in the first instance by the person most familiar with the case. Familiarity, however, can breed obscurity in the narrative. You may know the facts so well that you are unable to put yourself in the position of someone unacquainted with the case.

12.2.1 *What Facts Should Be Set Forth?*

Experienced appellate judges may form their first, and probably their most lasting, impression of your side of the case from reading your statement of facts. Do not let merely decorative facts obscure those that are important. In a murder case, for example, the installation of a stained glass window on the fiftieth floor of a building may be interesting, but what matters is that the victim was thrown out of the window.

In selecting the facts, the brief writer walks on a very tight rope. The job requires consummate skill, because the writer must constantly seek balance on several levels—the balance between being scrupulously accurate and putting the most favorable emphasis on your version of what happened; the balance between furnishing the relevant facts favoring your client and protecting yourself from a possible charge by your opponent that you have withheld vital facts from the court; and the balance between putting your best evidence before the appellate court and adhering to the

---

1. Carol Kort, A to Z of American Women Writers 29 (2014).
2. Barbara Tuchman, Practicing History 17–18 (1981).
3. Ruggero J. Aldisert, Winning on Appeal: Better Briefs and Oral Argument 165 (2d ed. 2003).

actual findings in the trial court. The exceptional advocate balances these conflicting duties and still conveys the impression that her client deserves to win.

Consider the weight of *stare decisis* when you select what facts to include in the statement. *Stare decisis* counsels us "to stand by the decisions," and a decision is a mix of the material facts and the legal consequences flowing from those facts. Material facts[4] must stand out because they form the predicate of the legal rule you are urging upon the court. The brief writer must ensure that all material facts necessary to the rule of law urged upon the court are set forth in the narrative. At this point in the brief writing task, it is worth recalling the words of a giant of the common law: "[Rules of law] are precepts attaching a definite detailed legal consequence to a definite, detailed state of facts."[5]

Do not forget your ethical duty of candor to the court when drafting the statement of facts. Under the Model Rules of Professional Conduct, "[a] lawyer shall not knowingly make a false statement of fact or law to a tribunal or fail to correct a false statement of material fact or law previously made to the tribunal by the lawyer."[6] Additionally, under the Model Rules, "In an ex parte proceeding, a lawyer shall inform the tribunal of all material facts known to the lawyer that will enable the tribunal to make an informed decision, whether or not the facts are adverse."[7]

Always address the "bad" material facts. Just like with adverse case law, including the material facts that could cut against you allows you to frame these facts in the best way possible for your case. You also do not want to be the lawyer with reputation among the judges for not being honest about the facts.[8] Justice Sarah B. Duncan of the Fourth Court of Appeals in Texas opined about the effect of misstatements or omissions of material facts in a brief by retelling a story from her own judicial experience:

> I was reading an appellant's brief, slowly but surely coming to believe we would have to reverse the judgment. Then I turned to the appellee's brief, which was replete with quotations from the record and the

---

4. For a discussion of what constitutes a material fact, see Chapter Seven.

5. Roscoe Pound, *Hierarchy of Sources and Forms in Different Systems of Law*, 7 Tul. L. Rev. 475, 482 (1933).

6. Model Rules of Prof'l Conduct r. 3.3(a)(1) (Am. Bar Ass'n 1983).

7. *Id.* at 3.3(d).

8. *See* Raymond T. Elligett, Jr. & John M. Scheb, *Stating the Case and the Facts: Foundation of the Appellate Brief*, 32 Stetson L. Rev. 415, 418 (2003); *see also* Wiesmueller v. Kosobucki, 547 F.3d 740, 741 (7th Cir. 2008) ("It is forbidden [under Seventh Circuit local rules] for the statement of facts to misstate the record or omit unfavorable material facts."); In re Guevera, 41 S.W.3d 169, 172–73 (Tx. Ct. App. 2001) (finding that an attorney "filed a petition in this court that grossly misstates obviously important and material facts"); Bryan A. Garner, *Interviews with United States Supreme Court Justices: Justice Antonin Scalia*, 13 Scribes J. Legal Writing 51, 72 (2010) ("Most important is citations to the portions of the record that support what you've said, and be rigorously accurate about what you say. A mistake in that portion is readily identifiable and will really undermine your credibility.").

relevant cases—no paraphrasing or ellipses to mistrust—and it began to become apparent that the appellant's lawyer had misrepresented the record and the applicable law. At that moment, the appellant's lawyer not only lost the case, but he also lost me to anger. And the reason I got angry? Volume and limited resources. At the end of a fifteen-hour day, I had just spent over an hour reading a brief that should never have been filed—an hour that could and should have been spent on a more deserving effort. Accuracy makes you a friend of the court and keeps you one throughout your career.[9]

You can, however, employ strategies to deemphasize bad facts, such as using the passive voice or using qualifiers to introduce the "troublesome," "imperfect," or "unfortunate" facts.[10]

Another category of facts to include in the statement is background facts. These are the facts that the court needs in order to understand your case. Be careful to not go overboard here. If your client's high school baseball career is not relevant to the background of the case, do not include it. Finally, be sure to also consider persuasive facts. These are facts that reflect favorably on your client. They may not be legally relevant, as material facts are, but the court wants to feel good about ruling in your favor. Again, just be careful to not overdo it. This is not a jury summation, it is an appellate brief.

In considering what facts to include, do not forget that what counts is the facts found by the fact-finder. When a jury determines the facts, the appellate court is required to assume that the jurors accepted the evidence presented by the verdict winner. Too often appellants attempt to argue evidence that was unsuccessfully presented to the jury.

The biggest offenders in this respect often are extremely effective trial lawyers. They are very successful before a jury, but when they appear before an appellate bench they conduct themselves as if they are still addressing the lay fact-finders. Summarizing the facts in an appellate brief is not a summation to a trial jury. In both briefs and oral arguments, these lawyers set forth the evidence they presented at trial rather than the facts found by the jurors.

The purpose of a brief is to persuade the court to your point of view. When you open your brief with a narrative of facts that picks and chooses those items of evidence favorable to your case at trial but ultimately rejected by the fact-finder, you immediately lose substantial credibility. Selecting only the bits and pieces of evidence favorable to your client will not go undetected. Appellate judges read trial court

---

9. Sarah B. Duncan, *Pursuing Quality: Writing a Helpful Brief*, 30 St. Mary's L.J. 1093, 1101 (1999).

10. *Guide to Appellate Briefs*, Duke Law, https://law.duke.edu/curriculum/appellateadvocacy/guide.html (last visited Mar. 20, 2017).

National Institute for Trial Advocacy

opinions and appellees' briefs. They soon get the complete picture. Judges may still respect and admire a lawyer with whom they disagree in interpreting the law, but the same measure of regard does not extend to the lawyer who misrepresents the facts.

Consider that some judges read the trial court's opinion before reading the statement of facts in either brief. You start off on the wrong foot when you try to pass off carefully selected bits of evidence as the facts found by the fact-finder. Judges need to see the picture with all its blemishes and imperfections; they do not want a retouched photograph. Reading a skewed statement of facts quickly disillusions the brief reader. It is bad enough when this occurs later in the brief-reading process, but when it occurs at the onset, you lose a serious initial impetus, one which you will never regain. You have destroyed the reader's initial neutral attitude, replacing it with a "What's-this-lawyer-trying-to-pull-off-here?" state of mind.

The advice to include facts and not evidence does come with a caveat. In some cases, the questions at issue require a detailed statement of the actual evidence that was presented. This is particularly true in appeals from the grant of summary judgment, from directed verdicts, from judgments as a matter of law or notwithstanding the verdict (j.n.o.v.) and in challenges to jury instructions. Here, the reviewing court will measure the quantum of evidence against the controlling legal precept in the same manner as did the trial court. Just be clear as to what constitutes evidence and what constitutes facts found by the fact-finder.

12.3   Distilling the Record into the Statement of Facts

Distilling a large record into a manageable statement of facts can be a daunting task.[11] While technology has made many aspects of brief writing much easier, there is no magic computer program that can review the record and spit out a fair, accurate, persuasive, complete (yet concise), and interesting statement of the facts. This means that you will have to do the hard work.

Before a statement of facts can be written, the record must be mastered. Margaret D. McGaughey, an appellate attorney with the United States Attorney's office in Maine, suggests that in all but the shortest cases, a digest of the record should be prepared for use by the brief writer.[12] One method of digesting the record is to make a page-by-page summary of the transcripts that converts the questions and answers into

---

11. *See* Laurie A. Lewis, *Winning the Game of Appellate Musical Shoes: When the Appeals Band Plays, Jump From The Client's to the Judge's Shoes to Write the Statement of the Facts Ballad*, 46 WAKE FOREST L. REV. 983, 1009 (2011) ("For the Statement of Facts in an appellate brief, [you must] first conduct[] a painstaking review of the record. Create an abstract that addresses all procedural matters and evidentiary rulings, and details all facts on the issues. Remember to include unfavorable as well as favorable facts. Sometimes students complain it is too time-consuming to create an abstract and then write an outline. In the long run, however, this initial process saves time.") (footnotes omitted); *see also* MARY BETH BEAZLEY, A PRACTICAL GUIDE TO APPELLATE ADVOCACY 36–40 (4th ed. 2014).

12. RUGGERO J. ALDISERT, WINNING ON APPEAL: BETTER BRIEFS AND ORAL ARGUMENT 167 (2d ed. 2003).

a few complete sentences that can later be joined together to make paragraphs in the statement of facts.[13] This summary can be tabbed with the names of the witnesses so that the writer can flip back and forth among them to fit the pertinent facts into their proper place in the organization. For those who prefer an electronic method of digesting the record, spreadsheets can be used to organize different aspects of the record.

Many experienced appellate attorneys believe that, when a digest has been prepared by someone else, the person who ultimately writes the brief and argues the case orally should read the actual record through at least once. This personal reading enables the writer to understand the complete story before becoming mired in collateral issues or excessive detail. It helps to ingrain the facts in the writer's mind for use in writing and in oral argument. It provides the greatest opportunity for the varying nuances in the record to be discovered and used to best advantage.

Although computers cannot write your statement of facts, there are programs and software available to help you in organizing the record, particularly those cases with large records. Thomson Reuters, the parent company of WestlawNext, offers Case Notebook, a program that assists attorneys in organizing case materials, including records and transcripts.[14] Testimony can be linked to specific issues, and then reports run on those issues to help in creating a statement of facts. LexisNexis offers a similar program, CaseMap.[15] Trial tools, such as Trial Director, allow you to annotate and keep track of exhibits and transcripts, which can be useful in organizing the record.[16] There are other programs available that seem to focus more on law practice management, but may also include a case management component.[17] Undoubtedly, technology will continue to advance in this area.

12.4   Writing the Statement of Facts

The basic theory behind writing a statement of facts is to make the case easy for the appellate judges to decide the advocate's way. This means preparing a statement of facts that is simple to follow and to accept as reliable. A statement of facts should read like an interesting story. As Chief Justice John G. Roberts, Jr., who was himself a gifted appellate advocate, said about the statement of facts in an interview:

> It's got to be a good story. Every lawsuit is a story. I don't care if it's about a dry contract interpretation; you've got two people who want to accomplish something, and they're coming together—that's a story.

---

13. *Id.*

14. *Case Notebook*, THOMSON REUTERS, http://legalsolutions.thomsonreuters.com/law-products/solutions/case-notebook/ (last visited Mar. 20, 2017).

15. *Id.*

16. Trial Director, http://indatacorp.com/TrialDirector.html (last visited Mar. 20, 2017).

17. *See, e.g.*, Clio, https://www.goclio.com/; Law Office Management Software, Legal Files, http://www.legalfiles.com/products/law-firms/; MyCase, http://www.mycase.com/ (all websites last visited Mar. 20, 2017).

And you've got to tell a good story. Believe it or not, no matter how dry it is, something's going on that got you to this point, and you want it to be a little bit of a page-turner, to have some sense of drama, some building up to the legal arguments.[18]

Because it is not fiction, however, literary license is unacceptable. As discussed above, a statement of facts should be an accurate reflection of *facts* found by the fact-finder, not simply the favored *evidence* you introduced at trial. Remember, in a jury verdict, the presumption is that the facts found are derived from the evidence presented by the verdict winner. Write them on the basis of evenhanded advocacy. Both the good and bad should appear. The aim is to have the appellate court rely on counsel's statement of facts, not the opponent's statement of facts. It must inspire and be worthy of the appellate court's trust. Justice Kennedy has said:

> the most important thing in a brief when you state the facts is you must be fair. Now, we know that the plaintiff's brief is going to be slanted for what the plaintiff wants to emphasize, and the defendant's too. We expect that. But I think the reader has to have confidence you're being fair.[19]

So how do you write a story that keeps a judge's interest, but that is also fair and reliable? Here are some important tips to follow.

Theme/Introduction. Your statement should adhere to a consistent theme, be written with true-to-life language, and have a cohesive organization. Start the statement off with a theme sentence that summarizes the story that follows or tells what the case is about. Remember though, this theme should not be argumentative. The introductory paragraph should also introduce the parties involved in the dispute.

Take a step back. After weeks, months, or maybe even years of handling a case, you know it inside out (or at least you should!). The statement of facts, however, will be read by a judge who knows nothing about the dispute and has a host of other demands on her attention. Write a statement of the facts that does not assume too much knowledge on behalf of the reader. This is especially important if your case involves a highly technical field, such as patent law, medical malpractice, or financial fraud.[20] Attorneys Hugh S. Balsam and Patrick C. Gallagher offer some excellent tips for attorneys writing briefs in technical cases, including:

---

18. Bryan A. Garner, *Interviews with United States Supreme Court Justices: Chief Justice John G. Roberts*, 13 SCRIBES J. LEGAL WRITING 5, 16 (2010).

19. Bryan A. Garner, *Interviews with United States Supreme Court Justices*, 13 SCRIBES J. LEGAL WRITING 79, 86 (2010).

20. Hugh S. Balsam & Patrick C. Gallagher, *How to Make Technical Briefs Understandable for Generalist Judges*, AMERICAN BAR ASSOCIATION, http://apps.americanbar.org/litigation/committees/appellate/email/winter2012/winter2012-how-to-make-technical-briefs-understandable-generalist-judges.html (last visited Mar. 20, 2017).

- "In selecting what information to give the judge, don't forget the product itself." When the subject of the case is a piece of technology, it can be very helpful to make the technology or invention in question, or at least an illustration of it, available to the judge.[21]

- "Select only the technical facts necessary to support the arguments in your brief." If at all possible, you should generalize the scientific or technical concepts in your brief.[22]

- "Build the technology [explanation] piece by piece." Do not be afraid to start basic when it comes to scientific material, and then carefully build up the concepts for the reader.[23]

- Use headings and topic sentences to better organize your statement of facts.[24] Headings in the statement of facts can help organize any long, or complicated, case. They allow the judge to better see the progression of the facts, much like the headings in the argument section show the progression of the argument.

- "Eliminate or define technical terms." As Balsam and Gallagher note, "just as you wouldn't write a brief in French, so you shouldn't write a brief in the technical language of the field you are dealing with." Try to omit as many technical terms as possible.[25]

Ask another attorney in your office, who is not familiar with the case, to read your statement of facts to ensure that it is accessible to an intelligent, but uninformed, reader.

Be brief but clear. In his noteworthy works, *Brief Writing & Oral Argument and Law Students Manual on Legal Writing*, Professor Edward D. Re refers to the ABCs of legal writing: Accuracy, Brevity, and Clarity.[26] Follow these guidelines in preparing your statement of facts. To achieve brevity, however, the brief writer will often sacrifice clarity. Do not do this. Avoid such shortcuts as resorting to initials or acronyms when identifying parties or participants in litigation—this can be both

---

21. *Id.* A recent example of judges benefitting from access to technology occurred when Justice Kagan and Justice Breyer decided to gain first-hand experience playing violent video games in order to decide the case of *Brown v. Entertainment Merchants Ass'n*, 564 U.S. 786 (2011), in which the state of California attempted to restrict the sale of such violent video games to minors. Fred Barbash, *Why Two Supreme Court Justices Played a Violent Video Game to Help Decide a Major Case*, THE WASH. POST (Sept. 18, 2015), https://www.washingtonpost.com/news/morning-mix/wp/2015/09/18/how-and-why-justices-kagan-and-breyer-faced-off-in-a-violent-video-game-to-help-decide-a-major-case/ (last visited Mar. 20, 2017).

22. Balsam & Gallagher, *supra* note 20.

23. *Id.*

24. *Id.*

25. *Id.*

26. EDWARD D. RE & JOSEPH R. RE, BRIEF WRITING & ORAL ARGUMENT 2–7 (8th ed. 1999).

annoying and cumbersome. "USS" may be the United States Steel Company, the Universal Statistics Service, or the Underwriters Society of San Francisco. The desirability of clarity is easier achieved by using a generic term such as "the company," or "the consortium," or "the underwriters," rather than making the reader of the brief fight the battle of trying to remember which initials go with which participant.[27]

Be inclusive. You also must be sure to include every fact referred to in the argument section in the statement of facts. This is one of the reasons that you write the statement of facts after the argument section. That is not to say that the level of detail for some event should be the same in both parts of a brief. It may be important to elaborate on an event in the argument section. If so, only a limited description of that event should appear in the statement of facts—do not unnecessarily burden the reader twice with all the details.

The reverse side of this rule is that if opposing counsel has, will, or should rely on a fact for argument, that fact should be covered as well. Including adverse facts fosters a sense of trustworthiness. At the same time it enables the advocate to blunt any negative impact. Do not fear that appellate judges will kill the messenger. They are much more likely to chastise the advocate who did not deliver the message of bad news about a case than they are to criticize the lawyer who faces the adverse facts squarely and attempts to place them in perspective.

Do not use opposing counsel's brief as the gauge of what is a significant fact in either the positive or the negative sense. Dangerous as it is to do, opposing counsel may ignore potentially adverse facts in the idle hope that they will be overlooked or disappear. It is equally common that opposing counsel fails to notice factual points that are helpful to that side of the case. In writing a statement of facts, your job is to make an independent judgment about whether each fact is important or not.

There is yet another reason to be objective and fair. Part of a judicial law clerk's unarticulated job description is to find critical facts and case authorities that the lawyers have not addressed. Doing so proves to the judge the law clerk's worth. Thus, when in doubt as to whether a fact is important, include it.

Be organized. In general, the statement of facts should be arranged in a manner that makes sense. Often, this is a chronological arrangement, or one that follows the orderly process of litigation from the initial pleading to verdict and the need to tell the underlying story. What happened before trial, during trial, and on post-trial motions should be handled in that order. Within that framework, the events should be described chronologically. Thus, if there was a hearing on a motion to dismiss

---

27. *See, e.g.*, Alex Kozinski, *The Wrong Stuff*, 1992 BYU L. Rev. 325, 328 (1992) ("In a recent brief I ran across this little gem: 'LBE's complaint more specifically alleges that NRB failed to make an appropriate determination of RPT and TIP in conformity to SIP.' Even if there was a winning argument buried in the midst of this gobbledegook, it was DOA.").

followed by a hearing on a motion for summary judgment two weeks later, those events should be handled in the order in which they took place in the district court.

By contrast, when including evidence is relevant to the statement of facts, the evidence from a testimonial hearing should never be organized witness by witness or exhibit by exhibit. That approach is repetitive and simply boring. Instead, the event that produced the litigation should be described chronologically from beginning to end, regardless of the order in which the evidence about it was presented at the hearing. Framed another way, the writer should present the historical facts as if a camera had begun to film them at the first operative point and had continued to run until the last event concluded. A statement of facts concerning a contract dispute, for example, should begin with the circumstances that led up to reaching an agreement, followed by a description of the how and when the contact was signed, and then explain how the breach occurred and what damage resulted.

Often, this chronological account can be accomplished best by organizing the evidence around one or two witnesses who have the broadest knowledge of the event being litigated.[28] The identity of these principal storytellers often surfaces during the initial broad-brush reading of the transcripts. Corroborating evidence or witnesses can be woven into the principal storytellers' account to keep the chronology moving forward in time. A witness who testified the first day of trial can be linked efficiently to a corroborating document that was admitted at the end of trial this way: "Corroborated by his telephone records and flight coupons, the informant testified that he called the defendant on January 1 just before the informant boarded a Delta Airlines flight to New York."

Include adequate, accurate citations. Under the rules of the Fifth Circuit, "every assertion in briefs regarding [a] matter in the record must be supported by a reference to the page number of the original record . . . where the matter is found."[29] Even if the rules of your jurisdiction do not require this level of citation, it is good practice to include sufficient citations.[30] Most courts today require citation to specific pages in the record, and in some appellate courts, those pages will be hyperlinked to an electronic record. This enables the appellate judges to focus directly on the disputed portions of the transcripts. Even the most experienced advocates cannot always anticipate accurately what fact an appellate judge will find to be critical. Rather than take chances, it is best to cover all bases with record citations.

---

28. A word of caution is in order. Care should be taken to avoid resting too heavily on any one witness or exhibit. Too much reliance on an isolated portion of the evidence may set the case up to fail on a harmless error analysis. Whenever possible, make clear that critical points find factual support in more than one source in the trial record.

29. 5TH CIR. R. 28.2.2.

30. What constitutes sufficient citations? It just depends on your jurisdiction and the preferences of the judges in your jurisdiction. Some judges do not believe that uncontroverted facts need citations. Judge Aldisert was one of those judges, but he noted that most of his law clerks disagreed with him. As he advised in an earlier version of this textbook, it is always best to play it safe.

Someone other than the writer should check the final draft of the statement of facts against the record. This means that every record reference at the end of each sentence should be verified against the transcripts and appendix to make certain that the cited pages say what the writer says they do. Numbers can become transposed in typing and render the record citation useless to a judge attempting to find that portion of the record. Moreover, different eyes can read the same passage different ways. This system of double-checking the record gives both inaccuracies and variations in interpretation a chance to be resolved before opposing counsel exposes them to anyone's embarrassment.

12.5   Special Considerations

In some cases, there may be other requirements for the statement of the facts that must be followed by the attorney. Be sure to fully understand the rules in your jurisdiction.

12.5.1   Summary Judgment

Since the U.S. Supreme Court's important 1986 trilogy of cases,[31] summary judgment has become an extraordinarily important part of modern litigation. Under Federal Rule of Civil Procedure 56, a party seeking to recover upon a claim, counterclaim, or cross-claim may move for summary judgment in the party's favor upon the entire case or any part thereof. The general practice is for the moving party to augment the motion with factual support contained in affidavits, depositions, or answers to interrogatories. Once the movant's papers are served, the adverse party responds with specific facts showing that there is a genuine issue as to any material fact. In many jurisdictions, the court rules require the moving party to support a summary judgment motion with fact statements set forth in numbered paragraphs, and the opposing party must then rebut or admit each fact statement in counterpart numbered paragraphs.[32]

Success in an appeal from summary judgment depends, of course, on the existence of a genuine issue of material fact—not just any fact, but a material fact, and not just any dispute, but one based on evidence sufficient to pass a minimum threshold. Accordingly, on an appeal from an adverse summary judgment, the statement of facts is crucial. Your appeal stands or falls in these few pages. Two critical requirements must be met:

1) *Material Facts.* The evidence must show a dispute about facts that are material, that is, essential to the adjudication. The evidence, if believed, must be substantial enough to justify a jury in returning a verdict for the nonmoving

---

31. Celotex Corp. v. Catrett, 477 U.S. 317 (1986); Anderson v. Liberty Lobby, Inc., 477 U.S. 242 (1986); Matsushita Elec. Indus. Co., Ltd. v. Zenith Radio Corp., 475 U.S. 574 (1986).

32. *See, e.g.*, S.D. FLA. R. 56.1; N.J. CT. R. 4:46-2.

party. Peripheral and incidental evidentiary data do not rise to the level of material facts.

2) *Appendix or Excerpt of Record.* In addition to indicating in your statement of facts where the evidence appears in, if available, an electronic record, include copies of the most significant documents in your appendix or excerpt of record filed in the appellate court.

12.5.2 Sufficiency of the Evidence

Sufficiency of the evidence often serves as a major point on appeal. We see it on the civil side after the plaintiff's suit is dismissed by the granting of a motion for failure to state a claim (at common law, a "demurrer"), by directed verdict, by j.n.o.v., and where a defendant is held not to have proved an affirmative defense. In criminal appeals, the defendant often argues that the government did not present sufficient evidence to prove the elements of the crime beyond a reasonable doubt.

In these cases, you must set forth the evidence presented at trial in your statement of facts. Do not pick and choose only those facts helpful to your case. Save yourself and the court valuable time by describing the evidence in the light of the verdict winner. Some judges, when confronted with a sufficiency issue, immediately read the appellee's statement of facts before trudging through the appellant's account. If you are writing a brief on issues questioning the sufficiency of evidence, write it in terms of the worst-case scenario—remember that the judges will be reading your opponent's statement of facts too. In so doing you will immediately win points with the court.

Unfortunately, many lawyers simply gamble. They are willing to take the chance that their factual presentation will sneak past a judge on appeal because of forensic fatigue or some other lapse of standards. But do not bet on it. Appeals are heard by more than one judge. You may get a fastball high and on the inside corner past one judge, but the odds are that you will not get it past the others.

12.5.3 Facts as Predicate for Jury Instructions

Often, your major issue on appeal is that the trial court improperly instructed the jury on a point or that it improperly rejected your suggested point for charge. Because this presents a mixed question of law and fact, your statement of facts must set forth the precise evidence of record which, if believed by the jury, would support the requested instruction. Narrate the facts carefully in your statement. Set forth a sufficient factual predicate, but do not clutter.

A jury instruction is a statement in lay terms of a rule of law. According to Roscoe Pound, legal rules are "precepts attaching a definite, detailed legal consequence to a definite, detailed state of facts."[33] Accordingly, the trial judge charges: "Members of

---

33. Pound, *supra* note 5, at 482.

the jury, if you find fact *A*, then you must reach conclusion *B*." In stating facts in your brief, all that must be shown is that evidence supporting fact *A* was in the record.

Here, the statement of facts must reflect quality, not quantity. Help the appellate judge reach your way of thinking by making the narrative of facts resemble as closely as possible the material facts set forth in the legal precedent upon which you hinge your assertion that the trial court erred in instructing the jury. You do not help the appellate court, or yourself, if the judge has to struggle through a thicket of extraneous narrative before finally discovering the relevant factual nuggets.

12.6   Appellee's Statement of the Facts

How should you write the statement of facts if you are the appellee? Under the rules of the United States Supreme Court[34] and the rules of many appellate courts,[35] the appellee is not required to include a statement of the case unless the appellee disagrees or is dissatisfied with the appellant's statement of the case. Here, you must strike a delicate balance. You do not want to write a lengthy, repetitive statement of the case that just adds to the judge's already heavy reading load. At the same time, however, you want to emphasis the facts that are important to your client. One way to strike this balance is to identify points of agreement with the appellant's statement and just emphasize or clarify the points of disagreement in a brief statement. Unless the rules of the court completely prohibit the appellee from including a statement of the case, this is a way to be both persuasive and brief.

12.7   Examples of Statements of Facts

See Appendix C.

12.8   Statement of the Procedural History

An appellate judge often will ask an advocate to describe the procedural path a case has taken so far. In a clever story involving such a question, attributed to more than one justice and with varying answers all to the same effect, it is said that Justice Holmes or Justice Frankfurter once asked an advocate "How did you get here?" In some accounts, the attorney answered, "By the B&O, sir," though perhaps the misapprehending lawyer said "by taxi," or even "the train from Houston to Washington, and a cab from Union Station to the Court." That was not what the justice wanted to know, of course. He was looking for a statement of the procedural history, a brief explanation of the nature of the appeal, the course of the proceedings, and the disposition in the tribunal below.

---

34. Sup. Ct. R. 24(2).
35. *See, e.g.*, Fed. R. App. P. 28(b); Fla. R. App. P. 9.210(c); Va. Sup. Ct. R. 5:28(b).

A succinct statement of the procedural history in the brief tells the appellate court "how you got here." In this portion of the brief the lawyer verifies the procedural history of the case by answering these questions:

Who: Who initiated the case? Who won in the court (or courts) below? Who is taking the appeal?

What: What is the general area of law implicated in the appeal, and what specifically are the issues? What claims were filed?

Where: Where has the case been so far? A trial court, administrative agency, or intermediate court?

When: When was the alleged error committed? During the pre-trial, trial, or post-trial stage?

How: How was the case resolved? By summary judgment, a directed verdict, a jury verdict, or a nonjury award? How did the lower court(s) decide the case?

The challenge here is expressed in Blaise Pascal's lament, "I am sorry to have wearied you with so long a letter but I did not have time to write a short one."[36] In writing the procedural history, be sure to briefly state on what grounds the issue or issues in the case were decided below. If the case has already been decided by an intermediate appellate court and the decision was divided, the appellant should mention the dissenting opinion.

12.9   Examples from the Briefs

As noted at the beginning of this chapter, the procedural history can come either before or after the statement of facts. Naturally, the content of the section will vary, depending on its placement. We have provided examples of both types of procedural history statements.

12.9.1   *Procedural History after Statement of Facts*

See Appendix C.

12.9.2   *Procedural History before Statement of Facts*

Consider the following examples of procedural history statements from briefs where the procedural history precedes the factual statement (and our comments on the examples):

---

36. Barbara Tuchman, Practicing History 17–18 (1981).

This case involves a prosecution of twenty-one defendants on charges, *inter alia*, of conspiring to violate the Racketeer Influenced Corrupt Organizations Act, 8 U.S.C. § 1962(d), under a twelve-count indictment returned August 19, 1985.

Appellant Matthew P. Boylan was retained specifically and solely as local counsel in pretrial proceedings for the defendant; Milton M. Ferrell, Jr. was also retained to participate in pretrial proceedings. Milton M. Ferrell, Sr., was the defendant's sole trial counsel. The trial commenced on November 16, 1986, before the Honorable Harold A. Ackerman in the United States District Court for the District of New Jersey.

On February 16, 1988, the trial was recessed when the defendant informed the court that Milton M. Ferrell had been diagnosed as having advanced and incurable cancer and could no longer continue to represent him.

The defendant asked the court to sever his prosecution from that of the other defendants as a result of his counsel's illness. On February 25, 1988, following a February 24 hearing, Judge Ackerman denied the defendant's motion for severance and ordered Mr. Boylan and his firm, Lowenstein, Sandler, Kohl, Fisher & Boylan, to represent the defendant at trial, which Judge Ackerman scheduled to resume on March 21, 1988. Judge Ackerman further ordered Douglas L. Williams, the new law partner of Milton M. Ferrell, Jr., to assist in that representation. Mr. Boylan and the Lowenstein firm refused to comply with that order and on February 29, 1988, were held in civil contempt by Judge Ackerman and subjected to sanctions of $2,500 and $10,000 per day, respectively, for that refusal.

That same day, a Notice of Appeal was filed, and a three-judge panel of this court entered an order staying the order of the district court and scheduling this matter for expedited appeal.

Comment: Does this statement explicitly explain that this is an appeal by the lawyers on contempt sanctions? Does the first sentence suggest this?

This case involves "the ongoing controversy over logging in old growth forests in Oregon and Washington and the impact of that logging on the northern spotted owl." Old-growth forests are favored natural habitat for the northern spotted owl, *Strix occidentalis caurina*. The bird's current range extends from northern California, through the coastal and cascade regions of Oregon and Washington, and into southern British Columbia. Because of logging and land conversion activities, approximately 90 percent of suitable habitat for northern spotted owls now occurs on government land. The Forest Service manages 79 percent of the habitat on federal land, and the Bureau of Land Management manages 14 percent of it; the remaining 7 percent is on National Park Service land. 60 percent of northern spotted owl habitat on federal land is in areas classified as "timber production land."

In the late 1980s, respondents—the Seattle Audubon Society, the Portland Audubon Society, and other environmental groups—filed actions in the Western District of Washington and the District of Oregon challenging the federal government's efforts to continue logging old-growth timber in government-owned forests located in the Pacific Northwest. During the pendency of those federal court proceedings, Congress enacted Section 318 of the Department of the Interior and Related Agencies Appropriations Act, 1990, Pub. L. 101–121, Tit. III, 103 Stat. 745–750 (1989), also known as the Northwest Timber Compromise. Section 318 "sets terms and conditions applicable only for fiscal year 1990 for making timber sales on Federal lands in Oregon and Washington, for managing habitat for northern spotted owls, and for minimizing fragmentation of significant old growth forest stands." H.R. Conf. Rep. No. 264, 101st Cong., 1st Sess. 87 (1989). Its purpose was to "balance the goals of ensuring a predictable flow of public timber for fiscal year 1990 and protecting the northern spotted owl and significant old growth forest stands." *Ibid.*

The district courts in Oregon and Washington concluded that Section 318 operated as a "temporary modification of the environmental laws" invoked by respondents in their lawsuits. Accordingly, the district courts determined that the statute by its terms precluded respondents' claims for relief.

The Ninth Circuit reversed, holding that one part of Section 318—the first sentence in Section 318(b)(6)(A)—violates the constitutional principle of separation of powers set forth in *United States v. Klein*, 80 U.S. (13 Wall.) 128 (1872). The court of appeals determined that Section 318(b)(6)(A) "does not establish new law, but directs the court to reach a specific result and make certain factual findings under existing law in connection with two cases pending in federal court." In the court's view, "[t]his is what *Klein* and subsequent cases agree is constitutionally proscribed." *Ibid.* The court of appeals thus remanded the cases to the district courts for consideration of the merits of respondents' challenges.

Comment: Clear writing explains a complicated problem. If the statement of facts appeared first in the brief, much of the discussion of the statutory structure could be moved to that section.

_____

Plaintiffs Nationwide Mutual Insurance Company, et al., by whom defendant H. Bruce Cornutt had formerly been employed, brought this action to enforce certain provisions of the contract by which Nationwide had employed Cornutt. Before a hearing on a preliminary injunction could be scheduled, Cornutt moved for summary judgment based on the provisions of the Agreement. The district court granted Cornutt's motion for summary judgment as to paragraph 11 the Agreement,* but left for trial Nationwide's entitlement to enforcement of paragraph 12 of the Agreement.

Thereafter, a settlement was reached among the parties to permit review of the trial court's grant of summary judgment. By this settlement, Cornutt agreed to a final injunction with respect to paragraph 12 of the Agreement, and agreed to the preservation of Nationwide's right to appeal from the trial court's summary judgment with respect to paragraph 11. A timely notice of appeal was thereafter filed by Nationwide.

[Text of footnote]

* Paragraph 11 of the Agreement provides:

> 11. Agent agrees that he/she will not, either directly or indirectly by and for himself or as agent for another or through others as agent, engage in or be licensed as an agent, solicitor, representative or broker in any way connected with the sale, advertising or solicitation of fire, casualty, health or life insurance in the area described below for a period of one year from the date of the voluntary or involuntary termination of employment with the Companies or, should the Companies find it necessary by legal action to enjoin Agent from competing with the Companies, one year after the date such injunction is obtained in the following area: within Twenty Five miles of the principal place of business . . . .

Comment: The crux of the appeal is the text of paragraph 11 of the Agreement. It should not have been demoted to a lowly footnote but summarized and included in the body of the statement.

_____

The appeal is from a decision of the U.S. Tax Court entered March 30, 1989. The appeal was timely filed on June 27, 1989.

The Tax Court opinion is reported as 92 T.C. No. 38 (March 1989).

Comment: The minimalist style is not effective, and it is never justified, even in a complicated and technical tax case. Always answer the five questions.

12.10   Conclusion

Take the time to write a compelling, but accurate, statement of the case. Human nature is hardwired to take interest in and respond to stories; thus, a statement of the facts that tells your client's story in a clear and compelling fashion will play a vital role in persuading the court to rule in your favor.

The narrative often forms, in large part, the appellate court's first impression of your client's cause. It is usually a lasting one. If you handle this job well, you give your entire case the high gloss that marks a professional. Conversely, stealing the facts and obscuring the issues, intentionally or through simple neglect, diminishes both the court's confidence in counsel and sympathy for his or her client.

CHAPTER THIRTEEN

THE BRIEF: SUMMARY OF THE ARGUMENT

13.1 Overview

Under Federal Rule of Appellate Procedure 28(a)(7), appellate briefs must include:

> a summary of the argument, which must contain a succinct, clear, and accurate statement of the arguments made in the body of the brief, and which must not merely repeat the argument headings.

Even for lawyers practicing in jurisdictions that do not require a summary, a good brief writer will still include a summary, unless it is prohibited by the rules of the jurisdiction. In many ways, the summary of the argument is the most important part of the brief.

The summary is critical because it gives the reader a concise preview of the argument. Justice Clarence Thomas has aptly likened it to a television preview.[1] The summary should be crafted so as to allow the judge to construct a practical outline of the argument that will follow. It is, in a sense, an expanded table of contents. Alas, the summary is often not as useful as it should be because the brief writer either has not prepared a summary or has slapped one together without the thought necessary to create a statement that is both comprehensive and concise. Justice Samuel A. Alito has noted that many lawyers spend little time on the summary of the argument, which he calls a "missed opportunity."[2] He considers the summary to be one of the most important parts of the brief, and that "somebody reading the summary of the argument should understand what the case is about and the essence of the argument that is being made and should be persuaded to agree with that argument by what's in the summary."[3]

Not all judges, or justices, share this view. The late Justice Antonin Scalia rarely read the summary of the argument, stating in an interview "Why would I read the

---

1. Interview by Bryan A. Garner with J. Thomas, *United States Supreme Court*, in Washington, DC (Mar. 28, 2007), *in* SCRIBES J. LEGAL WRITING, 99, 113 (Joseph Kimble ed., 2010).

2. Interview by Bryan A. Garner with J. Alito, *United States Supreme Court*, in Washington, DC (Mar. 2, 2007), *in* SCRIBES J. LEGAL WRITING, 169, 178 (Joseph Kimble ed., 2010).

3. *Id.*

summary if I'm going to read the brief?"[4] He found the only real purpose for the summary to be to refresh the recollection of a judge who read the brief weeks before.[5]

Because the summary of the argument is intended to summarize the argument section, it must be drafted after the main argument section is largely completed. You cannot summarize an argument that you have not written. Therefore, you must leave ample time in your brief writing schedule to draft the summary. Do not let your summary be that "missed opportunity." For judges and law clerks who read a brief from cover to cover, this will be the first explanation of the arguments that they read in the brief.

The summary should contain two parts: 1) the critical opening paragraph, and 2) summaries of the main arguments in the brief.

13.2   The Critical Opening Paragraph

Readers of appellate briefs tend to be very busy. As a result, they have highly selective reading habits. They need and expect to know what a given case is about, and the opening of the summary of the argument should tell them immediately. Detective mysteries and narratives with surprise endings have their place—in fiction. But apply these techniques to brief writing and you risk losing your audience. With the number of appeals constantly increasing, it is important that the brief writer give an early signal to the reader. That signal is the opening or orientation paragraph of the summary of the argument.

The introduction of your summary, or critical opening paragraph, must let the reader know, in a few sentences, the scope, theme, content, and outcome of the brief. It sets the stage for the discussion to follow. It dispatches your argument to the reader at once in succinct, concise, and minimal terms. It describes the equitable heart of the appeal. Judges crave an immediate sense of overview. At the beginning of a brief, they are not interested in hearing all the details of the case. They want to know what kind of case this is and what issues the brief addresses.

The critical opening paragraph has two key elements. The first is the orientation sentence or sentences that announce the theme of your argument. The second is the roadmap. This roadmap should be a clear, concise, and orderly list of the points presented in the brief. These points are then expounded on in the remainder of the summary of the argument.

The late Justice William A. Bablitch of the Wisconsin Supreme Court reminded us that, as a basic principle of good writing, "a reader should not be forced to confront

---

4. Interview by Bryan A. Garner with J. Scalia, *United States Supreme Court*, in Washington, DC (Oct. 2, 2006), *in* Scribes J. Legal Writing, 51, 74 (Joseph Kimble ed., 2010).
5. *Id.* at 75.

details before the writer has provided a framework for understanding."[6] Thus, the introductory paragraph must alert the reader to the upcoming issues, their importance, and any conclusions to be drawn.[7] You may have the opportunity to write an effective introductory paragraph in other parts of your brief, depending on the court's rules, but it is essential that you prepare one as the introduction to your argument summary and repeat it at the start of the argument section. Justice Bablitch aptly observed:

> It is not easy to write a good introductory paragraph. It takes great effort, but it is time well spent. A properly written introduction makes the rest of the brief-writing task comparatively easy. If you are unable to write a cogent, succinct, encompassing introduction, you probably do not have a solid grasp of the subject matter.
>
> The fundamental question is, "What does the reader need to know to decide the final resolution?" If the introduction offers context before detail, then the reader is able to discern the important from the unimportant.[8]

Answering the "fundamental question" before your write your brief and your summary will ensure that your brief remains focused on what really matters in the case.

13.2.1 Finding Your Theme

When a lawyer discusses a case informally with another lawyer, such as standing at a bar having a drink with a friend, he usually can encapsulate the issue in a few sentences: "This case I had this week . . . . The jury came in against me, but I think I have a good issue on appeal. The trial judge allowed this garage mechanic to testify as an expert witness and he challenged the design of a new gear box on a $100,000 BMW. I got socked to the tune of a million bucks!"

In those few sentences, the lawyer described the theme of the appeal: the trial court abused its discretion in allowing the testimony of an unqualified expert. That is it. Everything to be said in the appellate brief should relate to this theme and should not be hidden in thirty pages or thirteen thousand words analyzing six different and cluttered issues.

"Most cases can be woven into a simple and consistent theme," writes Professor Henry D. Gabriel, a longtime appellate litigator for the United States Department of Justice.[9] He says that the theme usually derives from a simple point: "You should take the opportunity to go beyond the technical, legal points of your case and give the

---

6. William A Bablitch, *Writing to Win*, COMPLEAT LAW, Winter 1988, at 11.
7. *Id.*
8. *Id.*
9. Henry D. Gabriel, *Preparation and Delivery or Oral Argument in Appellate Courts*, 22 AM. J. TRIAL ADVOC. 571, 583 (1999).

court a common sense, simple reason why all the technical stuff in your brief makes sense . . . . This theme, if possible, should be grounded in broad equitable reasons."[10]

The theme is the unifying focus of your brief. It directs the court's attention, as Judge Myron H. Bright of the Eighth Circuit said, to where "the heart of the matter lies,"[11] or to what Jordan Cherrick called "the equitable heart of the appeal."[12] It answers the question in the mind of every judge addressing a brief for the first time, the question succinctly phrased by the former Wyoming Chief Justice Walter Urbigkit as: "WHAT IN THE HECK IS THE MESSAGE?"

To craft the theme or focus of your argument takes skill and concentration. It is the *first* thing you write and the *last* thing you rewrite. It is the dominant argument of maximum potency that must be compatible with ruling case law or consistent with known policy considerations of the judicial tribunal before which you appear. The theme should be all-inclusive and subsume the various points to be discussed in the brief. It should be a short, pithy, pointed sentence containing some important legal precept, one that Cardozo, in a related context, described as "a brief and almost sententious statement at the outset of the problem to be attacked."[13] If you are proceeding on alternative theories, you may have multiple themes, or you may find a theme that pulls the different theories together.

If you have trouble expressing the theme of the brief in the introductory pages of your summary of the argument, look to the introductory paragraph of judicial opinions written by those judges who spend much care in fashioning the opening.[14] A sampling of some excellent opening sentences from United States Supreme Court justices in recent opinions discloses how one can combine tight writing with excellent orientation.

| **Chief Justice Roberts** | The Fourth Amendment prohibits "unreasonable searches and seizures." Under this standard, a search or seizure may be permissible even though the justification for the action includes a reasonable factual mistake . . . . But what if the police officer's reasonable mistake is not one of fact but of law? In this case, an officer stopped a vehicle because one of its two brake lights was out, but a court later determined that a single working brake light was all the law required. The question presented is whether such a mistake of law can nonetheless give rise to the reasonable suspicion necessary to uphold the seizure under the Fourth Amendment.[15] |

---

10. *Id.* at 584.

11. Myron H. Bright, *Appellate Briefwriting: Some "Golden" Rules*, 17 Creighton L. Rev. 1069, 1071 (1984).

12. Jordan B. Cherrick, *Issues, Facts, and Appellate Strategy*, 16 Litig. 15, 17 (1990).

13. Benjamin N. Cardozo, *Law and Literature*, 14 Yale L. J. 705 (1925), reprinted in Selected Writings of Benjamin Nathan Cardozo 339, 352–53 (M. Hall ed. 1967).

14. For examples of good openings in judicial opinions *see* Ruggero J. Aldisert, Opinion Writing 77–79 (2d ed. 1990).

15. Heien v. North Carolina, 135 S. Ct. 530, 534 (2014).

Justice Scalia	Title VII of the Civil Rights Act of 1964 prohibits a prospective employer from refusing to hire an applicant in order to avoid accommodating a religious practice that it could accommodate without undue hardship. The question presented is whether this prohibition applies only where an applicant has informed the employer of his need for an accommodation.[16]
Justice Kennedy	The Court must decide whether the town of Greece, New York, imposes an impermissible establishment of religion by opening its monthly board meetings with a prayer.[17]
Justice Thomas	To enforce the Fourth Amendment's prohibition against "unreasonable searches and seizures," this Court has at times required courts to exclude evidence obtained by unconstitutional police conduct. But the Court has also held that, even when there is a Fourth Amendment violation, this exclusionary rule does not apply when the costs of exclusion outweigh its deterrent benefits. In some cases, for example, the link between the unconstitutional conduct and the discovery of the evidence is too attenuated to justify suppression. The question in this case is whether this attenuation doctrine applies when an officer makes an unconstitutional investigatory stop; learns during that stop that the suspect is subject to a valid arrest warrant; and proceeds to arrest the suspect and seize incriminating evidence during a search incident to that arrest.[18]
Justice Ginsberg	In *Illinois v. Caballes*, 543 U. S. 405 (2005), this Court held that a dog sniff conducted during a lawful traffic stop does not violate the Fourth Amendment's proscription of unreasonable seizures. This case presents the question whether the Fourth Amendment tolerates a dog sniff conducted after completion of a traffic stop.[19]
Justice Breyer	The Pregnancy Discrimination Act makes clear that Title VII's prohibition against sex discrimination applies to discrimination based on pregnancy. It also says that employers must treat "women affected by pregnancy . . . the same for all employment-related purposes . . . as other persons not so affected but similar in their ability or inability to work." 42 U. S. C. § 2000e(k). We must decide how this latter provision applies in the context of an employer's policy that accommodates many, but not all, workers with nonpregnancy-related disabilities.[20]

---

16. EEOC v. Abercrombie & Fitch Stores, Inc., 135 S. Ct. 2028, 2031 (2015).
17. Town of Greece v. Galloway, 134 S. Ct. 1811, 1815 (2014).
18. Utah v. Strieff, 136 S. Ct. 2056, 2059 (2016).
19. Rodriguez v. United States, 135 S. Ct. 1609, 1612 (2015).
20. Young v. UPS, Inc., 135 S. Ct. 1338, 1343–44 (2015).

Justice Alito	This case presents the question whether the First Amendment permits a State to compel personal care providers to subsidize speech on matters of public concern by a union that they do not wish to join or support.[21]
Justice Sotomayor	Almost 50 years ago, this Court declared that citizens do not surrender their First Amendment rights by accepting public employment. Rather, the First Amendment protection of a public employee's speech depends on a careful balance "between the interests of the [employee], as a citizen, in commenting upon matters of public concern and the interest of the State, as an employer, in promoting the efficiency of the public services it performs through its employees." *Pickering v. Board of Ed. of Township High School Dist. 205, Will Cty.*, 391 U.S. 563, 568 (1968). In *Pickering*, the Court struck the balance in favor of the public employee, extending First Amendment protection to a teacher who was fired after writing a letter to the editor of a local newspaper criticizing the school board that employed him. Today, we consider whether the First Amendment similarly protects a public employee who provided truthful sworn testimony, compelled by subpoena, outside the course of his ordinary job responsibilities.[22]
Justice Kagan	Federal law prohibits any person convicted of a "misdemeanor crime of domestic violence" from possessing a firearm. That phrase is defined to include any misdemeanor committed against a domestic relation that necessarily involves the "use . . . of physical force." § 921(a)(33)(A). The question presented here is whether misdemeanor assault convictions for reckless (as contrasted to knowing or intentional) conduct trigger the statutory firearms ban.[23]

You might argue that because Supreme Court justices take only limited questions on certiorari (or petitions for review in the state systems), it is easier for them to fashion an opening in one or two sentences than it is for a lawyer writing a brief that raises more than one question. But remember that the theme or jugular issue in a brief may center on a single question of law. In expressing that point, you would do well to emulate the crisp, focused technique employed by judges and justices.

13.3   Examples of Good Openings

The following are good examples of the opening sentence or paragraph to the summary of the argument:

---

21. Harris v. Quinn, 134 S. Ct. 2618, 2623 (2014).
22. Lane v. Franks, 134 S. Ct. 2369, 2374–75 (2014).
23. Voisine v. United States, 136 S. Ct. 2272, 2276 (2016).

This case presents a basic question of statutory interpretation: Does the Religious Land Use and Institutionalized Persons Act mean what it says, or should the legislative history be interpreted to trump the statutory text and require extreme deference to defendant prison officials?[24]

Content neutrality is an objective test. Under that test, laws that facially classify speech based on content are content based. There is no need for a free speech litigant to also prove a content-based purpose to prevail. Moreover, the government cannot exonerate its content-based discrimination by the mere assertion of a content-neutral purpose.[25]

Every year, California law requires thousands of public-school teachers to pay hundreds of millions of dollars to the NEA, the CTA, and their local affiliates. This annual tribute subsidizes those unions for the quintessentially political act of extracting policy commitments from local elected officials on some of the most contested issues in education and fiscal policy. That regime presents the basic question whether the First Amendment permits states to compel their public-school teachers to fund specific, controversial viewpoints on fundamental matters of educational and fiscal policy.[26]

It is well established that the First Amendment bars public employers from politically-motivated retaliation against nonpolitical employees such as police officers. Respondents retaliated against Heffernan because they thought he was campaigning for Spagnola. Respondents' factual mistake did not cure their constitutional mistake.[27]

An evidentiary rule must yield when it seriously infringes a constitutional right without sufficient justification. Here, applying Rule 606(b) to bar evidence that racial bias infected jury deliberations seriously

---

24. Brief for Petitioner at 12, Holt v. Hobbs, No. 13-6827 (Jan. 20, 2015), http://sblog.s3.amazonaws.com/wp-content/uploads/2014/05/13-6827-ts.pdf (last visited Mar. 20, 2017).

25. Brief for Petitioners at 19, Reed v. Town of Gilbert, No. 13-502 (June 18, 2015), http://www.americanbar.org/content/dam/aba/publications/supreme_court_preview/BriefsV4/13-502_pet.authcheckdam.pdf (last visited Mar. 20, 2017).

26. Brief for Petitioners at 9, Friedrichs v. Cal. Teachers Ass'n, No. 14-915 (Mar. 29, 2016), http://www.scotusblog.com/wp-content/uploads/2015/09/friedrichs-opening-brief.pdf (last visited Mar. 20, 2017).

27. Brief for Petitioner at 9, Heffernan v. City of Paterson, No. 14-1280 (Apr. 26, 2016), http://www.scotusblog.com/wp-content/uploads/2015/11/14-1280-ts.pdf (last visited Mar. 20, 2017).

infringes a defendant's Sixth Amendment right to an impartial jury, and no state interest justifies that infringement.[28]

_____

In the Copyright Act of 1976, Congress did not intend to grant a century of monopoly protection to cheerleader-uniform design—or any garment designs for that matter. Quite the opposite, Congress first proposed and then deliberately excluded industrial-design protection in the Act, and it has declined every invitation to extend copyright protection to garment design, even for a period as short as three years.[29]

_____

13.4   The Summary of Summaries

The remainder of the summary of the argument should be a terse synopsis of the argument rather than a verbatim repetition of the statement of issues. The United States Supreme Court rules provide that all briefs on the merits must contain "[a] summary of the argument, suitably paragraphed. The summary should be a clear and concise condensation of the argument made in the body of the brief."[30] This rule cautions that "a mere repetition of the headings under which the argument is arranged is not sufficient." The Federal Rules of Appellate Procedure track this language.[31]

Philadelphia attorney James Crawford similarly advises: "In your summary of argument, do not merely restate your questions presented or headings. The summary should be a neat balance between the absolute condensation of the questions and headings and the extensive discussion contained in the argument itself." Include key legal rules and key facts that make up the heart of your argument, but distill these points to just a few sentences each. At this point, it is not important to include citations to authorities. Those will come later in your argument. Remember, this is the preview of the coming attractions.

If a judge has not read the entire brief prior to oral argument or has read it well in advance of argument, the summary of argument can serve as a valuable substitute or refresher which the judge can glance at prior to the hearing. Many advocates firmly believe, therefore, that the summary of argument is one of the most important sections of the brief, recapitulating the central issues in the case. But beware: most of these summaries are too long. Judge Leonard I. Garth of the Third Circuit

_____

28. Brief for Petitioner at 13, Peña Rodriguez v. Colorado, No. 15-606, http://www.scotusblog.com/wp-content/uploads/2016/06/15-606-pet-merits-brief.pdf (last visited Mar. 20, 2017).

29. Brief for Petitioner at 22, Star Athletica, LLC v. Varsity Brands, Inc., No. 15-866, http://www.scotusblog.com/wp-content/uploads/2016/07/15-866-Pet-Merits-Brief.pdf. (last visited Mar. 20, 2017).

30. SUP. CT. R. 24(g).

31. FED. R. APP. P. 28(a)(7).

recommends to his students that no summary should exceed one-and-a-half pages. Another rule of thumb is to have the summary no longer than one-tenth of the argument length. So, if the argument is twenty pages long, the summary should be about two pages long.

13.4.1 Examples of Summaries of Arguments

See Appendix D.

13.5 The Introduction

In the last few decades, advocates have started including introductions to their briefs. These introductions appear before the Statement of the Case and serve to provide the judges with a short explanation of what happened in the case and why the appeal is being brought. Practitioners and judges who like introductions believe that they are critically important for putting a case in context right from the start.[32] There is a danger, however, that the introduction will drone on too long, become argumentative, or be repetitive of the Summary of the Argument.[33] There is also a danger that your brief will be rejected by the clerk's office if the rules of the jurisdiction do not explicitly allow for an introduction.[34]

Chief Justice John G. Roberts, Jr., who used introductions in practice, explained in an interview with Bryan Garner his views on the difference between an introduction and the summary:

> [The introduction is] almost never, . . . "In part one I'm going to say this, and in part two I'm going to say this, and in part three I'm going to say this." It's more, "This is a story about what happened when this, this, and this, and the court below said this, and that's wrong because of this and this." And then go into it. But give them an idea of, not a road map, not a summary, but your main argument. Again, it's sort of the written equivalent of those first couple of sentences of oral argument.[35]

Should you include an introduction in your brief? It depends. First and foremost you must comply with the rules of your jurisdiction. Do the rules require an introduction? Do they permit an introduction even if it is not required? The rules of your jurisdiction must control. If the rules do permit an introduction, if your

---

32. Lance Curry, *No Introduction Needed? The Effectiveness of Introductions in Appellate Briefs*, 18 J. App. Prac. Sec. (The Florida Bar), Winter 2011, at 11, 13.

33. *Id.*

34. *Id.*; Interview by Bryan A. Garner with C.J. Roberts, United States Supreme Court, in Washington, DC (Mar. 2, 2007), *in* Scribes J. Legal Writing, 5, 30 (Joseph Kimble ed., 2010).

35. Interview by Bryan A. Garner with C.J. Roberts, United States Supreme Court, in Washington, DC (Mar. 2, 2007), *in* Scribes J. Legal Writing, 5, 30-31 (Joseph Kimble ed., 2010).

case is complicated, and you do not follow the "deep issue" formula discussed in Chapter Eight, then a brief introduction can be useful to judges. If, however, you are concerned about running afoul of court rules, you can simply include the introductory material at the start of the Statement of the Case. Regardless of the approach taken, be sure to keep the introductory material short and not overly argumentative, especially if it appears in the Statement of the Case.

13.5.1 *Introduction Examples*

Below are two examples of introductions in Supreme Court briefs. These examples are taken from the petitioner's and respondent's brief in the same case. As you are reading them, notice the persuasive, but not overly argumentative, language that each side uses to describe the facts of the case and the relevant law.

> Under Florida law, a defendant convicted of a capital felony cannot be sentenced to death unless the State proves beyond a reasonable doubt at least one statutory aggravating circumstance. Because the existence of a statutory aggravator is a condition of the defendant's eligibility for a death sentence, its determination must "be entrusted to the jury." *Ring v. Arizona*, 536 U.S. 584, 597 (2002).

> Florida law, however, assigns this factfinding role to the trial judge. In Florida, the court makes its own findings as to the existence of aggravating and mitigating circumstances and conducts its own weighing of those circumstances before imposing a sentence of its own determination. In doing so, the court may consider evidence that was never shown to a jury, and may find aggravators that were not found by or even presented to a jury. Only the judge's written findings of fact are relevant on appellate review of a death sentence.

> Florida juries play only an advisory role. The jury recommends a sentence of life or death based on its assessment of aggravating and mitigating circumstances, but that recommendation has no binding effect. Moreover, the jury renders its advisory verdict under procedures that degrade the integrity of the jury's function. Unanimity, and the deliberation often needed to achieve it, is not necessary; only a bare majority vote is required to recommend a death sentence. The jury makes no express findings on aggravating circumstances. And jurors voting for a death sentence need not even agree on which aggravating circumstance exists.

> In this case, for example, the State presented two aggravators in arguing that petitioner Timothy Lee Hurst should be sentenced to death. The jury recommended a death sentence by a bare majority of seven to five. The jury made no express findings as to any aggravator.

It is entirely possible that four jurors found one aggravator, and three found the other, but that at least two-thirds of the jurors rejected each. The trial court made its own findings that each aggravator existed beyond a reasonable doubt and imposed the death sentence based on its own weighing of the aggravating and mitigating circumstances.

Mr. Hurst's death sentence and the procedures it resulted from cannot stand. Florida's capital sentencing scheme contravenes this Court's holding in *Ring* that findings of fact necessary to authorize a death sentence may not be entrusted to the judge. It departs from the procedures that apply in every other State that allows death sentencing. And it undermines the jury's basic Sixth and Eighth Amendment functions as responsible factfinder and voice of the community's moral judgment. This case thus arises "at the intersection of [this Court's] decisions" according capital defendants basic Sixth and Eighth Amendment protections in sentencing. *Burch v. Louisiana*, 441 U.S. 130, 137 (1979). Even if a State can constitutionally assign the jury only an advisory role, or permit different aggravators to be found by different jurors on different theories, or allow the jury to find aggravating circumstances by a bare majority, a State cannot do all these things at once without transgressing those constitutional protections.[36]

For murdering Cynthia Harrison, Timothy Lee Hurst was tried, convicted, and sentenced to death. Hurst's death sentence came only after the court and the jury found beyond a reasonable doubt that Hurst's crime involved at least one aggravating circumstance. In a detailed written order, the trial court specifically found two: that Hurst committed the murder during the course of a robbery and that the crime was especially heinous, atrocious, or cruel. JA261-63. In the Florida Supreme Court, Hurst admitted the aggravating circumstances, characterizing the crime as a "robbery gone bad" and disclaiming any challenge to the aggravating circumstance findings. Appellant's Initial Br. 24-25 (No. SC12-1947). He nonetheless argues here that *Ring v. Arizona*, 536 U.S. 584 (2002), entitled him to specific jury findings regarding the aggravating factors he conceded. He further argues that only the jury—and not the judge—can impose a death sentence. Hurst asks too much of *Ring*.

This Court has consistently upheld Florida's capital sentencing scheme, which in essence treats the judge and the jury as

---

36. Brief for Petitioner at 3, Hurst v. Fla., No. 14-7505 (Jan. 12, 2016), http://sblog.s3.amazonaws.com/wp-content/uploads/2015/06/Hurst-merits-brief.pdf (last visited Mar. 20, 2017).

"cosentencer[s]." See *Lambrix v. Singletary*, 520 U.S. 518, 528 (1997). The Court has rejected claims that the jury must decide the sentence, *Spaziano v. Florida*, 468 U.S. 447, 465 (1984), that a court cannot rely on its own findings, *Hildwin v. Florida*, 490 U.S. 638, 640 (1989) (per curiam), and that the overall scheme leads to arbitrary sentences, *Proffitt v. Florida*, 428 U.S. 242, 251 (1976) (joint opinion of Stewart, Powell, Stevens, JJ.).

Ring undermined none of this. Instead, *Ring* narrowly held that the principle of *Apprendi v. New Jersey* applies to capital sentencing, meaning a defendant cannot become eligible for a death sentence based on facts found solely by a judge "sitting without a jury." *Ring*, 536 U.S. at 609 (citing 530 U.S. 446, 494 n.19 (2000)). Even under this rule, the judge may impose any sentence authorized "on the basis of the facts reflected in the jury verdict or admitted by the defendant." *Blakely v. Washington*, 542 U.S. 296, 303 (2004). And in this case, the "facts" necessary to make Hurst eligible for death were both reflected in the jury's decision and admitted by Hurst. Hurst's sentence complies with *Apprendi* and *Ring*.

Florida's capital sentencing scheme was constitutional before *Ring*, and it remains constitutional in light of *Ring*.[37]

13.5.2 *More Examples of Introductions*

See Appendix D.

13.6 Conclusion

The summary of the argument plays a critical role in your brief, either as a preview of the arguments to come, or as a refresher for judges prior to oral argument. Taking the time to craft an excellent summary will help solidify your argument section and the main theme that your case is centered around. Do not waste this opportunity.

An introduction has a different purpose than the summary of the argument. It sets the stage for the remainder of your brief by introducing the main characters and setting out the flashpoint of controversy between them. It is not a point-by-point summary of your argument. Think of it as the 30,000-foot level explanation to the court of what happened and why that is wrong (or right). For some matters, this explanation is best handled in a separate introduction section; for others, it can be done in the statement of the case.

---

37. Brief for Respondent at 2, Hurst v. Fla., No. 14-7505 (Jan. 12, 2016), http://www.scotus-blog.com/wp-content/uploads/2015/08/14-7505-bs.pdf (last visited Mar. 20, 2017).

CHAPTER FOURTEEN

THE BRIEF: FINALIZING AND FILING THE BRIEF, RESPONSIVE BRIEFS

14.1 Overview

Because requirements for briefs and supporting records, or excerpts thereof, vary throughout the country, this book is not intended to present a compendium. The purpose of this book is merely to touch on some features of United States Courts of Appeals and state systems and to emphasize that differences do exist, even among the federal circuits, and that lawyers must be aware of them. We also want to emphasize that you diminish the efficacy of your brief when you do not follow a court's briefing rules. Because of the extraordinary caseloads in appellate courts, judges are understandably disturbed when they turn to a particular section of a brief for information and find it wanting because the rules have not been observed. Nor are they pleased when parts of the briefs arrive in dribs and drabs after counsel discovers he has omitted something. When these arrive after the judge has already read the brief, lawyers run the risk that they will never be read.

Do not consider what we set forth about rules to be definitive; this book should not be cited as authoritative. It is not even intended as a secondary source. Only the latest edition of the Federal Rules of Appellate Procedure, the circuit rules or the state rules, and any local rules or operating procedures should be consulted in preparing an appeal.

The federal system will be discussed in detail because it affords some uniformity throughout the country. Rules in the state systems differ from jurisdiction to jurisdiction. Although it is difficult to generalize, we can offer a number of suggestions to alert you to problems relating to briefing rules. We will start with some key principles.

- *United States Courts of Appeals.* Do not rely exclusively on the Federal Rules of Appellate Procedure. They are only the starting point. You must always examine the rules of the individual circuits for local idiosyncrasies. If a difference does exist between the federal rules and the circuit rules, the circuit rules control to the extent that they are "not inconsistent with" the federal rules. You may obtain these rules from the clerk of the court of each circuit or on each circuit court's website.

- *State Appellate Courts.* Each state appellate court may have its own rules. Thus, do not assume that the rules of the state's highest court govern practice in the intermediate appellate court. In some instances, there may appear to be a conflict between a state appellate court's rules and the rules of the state's highest court. If in doubt, ask the clerk of court. You should also consult the state court's website.

- *Nomenclature.* Throughout these pages, we typically refer to the party bringing the appeal as the *appellant,* although in some states, in appeals from federal administrative agencies, and in the United States Supreme Court, the moving party is known as the *petitioner.* We will refer to the opposing party as the *appellee,* although in these same courts the answering party is known as the *respondent.* In most jurisdictions, the appellate proceeding is known as an *appeal,* although appeals from administrative agencies generally are termed *petitions for review.* Federal legislation has made most of the Supreme Court's jurisdiction discretionary, thus reducing direct appeals in favor of *petitions for writs of certiorari* either to a United States Court of Appeals or to a state appellate court. Some state appellate courts also have discretionary dockets. Accordingly, when we use the terms *appellant* and *appellee,* you may wish to read them as *petitioner* and *respondent.* We will also use the term *judge* rather than *justice.* Generally intermediate appellate courts are presided over by *judges* while the highest federal and state courts are made up of *justices.* Be sure you utilize the proper terms in your briefs. A simple online search should provide you with the right answer.

As a final introductory note, please remember that it takes a significant amount of time to finalize a brief and ensure that it meets all of the rule requirements. Even with the advent of readily available software programs that can create tables and the ability in many courts to electronically file a brief, you should always leave ample time to finalize and file your brief.

14.2 Requirements for Briefs: Federal Court

The general requirements for briefs filed in federal appellate courts are set forth in Federal Rule of Appellate Procedure 28. The federal rules outline these components in some detail, and most state courts follow a similar pattern.

The federal rules require the appellants to include the following elements, under appropriate headings and in the order indicated. Our comments follow each required element.

    (1) "a corporate disclosure statement if required by Rule 26.1;"[1]

---

1. FED. R. APP. P. 28(a)(1).

Comment: This requirement is designed to permit judges to recuse (or disqualify) themselves if they have a financial interest in any party, or in a parent or subsidiary company of party.

(2) "a table of contents, with page references;"[2]

Comment: This should serve as an outline of your argument that a judge can scan to refresh herself on the key points in your brief. Be certain that your page numbers are correct—judges rely on them.

(3) "a table of authorities—cases (alphabetically arranged), statutes, and other authorities—with references to the pages of the brief where they are cited;"[3]

Comment: A table of authorities is generally required in all state appellate courts. If it is not required but is not forbidden, you should include one. Be sure to follow carefully the court's rules on how to divide up the authorities. Some courts also require attorneys to put an asterisk by cases that are primarily relied upon.[4]

(4) "a jurisdictional statement, including:

    (A) the basis for the district court's or agency's subject-matter jurisdiction, with citations to applicable statutory provisions and stating relevant facts establishing jurisdiction;

    (B) the basis for the court of appeals' jurisdiction, with citations to applicable statutory provisions and stating relevant facts establishing jurisdiction;

    (C) the filing dates establishing the timeliness of the appeal or petition for review; and

    (D) an assertion that the appeal is from a final order or judgment that disposes of all parties' claims, or information establishing the court of appeals' jurisdiction on some other basis;"[5]

Comment: Please see Chapter Four for a detailed discussion of the jurisdictional statement. You must be certain that the court has jurisdiction.

---

2. *Id.* at 28(a)(2).

3. *Id.* at 28(a)(3).

4. *See* D.C. Cir. R. 28(a)(2) ("In the left-hand margin of the table of authorities in all briefs, an asterisk must be placed next to those authorities on which the brief principally relies, together with a notation at the bottom of the first page of the table stating: 'Authorities upon which we chiefly rely are marked with asterisks.' If there are no such authorities, the notation must so state.").

5. Fed. R. App. P. 28(a)(4).

(5) "a statement of the issues presented for review;"[6]

Comment: Please see Chapters Six and Eight for a detailed discussion of the statement of the issues. If permitted by the rules, write these persuasively.

(6) "a concise statement of the case setting out the facts relevant to the issues submitted for review, describing the relevant procedural history, and identifying the rulings presented for review, with appropriate references to the record (see Rule 28(e));"[7]

Comment: The references to the record should be done in accordance with Rule 28(e). Please see Chapter Twelve for a detailed discussion of the statement of the case.

(7) "a summary of the argument, which must contain a succinct, clear, and accurate statement of the arguments made in the body of the brief, and which must not merely repeat the argument headings;"[8]

Comment: Please see Chapter Thirteen for a detailed discussion of the summary of the argument. Remember that some judges might read this part of your brief first. Be sure that this is a persuasive overview of your argument.

(8) "the argument, which must contain:

(A) appellant's contentions and the reasons for them, with citations to the authorities and parts of the record on which the appellant relies; and

(B) for each issue, a concise statement of the applicable standard of review (which may appear in the discussion of the issue or under a separate heading placed before the discussion of the issues);"[9]

Comment: We recommend a separate standard of review section; however, your standard of review should be woven into your entire argument. Your issues presented and point headings should reflect the standard. Additionally, be sure to anticipate and rebut the appellee's argument. Remember that as appellant you face an uphill battle.

(9) "a short conclusion stating the precise relief sought; and"[10]

Comment: Be specific in your prayer for relief.

(10) "the certificate of compliance, if required by Rule 32(a)(7)."[11]

---

6. *Id.* at 28(a)(5).
7. *Id.* at 28(a)(6).
8. *Id.* at 28(a)(7).
9. *Id.* at 28(a)(8).
10. *Id.* at 28(a)(9).
11. *Id.* at 28(a)(10).

Comment: Your brief will probably require this certificate. Make it clear and accurate. Do not try to play games with the word limit.

The appellee's brief must conform to these requirements as well, except that the statement of jurisdiction, the statement of the issues, the statement of the case, and the standard of review may be omitted if the appellee is satisfied with those sections of the appellant's brief.[12] If the appellant has done her job, however, the appellee should not be satisfied with the statement of the issues, the entire statement of the case, or maybe even the standard of review. If, as appellee, you are satisfied with most of the statement of the case, feel free to include an abbreviated statement of the case that points out the areas of disagreement and includes the persuasive facts that the appellant likely left out.

An appellant may file a reply to the appellee's brief;[13] if the appellee has cross-appealed, the appellant may respond.[14] Where the appellant has responded, the appellee as cross-appellant may reply.[15] This is the *only* time an appellee is permitted to respond to a reply brief. All reply briefs must contain a table of contents and a table of authorities.[16]

Briefs should, indeed some courts say they must, refer to the relevant portions of the record. Until recent years, the portions of the record most important to the appeal were reproduced as an appendix or excerpt of the record.[17] Increasingly, appellate courts are subordinating the appendix—though it is still required—as the part of the record judges actually will use, and instead are requiring references to the actual, complete electronic record. You must be aware of the practice in your jurisdiction. The Fifth Circuit, for example, now requires the original record to be cited in briefs.[18] The Clerks' Office, by order, has established a special format for citation to be used in briefs so that the record citations will automatically become hyperlinks once the brief is electronically filed with the court. Judges can click on the links when reading briefs on an electronic medium and immediately be taken to that part of the record. Under the Fifth Circuit Local Rules, "record excerpts are intended primarily to assist the judges in making the screening decision on the need for oral argument and in preparing for oral argument. Counsel need excerpt only those parts of the record that will assist in these functions."[19]

---

12. FED. R. APP. P. 28(b).

13. *Id.* at 28(c).

14. *Id.* at 28.1(c)(3) ("In a case involving a cross-appeal: . . . "[t]he appellant must file a brief that responds to the principal brief in the cross-appeal and may, in the same brief, reply to the response in the appeal.").

15. *Id.* at 28.1(c)(4).

16. FED. R. APP. P. 28(c).

17. *Id.* at 28(e).

18. 5TH CIR. R. 30.1.

19. 5TH CIR. R. 30.1.1.

When an appendix is prepared, lawyers should understand that, both in theory and in actual use, an appendix is precisely what the word denotes—a supplement that adds supporting details to what was said in the text. An appropriate appendix should do no more and no less. Be sure to take the time to prepare an accurate appendix or excerpt of the record. Senior Judge Stephen S. Trott of the Ninth Circuit offers this comment:

> The excerpts we get are terrible, obviously prepared by paralegals or young associates. The excerpt is to your brief what your evidence in a trial is to your opening statement. Would you deliver a great opening statement and then ignore your evidence?
>
> I do not trust briefs when they describe or paraphrase something. I go immediately to the excerpt to see for myself what happened. However, often it is not in the excerpt, or the brief takes unwarranted liberties with the truth. Also, in cases where a defendant's liberty depends on whether or not a detective's photo lineup was unconstitutionally suggestive, I find a fuzzy fourth generation black and white copy of a color photo lineup. Can you spell *Strickland* on appeal?
>
> If you are going to make a claim or an argument, you better be able to prove it in your excerpt.
>
> Don't think of the process as "adversarial." Big mistake, because that will disconnect you from the truth. If you cheat or fudge or spin, it won't bother me because I am used to it, but my law clerks will want to tear you limb from limb. I always tell them, yes, but we do not visit the sins of the attorneys on their clients.
>
> [Attorneys must recognize] the importance of well-organized, judge-friendly excerpts in courts where we use them.

If a determination of the issues requires the court to examine particular statutes, rules, or regulations, court rules permit brief writers to place the relevant text of these sources in either the brief or an addendum to the brief. Where these sources are critical to understanding the argument, you should include the relevant portion—the heart of the issue—in the text, with the full source either footnoted or placed in the addendum. Requirements for the appendix are discussed below.

14.2.1   Special Rules of the United States Courts of Appeals

Each of the Courts of Appeals has promulgated local rules either supplementing or modifying the provisions of Rule 28 and the related rules. A lawyer appearing before these courts should carefully examine the court's current local rules, which can be found on that court's website.

The following is an indication of *some* additions or modifications to the general requirements of Rule 28, adopted by the various circuits: statement of related cases;[20] designation in the table of authorities of authorities principally relied on;[21] request for (or waiver of) oral argument;[22] copy of any unpublished disposition cited;[23] copy of the judgment or order appealed from;[24] relevant portions of any jury instructions.[25]

If the court dispenses with the requirement of an appendix, under Rule 30(f), it may "proceed on the original record with any copies of the record, or relevant parts, that the court may order the parties to file."[26] Some courts, like the Fifth Circuit, decide cases using the "Electronic Record on Appeal," which is prepared by the district court clerk.

14.3   Formatting Rules

In addition to the requirements for the contents of briefs, parties to an appeal must observe certain formatting rules regarding the form of the briefs, such as the print and paper size, the number of pages or words allowed,[27] the binding method required,[28] the color and content of the front cover,[29] and the number of copies to file.[30] Even though many jurisdictions, including all of the federal courts, permit or require electronic filing, some courts also require paper copies.[31]

In the United States Courts of Appeal, the appellant's brief cover must be blue; the appellee's brief, red; the reply brief, gray; and the intervenor or amicus brief, green.[32] The front cover generally shall contain the name of the court and case number, the title of the case, the nature of the appellate proceeding, the name of the lower court, the title of the document, and the names and addresses of counsel filing the brief.[33] It bears repeating that each appellate court—state or federal—is very exacting regarding these requirements. Do not try to play tricks to get around these requirements, especially the length requirements. Judges do not take kindly to

---

20. FED. CIR. R. 47.5.
21. D.C. CIR. R. 28(a)(2).
22. 5TH CIR. R. 28.2.3.
23. 6TH CIR. R. 28(b)(2).
24. 11TH CIR. R. 30-1(a)(5).
25. *Id.* at 30-1(a)(9).
26. FED. R. APP. P. 30(f).
27. FED. R. APP. P. 32 (a)(7) provides that principal briefs shall not exceed thirty pages or 13,000 words, and reply briefs shall not exceed fifteen pages.
28. *Id.* at 32(a)(3).
29. *Id.* at 32(a)(2).
30. *Id.* at 31(b).
31. 3D CIR. R. 31.1(a).
32. FED. R. APP. P. 32(a)(2).
33. *Id.*

such attempts.[34] Examine the rules every time you prepare a brief to ensure that each requirement of the court is met. Check to see if the court has a sample brief available on its website to help you visualize the formatting rules.[35]

14.4   Requirements for Briefs: State Courts

Unlike the federal appellate courts, the state courts do not follow a uniform briefing system. Requirements for briefs in state courts are as many and as varied as the states themselves.

Generally speaking, all states require the following: table of contents, table of authorities, statement of the case, statement of issues, statement of facts, and the argument and conclusion stating the precise relief sought. Some require a summary of argument, copies of relevant statutes, rules and regulations, a statement of jurisdiction, and specific references to the record. The length of briefs varies from thirty pages to seventy-five pages (if typewritten), with fifty pages being about the norm.[36] California has a unique rule: each point must be set off with a concise heading that generally describes the subject matter covered. Failure to comply can result in dismissal.[37] Some state appellate courts have sample briefs available online that lawyers can review to better understand state formatting rules.[38]

---

34. For example, in one case, a federal judge issued a serious warning to an attorney for "squeezing the spacing between lines" in order to fit more words into a 35-page limit. Debra Cassens Weiss, *Judge Scolds BP for Squeezing Extra Lines into Brief*, ABA JOURNAL (Sept. 18, 2014, 09:50 AM), http://www.abajournal.com/news/article/judge_scolds_bp_for_squeezing_extra_lines_into_brief (last visited Mar. 20, 2017). In another case, the judge dismissed an appeal altogether after the appellant twice submitted a brief which actually exceeded the word count but attempted to meet the limit by removing spaces from in between words and inventing unknown and confusing abbreviations. Pi-Net Int'l, Inc. v. JPMorgan Chase & Co., 600 F. App'x 774 (Fed. Cir. 2015) (Mem.). The Seventh Circuit also warned attorneys that misrepresenting the word count of the brief would result in dismissal of the appeal, after a party filed a brief that exceeded the word count limit, yet falsely stated in its certification that it was below the limit. Brad A. Catlin, *The Seventh Circuit Warns Lawyers Not to Misrepresent Their Word Counts*, PRICE-LAW (Mar. 9, 2011), http://www.price-law.com/news-blog/the-seventh-circuit-warns-lawyers-not-to-misrepresent-their-word-counts/ (last visited Mar. 20, 2017).

35. *See, e.g., Sample Brief Formats*, UNITED STATES COURT OF APPEALS FOR THE FIFTH CIRCUIT, http://www.ca5.uscourts.gov/documents/SampleBriefs.pdf (last visited Mar. 20, 2017).

36. The Council of Appellate Lawyers, *Comments on Proposed Amendments to the Federal Rules of Appellate Procedure Before the Advisory Committee on Appellate Rules*, ABOVE THE LAW, 1–2 & nn. 1–3 (Feb. 13, 2015), http://howappealing.abovethelaw.com/ABA_CAL_final_comments_re_proposed_FRAP_amendments(with_member_comments)_4833-2898-5890_v.pdf (citing multiple state court brief length requirements) (last visited Mar. 20, 2017).

37. CAL. R. CT. 8.204; *Superior Sand Co. v. Smith*, 64 P.2d 1149, 1149 (Cal. Ct. App. 1937).

38. *See, e.g., Appellate Court Sample Briefs*, OREGON COURTS, http://courts.oregon.gov/OJD/OSCA/acs/records/pages/samplebriefs.aspx (last visited Oct. 4, 2016); *Forms, Samples and Resources*, COURT OF APPEALS OF OHIO NINTH APPELLATE DISTRICT, http://www.ninth.courts.state.oh.us/Forms-Samples.htm (last visited Mar. 20, 2017).

14.5 The Brief's Conclusion

An important part of finalizing your brief is writing an effective conclusion, which is required by the federal rules. In this conclusion, you must advise the court precisely the relief you seek. Tell it what you want.

Some lawyers recapitulate the argument in the conclusion. Often, this is very effective, especially if the written argument has been lengthy, but the conclusion should be extremely concise; it should not be a reprint of your summary of argument and should not exceed a few sentences. In most cases, however, a recap is not necessary. Also, in most cases, the relief requested may be clear from the status of the case, but in a good number of cases this is not so. Either way, the federal rules require you to state "the precise relief sought."[39] If you are seeking a remand with a direction to enter judgment notwithstanding the verdict, say so. Otherwise, the court may conclude that you are requesting a new trial. If you are requesting a remand with a direction to dismiss the complaint or to enter judgment in favor of your client, say so. Be very specific.

Resist the urge to start your conclusion with the phrase "for the foregoing reasons" or something similar. Your conclusion naturally should follow from the arguments in the brief and these words simply contribute to pushing you closer to your word limit.

14.5.1 Examples of Conclusions

Here are some examples of appropriate conclusions.

> This Court should reverse the judgment against Smith and remand the case to the district court for entry of a judgment of acquittal. Alternatively, the judgment should be reversed and the case remanded for a new trial.

> The decision below should be reversed and remanded with instructions that the adoption be approved under state law.[40]

> This Court should reverse the judgment of the court of appeals.[41]

> The judgment should be reversed and the case remanded for further proceedings consistent with an opinion clearly stating that RLUIPA is

---

39. FED. R. APP. P. 28(a)(9).
40. Brief for Petitioners at 57, Adoptive Couple v. Baby Girl, 133 S. Ct. 2552 (2013) (No. 12-399).
41. Brief for Petitioners at 53, Reed v. Town of Gilbert, 135 S. Ct. 2218 (2015) (No. 13-502).

to be enforced according to its terms and that respondents have wholly failed to prove either compelling interest or least restrictive means.[42]

The Florida Supreme Court's judgment should be reversed and Hurst's sentence should be vacated.[43]

Arizona's triggered matching funds provision does not place a substantial burden on political speech, and it directly furthers the state's compelling interests in combating corruption and enhancing electoral debate and competition. The judgment of the Court of Appeals should accordingly be affirmed.[44]

[T]he Court should reverse the decision of the First Circuit, vacate the petitioners' convictions, and remand these cases for proceedings consistent with the exclusion of reckless conduct misdemeanors from the definition of a "misdemeanor crime of domestic violence."[45]

Complete the conclusion with a signature line signed by the party filing the brief or, if represented, the party's attorney.[46] If applicable, the signature block should also include the name of the law firm, followed by an address, the name of the party represented, and its role in the case, whether appellant, appellee, intervenor, or amicus. In some jurisdictions, the lawyer's bar number must be added to all court papers.

14.6 Requirements for the Record and Appendix: Federal Court

The record in federal appeals consists of all papers and exhibits filed in the district court, any transcript of proceedings, and a certified copy of the docket sheet.[47] Within fourteen days after filing a notice of appeal, the appellant must order from the court reporter a transcript of those portions of the proceedings not already

---

42. Brief for the Petitioner at 55, Holt v. Hobbs, 135 S. Ct. 853 (2015) (No. 13-6827).

43. Brief for Petitioner at 54, Hurst v. Florida, 136 S. Ct. 616 (2016) (No. 14-7505).

44. Brief of Respondent Clean Elections Institute, Inc. at 62, Arizona Free Enterprise Club's Freedom Club PAC v. Bennett, 564 U.S. 721 (2011) (Nos. 10-238 and 10-239).

45. Brief for Petitioners, Voisine v. United States, 136 S. Ct. 2272 (2016) (No. 14-10154).

46. FED. R. APP. P. 32(d).

47. FED. R. APP. P. 10(a).

on file that are relevant to the appeal.[48] Once the district clerk has received the transcript and the record on appeal is complete, the clerk generally has a duty to transmit the entire record to the clerk of the court of appeals.[49] However, a lawyer appearing before a particular court of appeals should ensure that the circuit's local rules do not modify these general rules. As noted above, increasingly records are being transmitted electronically, with the district court preparing an "Electronic Record on Appeal."

The appellant must also prepare and file an appendix to the briefs containing: "(1) the relevant docket entries in the proceeding below; (2) the relevant portions of the pleadings, charge, findings or opinion; (3) the judgment, order or decision in question; and (4) any other parts of the record to which the parties wish to direct the court's attention."[50] If the parties do not agree on the contents of the appendix, the appellee can compel the appellant to include items.[51]

Rule 30(f) allows courts of appeals to dispense with the requirement of an appendix. Some circuits, including the Ninth and Eleventh Circuits, take a moderate approach, requiring excerpts of the record in lieu of a full-blown appendix.[52] The Fifth Circuit requires record excerpts despite also relying on the full electronic record, but it states that the purpose of the excerpt is solely to assist a three-judge panel in determining whether oral argument should be scheduled.[53]

Some courts of appeals require both an appendix and an addendum to the briefs. The First Circuit, for example, requires the appellant to include at the end of the brief a copy of the judgment or order appealed from, any relevant jury instructions, and pertinent portions of any documents relevant to the issues on appeal.[54]

Many courts will excuse an appellant from filing an appendix for good cause shown.[55] Thus, if you have a good reason to omit the appendix, such as when the record is short or the appeal is expedited, you should consider filing a motion to dispense with the appendix. The court also may excuse the appendix requirement if the appellant is proceeding *in forma pauperis*.[56]

The most important lesson to be learned is that the local rules in the various courts of appeals do vary. An attorney appearing before one of these courts must study the local briefing rules carefully and follow them to the letter. A well-presented brief and appendix that adhere to the court's requirements will not only assist

---

48. Fed. R. App. P. 10(b)(1).
49. Fed. R. App. P. 11(b)(2).
50. Fed. R. App. P. 30(a).
51. Fed. R. App. P. 30(b).
52. 9th Cir. R. 30-1; 11th Cir. R. 30-1.
53. 5th Cir. R. 30.1, 30.1.1.
54. 1st Cir. R. 28(a).
55. D.C. Cir. R. 30(d).
56. *Id.* at 24.

the court, but will ensure that the court does not sanction the client or the attorney for noncompliance, as some local rules permit.[57] It also will present a professional image to the court.

14.6.1 *Whether to Provide an Appendix*

If you are not in a jurisdiction with electronic records and the appendix or record excerpt is optional under the rules, it may be prudent to file as an excerpt of record or as an addendum to the brief copies of 1) any opinion written by the district court; 2) if the issue relates to a jury instruction, the entire jury charge, the transcript of any jury instruction conference conducted under Federal Rule of Civil Procedure 51 or Federal Rule of Criminal Procedure 30, and if relevant, a transcript of testimony supporting your requested instruction; and 3) a rather detailed transcript of the proceedings when the issue is insufficiency of the evidence. You should also include copies of any opinion that cannot be easily obtained online from Lexis Advance or WestlawNext. Even though the rules may not require it, *always* paginate the documents in the appendix and include an accurate, detailed table of contents.

By following these recommendations, you will give each member of the panel the opportunity to examine these materials before, during, and after oral argument. That they are in the record and readily available to the circuit judge stationed at the seat of the court where the record is stored also is not sufficient. The good appellate lawyer will ensure that every member of the panel has easy access to them.

14.7 Requirements for the Record and Appendix: State Court

When appearing before a state appellate court, you must familiarize yourself with that court's rules, if any, regarding transmission of the record on appeal and preparation of an appendix for the court. Some states require both the record and an appendix; others require one or the other.[58] Generally speaking, you must file a copy of the judgment appealed from, the notice of appeal, and the entire trial court record.[59] Requirements for appendices vary: some require a table of contents, relevant docket entries, the judgment of the trial court or any intermediate court of appeals, the trial court opinion, the jury instructions and other pertinent portions

---

57. 3D CIR. R. 30.5(a) (providing that the court may impose sanctions "upon finding that any party has unreasonably and vexatiously caused the inclusion of materials in an appendix that are unnecessary for the determination of the issues presented on appeal").

58. FLA. R. APP. P. 9.220(a) (requiring an appendix containing "copies of those portions of the record deemed necessary to an understanding of the issues presented"); ME. R. APP. P. 5–6(a) (requiring a record on appeal to be filed); *id.* at 8(a) (requiring "[i]n every case the party who files the first notice of appeal shall file an appendix to the briefs.").

59. *See, e.g.,* N.Y. CT. APP. R. 500.14(a)–(b).

of the pleadings and transcript.[60] In some cases, the parties may file a joint appendix or the appellee is given the option of filing a separate one.

14.8   A Wrap-Up on Briefs and Records Rules

We cannot overemphasize the necessity of knowing and observing the rules governing briefs and the supporting record (whether by way of appendix, addendum, excerpt of record, or the entire transcript). Failure to respect these rules may not cause your case to be dismissed, but it may get you off on the wrong foot. The best you can hope for in an appeal is a sympathetic court; at the very least, you want a neutral tribunal, not one that is hostile. You certainly do not want to face a court that has formed the impression that "This lawyer is complaining that the trial judge did not follow the rules of the game, but in taking this appeal, this character isn't following ours!"

Philosopher Henry Habberly Price has emphasized the importance of first impressions. He has explained that a sort of mental occurrence takes place when we are in the process of acquiring a favorable or unfavorable initial impression, and that such a disposition is not necessarily a very long-lived one; it may last only a few seconds.[61] But the advice is clear: do not make an initial bad impression by filing a sloppy brief that fails to follow the court's requirements.

In some instances, failure to follow the rules may result in more drastic consequences. In *Kushner v. Winterthur Swiss Insurance Company*,[62] the Third Circuit dismissed an appeal for failure to file a brief and appendix conforming to the local rules. The appellant's brief failed to set forth the names and addresses of counsel, and the appendix omitted the relevant trial court docket entries and notice of appeal and was not paginated. The court stated:

> We have explained the practical reasons for our action. [Much valuable time had to be expended by three judges and personnel of the clerk's office repairing the incomplete brief and appendix.] There is jurisprudential justification for our decision as well. Each appellant in this court must of necessity allege that the district court violated some rule of substantive or procedural law relating to the finding of facts, the exercise of discretion, the choice of proper legal precept, the interpretation of the precept chosen, or its application to the facts as found. The litigant, then, who charges that the rules were not followed in the

---

60. *See, e.g.*, Va. Sup. Ct. R. 5:32(a)(1) (requiring, *inter alia*, the initial pleading, final judgments from all of the courts below, exhibits, a table of contents, and pertinent parts of the record).

61. Henry Habberly Price, *The Inaugural Address: Belief and Will*, *in* 28 Proceedings of the Aristotelian Society 1, 15–16 (1954).

62. 620 F.2d 404 (3d Cir. 1980).

district court should himself follow the rules when he applies for relief in this court. Sauce for the goose is sauce for the gander.[63]

Failure to follow briefing rules also may result in lesser sanctions, such as the striking of briefs[64] or monetary sanctions against counsel.[65]

14.9 Cover Page, Table of Contents, and Table of Authorities

The table of contents and table of authorities are important to judges. Take care to ensure that they are complete and accurate. How well you do this depends on when you do them. These tables comprise the first pages of most briefs, but they should not be completed until the brief is in its final stages. Even if you use computer programs to make these tables, be sure that you give yourself plenty of time to finish the tables and proof them before your brief is filed.

Judges constantly refer to these tables. They look to the table of contents to sense an overview of the case and for speedy references. They become frustrated when the tables omit crucial information or cite to incorrect page numbers or contain errors in citation. You want judges to be happy customers. They are not happy when your tables lead them astray.

Although the cover page may be prepared at any time, for administrative ease you should prepare the cover at the same time you prepare the tables of contents and authorities.

14.9.1 Cover Page

The cover page is used by the clerk's office and the court to identify the brief. Thus, it is important to set forth correctly on the cover page the information required by the court's rules. In many courts, that information will be the court in which the brief is being filed, the docket number, the case caption, the court below, the party filing the brief, and the attorneys on the brief. Federal Rule of Appellate Procedure 32(a) specifically provides:

> The front cover of a brief must contain: (A) the number of the case centered at the top; (B) the name of the court; (C) the title of the case (see Rule 12(a)); (D) the nature of the proceeding (e.g., Appeal, Petition for Review) and the name of the court, agency, or board below;

---

63. *Id.* at 407. Subsequent courts have dismissed appeals for failure to follow local rules. *See, e.g.,* Haugen v. Sutherlin, 804 F.2d 490, 491 (8th Cir. 1986) (violation of "all the rules in the Federal Rules of Appellate Procedure and [the] local Eighth Circuit rules pertaining to form for briefs and record"); Connecticut Gen. Life Ins. Co. v. Chicago Title & Trust Co., 690 F.2d 115, 116 (7th Cir. 1982) (failure to following briefing schedule), cert. denied, 464 U.S. 999 (1983).

64. *See, e.g.,* McGoldrick Oil Co. v. Campbell, Athey & Zukowski, 793 F.2d 649, 653 (5th Cir. 1986).

65. *See, e.g.,* Westinghouse Elec. Corp. v. NLRB, 809 F.2d 419, 425 (7th Cir. 1987).

(E) the title of the brief, identifying the party or parties for whom the brief is filed; and (F) the name, office address, and telephone number of counsel representing the party for whom the brief is filed.[66]

State rules follow the same general requirements. You should arrange the required information in the form suggested or mandated by the court, but the most important factor is accuracy. A brief containing an incorrect docket number or case caption could be misfiled or lost. If the court rules are unclear on order, you may politely ask the clerk's office for advice or review briefs filed by the solicitor general or attorney general of the state.

You also must ensure that the cover page is printed or formatted in the proper color. As stated before, the federal rules require that the appellant's brief cover be blue; the appellee's brief, red; the reply brief, gray; and any intervenor or amicus brief, green.[67] The cover of the appendix, if separately printed, should be white.[68] This color code may not be important to lawyers, but it is critically important to judges because of the time pressures under which they study the briefs. It enables them to quickly flick from one brief to another in a given case. You must keep in mind that some judges will read a point in the appellant's brief and immediately examine the appellee's response.

A valuable suggestion, often unheeded in appeals involving multiple parties or cases that are consolidated, is to set forth the name of the appellant or the appellee on the cover page. Instead of merely stating "Brief for Appellee," you should state "Brief for Appellee John J. Jones." This will allow the judge to identify immediately the party submitting the brief.

The following is a sample civil brief cover for a brief filed in the United States Court of Appeals for the Fifth Circuit.[69] Because it is an appellee's brief, it should be printed on red paper.

---

66. Fed. R. App. P. 32(a)(2).

67. *Id.*

68. *Id.* at 32(b)(1).

69. Brief of Appellees World Alliance Financial Corp. and Reverse Mortgage Solutions, Inc., Johnson v. World All. Financial Corp., 830 F.3d 192 (5th Cir. 2016) (No. 15-50881), 2016 WL 109802, http://www.ca5.uscourts.gov/docs/default-source/sample-briefs/appellee-39-s-civil-brief.pdf (last visited Mar. 20, 2017).

CASE NO. 15-50881

IN THE UNITED STATES COURT OF APPEALS
FOR THE FIFTH CIRCUIT

JILLIAN JOHNSON,
Plaintiff - Appellant,

v.

WORLD ALLIANCE FINANCIAL CORP.
AND REVERSE MORTGAGE SOLUTIONS, INC.,
Defendants - Appellees.

On Appeal from the United States District Court
For the Western District of Texas, San Antonio Division
Civil Action No. 5:14-CV-281

BRIEF OF APPELLEES WORLD ALLIANCE FINANCIAL CORP.
AND REVERSE MORTGAGE SOLUTIONS, INC.

Mark D. Hopkins
Texas State Bar No.: 00793975
Hopkins Law, PLLC
12117 Bee Caves Rd., Suite 260
Austin, Texas 78738
Telephone: (512) 600-4320
Facsimile: (512) 600-4326
mark@hopkinslawtexas.com

Crystal G. Roach
Texas State Bar No. 24027322
Barrett Daffin Frappier
Turner & Engel, LLP
15000 Surveyor Blvd., Ste 100
Addison, TX 75001
Telephone: (972) 340-7901
Facsimile: (972) 341-0743
crystalr@bdfgroup.com

ATTORNEYS FOR APPELLEES WORLD ALLIANCE
FINANCIAL CORP. AND REVERSE MORTGAGE
SOLUTIONS, INC.

14.9.2 *Table of Contents*

A good table of contents is very simple to prepare because it follows the logical pattern of your brief. In most instances, the task can be handled by a word-processing program, but you should always double check the program's work. The key is neatness and accuracy. Because many judges scan the table of contents to get a preview of coming attractions, a neat, accurate, and complete table of contents can help create a good first impression. Conversely, a sloppy, incomplete table can give the reader a negative impression of the entire brief. Carefully draft the table, and keep in mind the following advice:

> A well-organized and informative table of contents will allow the judges to quickly access your arguments—often in response to points made by your opponent—and will make assimilation of the elements of your position much easier for them . . . . If the table of contents is poorly done or incomplete—if it fails to separate and index the components of the arguments being made—the judge can easily take wrong turns and grow increasingly frustrated as he or she is forced to spend needless time paging back and forth through the briefs looking for points and counterpoints.[70]

Consider also these comments by Tenth Circuit Judge Harris L. Hartz:

> The table of contents (and the brief itself) should include helpful headings. When the headings are just "Point I," "Point II," etc., the judge who wants to double check what the party argues on a particular matter (perhaps after reading the opposing brief or while working on the opinion) must skim through the entire brief and may miss something important.

The table of contents should list by page each component of the brief.[71] Each issue and sub-issue should be included under the "Argument" heading. This allows the table of contents to serve as an outline of the brief. If the rules permit, you should frame each issue so that it becomes the heading in the argument portion of the brief. Your objective: cast the issue in language that the court can accept completely and adopt as a topic sentence in its opinion.

Consider form as well as substance. Because your purpose is to communicate, you should understand that a sentence typed in all capital letters is not as easy to read as one presented in caps and lower case. Moreover, reading is even more complicated when a single-spaced, all-caps sentence is underlined. Stating the headings in your brief is not the same as giving the title of a book or a play. Unless the court rules require otherwise, you need only capitalize the first word and any proper names in

---

70. Judge William Eich, *Writing the Persuasive Brief*, WIS. LAW., Feb. 2003, at 21, 22.
71. FED. R. APP. P. 28(a)(1).

your issue statement and in the table of contents headings. Capitalizing the first letter in every word in a sentence interferes with smooth reading. Additionally, any typographical formatting used to distinguish headings in the body of the argument, such as underlining, italics, or boldface, should be omitted from the table.

Finally, if the court rules permit, you should hyperlink your table of contents entries to take the reader to the specific location in the brief. Judges are increasingly reading briefs on computers and tablets. Hyperlinking permits a judge to quickly jump to various sections of your brief and can be incredibly useful to judges during oral argument. Again, be sure to check the accuracy of all the hyperlinks before e-filing your brief.

TABLE OF CONTENTS

Comment: This table of contents is particularly effective because the reader's eye is not distracted by unnecessary capitalization, underlining, or boldface print. The table also serves as a map of the entire brief; it succinctly tells the reader what the issues are and where each required element of the brief can be found. An effective alternative form utilizes all capital letters in the main point and lower case in the subpoints.

Consider the following examples of less effective tables of contents:

TABLE OF CONTENTS

Comment: The use of underlining makes this table much more difficult to read than the first model above. The point headings are also quite sparse and tell the reader very little about the arguments that will be raised in the case.

TABLE OF CONTENTS

Comment: Does this table of contents tell the reader anything about the appeal? Does the eye quickly follow to the precise page number without the dotted line?

14.9.2.1 Cross-Reference Indexing

In previous editions of this book, Judge Aldisert strongly recommended that the arguments in the appellee's brief track those set forth by the appellant. He reasoned that this allowed the reader to look at the table of contents and readily ascertain where the appellee has responded to a particular argument posed by the appellant. While this approach may be appropriate in some circumstances, the appellee should try always to lead from strength in his brief. This may require the appellee to order his arguments differently from the appellant.

If it is necessary for an appellee to place the various arguments in a different sequence than the appellant, the appellee should provide the court with a cross-reference index. The United States Court of Appeals for the Third Circuit, for example, requires the appellee to provide a cross-reference index when filing a single brief in response to consolidated appeals by several appellants.[72] The following is an example of an effective cross reference index which appeared in a brief responding to two consolidated petitions for a writ of mandamus:

CROSS-REFERENCE INDEX

Petitioners' Contentions	*Respondents' Answering Contentions*
1. Writ of mandamus should issue because district court abused its discretion and acted arbitrarily (Celotex brief 10–13; Eagle Picher brief 8–11).	Requirements for writ are not met; district court did not act arbitrarily nor did it usurp power (Respondents' brief 8–11).
2. Circumstances have changed since Third Circuit upheld class certification in 1986 (Celotex brief 13–30; Eagle Picher brief 18–28).	Petitioners have shown no change in circumstances sufficient to justify issuance of the writ (Respondents' brief 11–13).
3. District court's denial of class in *Davenport v. Gerber Baby Products* shows arbitrariness of its refusal to decertify the class in this case (Celotex brief 33–36).	District court properly distinguished *Davenport* (Respondents' brief 10).
4. The litigation is "unsettleable" (Celotex brief 36–39).	Several defendants have already settled; another settlement is being completed (Respondents' brief 13).

14.9.3   *Table of Authorities*

There are several word-processing programs out there that can help you automatically assemble a table of authorities.[73] Once again, the key is neatness and accuracy. Judges often use this table to refer to the place or places in a brief where a particular case, statute, or constitutional provision is discussed, or to quickly find the citation to a specific authority. It bears repeating that judges become disturbed when citations are incorrect or page references inaccurate. Carefully proofread the

---

72. 3D CIR. R. 28.2. This rule provides, in relevant part:

> The brief of an appellee who has been permitted to file one brief in consolidated appeals shall contain an appropriate cross-reference index that clearly identifies and relates appellee's answering contentions to the specific contentions of the various appellants.

73. *See* Michael R. Fortney, *Easily Create a Table of Authorities for a Legal Brief with Microsoft Word*, FORTNEY LAW GROUP (Sept. 29, 2014, 4:43 PM), http://www.fortneylawgroup.com/articles/Easily-Create-a-Table-of-Authorities-for-a-legal-brief-with-Microsoft-Word.html (last visited Mar. 20, 2017) (describing how to create a table of authorities using Microsoft Word); *Prepare Table of Authorities: Create a TOA Within Seconds*, LEXISNEXIS, http://www.lexisnexis.com/en-us/products/lexis-for-microsoft-office/prepare-table-of-authorities.page (last visited Mar. 20, 2017) (describing how to create a table of authorities using Lexis for Microsoft Office); *How to Create a Table of Authorities in WordPerfect*, COREL, https://support.corel.com/hc/en-us/articles/215963808-How-to-create-a-Table-of-Authorities-in-WordPerfect (last visited Mar. 20, 2017) (describing how to create a table of authorities in WordPerfect).

citations and verify the page numbers after the brief is in final form to ensure that any last-minute changes are incorporated in the table of authorities.

Federal Rule of Appellate Procedure 28(a)(3) requires that the table list "cases (alphabetically arranged), statutes, and other authorities with references to the pages of the brief where they are cited."[74] The local rules may require a different division of authorities, so be sure to verify the requirements of the jurisdiction in question. The citation to each authority should be complete and in *Bluebook* form unless the jurisdiction uses a different form of citation. List every page that the authority appears. Resist the urge to use "*passim*" even if the authority appears on numerous pages unless the rules specifically request that "*passim*" be used.

If you must gather the information for the table of authorities manually, we suggest that you or someone on your staff make a separate 3x5-inch index card for each authority or use a spreadsheet. After the complete citation for each authority has been placed on a card or in the spreadsheet, arrange the cards or entries in alphabetical order according to the type of authority. In most instances, you will have three separate groups of entries: one for cases; one for constitutions, statutes, and rules; and one for miscellaneous sources.

Once you cast the brief in final form and are reasonably certain that the page numbers will not change, have someone mark on each index card or in the spreadsheet the pages on which that particular authority appears. An administrative assistant or paralegal can then prepare the table of authorities simply by taking the information off the stacks of index cards.

Remember to begin working on the table of contents while you are writing the brief. Do not wait until the night before the deadline to start composing it in a frantic burst of overtime madness. Elements of the table should be assembled at the same time drafts of the argument are being prepared. Judges rely on your table in the decision-making process as well as the process of writing an opinion. The table must be complete and accurate. Save enough time to do it right—it is one of the most important parts of the brief.

You also should be aware that some courts, such as the Eleventh Circuit and the D.C. Circuit, require that the table indicate those authorities principally relied on.[75] If this is required, you should place an asterisk in the left-hand margin next to those authorities and note at the bottom of the first page of the table: "Authorities chiefly relied upon are marked with an asterisk." Additionally, some court rules, such as those of the D.C. Circuit, ask attorneys to list every page on which the authority is cited and not to use the term "*passim*."[76]

For briefs that are filed electronically, check the court's rules regarding hyperlinking authorities in your brief. For judges who read briefs on a computer or tablet,

---

74. Fed. R. App. P. 28(a)(3).
75. 11th Cir. R. 28-1(e); D.C. Cir. R. 28(a)(2).
76. D.C. Cir. R. 28(a)(2).

hyperlinking citations in your brief to the full text of the case can be a great time saver. WestlawNext and Lexis Advance offer software that can help attorneys add hyperlinked citations to their briefs.[77]

Consider the following example of a model table of authorities:

TABLE OF AUTHORITIES

Cases: Page(s)

Ashford v. State, 603 P.2d 1162 (Okla. Crim. App. 1987)............ 15

Brooks v. Tennessee, 406 U.S. 605 (1972)...................................24

Burgett v. Texas, 389 U.S. 109 (1967). 12

Carrizales v. Wainwright, 699 F.2d 1053 (11th Cir. 1983). 21

Commonwealth v. Rogers, 364 Pa. Super. 477,
    528 A.2d610 (1987)..15

Dowling v. United States, 110 S. Ct. 668 (1990). 12

Henderson v. Kibbe, 431 U.S. 145 (1977). 25

Lisenba v. California, 314 U.S. 219 (1941) 13, 14

Passman v. Blackburn, 652 F.2d 559 (5th Cir. 1981)...................21

People v. Jackson, 18 Cal. App. 3d 504, 95 Cal. Rptr.
    919 (1971) 15

State v. Lapage, 57 N.H. 245 (1876)..14

State v. Tanner, 675 P.2d 539 (Utah 1983) 15, 16

United States v. Bowers, 660 F.2d 527 (5th Cir. 1981)..................15

United States v. Rodriguez, 812 F.2d 414 (8th Cir. 1987) 19

Constitutions, statutes and rules:

U.S. CONST. amend. VI. 12

U.S. CONST. amend. XIV 1, 2, 9

28 U.S.C. § 2254(a)..22

FED. R. EVID. 404(b)...17

Miscellaneous:

EDWARD J. IMWINKELRIED, UNCHARGED MISCONDUCT
    EVIDENCE (1984)... 13, 14

A.H. McCoid, *The Battered Child and Other Assaults Upon
    the Family: Part One*, 50 MINN. L. REV. 1 (1965)...................14

---

77. Ellie Neiberger, *Judge-Friendly Briefs in the Electronic Age*, FLA. BAR J., Feb. 2015, at 46, http://www.floridabar.org/DIVCOM/JN/JNJournal01.nsf/c0d731e03de9828d852574580042ae7a/98d92d0040b87a1b85257dd40058dbc3!OpenDocument (last visited Mar. 20, 2017).

14.10   Filing the Brief

Today, all federal courts[78] and many state courts[79] allow (and sometimes mandate) briefs and related documents to be filed electronically. The federal courts' e-filing system, the Case Management/Electronic Case Files program—or CM/ECF—serves both as an electronic filing system and as the new case management system for the courts.[80] The National Center for State Courts' Court Technology Bulletin provides up-to-date information on the status of e-filing in state courts and links to the various state court e-filing systems.[81]

While e-filing can be very convenient for attorneys who would rather not have to worry about couriers and near deadline misses caused by unexpected traffic on the way to the courthouse, it does present its own unique set of difficulties. As the adage goes, "A computer lets you make more mistakes faster than any invention in human history—with the possible exceptions of handguns and tequila."[82]

Dallas attorneys W. Kelly Stewart and Jeffrey L. Mills have identified several key potential problems that attorneys should be aware of when e-filing documents with the courts.[83] Most of the problems that Stewart and Mills identify revolve around missing deadlines. For example, attorneys unfamiliar with e-filing and the amount of time it takes to register for an account, receive a password ("which may require human approval and might take longer than 24 hours"), prepare your document for filing, and check all of the online boxes can miss a deadline if they start the process too late.[84] Similarly, "even if you initially meet a deadline, a court can reject a filing if in filing it you did not choose from among the electronic fields properly, which can cause you to miss the deadline if you do not receive a rejection notice with sufficient time to correct mistakes."[85]

Attorneys can also miss deadlines by failing to calculate them properly. If you are e-filing a document, be sure that you know whether the filing deadline requires the

---

78. *FAQs: Case Management / Electronic Case Files (CM/ECF)*, U.S. Courts, http://www.uscourts.gov/courtrecords/electronic-filing-cmecf/faqs-case-management-electronic-case-files-cmecf (last visited Mar. 20, 2017) [hereinafter Case Management/Electronic Case Files].

79. *Status of State Court E-Filing – January 2016*, Nat'l Ctr. St. Cts. (Jan. 26, 2016), https://courttechbulletin.blogspot.com/2016/01/status-of-state-court-e-filing-january.html#more (last visited Mar. 20, 2017) [hereinafter Status of State Court E-Filing].

80. Case Management/Electronic Case Files, *supra* note 78.

81. Status of State Court E-Filing, *supra* note 79.

82. United States v. Carelock, 459 F.3d 437, 443 (3d Cir. 2006) (quoting Herb Brody, *The Pleasure Machine: Computers*, Tech. Rev., Apr. 1992, at 31.

83. W. Kelly Stewart & Jeffrey L. Mills, *New Risks Every Litigator Should Know*, For The Defense, June 2011, at 28, http://www.jonesday.com/files/Publication/efd9d946-2272-4493-9bb6-312e53bb8419/Presentation/PublicationAttachment/9398f37a-c4a0-4338-8a4e-35cdf2d69900/FTD-1106-Stewart-Mills.pdf (last visited Mar. 20, 2017).

84. *Id.* at 29.

85. *Id.*

document to be filed at the close of the business day or by midnight.[86] Be sure that you understand the service rules in your jurisdiction and what effect e-filing after the close of business may have on timely serving opposing counsel.[87] Also understand any relevant file size limits your jurisdiction has on e-filed documents.[88] Even if your document meets the court's page or word count limits, it could be rejected if the megabyte size exceeds the court's limits.[89]

Stewart and Mills advise attorneys to "confirm whether you uploaded the correct documents and attachments *before* you hit 'submit.'"[90] They cite two examples of federal appellate courts that found documents to be filed in an untimely manner when the attorney inadvertently uploaded the wrong document. As the Third Circuit noted in one of the cases, "Although the modern use of the computer is a great time-saver, its ease of use should not assuage the almost obsessive attentiveness that is required when filing any document with a court."[91]

Just because your jurisdiction allows e-filing does not mean that paper copies are not required.[92] You *must* carefully scour the court rules and local operating procedures to ascertain the requirements of your jurisdiction regarding any paper copies far in advance of any filing deadlines. If, after reviewing the rules, you are still in doubt with respect to the requirements, a politely inquiring call to the clerk's office will generally settle the issue.

14.11 The Appellee's Brief

The appellee's brief should follow the same suggestions we have made for the appellant: proper statement of issues, a summary of the argument, the enunciation of a theme or focus, and leading with strength while at the same time providing a clear cross-reference for the judges to follow. Some differences in appellate advocacy, however, present themselves. First, you have the advantage of defending a judgment, order, or decision in your favor and often are armed with the statement of reasons offered by the trial court or agency. It is your adversary, and not you, who has the burden proving that the judgment should be disturbed. Second, in the style of the Greco-Roman rhetoricians, your argument must be a combination of *confutatio* (refuting your opponent's argument) and *confirmatio* (confirming what the court did below).

---

86. *Id.*
87. *Id.*
88. *Id.*
89. *Id.*
90. *Id.* at 30.
91. *Carelock*, 459 F.3d at 443.
92. R. Laine Wilson Harris, *Ready Or Not Here We E-Come*, 12 Legal Comm. & Rhetoric: JALWD 83, 90–107 (2015) (listing state requirements for paper and electronic copies).

14.11.1   The Appellee's Statement of Facts

Where you agree with the appellant's statement of facts, even if the literary style or length is not what you would have offered, it may be well to say that you accept it. If you disagree, you probably have two choices: 1) accept with some modifications of your own, or 2) present your own statement.

Keep in mind the environment in which briefs are read, and seek to reduce the judges' reading time to a minimum. Also keep in mind the distinction between material or adjudicative facts on the one hand and surplus narrative on the other. If your quarrel is with the Mickey Mouse trivia in the appellant's statement of facts, you might state some phrase that fairly characterizes the fact-statement as excessive, but otherwise let it alone and save your big guns until later. (By all means, if you are going to say the appellant was too wordy, err on the side of being brief in doing so.) If there has been an omission or misrepresentation as to material facts, however, you may say, "We accept appellee's statement of facts, except that it omits the following [then insert the material with an appendix or record reference] and mistakenly says [so and so] when the record actually says [such and such with a page reference]."

If these factual omissions or errors are important, and you expose them, then your adversary's loses credibility points early in the judge's reading of the brief. If you have chosen to restate the facts because there are too many errors or omissions, it will be helpful to summarize the omissions and inaccuracies at the conclusion of your statement.

The late Ohio Supreme Court Chief Justice Thomas J. Moyer made the same point: "Conciseness in the writing of an appellee's brief includes the realization that the judge does not need to read the statement of facts twice. The appellee should indicate which portions of the statement of facts and statement of the case with which the appellee agrees and devote your efforts to clarifying the appellant's statement and adding facts that are favorable to the appellee's case that may not have been mentioned in the appellant's statement."

14.11.2   Comment on the Appellant's Authorities

The best case scenario for the appellee unfolds when the appellant has neglected to cite a controlling case of the highest court of the jurisdiction or of the court in which you now appear. When this occurs, you hit your adversary between the eyes as soon as possible. But do it skillfully, focusing on the *relevant* points that your opponent has failed to address. Avoid the ad hominem accusation that the appellant is deceiving the court. The judges will probably take it over from there at oral argument.

Does the appellee comment on all the authorities cited by the appellant? The conventional wisdom is that you should, but there are certain caveats. You are not in a law school class reciting the entire case cited by the appellant; you are before a busy appellate court. It is sufficient to note that the holding of the case is not as represented; if you can get a one-sentence direct quote laying out the law, put it in. It is sufficient also to note that the material facts in that case differ from the instant one and quickly show the distinction. It is sufficient also to show any difference in the procedural postures of the two cases. This may become very important when the appeal is from summary judgment or from a jury or bench trial and the cited case emanated from a Rule 12(b)(6) motion (judgment on the pleadings); point out the distinction and succinctly explain why it makes a difference.

The rule of thumb is that the appellee should have an answer to every authority cited by the appellant, but the response need not be unduly prolix. Often, totally irrelevant citations are thrown in as make-weights in the appellant's brief. These do not deserve the dignity of measured response, and here, perhaps, is where a footnote may tidily dispose of them.

But where the flashpoint of dispute is choosing among competing legal precepts, interpreting the legal material selected, or applying the resulting legal precept to the cause, it is not enough merely to say that your choice is the better (or majority) view, or that your interpretation or application is superior; you must explain why yours is the preferable view. Always give the court a supply of reasons, not only to persuade them to make the decision in your favor but also to furnish material that the judges may properly use in their justification of the decision—the opinion they will write.

A word about logic: it is not enough for the appellee to charge that the appellant's "reasoning was flawed." Be very specific and identify precisely why and how the logical progression fails. The judges will be impressed. Besides, it will straighten out your thinking. Often, when one says that the "reasoning is flawed," what is meant is that one disagrees with the judgment call used to choose the major premise; such is not a quarrel with canons of logical reasoning, but a disagreement with the value judgment employed by the court. Do not fall into this trap.

Finally, when you (and ostensibly the trial court) insist that a certain case is controlling, be sure to explain why.

14.12 The Reply Brief

The reply brief can be both the best of times and the worst of times. It is at its best when it addresses a point not raised in the appellant's opening brief, such as an argument or error in the appellee's brief, or a new decision handed down since the filing of the opening brief. It is at its worst when an appellant simply rewrites the opening brief and restates what was said before.

Someone who did not know a thing about how appellate judges decide cases has preached a gospel to many appellants' lawyers to file a reply brief in every case: "Always have the last word." While that may work in a schoolyard argument or a political debate, it is not always effective in appellate advocacy.

Judge Aldisert estimated that, of the thousands of reply briefs that he read since 1968, maybe 500 genuinely qualified as reply briefs. Most simply repeat arguments contained in the opening brief.

He believed that a reply brief should only be prepared in the following situations:

- if the appellee cites a case not covered in the opening brief and you are able to show that it is either not controlling or does not stand for the proposition asserted;

- if the appellee advances an important argument not covered by your opening brief and you have a convincing rebuttal to it;

- if the appellee has raised a question of jurisdiction not covered in your opening brief;

- if relevant cases have been handed down since filing your opening brief;

- if the appellee has made a misstatement of fact or an irrelevant argument;

- if the appellee has failed to respond to a principal argument you made in your opening brief. Here, you succinctly say that the appellee has apparently conceded this point.

Judge Aldisert's view on reply briefs, however, is not the only view out there. Some judges actually prefer to read the reply brief first, since they believe that is serves as the best synthesis of both sides' arguments. Other judges take the absence of a reply brief to be a surrender on anything in the appellee's brief that is new and for which some reply might have been helpful. Before you file a reply brief (or decide not to file) you need to try to ascertain the practice in your jurisdiction. Do the judges prefer reply briefs or view them as a bothersome addition?

In writing the reply brief, think of analogous situations at trial. Redirect examination is limited to new matters brought out in cross-examination. The reply brief serves the same function on appeal, so it should be subject to the same limitation. Your case in rebuttal is likewise limited to new matters that were brought up in your adversary's case. Again, the same considerations apply in an appeal. An attempt to use redirect or rebuttal simply to rehash points already made would call down the wrath of the trial court. Recycling your opening brief as a reply brief has the same effect on the appellate court.

Put your best foot forward in your opening brief. Never deliberately save for the reply the response to an argument you know that the appellee will advance. Draft the opening brief as persuasively and completely as possible. This means that you include all relevant arguments. Those who wait may be too late. Moreover, in courts that are absolutely current, often the judges will receive the briefs in chief before the reply brief, and they read these briefs and form tentative impressions before the reply briefs arrive. This is especially the case in accelerated briefing schedules.

Think carefully before filing a reply brief. Consider the advice in this book and the conventions in your jurisdiction.

University of South Carolina Law Professor Emeritus Thomas R. Haggard offers some additional impressive advice on reply briefs.

- Do not nitpick. Appellant should focus on the major, substantive errors that respondent has made in its brief. Appellant should not quibble over whether respondent has correctly stated the "holding" of some obscure precedent, whether respondent has slightly mischaracterized a minor factual point, whether some quotation has arguably been taken out of context, or whether all the cases the respondent cites truly support the proposition for which they are cited—except in extreme cases of abuse, of course. Judge Friedman in the Federal Circuit expressed it this way:

  > "Do not file a reply brief, as some lawyers do, that is primarily concerned with correcting minor errors the other side has made. Such a brief is a sign of weakness: it suggests that you have no good answers on the merits, and therefore are nitpicking at the periphery."

- Do not indulge in invective. Appellants generally feel that their original briefs were as sharp as the Excalibur sword and that respondent's brief has now blunted the point and severely nicked the edges of the blade. At this point, things begin to get a little personal, and the temptation is strong to refer to respondent's brief as a *viper pit of deception* and engage in other harangues. This is counterproductive.

- . . . The reply brief can be the *pièce de résistance* of the appeal; or it can be its Waterloo. Appellants should not be casual in how they approach the project. Realizing that appellate courts are always reluctant to reverse lower court decisions, that the burden is on the appellant, and that the chances of winning on appeal are not good, appellant's opening brief should have been a solid, legally compelling and well written effort. Respondent has had the opportunity to take its best shot, and the message of appellant's reply brief is that the shot missed.[93]

---

93. Thomas J. Haggard, *Writing the Reply Brief*, S.C. Law., Mar.–Apr. 2001, at 42, 45–46 (citation omitted).

National Institute for Trial Advocacy

14.13   Advice from an Appellate Specialist

Herb Fox, an attorney from Santa Barbara, California, specializes in appellate advocacy and authors articles on appellate court practice. He offers three suggestions to follow in drafting appellate briefs:

1)   Leave ample time to revise and edit the brief. If your analysis of the record, legal research, and first draft takes fifty hours, plan to spend another twenty-five hours rewriting and editing.

2)   Understand the reasons for revising and rewriting: The first draft is to demonstrate to yourself that you have command of the procedural history, facts, and law. The second draft is to demonstrate to opposing counsel why they are wrong. The third draft is to demonstrate to trial counsel and the client that you have a handle on the case and to invite their comments which, once received, should largely be discarded. The fourth through twenty-fifth draft is for the appellate court: by the fourth draft, you have a rough idea of what the case is really about, and now it is time to make the brief sparkle, sing, and persuade.

3)   Send a draft to trial counsel and clients for comments, they may catch grammatical errors. As a general rule, all other comments should be ignored. Trial counsel is usually making the case for the client, and both probably know little about the appellate standard of review, writing, or the art of obtaining reversal.

14.14   Brief Writing: A Summary

Above all else, the argument should be convincing. The brief should do its job even when the case poses difficult questions and your opponent's brief raises serious arguments that your brief may not answer completely. Your brief should state the strongest possible position for your client and should do so in a manner that convinces the court that your position is worthy of acceptance or at least serious consideration.

If you cannot do this, you should not be filing the brief at all. Except in the case of a criminal defendant who has a constitutional right to pursue even a weak argument that has a remote chance for success, there is no excuse for filing a brief that cannot convince its own author. Even in the criminal case, the brief should persuade the court that at least its author is convinced.

In addition to a strong argument, your brief should be polished. The cover, tables, and appendices should demonstrate the time and effort that you put into your brief. Leave yourself ample time to complete these sections and get your brief filed in a timely manner.

CHAPTER FIFTEEN

THE BRIEF: A COMPENDIUM OF ADVICE

15.1 Writing the Argument: A Recap

Brief writing for appellate advocates is not easy. As Judge Aldisert's Marine Corps boot camp drill instructor used to say in 1942: "We didn't promise you a rose garden!"

Your finished product must demonstrate substance, acceptability, and continuity. Your product must display an awareness of broad relevant considerations and be faithful to the canons of logic. Such an effort does not come about automatically. It results from the brief writer's participation in the scholarly life, succinctly described by Gilbert Highet:

> It is a curious life we lead, the life of scholarship . . . . Consider first the life of learning. It is based on certain principles which people outside the academic field seldom fully understand or appreciate.
>
> The first of these is devotion: devotion and diligence. The Germans pithily call it *Sitzfleisch*, "flesh to sit on" because they admire the will power that keeps a man at his desk or laboratory table hour after hour, while he penetrates inch by inch to the heart of a problem. But many of us now find that *Sitzfleisch* is not so important as what newspaper men call "leg work."
>
> The second principle of scholarship . . . is humility . . . .
>
> The third principle of scholarship is far easier to apply now than it has ever been throughout history. This is organization. Closely allied to this intellectual ideal is a fourth principle of scholarship . . . collaboration.[1]

Never dictate a brief. Prepare your first draft with whatever tool helps you to work and think most effectively: pen, pencil, computer, whatever. You will not be able to complete it in one sitting, so devise a strategy that will enable you to get back to it with a minimum of wheel spin. Ernest Hemingway is said to have stopped the day's work at a point when he had clearly in his head what he was going to write on the

---

1. Gilbert Highet, *The Scholarly Life*, 41 Am. Scholar 522 (1972).

following day. Judge Aldisert knew a professional who, when he started a day with writer's block, got back on track by retyping the last page he wrote the day before.

So, you have now battled through the "block" and written the argument. Now, rewrite it. Put it aside again and come back to it later. Let it cool off for a while. The length of time depends upon your schedule. Maybe put it aside for a few hours. Preferably a couple of days, or even a week. Then revise it again. Rewrite. Rewrite. Rewrite. Do not feel incompetent. Remember, when it comes to professional writing, appellate brief writers *are* professional writers.

There is no such thing as good writing; there is only good rewriting. Approach revision as a stranger, as an outside reader and editor who is seeing the copy fresh for the first time.

Edit your own work. *Edit like a reader*: identify the problems you encounter as a reader; determine whether the sequence of ideas flows smoothly and logically; determine whether the ideas are adequately supported; look for conspicuous omissions; look for needless repetition. Then edit like a writer: assess your writing techniques and mark up your draft like an editor would; read certain passages aloud, if necessary, and train your ear to detect errors reliably; avoid the trap of falling in love with your writing—love often blinds.

Consider the late Wisconsin Supreme Court Justice William A. Bablitch's phrase, "Develop the skill of distance." He described this as "the ability to distance yourself from your written work so as to see it through the eyes of a first time reader." He suggested that you "[r]oleplay yourself into being a first time reader."

> Next concentrate on the sentence and paragraph you are reading. Don't let your mind . . . wander ahead of your text. When you wrote it, you knew where you were going, but the first time reader does not. Then ask yourself, does this sentence make sense? Does this sentence and paragraph flow logically from the preceding?
>
> The more you force yourself to do this, the more you will see gaps, ambiguities, and lack of clarity in your writing. You will begin to understand the trap so many writers fall into when they know their subject either too well or not well enough. You will see where the connecting bridges are missing between sentences or between paragraphs, where sentences that seemed to make sense when you write them will make little sense to the first-time reader.[2]

Assess the "beat" of your writing. There is a difference between writing for reading and writing for speaking, even though each form has both mood and rhythm. Is the mood exaggerated? Do the words come through as a stentorian roar or as a "soft sell," soothing but nonetheless persuasive?

---

2. William A. Bablitch, *Writing to Win*, COMPLEAT LAW., Winter 1988, at 12.

Never become complacent with your writing. Remember, effective writing is a lifetime goal, never a final accomplishment. Become your own best critic. Try to write so that when you finish you can look at the result and honestly say, "I have just done the very best I am capable of at this stage in my literary development." Regularly review your past writing. Ask how it appeals to you now. Assess improvement or deterioration in your writing style. Ask yourself whether your words remain as persuasive as they first seemed and whether they do a good job of expressing the thoughts you intended when you began. Keep always in mind that writing is like exercising a muscle: The more you write, the easier it becomes.

Check and double-check your spelling. Run the entire brief through spell check, but do not stop there. Read the draft again because some words may be properly spelled but contextually erroneous. Obey the rules of grammar.[3]

Make certain that you include a year date for every citation. Some Supreme Court justices fail to do this, but you can excuse them, for rank hath its privileges. And never include a Federal Reporter citation without identifying the circuit.

15.2 Current and Former State Court Justices Speak

Below is writing advice from current and former state court justices.

Charles E. Jones
Former Chief Justice, Arizona Supreme Court

Be concise and direct. Written work should predominately reflect the active voice, not the passive. Omit weak arguments that are largely, if not completely irrelevant, and focus exclusively on the most persuasive, authoritative arguments that will lead to the disposition of issues. State the strongest and best arguments first.

Mary J. Mullarkey
Former Chief Justice, Colorado Supreme Court

Develop a coherent theory of the case. Give analytical framework to reach the result you want. Be as accurate and precise as possible. You build credibility by fairly characterizing the law and the facts. Limit the number of issues raised on appeal[.]

Ronald T.Y. Moon
Former Chief Justice, Supreme Court of Hawai'i

Follow the appellate rules on briefing scrupulously. Write in a concise and direct fashion, minimizing the utilization of long, rambling footnotes. Maintain credibility by presenting argument in a civil, reasonable, and professional manner.

---

3. *See* APPELLATE JUDICIAL OPINIONS 195–96 (Robert A. Leflar, ed. 1974) (offering a delightful spoof on writing style).

Rita B. Garman
Justice, Supreme Court of Illinois

Begin[] the Argument section with a clear "roadmap" of the issues to be addressed and the order in which they will be discussed, making the structure of the overall argument apparent.

[Use] [c]lear, concise language, without unnecessary "filler" [and] [w]ell-structured paragraphs, each dealing with one topic only, rather than single paragraphs that go on for pages.

Careful editing and proofreading. Errors in grammar, punctuation, and spelling suggest inattention to detail, which may indicate a similar lack of attention to legal reasoning.

Stephen N. Limbaugh, Jr.
Judge, U.S. District Court for the Eastern District of Missouri, formerly Chief Justice, Supreme Court of Missouri

Concede points that need to be conceded. To do so is no sign of weakness, and judges will appreciate the candidness. Double-space and use large type size, if not otherwise required by local rules of appellate practice. This makes the briefs more user-friendly for judges, like me, whose eyes glaze over from so much brief reading.

Karla M. Gray
Former Chief Justice, Montana Supreme Court

Be focused and concise: Say it once, say it well, and move on. Set out only the facts pertinent to the issues raised. Long statements of fact tend to leave the impression that you are making a jury argument because your legal issues are not going to be very strong. Meet adverse authorities head on and, where you cannot do so with a reasonable legal analysis, concede the issue and save your credibility for other issues.

Michael G. Heavican
Chief Justice, Supreme Court of Nebraska

[Briefs] [f]rame[] the issues presented for appeal, and provide[] guidance to court in beginning its research into the issue.

Patricio M. Serna
Former Chief Justice, New Mexico Supreme Court

Be conscientious in complying with appellate rules of procedure, such as informing the court of the manner in which an error was preserved in the lower court and including citations to the record for assertions of fact. Alert the appellate court to the proper standard of review and present the argument in the context of the standard of review. Be honest and forthright about the facts and the law, even if they appear to hinder an argument, because any perceived concealment will be far more damaging.

Thomas G. Saylor
Chief Justice, Supreme Court of Pennsylvania

Good briefs adhere closely to procedural requirements, are organized and concise, eschew irrelevant detail in favor of sharp focus upon what is material, and achieve resonance in the essential treatment without unnecessary repetition.

Frank J. Williams
Former Chief Justice, Supreme Court of Rhode Island

List [the] relevant standard of review before each argument and confine [the] argument to the applicable standard; use [the] summary of the case section to give more detailed background of the case so that reader may be educated before he or she proceeds to the argument sections; be vigilant about maintaining perfect organization, spelling, grammar, and citation.

Sharon Keller
Presiding Judge, Texas Court of Criminal Appeals

A good brief does the work I would otherwise have to do myself.

Nathan L. Hecht
Chief Justice, Supreme Court of Texas

The brief states the issues, presents the essential factual and procedural background with citations to the record, summarizes the arguments, lays them out in detail, and requests relief.

The written brief is the single most important part of the appeal. It is the resource for the court for the facts and arguments on which the parties [rely].

Gerry L. Alexander
Former Chief Justice, Washington Supreme Court

An argument presented efficiently requires editing. It is important for the attorneys to tell us up front and in conclusion what relief they seek from our court. It is helpful if the brief is divided into sections with good headings and clear transitions between issues.

Shirley S. Abrahamson
Justice, Wisconsin Supreme Court

When writing a brief, keep in mind that the result you want is an opinion in your favor. Make it easy for the judges to write that opinion by including all the necessary facts, legal precedent, and policy analysis in your brief. If the court will have to announce standards and criteria to be applied in future cases, try to suggest them in your brief. Adapt the style and mechanical details of your brief to human realities. Judges do not always have the law library and case record available to them. They read briefs in bed, in cars, and on planes. Quote the relevant statutes and make sure the appendix is sufficient to give the flavor of the record. Do not ignore unfavorable precedent. Ethically, you are obligated to inform the court of binding precedent in the controlling jurisdiction. Strategically, an unfavorable case will do far more damage when it is emphasized by your opponent, or worse, when the court discovers it after oral argument and you no longer have the opportunity to explain or distinguish it or ask that it be overruled.

15.3   Circuit Court Judges Speak

Michael Boudin
Senior Judge,
First Circuit

Be clear and concise—write and rewrite until the issue and answer can be identified in one short sentence. This will also aid the practitioner in culling out the real issues for appeal. Do not use footnotes—they distract and disrupt the reader. If the information is important enough to include, it is important enough to weave into the text. Remember your audience—the judge reading the brief has not spent the last few years living the case. Before filing the brief, let someone who has not been working on the case review it. If the argument is not clear to him, the brief is not finished.

Dennis Jacobs
Judge, Second Circuit

Pick the issues that make a difference. Discard distractions, such as attacks on adversary counsel and the trial judge. Adopt the pose of an officer of the court.

John M. Walker, Jr.
Senior Judge,
Second Circuit

Be concise; do not repeat arguments or facts. The poorest, least persuasive briefs are all too often those that the lawyer has not taken the time to reduce to its essence. Be highly selective in choosing the few points that have the best chance of prevailing. How often has the fourth or fifth point raised ever resulted in a victory for the appellant? Be careful with the mechanics of spelling, citation, and avoiding typographical errors (such as a line repeated or dropped on the word processor). Such mistakes subconsciously convey the lawyer's lack of concern for his client's cause.

Albert Diaz
Judge, Fourth Circuit

[In response to the attributes of a good brief] They 1) do not presume that use of the full word limit is the default; 2) focus their fire on no more than two or three of the strongest issues; 3) are tightly written and proofread; 4) tell an interesting (or at least bearable) story.

Jennifer Walker Elrod
Judge, Fifth Circuit

[In response to what about briefs irritate] Ignoring on-point case law. Treating the court as if it were a public policy committee rather than a court bound by the rule of law.

Carolyn Dineen King
Senior Judge, Fifth Circuit

Pick the most important issues, deal with them thoroughly, and omit the others. Deal directly with cases, statutes, and policy arguments that are adverse to your position. Be concise.

John M. Rogers
Judge, Sixth Circuit

[In response to what about briefs irritate] Misrepresentation of the record. Misrepresentation of a statute or a case. Failure to address arguments made by the other side.

Ilana Diamond Rovner
Judge, Seventh Circuit

[In response to what about briefs irritate] Taking a tone of outrage or extreme emotionalism is inappropriate and unhelpful. Engaging in personal attacks on parties, lawyers, or judges is unacceptable. Poor organization and repetition can make the briefs more difficult to read and understand. Before citing a case, read it in its entirety. Citing a case for a proposition that the case does not support wastes everyone's time.

Richard R. Clifton
Judge, Ninth Circuit

[In response to the attributes of a good brief] They get to the point. They present the case with an understanding of the target audience, namely judges and law clerks. They provide what those readers need to know to understand the case, meaning, for instance, no long statement of facts without a structure that helps the readers understand which facts are important and why. They explicitly identify what result is sought. They explain why that result is proper under the law and sensible from the judges' perspective. They are reliable. Citations to legal authorities and to the record fairly support the propositions for which they are cited. If they don't, our law clerks are likely to catch them and let us know, at a serious cost to the advocate's credibility on that subject and as to everything else as well. They are reasoned. Passion can matter, but adverbs, bold print, and exclamation points don't make an argument stronger.

N. Randy Smith
Judge, Ninth Circuit

[In response to the attributes of a good brief]

a) Accuracy, brevity, and clarity are the keys.

b) Use an introduction to explain the nature of the case and why your client should prevail—a highly useful roadmap for the reader.

c) State the facts accurately, objectively, and chronologically. Never include argument in this section; instead, craft the statement to be consistent with the standard of review.

d) Think from the judge's perspective. What would the judge want to know about that authoritative reference?

e) Not too many quotes, infras and supras, footnotes, different types of print, or legalese.

f) Use standard of review in argument.

g) A table of contents can provide an outline of your argument.

Harris L. Hartz
Judge, Tenth Circuit

I think all judges are particularly irritated by personal attacks on opposing counsel or the judge below. I do not know that a party who does that ever loses because of the disapproval by the appellate court. But the tactic is a pretty good indication that the lawyer is too emotional about the case and is not focusing on important legal issues. When a lawyer catches himself or herself engaging in personal attacks on a lawyer or judge, the lawyer should take a deep breath and regain focus. I should mention that it is particular[ly] important that attorneys who file a petition for rehearing or rehearing en banc not engage in personal attacks on the author of the panel opinion. Even if a member of the court has concerns about the panel opinion, the petition is going to have to be very convincing on the merits before the member will cast a vote that appears to endorse the personal attack on a colleague.

Carolyn B. McHugh
Judge, Tenth Circuit

[In response to the attributes of a good brief] A statement of the facts from the perspective of the reviewing court, i.e., all reasonable inferences in favor of the nonmoving party when the review is of a summary judgment ruling; a concise statement of the points to be covered in the summary of the argument; an argument that is focused, contains appropriate roadmaps, accurately cites to the record and authorities, applies the facts to the law under the applicable standard of review, and clearly indicates what relief is sought.

Joel F. Dubina
Senior Judge,
Eleventh Circuit

First, organize your thoughts and think about what you want to say to the court. Define the issues in your mind, and as you think about what the issues are, reduce your ideas to writing. A definition of the issues is important because the formulation of issues determines which facts are material and what legal principles govern. If you represent the appellant, you must review the record for possible grounds of error. If there is a transcript of an evidentiary hearing or trial, you need to read it in its entirety. No one right way of writing a brief exists. Anyone undertaking to announce authoritative rules of good writing invites debate and comparison. In a leading text on good writing, the authors acknowledged that "[s]tyle rules . . . are, of course, somewhat a matter of individual preference, and even the established rules of grammar are open to challenge." An exclusive style of writing does not exist. However, good writing can be distinguished from poor writing and I can assure you that appellate judges appreciate the former. A few characteristics of bad writing are worth discussing. Most lawyers write too much. More often than not, they try to convey too much information and cover too many issues. Lawyers fail to separate the material from the immaterial. When writing a brief, a lawyer should say no more and no less than he or she needs to say. A brief should express ideas accurately, briefly, and as clearly as possible, leaving little room for inappropriate interpretation. Precision is the main concern of good writing. Many legal writers lack the ability to write simple, straightforward prose. In order to write with clarity and precision, the writer must know precisely what he or she wants to say and must say that and nothing else. Frequently, lawyers have a tendency to overgeneralize. When lawyers are not sure of a legal principle or how to state it precisely, they decide to cover up by using vague expressions. Of course, painstaking and thoughtful editing is essential for precise writing. This means going over the brief, sentence by sentence, and eliminating the surplus. A sound brief is the reflection of a logical process of reasoning from premises through principles to conclusions. Good organization will be like a roadmap to the judges, enabling them to follow from the beginning to the end without getting lost.

Douglas H. Ginsburg
Senior Judge,
D.C. Circuit

Pick the most important issues, deal with them thoroughly, and omit the others. Deal directly with cases, statutes, and policy arguments that are adverse to your position. Be concise.

Visualize the whole before you begin. What overriding message is the document going to convey? What facts are essential to the argument? How does the argument take off from the facts? How do different arguments blend together? Better still, if it's a brief, visualize the way the judge's opinion should read if it goes your way. (Too many briefs read as if the paralegal summed up all conceivably relevant facts, and then the lawyer took over with the legal arguments, and never the twain doth meet.) Make the facts tell a story. The facts give the fix; spend time amassing them in a compelling way for your side, but do not omit the ones that go the other way. Tackle these uncooperative facts and put them in perspective (Too many times the judge reading both briefs will not recognize they are about the same case.). If you're appealing, make it seem like a close case, so any legal error will be pivotal. Above all, be accurate on the record; a mistaken citation or an overbroad reading can destroy your credibility vis-à-vis the entire brief. Describe what happened low-key ("Just the facts, ma'am") with no rhetorical or judgmental flourishes—well done, the facts should make your case by themselves. Think hard before writing what the "Issue" is. This provides the lens through which the judge-reader filters the rest of the brief.

Patricia M. Wald
*Chief Judge Emeritus, D.C.
Circuit*

Avoid abstractions; make it a concrete, easily understood question to which the answer is inevitable after you read the upcoming "Fact" section (if your facts are terribly unsympathetic, you may be driven to describing the issue in abstract, formalistic terms, but do so only as a last resort). Use neutral words; don't mix it up with argument or rhetoric; be especially fair in stating the real issue. Be sure and tell why it is important to come out your way, in part by explaining the consequences if we don't. The logic and common sense of your position should be stressed; its appropriateness in terms of precedent or statutory parsing comes later, i.e., the state of the law allows this result, rather than requires it. In complex cases, you need to fully understand the real-world dispute to write accurately or convincingly about consequences; more cases are decided wrongly by judges because they don't understand the underlying problem than because they read cases badly. Perceived confusion or ignorance on the part of counsel about "what really happened" can be fatal. In the same vein, don't over-rely on precedent; few cases are completely controlled by it. If yours isn't, don't pretend it is.

Haldane Robert Mayer
Senior Judge, Federal Circuit

Be clear and concise—write and rewrite until the issue and answer can be identified in one short sentence. This will also aid the practitioner in culling out the real issues for appeal. Do not use footnotes—they distract and disrupt the reader. If the information is important enough to include, it is important enough to weave into the text. Remember your audience—the judge reading the brief has not spent the last few years living the case. Before filing the brief, let someone who has not been working on the case review it. If the argument is not clear to him, the brief is not finished.

15.4   The Perfect Brief and Pet Peeves

At the 1990 Tenth Circuit Judicial Conference, two United States circuit judges were asked this question: "How do you define what a perfect brief is, and what would be your pet peeves in the briefs you do see?"[4]

---

4. These responses are reprinted from Robert R. Baldock, Carlos F. Lucero & Vicki Mandell-King, *What Appellate Advocates Seek from Appellate Judges and What Appellate Judge Seek from Appellate Advocates*, 31 N.M.L. Rev. 265, 265–67 (2000).

15.4.1 Perfection

Judge Bobby R. Baldock

[A] terrific brief that I enjoy is one that is very precise and gets to the point of the issues that have been raised, so that I know exactly what it is that you claim as an appellant. The brief needs to identify what the alleged reversible error is, taking into consideration the standards of review that we have to apply, because that standard in many instances determines the outcome. We can't substitute our judgment for the trial judge's, even if something that happened at the trial was very important to the outcome.

For an appellee, a good brief is one that goes directly to the heart of the matter. It is not one of those briefs that just says, 'Well, we won in the trial court; therefore, we should win in the appellate court.' Those briefs are absolutely no help. These issues sometimes are very close. A terrific brief is one that is straight to the point. It tells us what happened, why there was error, and what law supports the claim that the judgment below is reversible. The appellee, of course, does just the opposite, explaining why the judgment below should be upheld. So that is a terrific brief, and it doesn't take 150 pages to do that. You can do it easily with less than fifty pages.

Judge Carlos F. Lucero

To me a terrific brief is one that concisely, precisely, and meticulously states the issues for our consideration, and why they compel reversal of what the trial court did below.

15.4.2 Peeves

Judge Carlos F. Lucero

My . . . pet peeve is an unfocused statement of the issues that presents no compelling error that we should address or no novel and creative issue that is being advanced for the creation of law that should grab our attention.

Another pet peeve is a brief that does not contain a summary of the argument or that contains a summary of the argument that is of little, if any, help. A summary of the argument should be able to tell an appellate court precisely and concisely what error the trial court made below that requires us to take the extraordinary step and consume and utilize the judicial resources necessary to retry that case. I think litigants who don't put in a summary of the argument have done themselves a grave disservice, and those who don't use the summary properly are close behind.

The last of my pet peeves is briefs that use too much of their valuable space stating unnecessary facts and thereby consume too much of the judge's time, to the point that he or she loses interest. These briefs fail to isolate the really relevant facts on appeal—the facts that are truly critical to addressing the contended error. Some attorneys really blow it by failing to include citations to the record on those critical facts. That is the worst brief.

Judge Bobby R. Baldock

Why don't we see more concise briefs? That's the problem we have. I think those people who are frequently working at the appellate level understand these things and we don't usually see the type of briefs with the pet peeves we're talking about. Where we see these mistakes are from trial lawyers who only do an appellate brief once in a great while.

The Tenth Circuit has provided a guideline book on how to approach briefs. But it's amazing; time after time after time we get briefs that totally ignore those guidelines. We see briefs that appear to totally ignore the Tenth Circuit rules on how to prepare the brief. I think a lot of this is due to the fact that attorneys who don't have a very large appellate practice get a little bit negligent in really trying to conform to the rules. The time constraint is important too. But you've got one shot at the appellate court, and you really need to put your best foot forward. We see your brief first. That's why it's so important that you follow the court guidelines. We're aware of your time constraints. But you still have to follow the rules.

15.5   Rehearing En Banc

What do you do when the court decides against you and you are convinced that it is wrong? Under Federal Rules of Appellate Procedure 35 and 40, you may file for rehearing of a panel decision by the full court or by the three-judge panel that issued it. Be warned: the odds against obtaining rehearing are considerable. No procedural step should be taken without a searching inquiry into whether doing so would waste the client's time and money. Rehearing requests are confined to written presentations; no oral argument is available.

The essential difference between the two forms of review is that the Rule 40 rehearing seeks to persuade the original panel to correct errors of fact or law in its own opinion.[5] A Rule 35 petition seeks to persuade a majority of all the active judges in the circuit that the issues are important enough to invoke the extraordi-

---

5. FED. R. APP. P. 40.

National Institute for Trial Advocacy

nary step of consideration by the full court.[6] State practice regarding en banc rehearings generally tracks the federal experience: Granting the petition is the exception and not the rule.

Rule 35, the rule governing rehearing en banc by all the active judges of the circuit, provides:

> (a) **When Hearing or Rehearing En Banc May be Ordered.** A majority of the circuit judges who are in regular active service and who are not disqualified may order that an appeal or other proceeding be heard or reheard by the court of appeals en banc. An en banc hearing or rehearing is not favored and ordinarily will not be ordered unless:
>
> > (1) en banc consideration is necessary to secure or maintain uniformity of the court's decisions; or
> >
> > (2) the proceeding involves a question of exceptional importance.

Rule 35 states that the petition for rehearing must follow the form provided for briefs in Rule 32.[7] Some courts of appeals also provide additional requirements; many require that you file a separate petition for rehearing and petition for rehearing en banc, because the reasons for seeking panel rehearing are different from those governing rehearing en banc. Check your local rules. The Third Circuit, for example, treats all petitions as requests for both panel and en banc rehearing unless otherwise specified in the petition.

In a panel rehearing petition, be concise with the discussion of the proceedings and of the facts. Remember that you are speaking to the judges who decided the case earlier and to the law clerks who spent hours poring over your arguments and the record. They do not want you to rehash the same argument. Refresh their memory. Then get to the point.

In most courts of appeals, the authoring judge will pay the most attention to a petition for panel rehearing, although copies of it will be circulated to the chambers of each panel member. Realistically, however, the authoring judge is the one you should target. For petitions for rehearing en banc, there are likely judges who were not on the panel who will closely examine a focused, plausible argument that the panel got it wrong—particularly if the legal issues have special importance.

The petition for rehearing is also an opportunity to point out errors in the panel's treatment of the law. The lawyer may use the petition to ask the panel to tone down or excise aspects of its decision. A litigant may also have an interest in the development

---

6. Fed. R. App. P. 35.
7. Fed. R. App. P. 35(b)(2).

of law and may wish to shape the legal rules in ways that will not necessarily benefit him or her in the present case, but will be helpful later.

This too must be said. Judges have egos—and while sometimes willing to admit mistakes freely or grudgingly—they do not appreciate having their noses rubbed in an alleged mistake. Make it as easy as possible for judges to retract their earlier decision. Offer alternatives. Above all, do not accuse either the authoring judge or the panel of stupidity, bias, or prejudice. You may believe that, but personal attacks on those before whom you plead your case will not help. In one Fifth Circuit case, the court said that the "disturbingly unprofessional tone of the petition reveals a lack of respect for the court and constitutes an invitation to strike the petition." The court accepted the invitation.

Circuit rules generally warn against the filing of unnecessary suggestions for rehearing en banc. Because many circuits have penalties for frivolous petitions,[8] the en banc suggestion should be reserved for extraordinary situations. Be sure to adhere closely to the reasons for rehearing en banc set out in Rule 35.

In federal appeals, the boy-who-cried-wolf syndrome runs rampant. Far too many petitions and suggestions are filed. The rehearing rules are flagrantly abused; as a result, judges are universally aggravated. Too many lawyers file these requests routinely every time they get an adverse result. They make no effort to demonstrate that the panel decision conflicts with circuit or Supreme Court precedent. They simply want to get a second bite of the apple. Too many lawyers describe every holding as a question of exceptional importance. Because active circuit judges are inundated by so many frivolous requests, the sheer volume infects the rehearing process. The inundation minimizes the efficacy of those rare requests that are worthy of reconsideration by the panel or the full court.

The Third Circuit attempted to stem this tide by setting forth guidelines in its circuit rules:

- Rehearing en banc is not favored.[9]

- "[The] court does not ordinarily grant rehearing en banc where the panel's statement of the law is correct and the controverted issue is solely the application of the law to the circumstances of the case."[10]

- "Where the petitioner for rehearing en banc is represented by counsel, the petition shall contain, so far as is pertinent, the following statement of counsel:

    'I express a belief, based on a reasoned and studied professional judgment, that the panel decision is contrary to the decisions of the

---

8. *See, e.g.,* 8TH CIR. R. 35A(2); 5TH CIR. R. 35.1.
9. 3D CIR. R. 35.4.
10. 3D CIR I.O.P. 9.3.2.

National Institute for Trial Advocacy

United States Court of Appeals for the Third Circuit or the Supreme Court of the United States, and that consideration by the full court is necessary to secure and maintain uniformity of decisions in this court, *i.e.*, the panel's decision is contrary to the decision of the court or the Supreme Court in [citation to the case or cases] OR, that this appeal involves a question of exceptional importance, *i.e.*, [set forth in one sentence].'"[11]

Perhaps the Third Circuit rule has had a minimal effect on the tide. Judge Aldisert opined in an earlier edition of this book that, from where he sat, many lawyers were willing to certify a "reasoned and studied professional judgment" that a case qualifies for consideration under the rules when, in fact, it was little more than an exercise in both frivolity and futility.

15.5.1 Judge Patricia M. Wald's Comments Regarding En Bancs

Patricia M. Wald, Chief Judge Emeritus of the United States Court of Appeals for the D.C. Circuit, discusses en banc in her delightful essay, *19 Tips from 19 Years on the Appellate Bench*.[12] Although her comments describe the experience on her court, her observations are generally descriptive of most en bancs. Her commentary follows:

> Let me talk a bit about en bancs. They spell cruel and unusual punishment for all concerned. Think before you ask for one. We get hundreds of petitions but grant on average less than six a year . . . . Fed. R. App. P. 35 says that en bancs are disfavored and ordinarily will not be ordered except when necessary to secure uniformity or for a question of exceptional importance.
>
> Those have not been the de facto criteria in my experience. En bancs most often occur when a majority feels strongly that the panel is wrong about something they care a lot about or which may be precedential outside the confines of the immediate case. Every judge writes panel opinions (or dissents) in the shadow of an en banc and when there is the threat of one, panel majorities will often try to conciliate opponents or temper rhetoric in a supplemental opinion on rehearing; they may pull back from excessive rhetoric, too-broad holdings, or clarify the scope of the original opinion.
>
> En bancs usually follow a strong dissent, but can also be provoked by a unanimous panel composed of a philosophical minority on the court. I once sat on a now-notorious panel that had three unanimous decisions en banc-ed and one reheard by the panel to forestall an en banc . . . .

---

11. 3D Cir. R. 35.1.
12. 1 J. App. Prac. & Process 7, 15 (1999).

At any rate, remember four things about en bancs before you jump to ask for one when you lose before a panel:

(1) They take a long time, often up to two years before the court can assemble itself and get all the opinions written. If your case is really hot, you could be up on certiorari long before, and chances are either you or your opponent will go for certiorari anyway afterwards. As court of appeals dockets go up, the Supreme Court's steadily declines—only eighty-six cases argued last year.

(2) There are apt to be many en banc opinions written— likely a plurality and several other unclassifiable opinions rather than just a majority and dissent—so that the law is not necessarily the clearer or cleaner for the exercise.

(3) An en banc is like a constitutional convention. Everything— in circuit law—is up for grabs. The decision may emerge on grounds argued by neither party and desired by neither party. Advocates lose control since judge power is at its zenith; except for Supreme Court precedent, the decision can go anywhere. You, the counsel, no longer hold the road map.

(4) Since en bancs so often occur in fundamental value-conflicted cases, astute counsel can pretty well predict the outcomes on the basis of past positions taken by the judges. If you don't have a shot at winning an en banc, all you do is risk an even stronger set of nails in your coffin.

Oral argument in an en banc is an especially perilous undertaking. The mere fact that an en banc has been commenced usually means that the court is divided and panel members in the majority are already unhappy. Many more of the judges' questions in en banc arguments seem to be motivated by the desire to establish rather than explore positions or to defuse the positions of other judges. The counsel is often the woman in the middle of an intramural contest. She may not be aware of the real reason why the en banc was voted or what the court thinks is really at stake. The judges may have their own agendas as to what precedential underbrush the en banc will clear out or even what brand new doctrinal formula it will encapsule into law—with or without aid of counsel. It's also harder to control the flow of questioning from [eleven] judges than from [three]. More judges means more interruptions, cross-conversations between judges, and attempts to bind counsel to or divorce him from another judge's articulation of the issue or the acceptable resolution of it.

In sum, more is not always better, so think before en banc-ing. A really important case will likely go up anyway; a really wrong decision is worth a preliminary try at the en banc, but most of the rest brings much hassle and little success.

In our experience, much as Judge Wald states, the result of an en banc is often not a tighter, more likely correct explanation of the law. Sometimes it is, sometimes not. The result will be, though, the explanation that garnered at least a plurality of the votes from the full court. Those somewhat gloomy considerations are more for the judges as they decide whether to vote in favor of taking a case en banc. For the losing litigant considering whether to petition, unless there is a fear the loss could be made worse, the principal considerations include timing, as en banc may take a while; financial cost; and whether in fact this is a case in which a good faith argument can be made that the legal issues are of sufficient important to deserve the full court's attention.

15.6   Advice from Paul D. Clement, Kirkland & Ellis

Former U.S. Solicitor General Paul D. Clement, now with Kirkland & Ellis, offers the following advice for writing a successful brief.

> Think about the oral argument while writing the brief. In an appellate argument, it is critical to have a theory of the case—a concise theory of why your client should prevail. Moot courts are helpful in refining your theory of the case (nothing concentrates the mind like an upcoming oral argument), but you cannot wait for the moot courts to develop your theory of the case. You need to have it before you start drafting your brief. With your theory of the case in mind, you are much better positioned to decide which arguments to emphasize and which to omit. Thinking ahead to the oral argument ensures that you confront adverse facts and precedents in the brief and explain why they are not fatal to your client's cause. Appellate judges are likely to question you about these problems at oral argument, and you are well served to address them in the brief. Keep in mind that some answers (especially those that require multiple steps or depend on close parsing of the text) work much better in a brief than at the podium.
>
> Do not neglect the statement of the facts. The portions of an appellate brief that precede the summary of the argument are not just a series of technical requirements or a throat-clearing exercise. They are an integral part of the brief. If the statement of facts will make more sense in the context of the relevant statutory or regulatory regime, consider including a brief, non-argumentative statutory background section in the statement of the case. While the factual sections of the brief should not be argumentative, they can tell a compelling story

of why your client should prevail. By the time the reader reaches the summary of the argument, the reader should be predisposed to think your client should prevail and should look to the argument section to understand precisely why your client wins.

In the argument section, be wary of breaking up the flow of your argument. The argument section of a brief needs to make a compelling case for why your client prevails on each of the issues included in the appeal. Anything that breaks up the flow of the argument should be avoided. For example, long block quotes frequently break up the flow of the argument and tempt a reader to skim. Once your readers start skimming, you have little control over when they stop. Unless every sentence in the block quote advances your argument and benefits from coming from an authoritative source, quote the "money" sentence and work it into the flow of the argument. Similarly, avoid long strings of citations with parenthetical quotations after each case. Occasionally, a string cite is appropriate to emphasize the depth of authority for a proposition or that every circuit has accepted or rejected a point. But in such cases, parenthetical quotations for each case are generally unnecessary. If a particular quotation is too good to omit, include it in your main argument, where the reader is more likely to read and appreciate it.

PART FOUR

THE NUTS AND BOLTS OF PREPARING AND DELIVERING ORAL ARGUMENT

CHAPTER SIXTEEN

PREPARING FOR ORAL ARGUMENT

16.1 How Judges Prepare

Judges follow different chambers practices. Our work habits differ. Our experiences differ. In earlier editions of this book, Judge Aldisert set out his preparations for oral argument. In our experience, his habits are not common ones. A brief summary, though, will give the details.

1) Judge Aldisert was the first person in chambers to read the briefs and the appendices. He would first read the appellant's statement of issues, then read the district court's opinion with special focus on those issues. Next, he would read the summary of both side's arguments, then read each brief cover to cover.

2) Judge Aldisert would reach a tentative decision based on those readings, then dictate a memo to himself. He made three decisions at that time: a) whether he desired oral argument; b) whether his clerks should do further work on the case; and c) a very tentative decision as to disposition.

3) His law clerks would prepare a lengthier bench memo for those cases that were to be argued.

4) In the week prior to argument, he would devote along with his clerks at least a day to a conference in which each case would be discussed

Each judge has his or her method of preparation. We boil at different degrees. At the Tenth Circuit Judicial Conference in 2000, Judges Bobby R. Baldock and Carlos F. Lucero were members of a panel and asked by the panel's moderator about chambers preparation. Their responses follow.[1]

16.1.1 Judge Bobby R. Baldock, Senior Judge, Tenth Circuit

Moderator: What part of the brief do you think is most important and which brief do you read first? Do you read the reply brief first because that's where the issues are joined?

---

[1]. These responses are reprinted from Robert R. Baldock, Carlos F. Lucero, & Vicki Mandell-King, *What Appellate Advocates Seek from Appellate Judges and What Appellate Judges Seek from Appellate Advocates*, 31 N.M.L. Rev. 265, 265–79 (2001).

Judge Baldock: I know each judge does things differently. I start with what the trial court did below. It doesn't matter whether it's a criminal or civil case. I want to know what the trial judge was looking at, and what he or she did. Normally, if it's a jury trial, I read the appellant's brief first, since the burden is on the appellant to convince me to overturn the conviction. Then, after making my notes and looking at that, I go to the appellee's brief, and then I go to the reply, if there is one. Doing it in this order helps formulate the issues in my mind. At the end, hopefully I have a clear understanding of what the issue is. And I do my homework. My law clerks don't do a synopsis for me and come tell me what the case is about. The lawyers are trying to convince me—I'm the judge—why I should do something or the other. So I do my own bench memos. The law clerks and I fight a lot about some of these things. Now, I may rely later on a clerk's judgment if the clerk sees the issue differently. But it's your argument to me, and my understanding of your argument, that's important.

Moderator: Let's say there are three issues. When you read the briefs, do you read the first issue through all three briefs and the second through all three briefs?

Judge Baldock: I read each whole brief, because so many times the arguments are integrated. You can't separate them because some of the facts will pour over into the other issues. That way I get a clear picture. Then in my analysis I will separate and outline each issue. As I'm trying to formulate my bench memo I do an outline of each issue. But first I have to know how all the facts come into play . . . .

When the briefs are really far apart, or I see citations to cases that are going off in different directions, then I may call the law clerk in and say, "Look, there's something strange here." The lawyers should pretty much be looking at the same line of cases and arguing different analysis. So when lawyers are arguing entirely different cases, then I know that something is wrong with one side or the other. Then I may call the law clerk to do some more extensive research.

16.1.2   *Judge Carlos F. Lucero, Tenth Circuit*

At the same judicial conference, Judge Carlos F. Lucero of the Tenth Circuit describes his chamber preparations as follows:

I'm a creature of habit in reading briefs, and I pretty well follow the same model each time. I pick up the appellant's brief, and I read the statement of the issues and the summary of the argument. I do this because I want to know what the case is about and what the dispute is. The statement and the summary tell me that very quickly. If somebody doesn't include a statement of the issues, they've blown it in a big way because now they're putting a judge in a bad frame of mind by making him try to figure out what the appeal is about.

Having read those two parts of the appellant's brief, I then turn to the appendix and read the trial court's order and judgment. Now, knowing what the issues are, I can focus on what the trial court did, to see whether the judgment of the trial court was right or wrong. This is sort of a preview of coming attractions. Then I turn back to the arguments in the appellant's brief, and, to the extent that I've been persuaded, I carefully consider every aspect of the appellant's brief. If I have not been persuaded by the appellant's argument, I still read the appellee's brief, but with less concern. Finally, I turn to the reply brief, and I come to my preliminary opinion.

Now, where Judge Baldock and I differ is I do use bench memos from my clerks. I will not read the bench memo before reading the briefs, but having read the briefs and come to my preliminary conclusions on the case, I then turn to the bench memos. It is remarkable, quite remarkable, how often you agree pretty well with the bench memo. At that point, I come to closure in my mind. Now, if the clerk's recommendation and mine don't square, that is a red flag, and you've got a hot issue here. Then I'll direct more research, and I'll pull cases. The law clerk always attaches key cases to the bench memo, and I'll read those as well. Now the case is ready for oral argument.

16.2   The Importance of Preparation

The tradition and the majestic history of any courtroom always electrifies, but you feel the atmosphere in the court of appeals to be especially charged; it is the court of last resort for more than 99 percent of the cases.[2] The history, tradition, and heavy responsibility all contribute to the massive discharge of psychic energy by the judges, because the argument demands high concentration and unflagging attention. Judges recognize the importance of oral argument because, insofar as the case is concerned, it is the bottom half of the ninth inning.

All the weeks of preparation in chambers—reading the briefs, researching the authorities, contemplating the outer perimeters to which a decision one way or

---

2. In the twelve months ending September 30, 2015, the federal courts of appeals terminated 53,213 cases. ADMIN. OFFICE OF THE U.S. COURTS, TABLE B. U.S. COURTS OF APPEALS—CASES COMMENCED, TERMINATED, AND PENDING DURING THE 12-MONTH PERIODS ENDING SEPTEMBER 30, 2014 AND 2015 (2015). During the same period, the Supreme Court received 5,781 petitions for certiorari in federal cases; of these, 136 were granted. ADMIN. OFFICE OF THE U.S. COURTS, TABLE B-2. PETITIONS FOR REVIEW ON WRIT OF CERTIORARI TO THE SUPREME COURT COMMENCED, TERMINATED, AND PENDING DURING THE 12-MONTH PERIOD ENDING SEPTEMBER 30, 2015 (2015).

another will take the law, ruminating the broad policy questions involved in the issues—all of this, comes down to an oral presentation of fifteen minutes, at the most thirty minutes, per side. And for all of this, the lawyers must be prepared. Prepared for the most intensive courtroom participation in the life of a litigator. Yet some lawyers are not ready.

You must prepare. When you look at the black-robed figures sitting on the dais, your first thought should be, "Lemme at 'em." You should be straining at the leash to get to the judges. An attorney once told Judge Aldisert, "If you feel comfortable sitting, waiting for your turn to argue, your mental attitude is all wrong. You should feel that you are in the starting blocks, totally trained and ready, longing for the starting gun to go off, longing to let the judges know what you know about the important parts of the case, and thus believe what you believe about the Rightness, not just correctness, but the Rightness or Righteousness of your position."

You must prepare. The most important step in getting to the "lemme at 'em" frame of mind is total preparation on the facts and the law.

You must prepare. You must know and—what is important—you must *believe* that you know more about the case than anyone else in the courtroom, including the judges. You want the judges to think that you are the "Master of the Universe" insofar as this case is concerned. If the judges get this feeling, then they will be more likely to trust what you say and believe what you believe. And if you have this feeling, then you will have no apprehension about having hypotheticals thrown to you at oral argument. You will have the attitude that you are ready for anything. Advice on how to acquire this attitude is contained in the pages that follow.

16.3 Advice from Current and Former State Court Justices

Mary J. Mullarkey *Former Chief Justice,* *Colorado Supreme Court*	Practice your argument before you appear. Review the record. Nothing is more disheartening to the judge than asking questions about the record and being told that the attorney has not looked at the record since writing the brief. Respond to questions as they are raised. Don't try to postpone or evade answering the judge. The point of oral argument is to address the court's concerns, not to give a flawless speech.
Chase T. Rogers *Chief Justice, Connecticut* *Supreme Court*	Anticipate what the problems are as opposed to [your] best points.
Sabrina McKenna *Associate Justice, Supreme* *Court of Hawai'i*	Know the record, the briefs, and the law. Know what relief you're actually requesting. Suggest holdings, limited to broad.
Ronald T. Y. Moon *Former Chief Justice,* *Supreme Court of Hawai'i*	Oral argument is not a speech but a discussion with the appellate judges. Prepare thoroughly by knowing the facts, the record, and the applicable case law. Anticipate touching

upon the weaknesses in your case and the reasonable arguments of your opponent; practice your answers.

Rita B. Garman
Justice, Illinois Supreme Court

Practice out loud—in the car, in the shower, or while walking your dog. Phrases that look good on paper may not roll trippingly off the tongue. Have an imaginary conversation in your head. Think about what you are likely to be asked and rehearse your answer.

That said, do not memorize a script. Make a list of bullet points that you will address if the bench is not "hot."

Know the record backwards and forwards. Nothing undermines your credibility more than being unable to answer a question about the state of the record or the procedural history of the case.

Bill Cunningham
Justice, Supreme Court of Kentucky

Watch other oral arguments before the same court.

Maura D. Corrigan
Former Chief Justice, Michigan Supreme Court

To succeed at oral argument, you should: Prepare. Advocates should participate in as many moot court arguments as possible. You must know every aspect of your case, from the record to the standard of review, in order to successfully address the questions asked. Answer truthfully. Don't be afraid to concede that you haven't thought about a particular line of questioning. Answering truthfully and asking to file a supplemental brief on the issue is far better than talking yourself into a corner and compromising your argument. Know your audience. Take the time to research the particular concerns of the court and tailor your argument accordingly. You do your client a great disservice if you fail to focus on issues and arguments the court considers important.

Stephen N. Limbaugh, Jr.
Judge, U.S. District Court for the Eastern District of Missouri, formerly Chief Justice, Supreme Court of Missouri

Concede points that should be conceded. Understand the purpose of oral argument, which is not so much to allow the lawyers to rehash the argument in their briefs, but, instead, to allow the judges to ask questions in order to better understand those arguments. Supplement charts, graphs, blown-up photographs, or other visual aids, for use in oral argument with small, individual copies for each judge that the Marshal can distribute beforehand. This makes the argument more user friendly.

Karla M. Gray
Former Chief Justice,
Montana Supreme Court

Think long and hard before attempting to "split" your oral argument time with another lawyer. It almost never works out well. Answer questions from the bench when they are asked; do not say you will get to it later. Sometimes you run out of time and, in any event, the question may remain in the judge or justice's mind until answered and distract attention from your other points. During preparation, check for—and be familiar with—related cases decided after the briefs were filed in your case.

Michael G. Heavican
Chief Justice, Nebraska
Supreme Court

(1) Know the record and the law. (2) Understand what issues you've preserved for appeal. (3) Know the standard of review and how it applies. (4) Watch our webcast oral arguments so you have some familiarity with the court before you argue.

Thomas G. Saylor
Chief Justice, Supreme
Court of Pennsylvania

It is essential to have a complete understanding of all material facts and legal principles and to plan to proceed in an organized and direct fashion, but with full awareness that things may not go as planned. Certainly, mock court exercises can be very useful.

Frank J. Williams
Former Chief Justice, Rhode
Island Supreme Court

State the standard of review during argument and confine argument to the applicable standard. If you don't know the answer to a question, say so directly and move on to the next point. Do not give detailed background of the case. Assume the justices are familiar with the facts and begin and limit your discussion to the most important issues.

Frank F. Drowota II
Former Chief Justice,
Tennessee Supreme Court

Be familiar with the court, the judges, and the court rules. Preparation for oral argument will vary depending upon whether the court is "hot" or "cold." Do not treat questions from the bench as interruptions. Be flexible. Be candid. Be honest. Shading the facts or law will undermine your credibility as an advocate. Be attentive when opposing counsel is presenting argument so that you will be able to respond to questions the judges asked opposing counsel. These questions sometimes emphasize areas in your adversary's case that the judges consider weak.

Nathan L. Hecht
Chief Justice, Supreme
Court of Texas

Practice it in front of lawyers and non-lawyers unfamiliar with the case.

16.4 Advice from Circuit Court Judges

Bruce M. Selya
Senior Judge, First Circuit

Know the record, know the law, and learn in advance about the judges.

Dennis Jacobs
Judge, Second Circuit

Find somebody who does not know the case to read the briefs fast, and have that lawyer ask the questions that come to mind.

Prepare for argument by thinking about how many different ways you can win and, if a judge is rejecting one of your arguments, back away by explaining how you win anyway, without (however) conceding the point. And do not panic, because one judge on a panel may very well turn out to be just one judge.

John M. Walker, Jr.
Senior Judge,
Second Circuit

Be completely prepared for all foreseeable questions. Master the record and the relevant statutes and case law. Practice with a moot court. Have a strategy that, amidst all of the questioning, results in bringing home the two or three points that you want the court to absorb, if nothing else. Open your argument with a carefully planned statement that plays to your strength: the law, the facts or, hopefully, both.

Thomas L. Ambro
Judge, Third Circuit

Review the record and law, revisit themes of analysis, moot case before experienced panel, create succinct and direct responses to questions that can be anticipated (especially questions that focus on possible weak areas), and prepare how you would suggest writing a narrow opinion that rules in your favor.

D. Michael Fisher
Judge, Third Circuit

Moot the argument; use some non-lawyers in moot.

Marjorie Rendell
Senior Judge,
Third Circuit

[Regarding how to best prepare for argument] Write the opinion your way before you write the brief; definitely before oral argument.

Kent Jordan
Judge, Third Circuit

Anticipate the obvious lines of attack from the other side and be prepared to address them with logic tied to the record and controlling law.

Anthony J. Scirica
Senior Judge,
Third Circuit

You must prepare. You know the record and the law. Although you are necessarily focused on winning your case, be aware of the appellate court's role in enunciating the law in similar cases. If you are asked what legal standard the court should adopt, you should have an answer.

Albert Diaz
Judge, Fourth Circuit

There is no substitute for putting in the time necessary to know the case. There is no excuse for allowing a judge (who must familiarize himself with many cases on an argument calendar) to know more about the case than the advocates.

Gregg J. Costa
Judge, Fifth Circuit

In addition to the obvious need to thoroughly study the record and relevant case law, I recommend the following: Moot courts with lawyers who have argued before the before the same court; listen to recordings of recent arguments involving the same judges (or better yet, watch the same panel the day before your argument) to get a sense of the judges' style.

Jennifer Walker Elrod
Judge, Fifth Circuit

Read the record. Read the district court opinion and the briefs. Make a road map. Spend some time thinking about what you would want to know if you were looking at the case fresh. Moot the case.

Carolyn Dineen King
Senior Judge, Fifth Circuit

Prepare thoroughly—have an excellent grasp of the record and the law on the subject; start out by focusing on the most important issue, the one you have to win on.

Edward C. Prado
Judge, Fifth Circuit

[Regarding how to best prepare for argument] Case was set for argument for a reason, figure out [what] the reason is and be prepared to address it.

Jerry E. Smith
Judge, Fifth Circuit

[Regarding how to best prepare for argument] Assume that the purpose of argument is to help the judges do their job, not to convince them that your client should win.

Jacques L. Wiener, Jr.
Senior Judge, Fifth Circuit

Overarching the preparation of an appellate brief is the recognition that it will be the appellate judges' first exposure to the case. So, counsel for both appellant and appellee must keep that in mind to ensure that the judges are fully apprised of the salient facts and the key legal issues presented. By contrast, counsel preparing for oral argument must assume that the members of the panel will have read the briefs and the record excerpts and are fully familiar with the facts and the legal issues on which the appeal turns. Preparation for argument thus requires counsel to (1) decide which of those factual and legal issues are most likely to concern the panel members and (2) become sufficiently conversant with them to lay out the case and respond cogently to questions from the bench. Counsel should keep in mind that oral argument on appeal is essentially a discussion between experienced lawyers, viz., counsel and the members of the panel, all of whom have narrowed the issues and are seeking dispositive answers.

John M. Rogers
Judge, Sixth Circuit

[To best prepare you need] [g]reat familiarity with the record and the law, focus on one or two central points, know your argument's structure and keep it simple, plus at least one ex parte practice before a lawyer friend or two whose only familiarity with the case is having read the briefs.

David F. Hamilton
Judge, Seventh Circuit

(a) Ask a couple of colleagues to read the briefs and the decision being appealed from, and then have them ask lots of questions—both friendly and not friendly. If the area of law is one that will not be thoroughly familiar to the judges (e.g., tax, utility or other specialty regulation), ask colleagues who also are not specialists in the area. If the area will be familiar to the judges (e.g., employment discrimination, civil rights, habeas, most criminal law), try to find colleagues who also know the area pretty well. (b) Be prepared to give the "elevator talk," a persuasive summary lasting no more than [sixty to ninety] seconds that will make a judge comfortable ruling in your favor.

Ilana Diamond Rovner
Judge, Seventh Circuit

A lawyer should review the record and the cases cited by both sides. Practicing with colleagues who can moot the argument is an excellent approach. Lawyers should also think through the ramifications of the positions they advocate beyond the facts of the case at hand. They must be prepared to argue not only why the outcome they seek is desirable on their facts, but why it is consistent with both prior law and future scenarios that may arise.

Richard R. Clifton
Judge, Ninth Circuit

Thoroughly familiarize yourself with the briefs and records. The judges and their law clerks have worked on the case recently. Relying upon memory of what happened months or years before is dangerous, and memory won't tell you where to find something in the record. If I discover as a judge that I know more about the case than you appear to know—and that happens much too often—there is little reason to listen to anything else you might have to say. Try to approach the case from the judges' perspective. What are they likely to ask about? If you don't think about questions in advance, your responses are likely to be rough first drafts. A response that has been thought through beforehand is almost always more effective.

Andrew Kleinfield
Senior Judge,
Ninth Circuit

Know the excerpts of record, know the law, and have the excerpts and law tabbed and highlighted, so that accurate answers can be found rapidly.

N. Randy Smith
Judge, Ninth Circuit

a. Know the record from cover to cover.

b. Limit the material you will try to cover.

c. Know the appellate posture of the case you are arguing.

d. Know thoroughly the cases in your brief and the opponent's brief.

e. Know what you want the court to do and for what reason.

f. Think about questions that may be asked/participate in a moot court.

Harris L. Hartz
Judge, Tenth Circuit

The lawyer must become intimately familiar with the record. When the panel asks a question about what happened, it expects an answer in pretty short order. The lawyer must also be familiar with the cases cited by both parties. The lawyer must also try to anticipate questions from the panel so that he or she can give short, persuasive responses. That is probably why more and more appellate attorneys seek input from others about questions that could arise. Also, the lawyer should be thinking about how to make the court want to rule in the client's favor, not just rule that way because it has to.

Carolyn B. McHugh
Judge, Tenth Circuit

Every lawyer is different in how she prepares. My practice was to write out my argument and practice it, knowing that I would not recite it verbatim. I would then condense to an outline that I took with me to the podium. By having practiced the full version, I could easily move among issues in response to questions. Once I covered a topic, I crossed it out on my outline. That way when I returned to my argument, I could avoid repetition. I also practiced answering questions posed by another lawyer familiar with the case.

Deanell Reece Tacha
*Former Judge,
Tenth Circuit*

The most common failing I see in both oral argument and brief writing is the failure to be analytically precise about the issues addressed on appeal. It seems to me that before ever writing a brief, and certainly before oral argument, counsel should have a very candid discussion with himself or herself about what precisely the issues are that will result in a favorable decision on appeal. The most common complaints I hear from appellate judges relate to . . . lack of focus, covering too many issues, and scattering case authority and facts throughout the brief and argument so that they lose their impact on the issues to which they are most germane. I therefore urge discipline in both brief writing and preparation for oral argument with respect to answering with clarity these central questions.

Joel F. Dubina
Senior Judge,
Eleventh Circuit

The following are sixteen simple suggestions that should help a lawyer achieve success in orally arguing a case:

1. Be courteous and polite.

2. Get right to the issues.

3. Don't dwell on the facts.

4. Answer the judges' questions directly and precisely.

5. Learn to overcome fear.

6. Cite to Supreme Court authority and [circuit or state] authority.

7. Check slip opinions the day before oral argument to see whether recent law impacts your case.

8. Keep in mind that the brief is critical.

9. Know the standards of review.

10. If you represent the appellee, track the argument of the appellant.

11. Know the record.

12. Don't make a jury argument.

13. If you represent the appellee and the district judge committed error, you will do better to admit it and argue that it was harmless.

14. When concluding your argument, tell the court what you want.

15. Educate and teach the court.

16. PREPARE!

Robin S. Rosenbaum
Judge, Eleventh Circuit

Great advocates are well prepared, have a conversational style, and directly answer questions from the bench. They recognize what about a case may bother a particular judge and they focus on why that issue is not really a problem.

Patricia M. Wald
Chief Judge Emeritus, D.C.
Circuit

Apart from an acceptance of the "life is not fair" motif to oral argument, probably the most important thing for an appellate lawyer is to "know the record." It is not good enough that the paralegal or the associate who drafted the brief knows the record inside and out; the lawyer who argues the case must.

I concur with Chief Justice Rehnquist's lament about oral advocates who depend too heavily on their subordinates in writing the brief, and who cannot answer questions about the basic case or the record. The more arcane the subject matter, the more intimate with the record the advocate needs to be. All the questions of fact and expert opinion that the brief may have raised in the judges' minds will surface at argument, and nothing frustrates a bench more than a lawyer who does not know the answers. Your credibility as a legal maven spurts as soon as you show familiarity with the facts of the underlying dispute. When a lawyer cannot smoothly answer a question securely rooted in his knowledge of the record, the specter of a remand for inadequate explanation by the agency comes quickly to the fore. If you watch, we don't ask you so many questions about the meaning of precedent as we do about the underlying dispute in the case: What is it really all about? Why does one party care so much about a few words in an agency rule? Of course counsel can always offer to submit record cites after argument, but inability to locate them onsite definitely detracts from the image of her being in complete control of the case.

16.5   Advice from Chief Justice John G. Roberts, Jr.

Before ascending the federal bench, Chief Justice John G. Roberts, Jr. was a well-known Supreme Court advocate who argued thirty-nine cases before the high court, with his side winning twenty-five of those cases.[3] In 2007, he sat down with legal writing expert Bryan Garner to discuss, among other things, how he prepared for his Supreme Court arguments:

> One thing I did preparing for oral arguments: I would do countless moot courts early on. For a Supreme Court case, certainly five, maybe as many as ten. I'd do them over and over again, and it paid off enormously in terms of generating familiarity with the types of questions people would ask and also developing a comfort level with answering. You'd give an answer in moot court, and you'd stumbled over a name, a name of one of the parties in the case. Well, then, don't use it. Call him the engineer instead of Mr. Whoever, whose name you can't say. And then you don't have to worry about that. The same thing with any other type of verbal formulation—just get comfortable with it.[4]

---

3. Charles Lane, *Nominee Excelled as an Advocate Before Court*, Wash. Post (July 24, 2005), http://www.washingtonpost.com/wp-dyn/content/article/2005/07/23/AR2005072300881_2.html (last visited Mar. 20, 2017).

4. Bryan A. Garner, *Interviews with United States Supreme Court Justices: John G. Roberts Jr.*, 13 Scribes J. Legal Writing 5, 19 (2010).

National Institute for Trial Advocacy

Rather than memorizing your argument, Chief Justice Roberts instructs advocates to internalize it:

> I don't believe in memorizing what you're going to say. But when you've practiced it as many times as you need to do, in effect you are memorizing it. You're internalizing it. You're not sitting down and memorizing [as if to say] this is my answer to this question. But if you practice giving the answer to that question [twelve, fifteen, twenty] times, your mind has got it there, and you may not give it precisely the way you would as if you'd memorized it, as if you'd memorized *The Midnight Ride of Paul Revere* in fourth grade or whatever. But your mind is going to click into that and be able to give it without too much thought about exactly how to formulate it. Now, the opening in the Supreme Court, you're only guaranteed usually about a minute or so, a minute and a half, before a Justice is going to jump in. So I always thought it was very important to work very hard on those first few sentences. You want to convey exactly what you think the case turns on and why you should win—not just the issue in this case is blah, blah, blah. One, they already know that. And two, you're not doing anything; you're not moving the ball if you're just telling them what the issue is. You've got to frame it in a way that makes your main argument, so they understand right from the beginning: the focus is on this particular statutory phrase; the focus is on this particular precedent; the focus is on this particular consequence that'll happen if you don't rule in my favor.[5]

Finally, Chief Justice Roberts explains the importance of being able to transition between your different points in the argument. When he was practicing for an argument, he would identify the four or five key points in the case and write them on cards. As he explains:

> I don't care how complicated your case is; it usually reduces to at most four or five major points: here's the key precedent, here's the key language, here's the key regulation, here are the key consequences. You have four or five points. It's called A, B, C, D, and E. And when I'm practicing giving the argument, I'll go through it, and then I'll just shuffle those cards—A, B, C, D, and E—without knowing what they are. Then I'll start again and I'll look down. Okay, my first point is going to be C; and then from point C, I'm going to move to point E; and then from point E to point A. You develop practice on those transitions . . . because that's how it always works, at any appellate court. You can't guarantee the first question you're going to get is going to be on your first point. It may be on your third point. And everyone has seen this,

---

5. *Id.* at 20.

and it's very awkward for somebody to say after they answer that third point, "And now I'd like to go back to the point I was making." Well, okay, it's not very smooth, and you kind of lose a little bit of traction. If you've practiced giving that argument [on your] third point and then to the first point and then to whatever, you can make those transitions, and it's much smoother. And again, one, it conveys a greater degree of confidence on your part in your presentation—that you're not pausing and saying, "Now I'll go back to something else." It prevents the argument from seeming disrupted, and it makes the argument look fluid no matter what questions you get or in what order the points come out.[6]

16.6   Is It a Hot or Cold Court?

Should you proceed to oral argument on the assumption that the court has read the briefs? It depends. You must learn in advance as much as possible about any appellate bench before whom you appear. Find out if the judges traditionally receive the briefs before oral argument and if so, how far in advance. If the judges receive briefs at the last minute, as is the case in some state appellate courts, you may assume that it is a cold court and that there has not been much advance study of the briefs.

Investigate to see if the court has published internal operating procedures, or communicate with a former law clerk who has served with the court to learn their practices. For example, from the Third Circuit's Internal Operating Procedures you can learn that "Briefs and appendices are distributed sufficiently in advance to afford four full weeks' study in chambers prior to the panel sitting."[7] As discussed in § 16.9, previewing arguments online or in person before the court in advance of your argument will also provide insight into how hot or cold the court tends to be at argument.

16.7   Preparing for the Questions: A Checklist

The judges will question you. Prepare for it.

Every brief submitted by counsel and every point to be covered at oral argument must be meticulously examined and reviewed from the point of view of a judge who is either skeptical or downright hostile. That judge will toss hypotheticals at you in an attempt to show that your position will damage controlling case law or clash with traditional legal precepts. Prepare for this inquisition.

The very process of preparing for the worst onslaught will strengthen your hand. It will help build a strong intellectual framework for your presentation. Step aside from your written brief and argument outline and go through a check list of questions.

---

6. *Id.* at 23–24.
7. 3D CIR. I.O.P. 1.1.

National Institute for Trial Advocacy

- What do you want? What are you asking the court to hold?

- What rule do you want the court to adopt to justify the holding you request? Is there any other rule that would satisfy you?

- How will the rule work? What are the practical consequences? How far will the rule carry? How far will the law go? Will it expand or contract existing case law? If we extend claims, demands, or defenses, at what point can we draw the line before it conflicts with a competing legal precept? If we contract claims, demands, or defenses, will we now or in the immediate future be overruling settled case law (recall that a panel cannot overrule circuit precedent, though the en banc court has that authority)? Would we be modifying it? If so, are there strong policy reasons for a potential change in the law? Will it change current practice? Will it generate additional litigation?

- Is there a legally respectable argument for the rule? Is it supported by relevant authorities? Is it consistent with what the court has done before? Is it coherent in the sense that it hangs together in fact and law?

- Why should the court accept your argument and your proposed rule? What values and interests would be advanced? Would opposing values and interests be accommodated? How thoughtfully and disinterestedly have the social interests been weighed? How fair and durable does the adjustment of any interest-conflicts promise to be?

- Why is your rule superior to an alternative? To the one advanced by the trial court? By your opponent?

- Is the court in a position to announce your rule? Do the record facts and procedural posture furnish the adequate background? If it is a Rule 12(b)(6) matter (judgment on the pleadings), would it be better cast as a grant of summary judgment? If a summary judgment, should the court have the benefit of a full trial record?

- Where is the flashpoint of conflict between you and your adversary? Is it in the choice of competing legal precepts? Are you quarreling simply over construction of a controlling precept? Or only over application of a chosen and interpreted precept to the facts found by the fact-finder?

- Are the points constituting your argument mutually independent? Does the whole argument depend upon the court accepting your first point? If the court rejects one point can it still rule in your favor?

- Are there any formal fallacies in the argument? Any material fallacies?

- In reviewing your brief at this eleventh hour, do you spot any weakness? To avoid a grilling from hostile judges, are you willing to concede any points? If so, does this strengthen or weaken your remaining arguments?

- Do you know the essential part of the record like the back of your hand? Will you be able to turn to it in a moment, or will you leaf through pages, or look with dismay at your junior colleague at the counsel table?

Go through an inventory of questions like these in order to frame answers to possible questions in the calm and friendly environment of your office, where you will have the advantage of time and research and consultation with colleagues. If you do not do this, consider the alternative: standing alone at the lectern with the minutes and seconds of rationed time ticking away and being forced to think of an immediate answer to a question that never before had entered your mind.

16.8 The Mandatory Rehearsal

Nearly every federal and state judge surveyed strongly recommends that you rehearse your presentation before several office colleagues (and maybe even a non-attorney), not intimately familiar and emotionally influenced by the case, but who have taken the time to read the briefs and are willing to assume the role of judges and that of your adversary. This is as important as any other phase of preparation. To do this is not to demean your abilities; rather, it is to demonstrate high professionalism. It is not a waste of time and is a legitimate part of your billable hours.

Here, you do not want to engender tunnel vision or participate in a sycophantic romance with your associates telling you what a fantastic lawyer you are. It is important that the "judges" study both sets of briefs in advance and thus acquire more than a superficial understanding of what the case is all about. They should be prepared to interrupt you with the type of questions that you might expect at the official performance. In particular, they should throw at you hypotheticals: "Counsel, before us are facts *A*, *B*, and *C*, and you are asking us to accept a legal proposition, *X*, to govern them. Suppose the next case we have includes an additional fact, *D*. Would we apply your rule? Or suppose we have only facts *A* and *B*?" Anticipate such questions and be prepared to answer them. Do not simply say, "Of course, Your Honors, but that is not the case before the court." The judges know this.

Your office "judges" should test both your inductive and deductive reasoning. Be prepared to defend your analogies. Know the resemblances and differences in the compared cases, vindicate your major premise, and demonstrate that your conclusion logically flows from it.

Prepare for oral argument the way the president might prepare for a press conference. His aides pitch him the hard balls and curves that the press will be throwing. And if such a rehearsal is mandatory for the president, it should be mandatory for you.

You may even ask an attorney from your office to play the role of opposing counsel. Have him give his argument and let the "judges" work him over. You will gain valuable insights from this. You will hear how the strong arguments against you will sound in court. This may influence you to alter your presentation. If you are the appellant, it may give you some intuition in preparing some "spontaneous" rebuttal.

Such a rehearsal is not playacting. It is serious preparation for a fifteen-minute oral presentation that may make or break your case. You should also record the rehearsal and watch it with an eye towards any distracting mannerism that could negatively impact your argument.

But the question comes: if you are the appellee, how do you rehearse? The best answer is to have one of your colleagues argue your opponent's case as a preliminary so that you may then proceed into a response. Here, it is important that the panel of your "judges" fire away with questions directed to both your opponent and you.

We cannot emphasize too strongly the need to rehearse. Oral arguments before an appellate court do not come every day. The late Philadelphia attorney Irving R. "Buddy" Seigal explained that this rehearsal should include

> sessions with experienced as well as inexperienced lawyers in counsel's firm. This kind of preparation is essential. If the case is not "important enough" to justify the legal time necessary for such thorough preparation insofar as fees are concerned, then, having accepted the appellate assignment, counsel must do what is necessary in the fee area, but still prepare just as if he was being adequately compensated. That is the duty of the lawyer, and particularly the lawyer appearing in the appellate courts.

The rehearsal requires law office teamwork. If properly conducted, you will indeed develop the necessary "lemme at 'em" frame of mind. You will be thoroughly prepared. You will be ready for the questions. You will be alert to the potential hypotheticals.

Notwithstanding these views, other distinguished lawyers have different ideas.

As noted in the Foreword to an earlier version of this book, Charles Alan Wright, the late scholar, author, professor, and appellate lawyer, made this comment:

> I would not dream of rehearsing an argument. Indeed I refuse even to discuss a case in the period leading up to when I am going to argue it. At least for my style of argument, freshness and spontaneity are vitally important. I think long and hard about what may be said at oral argument, but I do not put words on paper nor do I discuss the case with others.

Similarly, veteran Philadelphia appellate lawyer James D. Crawford shared Professor Wright's view insofar as he, himself, is concerned, but he seems to think that it is helpful for others in his firm:

In more than forty years of making appellate arguments, I have never practiced before a moot court—although I have participated in many as a "judge." Even when clients have told me that they require moot courts of their lawyers, I have persuaded them that it doesn't work for me. (Of course, I am always willing to discuss my tentative approach to the argument and to explain how I would answer particular questions; what I won't do is try to get "psyched up" for an argument that doesn't count.)

I recognize that most appellate lawyers don't agree with me. But I have always believed that I would read too much into the moot court and would tend to search for the answers that worked there even if the question or the questioner at oral argument is very different from those in the moot court. That doesn't mean that I don't regularly seek the help of colleagues in preparing an argument; I will discuss problems in the case, approaches to the argument or even proposed answers to expected questions; I just think it is at best useless, and sometimes harmful, to do this in a formal moot court setting.

16.9   Previewing the Court

For important arguments in unfamiliar locations or before unfamiliar judges, you should take the necessary steps to preview the court. Your preview should consist of two separate steps. First, during your argument preparatory time you should seek to watch or listen to several oral arguments before the court in general, or your panel in particular. If the court is too far away for you to reasonably travel to it in advance of your actual argument, you should see if the court live streams arguments online. Increasingly, state supreme courts (and some state appellate courts) are offering live streaming of oral arguments.[8] Many of these courts also offer archived video of past arguments.

The federal appellate courts are not as open to cameras in the courtroom, but many federal appellate courts, including the Fifth Circuit, do offer online audio archives of past arguments.[9] Chicago-Kent College of Law's Oyez project also offers audio of past United States Supreme Court arguments.[10] You may consider listening to the oral argument in key cases that your brief relies on.

---

8. Tessa L. Dysart, *Live Streaming of Appellate Arguments*, Appellate Advocacy Blog (Sept. 12, 2016), http://lawprofessors.typepad.com/appellate_advocacy/2016/09/live-streaming-of-appellate-arguments.html (last visited Mar. 20, 2017).

9. *See, e.g., Listen to Oral Arguments*, U.S. Court of Appeals for the Fourth Circuit, https://www.ca4.uscourts.gov/oral-argument/listen-to-oral-arguments (last visited Mar. 20, 2017); *Oral Argument Recordings*, U.S. Court of Appeals for the Fifth Circuit, http://www.ca5.uscourts.gov/oral-argument-information/oral-argument-recordings (last visited Mar. 20, 2017).

10. Oyez, https://www.oyez.org/ (last visited Mar. 20, 2017).

National Institute for Trial Advocacy

In addition to previewing arguments during your preparatory stage, you should also arrive a day or so before your oral argument to preview the actual court building. If you can possibly do so, watch the arguments of others the day before you argue. Learn something about the acoustics of the room.

The late Pittsburgh attorney John H. Bingler Jr. offered this advice in an earlier edition of this book:

> On the day before your argument, go through the routine you expect to follow on the day you[] argue, even the walk/drive to the courthouse. If at all possible, stay at a hotel within walking distance of the courthouse. Get up at the same time, eat the same breakfast, drink the same number of cups of coffee, so you'll know how you will feel the day you argue and so you won't need to think about much else on argument day besides your argument.

At a bare minimum, if you have never been to the court, find out first where the lawyers must report in. Learn whether there is more than one courtroom; how cases are called; whether there is a daily calendar for distribution; where you can find your case on the list; the arrangement of counsel tables (who sits where); how the court controls the length of argument (by lights or cards or whatever); whether a clock can be seen from the lectern; where counsel may place notes or other materials; whether a sound system is used. Learn something about the acoustics; judges do not want to be shouted at, but they should not have to strain to hear what is being said. If you plan on driving to the courthouse, learn in advance where you can park and how you must pay for parking. Scope out the courthouse too. Know where the restrooms are and whether there is a cafeteria if you think that you will need a snack. These details might be trivial, but you do not want to be in a situation where you do not know where to find the bathroom in case pre-argument jitters hit.

16.10   Supplemental Citations

If you have cases that you have discovered or which have come up subsequent to the filing of your brief, forward them to the court under the procedures set by the court. Do not wait until the day of the argument. United States circuit judges are rather liberal in permitting "late citations" in the form of a letter to the clerk with copies to the panel, including some courts allowing citations to be handed up to the bench at the beginning of the argument. Just because it is permissible, however, does not make it a good idea.

If you wait until the day of the argument, you are losing much of the zip. If the case is important enough to be cited, the judges should have the opportunity of studying it before hearing your oral argument. At a minimum, the judges should be permitted to examine it before participating in the decision conference, which usually takes place immediately after the oral argument.

Technically, late citations should be limited to cases which have been handed down by a court subsequent to the filing of the brief. Often, however, it is simply tardy research that is responsible for these late citations. Submitting cases at the last minute that should have been in the brief is a sign of sloppy lawyering. The Fifth Circuit, inconsistently, will reject letters citing authorities that predate the briefing that has already been done. Finding an older authority after a brief has been filed is technically not a sufficient basis to submit it as supplemental authority.

It is extremely important to give a reason for the citation. The judges should be told what point the late citation is supporting with a one- or two-sentence summary of the holding of the case or a parenthetical quotation. Federal Rule of Appellate Procedure 28(j) concerning Supplemental Authorities states, "The letter must state the reasons for the supplemental citations, referring either to the page of the brief or to a point argued orally." In a previous edition of this book, Judge Aldisert recounted a case in which the panel's attention was drawn to a last-minute citation represented by counsel to be controlling on a point. He sent for the case, glanced at it on the bench, and discovered immediately that the holding was the exact opposite from the characterization given by counsel. He noted also that the presiding judge had written the opinion. He turned to him, handed him the book, and pointed out the relevant part. Whereupon the presiding judge, who previously had been silent, took over the questioning and destroyed the oral presentation. This late citation turned out to be a disaster. Not really understanding the case, the attorney who offered it committed forensic suicide in open court.

CHAPTER SEVENTEEN

HOW APPELLATE LAWYERS PREPARE

You have written, edited, rewritten, edited again, and finally perfected your brief. You filed it with the appellate court, and the court granted oral argument on the matter. How do you prepare? The first step in preparation is to remember the purpose of oral argument. Look back at Chapter Three and review what judges expect oral argument to accomplish. As noted in Chapter Three, you also have your own expectations, most notably to face the decision makers and answer any questions and misunderstandings that they have about your case. Your preparation should be aimed at achieving both these sets of expectations. The challenges in oral argument are many, not the least of which is the fact that you wrote your brief months ago and have other important matters demanding your time. Furthermore, there are several key issues that you want to address, but you only have a few minutes before the court. This chapter offers advice on how best to meet these challenges head on and prepare for argument.

Advice on how to prepare for oral argument comes largely from expert lawyers, rather than from the judges. Judges may offer suggestions on how to make the presentation. They can also sketch out in broad strokes the nature of the preparation necessary to satisfy them. But the nuts and bolts on how to prepare must come from experienced appellate advocates, so it is to them that we now turn.

17.1 Howard J. Bashman, Law Offices of Howard J. Bashman

Howard J. Bashman, a solo appellate practitioner based in Willow Grove, Pennsylvania, is a nationally known appellate practitioner and the presence behind *How Appealing*, a delightful and informative blog devoted to appellate matters.[1] He offers this advice.

> The first one or two sentences of your presentation should deliver a roadmap to the main points you plan to address during your time at the podium. "The trial court's judgment should be reversed for three reasons. First, second, and third."

---

1. Howard Bashman, HOW APPEALING, at http://howappealing.abovethelaw.com/ (last visited Mar. 20, 2017).

Respond immediately to the substance of questions from the bench, in a manner that is forthright, not evasive. If you are asked about issue two while you are addressing issue one, answer the question. You can then return to your intended presentation or stay with the issue raised by the question should the judges appear especially interested in it.

If, before your allotted time has expired, you have answered all of the judges' questions and have addressed the matters you intended to cover, thank the court for its attention and sit down.

17.2 Bobby R. Burchfield, King & Spalding

Bobby R. Burchfield—one of Judge Aldisert's former clerks—is a partner in the Washington, D.C., office of King & Spalding. He has argued before the United States Supreme Court and numerous federal and state appellate courts throughout the country. He offers this advice.

Work hard to find the winning argument. To be in this business, we almost have to believe that every case is winnable if only we can find the right argument and make it effectively. Sometimes the winning argument will be unconventional, but if a candid evaluation of the available arguments leads to the conclusion that the conventional arguments cannot succeed, a more creative approach may be necessary.

Believe in your position. Critique your own argument mercilessly, and take account of its weaknesses. By the time of oral argument, you should be confident that your argument is logical, consistent with the record, supported (or at least not foreclosed) by pertinent precedent, and responsive to any argument advanced by your adversary. Until you reach the point of believing in your own argument, it is difficult to expect an appellate court to do so.

State clearly and early why you should win. At the outset of the argument, express concisely and precisely why your client should win. The opening sentence of the argument should simply but powerfully tell the court why you win the case. The rest of the argument should elaborate upon that statement. This principle discourages, and is intended to discourage, [buffet-style] arguments.

Be authoritative. Both in the briefs and at argument your goal should be for the court to look to you as the most authoritative person in the courtroom with regard to your case. This requires extensive preparation on both the law and the record, as well as painstaking candor. If relying upon critical evidence, direct the court to the location of the document or testimony in the record, give the court time to find it, and read the pertinent language to the court. By doing so, you will assure that the court sees the evidence and appreciates its importance to your case.

Whenever possible, follow the judges. Understand and associate yourself with the views of the judges on your panel to the maximum extent possible. If you know the panel in advance, determine what each judge has written about the issues in your case, and attempt to reconcile your position to that of each judge. Even when the panel in not known in advance, your typed summaries of the important decisions should indicate the author and participating judges so that quick reference is possible immediately before argument. During argument, seize upon questioning by the court to align your position with the questioning judge. If you are the appellee, you might even pick up on a question asked of the appellant's counsel to demonstrate how the inquiry helps your case.

Simplify complex issues. It is important to understand complex issues, but just as important to simplify them. The goal is to communicate even the most complex factual and legal issues in an accurate but simple and understandable way. Excellent advocates especially excel at this.

Finally, do not neglect the equities. It is as important to explain why a ruling for your client is fair as it is to explain why a ruling for your client is required by existing precedent. Judges strive to reach fair results within the confines of existing precedent. You should strive to make the judges want to rule for you, rather than persuading them that they must rule for you. A judge will often find the way to a fair result, even if apparently applicable precedent seems at first blush to stand in the way. The best "one-two" punch is to explain why a ruling for your client would be fair, and then how precedent compels (or at least allows) your client to win.

Nuts and Bolts of Preparing for an Argument. Over the years, I have developed a standard routine to prepare for an appellate argument. Preparation begins about a month before the argument date. First, I carefully reread the lower court decision, often for the fourth or fifth time, and note the points with which my client agrees and the ones with which it disagrees. Second, I carefully reread the briefs and take copious notes, focusing especially on selecting the theme for my argument and anticipating responses to that theme. Third, I identify the handful of decisions that will govern the case, that the lower court relied on, or that my adversary contends may govern the case. I read each of them carefully, and then dictate out a paragraph listing the author of the majority opinion, noting any dissents, stating the holding (e.g., "reversing summary judgment in favor of plaintiff, and holding that the direct purchaser doctrine bars the action"), and then setting forth the reasoning in the court's decision. Fourth, I dictate the argument as if I could give it uninterrupted, and then edit it numerous times until it is boiled down to its essence, with my key point in the very first sentence. I know that I will never be able to give the entire argument uninterrupted, but this process of outlining, dictating, and editing helps me to develop the appropriate phrasing for the argument and prepares me to work in the key points in response to questions. Simultaneously, I spend time writing out possible questions and answers to the questions, editing the responses to make them crisp and persuasive. Then, a week or so before the argument, I hold one or more moot courts with my team and often the client, allowing sufficient time between the moot court and the actual argument to revise the argument and answers to questions to take account of what I have learned. The night before the argument, I always make it a point to get a good night's sleep.

17.3   G. Todd Butler, Phelps Dunbar

G. Todd Butler is a partner in the Jackson, Mississippi, office of the firm Phelps Dunbar, where he has handled appellate matters before the federal and state courts. He is a former clerk to Judge Southwick, and he offers this advice.

1) **Update Your Argument**

   a) Search for new legal authorities issued after briefing has closed. This goes for authorities relied on by both you and your opponent.

   b) You might have an obligation to provide new legal authorities to the court and the other side under governing procedural rules (e.g., F.R.A.P. 28(j)) in advance of oral argument, but certainly be prepared to discuss them during oral argument.

2) **Review Writings From The Judges Hearing Your Case**

   a) Most courts release the names of the judges deciding a case in advance of oral argument, so be sure to review any decisions by those judges that may be pertinent to your argument.

   b) In one appeal, I was able to find a law review article written by a member of the court during the judge's law school days. So don't limit your research to published opinions.

3) **Listen To Oral Argument Recordings**

   a) Many courts offer oral argument recordings on their websites. These recordings are useful in identifying judicial concerns that sometimes don't show up in written opinions. Listen to the recordings of any big cases involved in your appeal, and especially do so if one of those prior cases included a judge that will be deciding your case.

b) Listen to oral arguments from your opponent. Most court websites allow you to search by "attorney name," in addition to by "case name" or "case number." If the lawyer on the other side is a specialist, it is likely that he or she may take the same approach to your case that was taken in a previous case.

c) Be efficient and multitask. I listen to oral arguments while traveling or exercising. Smartphones make it easy to combine argument preparation with life outside of the office.

4) Get Mooted And Moot Yourself

a) I am fortunate to have colleagues and friends who are either seasoned appellate litigators or former judicial law clerks. They don't always like it, but I make them review briefs and pepper me with questions. If a particular judge deciding my case is known for a certain approach to oral argument, I ask the person mooting me to assume that role. If one of the judges is a combative questioner, for example, I can expect a heated practice round. I like to compare the experience to a quarterback who faces an intense practice squad before the Sunday game.

b) Practice alone, too. And make the experience as formal as possible. Stand in front of a mirror or a lectern. Even if you have good ideas in your head, you will benefit from articulating them aloud for clarity in organization.

17.4 Kyle Duncan, Schaerr Duncan LLP

Kyle Duncan is one of the founding partners of the Washington, D.C., law firm Schaerr Duncan LLP. He has argued many appeals in federal courts including the U.S. Supreme Court and served as Louisiana's first Solicitor General. He offers this advice.

1) *"Smile and let them know you are glad to be there."* This last-minute advice was texted to me by the brilliant appellate lawyer, the late Greg Coleman, as I rode terrified in a taxi to my first argument before the U.S. Supreme Court. What Greg meant was that the attitude you bring to the bar is critical.

Arguing any appeal is a privilege. I think judges want to know that lawyers are grateful for the chance to explain why their client's cause is just. Whenever I make an argument, remembering Greg's advice helps me remember why I am there.

Greg was one of the finest appellate lawyers of his generation. He was the first Solicitor General of Texas and successfully argued many times before the High Court. I had the great good fortune to work for him and learn from him early on. Greg died in a tragic plane crash in 2010. Whenever I make an argument, I hope Greg likes it.

2) *"Once you are up on your feet, you are on your own[.]"* This quote is from a good book, *Effective Appellate Advocacy* by Frederick Wiener, and it is true: you feel alone at argument because the whole case is distilled in one short event, you want to do your best for the client, and you're up there by yourself. How to deal with that? Here are some ideas that have been helpful to me.

First, I must have a clear game plan. A simple theme; three or four main points; a few key cases, record cites, or quotes I want to emphasize. Appellate argument is not like defending a doctoral thesis. You must make your best points succinctly while the few minutes you have dribble away under a barrage of questions. A game plan is necessary to prevent wilting under that pressure.

Second, the game plan must be in my head. Not in the seventeen-page, single-spaced "Oral Argument Outline"; not in the massive colorfully tabbed binder on the podium. At most, I may bring to the podium two pages with a sketch of my main points, a few pointed phrases I want to work in, and any key record cites. Anything more is a distraction at best. At worst, it is a sign that I have not yet grasped what I want to tell the court. By the time you are alone at the podium, it is too late.

Third, I must be able to sum up why my client should win the case in about forty-five seconds. It is very comforting to be able to do this. I try to practice it over and over again, using different words and phrases, until it is embedded in my brain. This is the reference point for the entire argument. In some way, it must be the ultimate answer to every question, even the most hostile.

17.5   Miguel Estrada, Gibson Dunn & Crutcher

Miguel Estrada, a partner in Gibson Dunn's D.C. office, has argued twenty-two cases before the United States Supreme Court. He has also served as an Assistant to the Solicitor General of the United States and as an Assistant U.S. Attorney and the Deputy Chief of the Appellate Section in the Southern District of New York's U.S. Attorney's Office. He offers this advice.

Too many lawyers give oral argument preparation short shrift. After researching and writing the briefs, they think they can prepare by rereading the briefs a day in advance and reciting topic sentences to the court. Nothing could be further from the truth. Although cases often enough are won or lost on the papers, some winning briefs are lost (and even the occasional losing brief is salvaged) at the podium. The key, then, is to prepare for argument on the assumption the judges will be skeptical of the arguments in your briefs.

Because courts increasingly allocate oral argument time only when the judges have actual questions, some members of the panel likely will have significant questions about the record and the logical implications—and limitations—of your legal position. Oral argument is the time to keep friendly judges on your side, persuade judges who are on the fence, and manage hostile judges so they do not swing others to their side. To succeed, you will need to read the court and direct skeptical judges to a satisfactory resolution in your favor. The following guidelines should help prepare you to do just that.

Rethink your case. Oral argument typically requires you to rethink—not merely to reargue—your case. If you failed to win over a judge with the arguments in your brief, repeating those same arguments at the podium is unlikely to move the needle. For judges who are hostile or on the fence, you will need to provide, instead, a fresh perspective on the case. You must be facile enough that you can direct the court to a plausible basis for a majority decision in your favor—all while answering the court's questions.

As you reread the briefs, take a step back and consider how opposing counsel or a skeptical judge may view the case. Give yourself enough distance from your arguments that you can identify weaknesses where a judge is less likely to join your side. Then boil your case down to its essentials: which arguments you absolutely need to win, and which you need not discuss at argument (or even concede if necessary). This process will help you to identify the strongest paths to victory and, in turn, to direct the court to one of those paths for deciding the case in your favor. It also will make clear which one or two points you absolutely must convey to the court during your argument.

Prepare, prepare, prepare. Air time during oral argument is at a premium; you should prepare accordingly. You should of course have an outline of the one or two indispensable points in your argument; but there is no need to write out and polish a long, uninterrupted argument that you almost assuredly will not deliver. Focus your preparation instead on learning how to answer questions succinctly and adroitly.

About 75 percent of questions are wholly predictable to counsel who has prepared. To get ready for these questions, first make sure you know the relevant portions of the record and case law. Begin by rereading key portions of the district court record and the key cases for each side—especially if there is a long lag between briefing and oral argument. As you read, think of questions that could arise at oral argument, including those that are critical of your argument. Then update your research and see if there are any new authorities for a [Federal Rule of Appellate Procedure] 28(j) letter. You do not want to be blindsided by a harmful 28(j) letter on the eve of oral argument.

Next, write out in advance your best response to every question you think a judge—friendly or hostile—could reasonably ask. To save time at oral argument, a good answer should be distilled ahead of time until it is crisp and succinct. Make no more than two or three points, then transition back to your main argument. This sort of answer must be prepared in advance; you will waste valuable time trying to create an answer on the fly during oral argument. Of course, you will not be reading your responses, but this type of advance editorial effort will help ensure that you recall your key points when you hear the same questions at argument.

You also need to plan an exit strategy for escaping difficult questions that expose a weakness in your case or risk miring the court in a distracting or unhelpful issue. As you prepare, confront the weaknesses in your case head-on (you know them better than anyone), and determine what can be conceded without losing the case or losing credibility before the court. Then prepare your two or three best points in response to a difficult question and include a concession as appropriate. It is far better to concede a non-essential point than to waste time arguing it.

Audition. The best preparation for unpredictable questions is live argument before a moot court. I typically will go through at least two moots before an oral argument because a properly assembled moot panel can provide helpful perspective on the case. Assemble a mix of people who know the record and can grill you on the case, and people who are reading the briefs for the first time and can bring a fresh perspective. After each moot, go back and continue your preparations by incorporating points from the moot panel and preparing your best response to any new questions that arose. The moot process also will help solidify responses to questions you had already anticipated.

Be responsive. At oral argument, greet the court and provide a concise roadmap of the indispensable points of your argument—one or two sentences, at most. "This Court should affirm the district court's judgment for two reasons. First, second." If you are the appellee or respondent, consider picking up where the court seemed to be heading during your opponent's argument. Many judges may not let you even finish your introduction before they jump in with questions.

As you field questions, remember that oral argument time is for the benefit of judges, not attorneys. You should view questions as a welcome opportunity to clear up any confusion or eliminate obstacles to ruling in your favor. So stop talking when a judge begins a question, never interrupt a judge, and always be responsive. When answering a question, promptly give a direct response—"Yes" or "No" (or "Yes, but" or "No, but")—before explaining your answer. As you transition out of a response, try to read the court to see if you should say more about that issue or switch to a different point. If the court stops asking questions, try to gauge whether the court is already convinced by one side. One much appreciated strategy is to ask if the court has any other questions—and if not, thank the court and sit down.

17.6   Wes Hendrix, U.S. Attorney's Office for the Northern District of Texas

Wes Hendrix is an Assistant United States Attorney and the Appellate Chief in the Northern District of Texas. He is a veteran appellate lawyer with extensive experience in the United States Courts of Appeals. He regularly teaches appellate advocacy at the National Advocacy Center. He offers this advice.

Before diving into how I prepare for oral argument, it is important to note the characteristics of the most effective oral advocates. No one can plot a course without first knowing the destination. Or, as Yogi Berra would say, "If you don't know where you're going, you might not get there." The following traits serve as my inspiration when preparing for argument, and they drive the nuts-and-bolts of my preparation.

Be helpful to the court. Lawyers are, of course, advocates for their clients, but the most effective advocates understand that they must be viewed by the court as helpful. They recognize that they are on the court's time—not the other way around—and that their role is in large part to answer the court's questions. They see questions as an opportunity to address the court's concerns, not as an interruption. They also understand that being helpful and being persuasive are not mutually exclusive. Most judges will be more receptive to an argument when the lawyer demonstrates a willingness and ability to answer questions candidly and directly. Being thoroughly prepared and helpful engenders trust and increases the likelihood that the court will carefully consider your position when you pivot from questions to your argument.

Be precise with the record and the law. The best advocates master the record and relevant law because they know appellate panels expect precision. The quickest way to get a panel to stop listening to, or trusting, your argument is to show that you do not know the record or the law—or, worse still, that you are overstating them. Thankfully, however, the opposite is usually true as well. Demonstrating a mastery of the record and the law—and speaking precisely about them—increases the likelihood that a panel will trust your view of the case.

Be confident and passionate. It is often said that while it may be difficult to win an appeal at oral argument, it is possible to lose the appeal at that stage. One way to do so is to show a lack of confidence and passion in your position, which might naturally cause the judges to feel the same. No case is perfect, and advocates must admit weaknesses and cede ground where necessary, but we must also identify where to stand and fight—and do so confidently.

Be able to pivot. It is important to refine your argument to a few critical points and identify natural connections between them. The more connections you see, the easier it will be to answer questions and address weaknesses without getting completely sidetracked. Answering questions is paramount, of course, but you must be ready to pivot from your answers back to your view of the case. The best advocates make this look easy and provide a roadmap to resolving the case, but it comes only from earnest preparation.

These traits are much easier to identify than embody. To accomplish them, I recommend a systematic approach that includes the following steps:

1) *Gear up.* If you work in hard copy, make binders of the briefing, record, and case law. The simple process of gathering these often voluminous materials is a sobering reminder of how much work lies ahead. If you prefer to work electronically, get these materials loaded onto your iPad or tablet. I work mostly electronically, and I find it helpful to combine all the cases into one searchable, bookmarked PDF. I do the same with the briefing and the record, so at argument I can have only three tabs open in my e-reader application—the briefing, record, and case law—and everything is searchable.

2) *Master the record.* Reread the record closely, taking notes and pulling key excerpts. I use the notes later when distilling my argument, and I incorporate the excerpts into the argument binder I take to the podium.

3) *Know the briefs.* Reread the briefs closely, taking notes and reading the key cases. In most cases, the briefs define the boundaries of your argument, and it is important to remember their scope if additional, unexpected issues arise during oral argument. And if you are the appellee, it is especially critical to understand the reply brief and prepare responses to it.

4) *List tough questions.* As you take notes on the record and case law, you should inevitably begin to see weaknesses in your position and anticipate difficult questions. As they arise, list them in a "Tough Questions" section of your notes. If you can answer the question at that point, do so. If not, you have left a visual reminder to revisit the question later.

5) *List key points and themes.* Also during the note-taking process, list your most helpful points and the themes you may want to pursue at argument.

6) *Confirm that the law remains the same.* Time will have passed between briefing and oral argument—sometimes a substantial amount of time. Thus, it is necessary to research the relevant issues to check for material changes in the law. If material changes have occurred (or the briefing overlooked a critical case), inform the court by filing a letter pursuant to Federal Rule of Appellate Procedure 28(j), which permits letters no longer than 350 words to advise the court of "pertinent and significant authorities."

7) *Draft an argument outline.* Review your notes and distill them into two to three critical points. The argument outline should list these critical points and include any necessary case and record citations. You should not plan to restate or summarize your brief. Nor should the outline include complete sentences or paragraphs, which are too tempting to read at argument and disrupt a dialogue with the court. Your time is short, and you must decide the most important points to communicate before you sit down.

8) *Practice answers and talk to colleagues.* Practicing your answers out loud will help you speak more easily with the court and reduce unnecessary stumbling over names, facts, and explanations. And speaking with your colleagues will help crystallize your argument.

9) *Do reconnaissance on the panel.* Most courts permit enough time between the panel's announcement and the day of argument to research the judges. Were any of them involved in the key opinions? Do any of them ask particular types of questions at argument? Know your audience.

10) *Moot and refine.* You must conduct at least one moot court. There is no substitute for standing on your feet in front of your colleagues, presenting your argument, answering questions, and receiving immediate feedback. Take the feedback and refine your argument as necessary. It is not easy, but your argument will be much better for it.

11) *Trust yourself.* When you walk to the podium, trust that your preparation will make you helpful, precise, confident, and persuasive. Know that because of your hard work, you can have a meaningful dialogue with the court and put your client in the best possible position to prevail.

17.7   Peter Keisler, Sidley Austin LLP

Peter Keisler is the co-leader of Sidley Austin's Supreme Court and appellate practice and has argued numerous cases before federal appellate courts, including the United Supreme Court. He has also served as Acting Attorney General and clerked on the United States Supreme Court for Associate Justice Anthony Kennedy. He offers this advice.

> The advocates in every case have a wonderful opportunity to present a full, detailed and uninterrupted exposition of their position and the legal and factual support for it. But that opportunity is called a *brief.* Oral argument is something else entirely. It's not simply a condensed, spoken version of a brief, but a very different enterprise that offers different opportunities.
>
> In particular, it offers the opportunity to focus the judges' attention on a small number of your most important and compelling points, to learn through the judges' questions some of the objections or doubts—or perhaps misunderstandings—they might harbor that could keep them from embracing your position, and to respond directly (and one hopes, convincingly) to those concerns. An advocate who complains that a judge's questions kept him or her from getting out the argument they had planned to make has missed the whole point of oral argument. The judges have already spent plenty of time "listening quietly" to the advocates' theories in reading their briefs. The oral questions (and answers) are the reasons for making oral argument part of the process in the first place, because they provide the opportunity for the judges to react to what they're reviewed up to that point, and for the judges and advocates together to take the dialogue to the next level.
>
> So with that in mind, how would I suggest one prepare? I would urge the advocate to do three things on his or her own, a fourth involving others, and a fifth and sixth at the argument itself.
>
> *First,* re-read carefully all the materials the judges will be reviewing—the principal statutes, decisions, and other pertinent authorities, the portions of the record at issue, and the briefs. Although you already examined these documents in detail when you prepared your brief, try to do it again with a fresh and open mind, as if you were reading

them for the first time, without predispositions about what is and isn't important within them and what they do and do not establish. To begin with, you need to internalize these materials well, because you may get a question at argument about any aspect of them and at that point there's really no time look up things you don't already know. (If you undertake this reexamination comprehensively, 95 percent of what you review will never come up at argument, but it's impossible to predict which specific elements will fall within that otherwise infuriating 5 percent.)

But even apart from that, I've yet to go through that review process without seeing something new in what I'm reading, with the benefit of some time and distance from the brief-writing process. Perhaps it's a new way of understanding a feature of the law or the facts that helps my case, or perhaps it's something that might undermine my case and that I need to better consider in order to be properly prepared. Either way, I've yet to encounter a case in which I discover that I already had it all fully figured out.

Second, sketch out what you would say if you were living in the alternative universe in which you could speak without interruption. Keep in mind when you do this how much more limited our human abilities are to convey and to understand complex multi-step points orally rather than in writing. And remember also that while you may have been living and breathing your case day and night (perhaps even dreaming about it), it is merely one of many cases that the judges are hearing during the sitting to which it's been assigned, and they do not have at their mental fingertips all the details that you have at yours.

A fifty-page brief that the reader can study and return to may have room for complicated roadmaps, footnotes with string cites, and multiple alternative arguments (although even in the brief, not as much room as people tend to think). A fifteen-minute oral presentation cannot. So decide on your most compelling arguments and how they can be most simply, directly, and convincingly communicated. And if you have not yet done a sufficient number of arguments to have a sure instinct for how much you can present in a specified number of minutes, time yourself making those points and see whether you're being realistic. You may be surprised how quickly time passes when there's a lot you want to say.

Why do this even though you are so unlikely ever to deliver that hypothetical speech you've just outlined? Because you will then have boiled your argument down to its most effective core. If you represent the appellant, you will then know how to begin. If one or more of the panel's questions can be related to those core points, you will have a head start in formulating your response. And if there's a pause in the questioning, you will be best positioned to fill that space by directing the panel's attention to your most persuasive points.

Third, make a list of the toughest and most likely questions you might get and consider your best responses. You won't be able to anticipate every question you get, but you'll be able to anticipate many of them. When you first picked up the case, you probably saw some initial vulnerabilities for your side immediately, as a first reaction. As you dug deeper, you found other vulnerabilities. And your adversary has forcefully pointed out many of those vulnerabilities in his or her brief and likely added some more. All of those can go on your list, and then you can methodically work through them and decide how you would address each one most effectively.

One of the most valuable decisions you can make in advance of the argument is to identify the single best response to each potential vulnerability. We're trained as lawyers to come up with four arguments for every point. The other side claims your suit was barred by the three-year statute of limitations. You respond in your brief that the applicable limitations period is five years, not three; that you filed within three years anyway; that the limitations period was tolled by a discovery rule; and that the statute of limitations is in any event unconstitutional. When a judge raises the issue and you respond with one of those four points, the judge may well follow up, and you will never get to the other three. One of those arguments is the best of the four, and it's important to have figured out in advance which one it is.

Fourth, after you've done all this, have two or three colleagues read the briefs who (a) have experience arguing appellate cases, and (b) have no prior experience with your case. Make them your moot court judges, try out your arguments, and see what questions they ask and what they think of your responses. (Moot courts are usually much more difficult than actual arguments, because moot court judges are playing the role of the skeptical or even hostile judge, and actual judges tend to be more open-minded than pretend judges; one or more members of the actual panel may even enter the courtroom inclined towards your position.) It's absolutely critical, I believe, that the "no-prior-experience-with-your-case" rule be followed in selecting mooters. It's the best way to break out of the groupthink that can settle in among the people that have been working together on the case—and to discover how many things that group thought "clear" or "obvious" can in fact be a source of confusion or legitimate disagreement. The feedback from well-structured moot courts virtually always leads the advocate to modify his or her approach in some significant and helpful respects.

Fifth, when you then get to the argument, try to let all this preparation be a source of liberation: you know your case, you've thought through its strong and weak points, you've strategized about how to pitch your points, and ideally this can give you the confidence and freedom to engage in a genuine give-and-take with the panel. If the careful preparation instead makes you heavily scripted, it's taken you in precisely the wrong direction. And most importantly, to engage in that more natural give-and-take, be sure you are genuinely listening to what the judges on the panel are saying in their questions rather than immediately categorizing those questions in your mind and launching into "Prepared Response No. 9." It's remarkable how frequently advocates make that mistake—and, for example, react to a friendly or at least neutral question as if it were an adversarial one, simply because that is what they have mentally geared themselves for and they're not listening carefully enough to what the judge is actually saying.

Finally, enjoy yourself. Oral argument is one of the moments in which you will most "feel like a lawyer"—engaging in real time with judges and your opposing counsel in seeking to be persuasive on behalf of your client. The judicial branch is unique in our system of government—nowhere else, certainly not in the White House nor in the halls of Congress, does the interested party regularly get to be in the room with the key decision-makers and engage directly with them, one on one, on the matter they're about to resolve. Be proud of the process you're participating in and the central role you're playing in it.

17.8   Scott Keller, Solicitor General of Texas

Scott Keller is the Solicitor General of Texas. He clerked for then-Chief Judge Alex Kozinski of the United States Court of Appeals for the Ninth Circuit and Associate Justice Anthony Kennedy. He also served as Bristow Fellow in the Office of the Solicitor General at the United States Department of Justice. As Solicitor General, he has argued before the United States Supreme Court. He offers this advice.

1) *Oral argument ideally should be a conversation.* Your role as an advocate, of course, is to persuade judges of your position. But the most effective way to accomplish that in an appellate oral argument is to be unflappable and maintain a conversational tone. This enhances your credibility by focusing on legal arguments rather than emotional appeals. A conversational style also prevents your presentation from turning into scripted oratory—which rarely has a place in appellate oral arguments today.

2) *Do multiple moot (practice) arguments before the actual oral argument.* Moot arguments allow an advocate to anticipate the questions asked at the actual oral argument. If the moots are conducted properly with engaged mock judges, the moot arguments may very well be more difficult than the actual oral argument. In the Texas Solicitor General's Office, each attorney will do at least two moots before every oral argument. With each additional moot, your arguments will become more crystallized and your responses more succinct.

3) *Pay very close attention to the precise question asked by the judge.* When a judge asks a question, the advocate should stop talking. Talking over judges is disrespectful, and any points the advocate tries to make while doing so will probably not be heard by the judges. Moreover, a judge's question is a valuable opportunity to understand what the judge believes is crucial to the case. Good advocates take advantage of this information by listening to the question, comprehending what precise issue the judge is concerned about, and responding with the most persuasive answer.

4) *Answer questions as succinctly as possible.* Often, you will only be able to answer in a few sentences before a judge asks you an additional question. So answer each question succinctly while raising your best points. Respond with "yes" or "no" when possible. Fighting against a question that can easily be answered "yes" or "no" wastes your time and annoys judges. However, you need to understand the issues in your case thoroughly to know when it is not possible to answer with just "yes" or "no." For example, if a simple "yes" or "no" would concede away a key point, you would want to clarify that the answer depends on certain circumstances.

5) *Don't try to say too much.* You will not have time at oral argument to review every point made in your briefs—and strategically you don't want to do that anyway. The main purpose of oral argument is for judges to probe the arguments they believe will be dispositive to the resolution of the case. So rather than trying to rehash every point you made in your brief, figure out what points the case probably turns on and be sure to give your most persuasive arguments addressing those points in your precious time at the podium.

17.9 George A. Somerville, Harman Claytor Corrigan Wellman

George A. Somerville is Senior Counsel in the Richmond, Virginia, office of Harman Claytor Corrigan Wellman, where he focuses on appellate litigation in federal and state court. He is a former clerk to Judge Aldisert and a frequent lecturer on appellate practice. He offers the following advice.

> *Rule 1*: PREPARE! It is quite difficult to over-prepare for an oral argument (but it is not nearly so difficult to prepare poorly).

Prepare over an extended period of time—several weeks, if at all possible. Read and reread the opinion(s) below, the briefs, every significant authority, and the entire Appendix (not merely the passages cited in the briefs). Be aware that in a significant number of cases, one or more questions from the bench will ask counsel to clarify apparent ambiguities in the factual record. "I didn't try the case" is the worst possible answer to such a question. Consider the possibility that you may need to be ready to cite additional materials in the Record, to address unanticipated arguments made in an opposing brief or even at the podium. (These points are discussed further in Rule 1(e), below.)

When you walk into the courtroom, you should know both the evidence and the authorities like the proverbial back of your hand. "While familiarity with your own authorities is key, knowledge of your opponent's authorities is equally important. For example, you are more likely to be asked during oral argument to comment upon or distinguish your opponent's authorities than your own."[2]

Appellate oral arguments seldom explore more than a few of the most important cases, but you cannot always predict which will fall into that category in the mind of one or more judges. If the significant cases are so numerous that you worry about keeping all of them straight in your mind, prepare a list of *very brief* descriptions of those whose short-form captions may not immediately call up the important memories, and keep it in an accessible location when you are at the podium. But *do not* rely on it to remind you what is significant about each such case. You need to *know* what is significant (including not only the points of law decided but also the essential facts and the procedural postures of each case). The list should be designed and used only to remind you which case is which.

Plan to argue only your one or two key points—usually your strongest points, but necessarily including any point on which you *must* prevail to win—but *prepare* to argue *every* issue in the appeal. Many a lawyer has been surprised by appellate judges' interest in an issue that he or she regarded as having only secondary importance.

Do not plan to deliver an argument that encompasses all of your allocated time. The court rarely will cooperate with such a plan; and if you get few or no questions, you will do well either to yield a part of your time or to reserve it for rebuttal. (A silent bench is usually either very good or very bad news, and it is more frequently the former. In either event, an overly lengthy argument is not likely to advance your case; but by rambling on too long, you risk sticking your neck out too far or inviting questions that ultimately torpedo your position.)

Do not plan to regurgitate your brief in a more condensed form. Almost all appellate jurists today are familiar with the briefs, and most quickly grow bored with repetition of the same arguments from the podium. The oral argument is your opportunity to approach the case from a new direction. Your purpose is to drive home the arguments that you made on brief, but you will do that most effectively by presenting them from a fresh perspective.

Incorporate the principles of primacy and recency. The justices or judges will usually (though *not always*) allow you to speak without interruption for a minute or two at the beginning of your argument. That may be the only time that you are allowed to capsulize your strongest argument, and it is one of your best opportunities to leave a lasting impression. Make good use of it.

Study the biographies and relevant opinions of the judges who will be on your panel. (You may not want to launch a broadside attack on the Federal Trade Commission, for example, if one of the judges on your panel is a former General Counsel of the FTC.) In a court that does not identify the judges on panels until the day of argument, arrive with biographical sketches of each active and senior judge and short summaries of how they have addressed similar issues in previous cases. (That won't help if you are surprised by the presence of a visiting judge from another court, but there are limits on the extent of possible preparation. Even in those cases, however, a telephone call to an associate at your office may glean some helpful information.)

Rule 1(b): Be sure that you are current on the law. You should have been sufficiently alert while the case was pending that you are aware of every new decision, statute, or regulation that might have some impact on your case. But whether you have been monitoring the appropriate sources or not, you should Shepardize every significant case cited in any of the briefs and—in any area that might be governed by a statute or regulation—to investigate the possibility that significant new enactments may alter the outcome or analysis. If you identify pertinent new authorities, send a [Federal Rule of Appellate Procedure] 28(j) letter to the Clerk). (Send a letter even if you are in a jurisdiction without a similar rule. Rarely, if ever, will a court find fault; but attempting to argue a new authority orally, without notifying the court and opposing counsel in advance, will gain you nothing but judicial opprobrium.)

Rule 1(c): Develop one or *perhaps* two themes around which you will build your argument. (Usually your theme will be apparent from rereading your brief.) A perfect theme is *concise, comprehensive,* and *compelling*. Short phrases that quickly evoke recognition in the minds of the listeners also can be employed repeatedly (without overdoing it) to hammer home an essential point. I have in mind pithy expressions such as "straw man" or "the dog that didn't bark." But do not wander too far into the realm of the informal and colloquial; "that dog don't hunt," for example, while likely familiar to most judges, is over the line.

Rule 1(d): Be your own devil's advocate. Figure out the *hard* questions that other side did *not*. Anticipate questions regarding whether the trial or appellate courts have jurisdiction and whether your arguments were preserved in the court below. Appellate judges are obligated to address those issues even if the parties do not. Consider issues of policy that may concern the court. Prepare to discuss the consequences of the rules of decision that you are advocating. Anticipate hypothetical questions designed to test the limits and consequences of those rules. Expect the judges to push you for legal or factual concessions, know what you may have to concede and how far you can go without conceding away your case, and stiffen your backbone to resist if you are pushed beyond those points.

Rule 1(e): KNOW the record. This can be extremely important at oral argument. "The attorney who cannot turn, in a moment, to an essential part of the record, or who cannot answer questions about the state of the record, will not command the confidence of the Justices."[3]

Here is how I prepare to be able to "turn, in a moment, to [any] essential part of the record": For each such "essential part," I prepare a very brief description, handwritten on a small yellow post-it note, and attach it to the pertinent page of the Appendix. When I am done, I typically have a series of such notes running across the top of the pages, down the right side, and often across the bottom. I append them in such a way that if I grasp the pertinent note and use it to open the volume, I will be looking at the relevant page. The post-it notes are firmly

---

3. Stephen M. Shapiro, *Oral Argument in the Supreme Court of the United States*, 33 Cath. U. L. Rev. 529, 532 (1984).

attached to the Appendix pages with scotch tape, on the back side (opposite the gummy side of the note). That is not purely obsessive-compulsive; I do not want one of my notes to detach when I take hold of it at a critical moment in the discussion.

Many skilled advocates rely on record indices prepared as separate documents or spreadsheets. My method works for me, because it requires a minimum of fumbling with multiple documents and flipping through pages for the right location. But just as with oral argument notes (*see* Rule 2, below), you need to develop and employ the method that works best *for you*.

Rule 1(f): PRACTICE! Practice out loud to hear your own prepared remarks, which often sound very different from what you "hear" when you read silently to yourself, and revise your presentation as needed. Practice in front of a mirror can be beneficial, but a video camera is better. When you watch the [recording], you will see the annoying mannerisms that would be so apparent to the judges.

Many skilled and experienced appellate advocates regard "moot court" practices as essential. I am one of them. All your "judges" need to do (at minimum) is to read the briefs, one time, and then listen and ask questions. They often will think of hard questions that did not occur to you. But don't wait until the last minute to conduct this practice. Allow yourself at least a few days to incorporate the lessons learned *and* to recover from the deflation that you may experience at the hands of your inquisitors.

Test oral arguments on your spouse, your teenagers, or taxi drivers (people who may give you honest advice, because they have no incentive to flatter you). Among other things, this will force you to boil your overly convoluted argument down to its essence. If those audiences understand your points, then the court likely will also.

Rule 2: Oral argument notes:

Develop a style that is effective and comfortable for *you*, and follow it in your preparation and argument. My own style is essentially to script the entire argument that I would deliver if I get no questions (which occurs rarely, but occasionally) and dictate it to a Word file with a large, easily readable font and spacing designed to mimic the rhythms of my speaking, more or less like this example:

This case is like *Calvin* and *Hobbes*.

In both of those cases, the Court applied the provision in 88 U.S.C. § 844 which says that "if a party has *no opportunity*

to object to a ruling or order at the time it is made,

the absence of an objection

shall not preclude assignment of error

to that ruling or order on appeal."

That's the case here. The circumstances are different,

but these plaintiffs, like the defendants in *Calvin* and *Hobbes*,

had no opportunity to object to the Judge's rulings

on the theories that he developed by himself.

I print my prepared argument, two-sided, and put it in a three-ring binder; and I rehearse it to the point where I can make eye contact with any audience, speak conversationally, and turn each page at the proper time without ever looking down at my notes. I make frequent revisions during the course of rehearsal, often even while I am in the courtroom waiting for my case to be called. I do not expect to present that argument without interruption; but the effort that goes into the document leaves me well prepared to transition from answering questions back into my key points. The printed document is available as a crutch, in case it is needed, but that is rare. Above all, I prepare sufficiently that I will never need to read from my notes (aside from very occasional, brief quotations from statutes or other authorities—when I *want* to be observed as reading).

Other skilled advocates have different styles. Some handwrite their argument notes on the inside facing pages of a single manila folder. Some use a small handful of 3x5 file cards with nothing written on them but brief reminders of their principal points. (Chief Justice John Roberts reportedly practiced randomly shuffling the cards while practicing, to be prepared to move smoothly from answering questions back into any point in his prepared argument.) Some begin with a detailed script, similar to mine, but throw it in the trash before they go to court. At least a few lawyers prepare extensively but argue extemporaneously. There is no right or wrong in this area; it is art, not science, and no one size fits all. Each of us must develop a set of practices that works for him or her.

Rule 3: Different rules apply to counsel for appellees. An appellee's preparation is divided, though not equally, between advance preparation in the office and ad hoc preparation in the course of the appellant's argument. If you represent an appellee, you must be flexible. You must prepare in advance with an agenda for the argument and adjust it as necessary during the appellant's argument. I emphasize *adjust*; in most cases, at least, it would be foolhardy to throw your own agenda out the window or to allow the appellant to dictate the course of your argument. The best approach usually is to incorporate responses to the appellant's arguments at the most appropriate points in the remarks that you intended to deliver anyway.

That obviously falls almost entirely in the realm of art rather than science. In some cases, the most appropriate moment for rebutting an appellant's best *or* weakest argument may be immediately after "May it please the Court, I am Stan Laurel, counsel for appellee Oliver Hardy." In others, those rebuttals may best be interjected at various points. The only true imperative is not to fail to respond to any arguments that scored with the panel; and the judges will usually, but *not* always, guide you there with their questions.

17.10 Michael B. Wallace, Wise Carter Child Caraway, P.A.

Michael B. Wallace is a shareholder in the Jackson, Mississippi, firm of Wise Carter Child Caraway, P.A. He has extensive appellate practice in federal and state courts. He clerked for the Honorable Harry Walker of the Supreme Court of Mississippi and then-Justice William Rehnquist of the Supreme Court of the United States. He provides the following advice.

Bear Bryant famously said, "It's not the will to win that matters . . . . It's the will to prepare to win." Preparation to win an oral argument begins long before the advocate gets the notice of hearing. Making the right decisions at the outset makes it possible to make a winning argument at the end.

Preparation, of course, necessarily varies with the nature of the case and the resources of the client. Even the wealthiest clients have no interest in spending massive sums to litigate a small claim. Many clients, no matter the importance of the claim to them, simply cannot afford all of the efforts that might be brought to bear in a contest between two well-financed adversaries. Nevertheless, there are some things that any lawyer can and should do in every case. Both the client and the court deserve your best efforts, and these are things that can be done on the smallest of budgets.

Know what you want. The great legal philosopher Yogi Berra once said, "If you don't know where you are going, you might wind up someplace else." Notwithstanding the requirement of Rule 28(a) that the appellant's brief conclude by "stating the precise relief sought," I am always amazed by oral advocates who cannot answer the question,

"What is it you want us to do?" Indeed, you should generally begin your argument with a short statement of exactly what you want and why, because the pace of questions may keep you from getting to it later. It is not enough to express unhappiness with the result below; the advocate and client need to sit down at the beginning to decide exactly what they want the appellate court to do about it.

Every appellant wants the appellate court to render judgment in its favor, but it is not always possible to find a legal theory to achieve that result. Sometimes a new trial is the best you can do, and you have to think about whether a new trial can cover all issues or just, for instance, damages. In some cases, a new trial is a complete waste of time and money if you have to face the same judge in the same venue. If you think you cannot win without changing one or the other, then you need to be prepared to address recusal and venue issues at the outset.

In most cases, the appellee simply wants the appellate court to think that the trial judge is a genius. That is why a cross-appeal is very often a bad idea. Even if the appellee is unhappy with some aspects of the decision, where everyone is complaining about the result, the appellate court might be inclined to suspect that there is some error somewhere. Sometimes the error is pretty obvious, and the appellee must antici-pate a reversal. In that case, the advocate must consider how to limit the damage. It may be possible to preserve liability while limiting a new trial to damages. An appellate court may well be inclined to try to salvage as much as possible from an expensive trial, so an appellee's counsel should be prepared to help the court reach a result the client can live with.

Everything else follows from the determination of the objective. Only when you know where you are going can you decide how best to get there.

Know your court. The process of knowing your court should begin long before you learn the identity of your panel, often just a few days before oral argument. Certainly, at that point you want to review all of the relevant cases to see if any of your panelists participated in the decisions. You also want to review each judge's history for clues about likely positions on the issues in your case. A former trial judge is very likely to sympathize with the lower court's exercise of discretion. A federal judge who comes from the state system is very likely to have a realistic appraisal of the state courts and state law.

That process, however, comes much too late in the game to be of much help in determining how to achieve your objectives. An appel-late advocate must have some idea of the tendencies and the priori-ties of the court that will consider his appeal even before he begins the briefing process. Even a distinction as crude as varying levels of sympathy for plaintiffs or defendants can be of some use. A plaintiff appearing before a pro-defense court should devise an argument that will permit his client to win without opening the proverbial floodgates that conservative courts are supposed to fear.

For most lawyers, who do most of their practice in a single locality, this simply involves paying attention over time. I clerked at the Supreme Court of Mississippi forty years ago, and my practice has been centered there ever since. Their sympathies have varied between defendants and plaintiffs over the years, but there are some characteristics that remain constant. They want to keep the law relatively simple, because lawyers and trial judges like it that way; if your argument depends on an eight-factor balancing test, you are probably going to lose. Likewise, if your victory depends on the trial judge being branded a fool, you are going to lose. The Supreme Court knows very well which trial judges are fools, but your job as an advocate is to give them a reason to reverse without having to say so.

Even when an advocate appears before an unfamiliar court, there are certain characteristics that most courts have in common. A Fifth Circuit judge once told me that the Court's first judgment over a century ago was a dismissal for lack of jurisdiction, and that it has been their favorite disposition ever since. I presented my first argument before the Second Circuit to a panel composed of President Bush's cousin, a Nixon appointee from San Diego, and Judge Sotomayor just before her elevation to the Supreme Court; despite their diverse backgrounds, all three of them wanted to talk about jurisdiction.

Most courts want to resolve cases with as much clarity and simplicity as possible. Complicated and contingent rules of law invite trial court error and endless appeals. The job of the advocate, then, is usually to help the court find the simplest method to help his client.

Just as knowing the court begins before writing the brief, it continues to the end of oral argument. Each question is a gift, offering insight into the mind of that judge. The advocate's task only begins with giving a direct and clear answer. The art of oral argument is to discern where each judge is inclined to go and to steer the judge in a direction that best helps your client. Remember that a judge's question may really be directed to a colleague, as much as to the advocate. Recognizing and understanding that dynamic gives the advocate an opportunity to help those judges find common ground. Oral argument is a discussion, not an inquisition; once the advocate grasps the court's inclinations, he must explain why those inclinations can best be served by giving his client the result he wants.

Know yourself. Every lawyer has blind spots. Every lawyer has concerns that may not be shared by the courts. Every lawyer needs guidance to avoid chasing rabbits into the wilderness.

In many cases, the last opportunity for a sanity check is the moot court. When a client can afford to gather a group of lawyers to interrogate the advocate, it can be incalculably beneficial. The group can help to weed out weak arguments and to fill holes in the strong ones. That collaborative process can be the best preparation for a successful oral argument.

Many clients, however, cannot afford such an effort, and some cases simply cannot justify the expense. Still, every advocate needs to test his theories before oral argument. The echo chamber of an individual mind is not good enough to prepare for the give and take of argument.

Every advocate, whether he practices in a firm or is one of the few remaining sole practitioners, needs somebody to keep him honest. Find somebody you respect to listen to your ideas. Start that process at the outset, as soon as you and the client have determined your objectives. Find a good lawyer who will listen to your ideas and knows you well enough to tell you when you are out your mind. Good advice from a good lawyer will go a long way in helping to select your issues and sharpen your presentation.

It is still possible, at least in most communities, to find lawyers who are willing to offer their thoughts at no expense to your client, and the best way to find somebody is to be willing to do it for others. The practice of law should to be a collaborative exercise. Lawyers are supposed to work together with the courts and with each other to improve the administration of justice. Any appellate advocate should be willing to help any young lawyer learning his trade and, indeed, any lawyer who asks for it. A good friend, then, can be just as beneficial as a good moot court.

Know the record. You don't have to read the whole record. The court won't read the whole record either, but the court will read enough of the record to understand the issues presented by the appeal. The advocate should know that part of the record well enough to answer any imaginable questions the judges might pose.

Of course, the advocate must read much more of the record at the outset to know what issues to raise. That process should be completed before the advocate and the client sit down to determine the course of action. More often than not, the client will want to dwell at great length on the factual errors made by the court. You don't have to read every word of the testimony to explain to the client that appellate courts don't reverse on the facts. Your job is to find the legal errors that caused the factual errors.

Know the law. No, the law is not the least important part of an appeal, but it is rarely as important as the advocate thinks. Certainly, there are cases where legal error is all you need. Years ago, a Mississippi federal judge, when reminded by a lawyer that the Fifth Circuit had already reversed him four times on the same issue, replied, "I know. One more and I bingo." With that judge and that case, the law is all you need.

Most of the time, however, legal error is not enough to secure a reversal. The harmless error rule codified for district courts by Rule 61 is equally applicable on appeal. The advocate must be able to combine his knowledge of the law with his knowledge of the record to convince the court that the error made a difference.

Legal rules, at least most of the time, are not arbitrary dictates but tools to achieve substantial justice. Appellate courts, at least most of the time, do not sit for the enjoyment of throwing penalty flags on the misuse of legal rules, but seek to achieve substantial justice. It is true that an appellate court's primary responsibility is to devise and apply legal rules that can be fairly administered in a whole host of cases, not just the one before it. Nevertheless, it is foolish to think that judges do not care how the individual case comes out. Your task as an advocate is to show how the legal rule you have identified produces substantial justice for your client and improves the administration of justice across the board. That task requires not only knowledge, but imagination. You have a story to tell, and rarely more than twenty minutes to tell it, so make it good.

17.11 Julie A. Warren, West Virginia Attorney General's Office

Julie Warren works in the West Virginia Attorney General's Office, where she argues appeals before the West Virginia Supreme Court and serves as legislative counsel to the Attorney General. She has also worked in private practice and for the United States Department of Justice. She offers this advice.

1) The majority of appeals are won on the strength of the briefs. Thus, oral advocates may find that their case is best served by adopting a protectionist role that focuses on defending the strength of their arguments, rather than viewing oral argument as a tool to advance their position.

   a) One approach to ensuring that the strength of an advocate's case is not weakened at oral argument is to view the oral advocacy process as an opportunity to answer the Court's questions. An advocate's focus should be on her ability to answer the court's questions, rather than pitching her argument to the court and ensuring that she has hit all of her points.

      i) In order to address the court's questions, an appellate advocate must know the case, this includes the record and each legal authority cited in support of the arguments proffered by both sides, including amicus.

      ii) Write down every conceivable question that may be asked by the court during oral argument and be prepared to address each question.

      iii) At oral argument, an advocate should carefully listen to the court's questions, and take caution not to focus her attention on her anticipated response while the court is presenting its inquiry. Also, if needed, an advocate should take a moment to consider the question before responding to the court's question. A momentary deliberation that results in a thoughtful response is preferred to an immediate and rushed reaction to the court's inquiry.

      iv) The best response to a question for which an advocate may not know the answer is an honest one. Failed attempts to fake or fumble through a response may damage both the credibility of the advocate's case and the advocate's credibility before the court. For instance, if the court refers an advocate to a case that she is unfamiliar with, then the best response is to admit ignorance and offer supplemental briefing if the court signals that it finds the case to be relevant to the arguments presented.

      v) An oral advocate should avoid being combative when addressing the court's questions or comments, and take care to ensure that all responses are measured and deferential.

   b) An oral advocate should have a short introduction prepared that highlights the points that support her arguments. The theme of the brief should be the theme of the oral argument. However, she should be prepared to abandon the introduction once the court directs questions. Also, advocates must be prepared to adjust the presentation of their argument if it becomes clear that the court's attention is more narrowly focused.

c) It is important for an oral advocate to moot her argument at least once prior to oral argument.

2) Impressions matter. A successful oral advocate will focus on making a strong first impression when presenting oral argument, and strive to maintain honor and credibility in every aspect of her appellate practice.

17.12 Former United States Solicitor General Seth P. Waxman, WilmerHale

Seth P. Waxman—Solicitor General of the United States from 1997 to 2001—has argued seventy-five cases in the United States Supreme Court and is now a partner at WilmerHale in Washington, D.C. He is considered to be among the country's premier oral advocates. He offers this advice in his essay, *In the Shadow of Daniel Webster: Arguing Appeals in the Twenty-First Century*:[4]

> I mention Daniel Webster not because of his mastery of American politics, but rather because he is widely regarded as the greatest advocate ever to argue in an American court. *McCulloch v. Maryland, Gibbons v. Ogden, Luther v. Borden*, the *Charles River Bridge Case*. Webster argued them all. Webster's qualities and accomplishments as an advocate have been extolled so often that the highest praise to which any modem lawyer can aspire is to be deemed "almost as good as Daniel Webster." In the realm of advocacy, Webster doesn't merely sit in the Pantheon: He is Zeus himself.
>
> *Passion.* This first principle is the most fundamental. If you want to be a great oral advocate, you must care passionately about your work. Justice Story recalled Webster's "earnestness of manner, and a depth of research, and a potency of phrase, which at once convinced you that his whole soul was in the cause . . . ." You need only read Webster's published letters to understand that he saw complete dedication as the key to his work—dedication to his client, to his craft, and to the principles to which he believed his profession should aspire. As Chief Justice Fuller once observed, "It is impossible to overestimate the support the

---

4. Seth P. Waxman, *In the Shadow of Daniel Webster: Arguing Appeals in the Twenty-First Century*, 3 J. App. Prac. & Process 521 (2001).

Court derives from the bar, and in Mr. Webster's arguments fidelity to the Court is as conspicuous as fidelity to his client. It is not the client first and the conscience afterwards, but duty to both together, one and inseparable."

That passionate devotion to duty has continued to resonate with judges and lawyers from generation to generation. The attitude and preparation of some show that they have no conception of their effort higher than to make a living. Others are dutiful but uninspired in trying to shape their little cases to a winning pattern. But it lifts up the heart of a judge when an advocate stands at the bar who knows that he is building a cathedral.

Preparation. The second principle that Webster's work exemplifies builds on the first. Webster acknowledged, as we all know we should, the absolute importance of comprehensive preparation. Things may not—indeed, they will not—always turn out precisely as we hope, but for lawyers like Webster, it will not be for lack of effort. For lawyers building a cathedral, every argument demands what others might deride as over-preparation. "Accuracy and diligence," Webster said, "are much more necessary to a lawyer than great comprehension of mind, or brilliancy of talent." To be a great lawyer, he recognized, one "must first consent to be only a great drudge." The night before his grand performance in *Gibbons v. Ogden,* Webster worked for eleven straight hours, pausing only to shave, eat, and read the morning paper before appearing at the Court. As Webster understood, the goal of preparation is simply this: *When you walk into the courtroom to make your oral argument, you should know every aspect of the case better than anyone else does.*

Certainly you should know it far better than any judge. You must know the entire factual record. You must comfortably understand all of the relevant law, whatever its source. And finally you must do something else that is far more difficult—you must understand the implications of every principle upon which your case depends.

Every advocate follows his own path, but I generally try to do this in two ways. First, I think about questions. I attempt to identify every question a judge could reasonably ask. I think as hard as I can about what the best possible answer is. And finally I consider what further questions might follow from that answer, and what the answers to those questions should be. This is, for me at least, hard, hard work. It is generally easy to think of a few difficult questions; it is impossible to think of them all. How far down the list of conceivable questions you get, though, is a pretty good indicator of how well prepared you are.

The other thing I often do is to try to explain the case to a non-lawyer. This may seem peculiar, since judges, after all, are lawyers. But I find that explaining the case to someone who is not a lawyer helps me to discern whether there is a basic flaw in my reasoning, and whether I am really able to distinguish what is fundamental about my case from what is not. Preparing to answer all sorts of doctrinally tricky questions is essential, but it may also obscure the forest for the trees. You must be able to see both very clearly when you stand up to argue.

Planting the Kernel. My third and final point relates to the argument itself. Because oral argument is now so very different from what it was in Webster's day, it is difficult to translate the principles for appellate advocacy that might have been used in his time into precepts that will apply today. In all but the rarest of modern appellate courtrooms, for example, we litigate in an environment of interruption, not oration. But even in this very different world, there is a fundamental principle from Webster's day that still prevails, and it is this: When you stand up to present your oral argument facts and law at your command and head crammed with answers to every conceivable question, something else must be at the forefront of your mind. Daniel Webster certainly had it clearly in focus when he stood up to argue.

It is the kernel of the case—the one or two, or at the very most, three points that you must impress upon the court before you sit down.

These points may or may not be those you emphasized in your briefs. Sometimes, in fact, the thorough preparation you make for oral argument leads you to see the fundamentals of your case in a different way. I once came to reconceptualize a case on the very night before oral argument, because, although I had conducted two moot courts in the case, each using a different theme, neither had worked to my satisfaction. My last-minute change worked beautifully in that case, but I would never counsel brinksmanship like this for its own sake, for it is fraught with risk. But my own experience in this unusual case does demonstrate, I think, that however difficult the kernel may be to discern, and however late it reveals itself, you must have it in mind when you appear before the court.

Once you have found the kernel, polish and refine it into its purest, simplest form. And consider carefully how best to present it to the court. Webster understood this precept well, demanding of himself "the greatest effort of power in the tersest and fewest words." In Webster's day the kernel was often planted only after hours spent carefully tilling the judicial mind. Nowadays, the best strategy before a fully prepared court may be to make your point, pellucidly, as soon as you begin. But however you plan to do it, you must be absolutely clear in your mind about what the essentials are, and you must also be confident that when you sit down, the judges will understand both what they are and why they are important.

Questions will come. In the Supreme Court they come in a torrent. You should welcome and embrace questions, not be annoyed by them. An oral argument punctuated by questions may not be as transiently satisfying as a perfectly de-claimed speech. Almost certainly, it will not be studied with admiration through the generations. But if those are your objectives, stick to giving speeches or lectures. The oral advocate's job is to convince judges, and questions provide the clearest window of insight into what will accomplish that. Treat each question as a sincere effort to understand your point—even if that might not be the judge's true reason for asking. And answer every question frankly, respectfully, and directly. If you are sufficiently well prepared, you will often see how a judge's question can lead you to a point you need to make in order to help the court understand the kernel of your case. Fish are more assertive today than they were in Webster's time; they will not simply jump into your pocket at the sight of your fishing rod. But once judges start to nibble with questions, with direct and thoughtful answers you can still hope to reel them in.

Before I drown you in metaphor. I will close with one further thought: In modern oral argument, the very best strategy, whether answering questions or making your essential affirmative point, may be to heed the advice with which the great Admiral Nelson admonished his captains: "Never mind maneuvers," he used to say, "always go at 'em." In his own way, in his own time, that is just what Daniel Webster did.

CHAPTER EIGHTEEN

DELIVERING THE ARGUMENT

18.1 Appearance and Demeanor

The day for oral argument has finally arrived. Soon, you will be standing before a panel of appellate court judges and persuading them to rule for your client. As you prepare for court that morning, consider your attire. You should dress conservatively. Men should wear a dark business suit, a white or light-colored dress shirt, and a conservative tie. For women, a traditionally tailored, dark-colored suit or dress with jacket is appropriate. Judges are more tolerant today—much more tolerant than they were just a few decades ago—but it would not hurt to remember the words of King Lear: "Through tattered clothes small vices do appear."[1] No court will stop a lawyer from arguing if he or she shows up in technicolor splendor; yet keep in mind that the judges appear in black robes in the appellate courtroom—the most formal of settings. How you dress may be of little moment to most judges, but if your appearance offends one judge who is a stickler for proper deportment, then you are starting off on the wrong foot in your responsibility to persuade. You want the judges to leave the courtroom discussing the persuasive power of your argument, not the outlandish pattern on your tie or blouse.

One Fifth Circuit story, much retold, is of the advocate who appeared in the courtroom for argument in New Orleans in casual clothes. He explained he had checked his bag with his suit, and the airline lost the bag. The judges were sympathetic until he said, "This is the second time that has happened." If true, he effectively conceded he had learned nothing from the first experience. Court lore does not include a record of what the judges said to that admission.

Arrive at the courthouse with plenty of time to spare. This allows you time to calm any remaining jitters and get settled in before your case is called. When your case is called, you approach the lectern and, if you have not already been identified by the clerk or marshal, identify yourself: "I am attorney So and So representing the appellant Such and Such." This is not only necessary for the moment of the argument, but

---

1. WILLIAM SHAKESPEARE, KING LEAR act 4, sc. 6.

if the case is being recorded, in reviewing the tape or a transcript of it, the judges will know exactly who is speaking.

Keep your voice well modulated. Your appearance before san appellate court is not an appearance before a jury. If the lectern is fairly close to the bench, it is well to keep your voice on the same level and in the same tone that you would use in a conversation at a dinner table with one sitting across from you. The acoustics in many courtrooms will not permit this, and you may have to project your voice. In many courtrooms, the bench is somewhat elevated and is set at some distance from the lectern. In this situation, you should pitch your voice accordingly. Some microphones are placed on the podium for amplification purposes. Others are there for recording purposes only. Find out in advance what the situation is.

You should attempt to make your presentation as if you and the judges are sitting around a conference table. When the present courtrooms in the Third Circuit were designed, the judges deliberately arranged the design so that the attorney and the judges were almost on eye level. This was to encourage the private conversational give-and-take between counsel and the court. Even in courtrooms without that intimacy, strive for a conversation, not a speech.

Should the client be present at oral argument? We do not think so. Clients have a tendency to make the sort of suggestions that are least admired by judges. Consider the experiences described by Justice Robert H. Jackson:

> When I hear counsel launch into personal attacks on the opposition or praise of a client, I instinctively look about to see if I can identify the client in the room—and often succeed. Some counsel have become conspicuous for the gallery that listens to their argument and, when it is finished, ostentatiously departs. The case that is argued to please a client, impress a following in the audience, or attract notice from the press, will not often make a favorable impression on the bench. An argument is not a spectacle.[2]

While it is important to retain a conversational approach to oral argument, it is extremely important that you speak loud enough for the judges to hear you. Many lawyers are understandably quite nervous and have difficulty projecting. This is unfortunate. All is lost in oral argument unless the judges understand you—and we cannot understand you unless we hear you. Justice Jackson also adds:

> If your voice is low, it burdens the hearing, and parts of what you say may be missed. On the other hand, no judge likes to be shouted at as if he were an ox. I know of nothing you can do except to bear the

---

2. Robert H. Jackson, *Advocacy Before the United States Supreme Court*, 37 CORNELL L.Q. 1, 10 (1951).

difficulty in mind, watch the bench, and adapt your delivery to avoid causing apparent strain.[3]

18.2   Nervous? Yes, We Know

Judges know that appearing before a panel of the court is a formidable experience. There is an accompanying nervousness, and this is to be expected. The stress level is always high as the lawyer stands, ready to sell the case. Alan L. Dworsky put it very well:

> Experienced lawyers feel that way too. In fact, polls show that most people are more afraid of public speaking than dying. To me this only proves that most people who are polled don't think much about the questions. My point is: you're human. Don't interpret your nervousness as personal flaw. Be gentle with yourself. Nervousness is a normal human experience in an exciting and scary challenge. It shows that you care about your performance and your case. When you stop being nervous, start worrying. You've either stopped caring or stopped breathing.[4]

There is, however, one antidote to this that will work every time. If you walk into that courtroom better prepared on the subject than anyone else in the room, you have nothing to be nervous about. It is your case. You have lived with it. You have written the brief after researching and becoming familiar with every case touching the subject matter. You now know more about the subject matter than any judge on the bench. Judges are generalists, not specialists in any idiosyncratic part of the law. It is you who is the specialist. You are there to help the judges by sharing your knowledge.

Notice that we used the phrase "know more about the *subject matter*." We did not say "know more about *your case*," but you certainly need that too. You must have a broad comprehension of the entire branch of the law of which your case is but a part. You will have a ready answer for any hypothetical thrown at you, and *you*, not the judges, are now the master in this little domain.

Assume that you are still nervous. Not to worry. Ultimately, judges are interested in what you say; not how you say it. We are not out there judging a debate or a law school moot court competition. We have asked for oral argument because we need a little more substantive help from the lawyers, not an Oscar-worthy performance.

Do not mumble. Always speak clearly so that you may be understood. Oklahoma Supreme Court Justice Yvonne Kauger adds:

> Don't whine. . . . Nervous tension seems to raise voices by octaves. Take a deep breath and lower your register. It should go without saying—but don't chew gum! As incredible as this sounds, it has happened.

---

3. *Id.*
4. ALAN L. DWORSKY, THE LITTLE BOOK ON ORAL ARGUMENT 3–4 (2000).

18.3 The Actual Delivery

We all have our own personality, our own way of speaking, our own way of convincing. We say things in a certain manner, communicate in individual styles of tone, inflection, and gesture. We are comfortable as we do this, and we are usually effective.

In oral argument be as natural and comfortable as possible. Be yourself. Do not try to cast yourself in the image of another, because you run the risk of appearing artificial and insincere; you fail to project the appearance of confidence and credibility. When this happens, you lack persuasion. If you have prepared enough, you can afford to be yourself.

To launch your argument you might wish to commit to memory a few opening sentences, but do not start out by reading. To read your argument is to antagonize the court. Never, never do it. Do not even think about it. Have an outline or notes, but your notes must be a safety net, not a crutch. Look at your notes when you are making a short quote from the record or a case. Referring to your notes at this time adds the appearance of reliability to your quoting. If you have prepared sufficiently, or have rehearsed adequately, you should know exactly what to say.

Your oral argument should never exceed three points. You do not have the time to develop more. After identifying yourself, it is imperative to inform the court what issues you intend to discuss. You will then explain that you are relying on the brief for the others. At this point, you may be interrupted by one of the judges who wishes to hear argument on another issue. You should be sufficiently prepared to accommodate the court.

You always lead off with your best point—your strongest one. Your strongest point is *the argument that objectively considered, and based on precedent, and stated policy concerns of the court, is most likely to persuade the court to your point of view.*

It is what John W. Davis characterized as the "cardinal point around which lesser points revolve like planets around the sun."[5] This determination must be made dispassionately. No matter how great the cause you hope to advance, no matter how deep the passions run, your presentation must be at all stages cool, calculating, and logical.

After setting out your first point, you then move to your second strongest argument, and if there is more, then to the final one. The presentation should be in the form of an inverted pyramid, with the best material presented first and the lesser following after in order of diminishing importance. This is how reporters are taught to write a newspaper article—to permit the editor to cut it off at the end and still leave a complete and important story.

Ideally, your second or third points should be self-sufficient and independent of the court's acceptance of the first argument. If the first point is rejected by the court,

---

5. John W. Davis, *The Argument of an Appeal*, 26 A.B.A. J. 895, 897 (1940).

be prepared to shift ground immediately. Do not try to slug it out with the judges on the first point—all that accomplishes is wasting valuable time that could be spent on a more persuasive point.

18.3.1 Do Not Hide Facts and Cases that Hurt

You are the appellant. There are facts in the record and a case or two that may hurt you. Your opponent is sitting at the counsel table waiting to slam you with them as soon as you sit down. Or even worse, the judges are about to trump your opponent and launch an attack of their own. It is time to take the wind out of your adversary's sails. Mention these facts up front and tell us why they do not hurt you. Explain why the adverse case really is not a death knell. This will defuse any potential attack.

If you do this well, some of the fire and brimstone is taken out of the appellee's main argument. What is more, you have earned the respect of the court because this has heightened your credibility. This does not mean that you should pitch your entire argument as a rebuttal to the appellee's case. Rather, you, not your opponent, must control the direction of your argument.

If this is not done, you will surely get a question from one of the judges: "Help us out. In a few minutes, your friend is going to talk about these facts or this case, may we have your views on this now." Address these points before the court has an opportunity to ask. Where the case is fact driven, as in a sufficiency of the evidence case, too often the appellant gives us a reprise of a jury speech, arguing evidence that has been rejected by the jury. Avoid this temptation and provide the court, up front, a worse-case scenario of facts against you. This will engender respect every time.

There is another important reason to be upfront with the court about bad cases and facts, and to be scrupulously accurate in your case descriptions and record cites: your panel may be checking cases from the bench. Increasingly, federal and state appellate judges are taking computers and tablets to the bench during oral argument, which brings cite checking to a whole new level. These devices provide access to electronically filed documents and the whole array of electronic legal research. As one judge told us, "Sometimes I check on citations to cases or the record right on the spot, occasionally to the lawyer's regret." If you have prepared well, you should not be troubled by these instantaneous checks, but if you have not, your lack of preparation will be crystal clear to the judges.

18.3.2 How to Say It

Spicing your argument with a quote from one of the literary masters can be effective if used properly. A familiar quotation can eloquently sum up your position or vividly illustrate the equities that favor your client. Do not repeat it if it appears already in your brief. Do use it if the quote fits perfectly, is memorable, and you are confident that it is well known to the judges. Make certain that it does not provide fodder to your adversary and thus boomerang on you.

Keep your main points simple and hard hitting. Limit discussion of citations and precedents. It is better to leave detailed discussion of cases to the briefs. Concentrate instead on the logic and force of your position. Keep always in mind the focus of your argument and do not get sidetracked, even by a single judge. But be alert to clues that the judges want to move to a different part of your argument or briefs. Stay with the theme that represents your best hope of winning. Do not waste your severely rationed time on unnecessary elaboration.

Tell the court what you want and why. Explain how the rule you want the court to adopt will work, and show how it is consistent with what these judges have said before. Explain that there is impressive, respectable authority for it and that it fairly accommodates relevant values and interests. Your argument should confirm the acceptability of the proposition you are urging before the court. It proves the case. At the same time, you must refute the proposition urged by your adversary.[6] Quickly, forcefully, and effectively show why that position should not be accepted, why it is not supported by good reason or authority, and why it will not work.

Know your record cold. Be prepared to answer questions about *all* its relevant parts. Remember, different judges may focus on different aspects of the prior proceeding. One judge may question you about an event or finding, because that judge has already studied the record and is seeking only to question the factual predicate of your position. This is simply a quiz. Another judge may ask about a portion of the record to substantiate that judge's support of your proposition. As we will develop later in this chapter, not all questions asked by judges are zingers. Many are "softballs" designed to help you. Many are designed as part of an open internal advocacy of positions on the bench.

The corollary of knowing the record is sticking to it. Unless asked by a judge, never go outside the record in oral argument.

As soon as you perceive that the judges understand your point, move to the other issues. When you perceive that they understand these arguments, *sit down*. We cannot emphasize too much the necessity to quit while you are ahead. To be clear, though, usually an advocate will not reach that point before time has run out on the argument. Be alert to those occasional situations and respond as suggested.

A certain atmosphere or mood characterizes an argument in every case. Experienced lawyer-observers can sense this as they watch other lawyers' performances. Even law clerks, fresh out of law school but thoroughly acquainted with the case, can sense this. There comes a time when the advocate at the lectern reaches the maximum

---

6. For an analysis of argument by the Greco-Roman rhetoricians, see RUGGERO J. ALDISERT, OPINION WRITING 72 (1990).

possible advantage of the oral presentation. That is the moment to quit talking and sit down. Do not think that talking for a few more minutes cannot hurt. It *will* hurt. It can dispel the positive, confident atmosphere created by your presentation.

There is a level of theater in appellate courtroom rhetoric, with recognized highs and lows. To abandon a high point that has been successfully reached and then proceed to fill the air with meaningless padding and verbal filler is to transform your sizzle into drizzle. But even more dangerous, the anticlimactic speech used to fill the air between the close of your real argument and the expiration of your allotted time may call attention to a weaker point in your position. One of the judges may pick up on this, start probing and wind up destroying the court's prior willingness to accept your argument. Judges carry impressions—weak or strong, good or bad—from the close of oral argument to the decision conference that immediately follows the day's calendar.

18.3.3 The Delivery: A Summary

The Opening. Walk to the lectern. Be aware of the practice of that court on whether you should wait to be recognized by the presiding judge or instead introduce yourself. Then open by saying:

> If it please the court. My name is John J. Jones, and I represent the appellant, Santa Barbara Olive Company. We request this court to reverse the judgment of the trial court for the reasons set forth in our brief. Today, I will address two points in support of our position. We will rely on our brief for the other arguments. I respectfully request two minutes for rebuttal time. [*Pause for reaction from the presiding judge.*]

Some judges see it as simply courteous and appropriate for you to introduce any co-counsel at the table who will not be arguing. Likely none will be bothered by such an introduction.

Your outline. Have an outline of your argument, together with supporting papers, at the lectern. Remember: your outline is a safety net, not a crutch.

Maintain eye contact. You look directly at the judges at all times. It is eyeball-to-eyeball time.

Be courteous and respectful. But do not be timorous or overawed. Maintain a position of respectful equality. Think of your oral argument as a conversation with a respected elder, such as a family member, professor, or civic leader. Do not be disturbed or pushed around simply because a judge disagrees with your position. Stand your ground firmly but with courtesy and dignity.

Be prepared to modify your planned presentation. You may have to modify your argument for several reasons. The judges may agree immediately with one point. If you sense this, move quickly to another point. Similarly, you may find the judges seem quite unconvinced (and inconvincible). In that case, if you have an alternative, move to it. A series of questions may have taken much time from your planned presentation on one point; when you move to the next point, deliver it in truncated fashion—otherwise, time may run out. If you are the appellee and the questions put to the appellant demonstrate that the judges understand your position on one point, alter your planned argument.

Your closing. Do not let the presentation peter out simply because time has been called. Save time for a concise, punchy summary that clearly states your requested relief.

Sit Down. Exactly that. Unless you are in a moot court competition, do not feel the need to use all of your time if you are done with your argument. Doing so could snatch defeat from the jaws of victory.

18.4 Watch Your Time

Most courts will have some mechanism to assist you in keeping track of your time. In some courts, a series of lights are placed on the podium. The green light signals the start of your argument; the amber comes on when you have two minutes remaining, and the red light signifies that you should stop. When the red light comes on, stop speaking; do not antagonize the judges by prolonging the discussion when your time has expired. If you need more time to conclude a point, ask the presiding judge for more time. If there is not a time-keeping method in the courtroom, place a watch on the lectern to keep track of your time.

Watch your rebuttal time. If you are the appellant, arrange in advance how much time you are reserving for rebuttal. In some courts, you may ask the presiding judge at the beginning of the argument for rebuttal time. In other courts, you make arrangements with the clerk, in which case you advise the court what you have done.

Do not intrude on your rebuttal time by prolonging your argument in chief. Depending on the court, the time may be subtracted from you. Do not expect to use rebuttal simply as a chance to include arguments that should have been made in the case in chief. There are presiding judges who are very strict about what can be said in rebuttal. It is not spillover time from your case in chief. The appellee always has the right to respond, so you may not save for rebuttal material what should have been stated earlier. It is standard practice in the Fifth Circuit, for example, for the presiding judge to include among a very few opening comments before each case is argued that "rebuttal is for rebuttal only." So courts do take that point seriously, for fairness to the appellee.

18.5 Be Flexible

In the modern appellate argument, you must be able to think on your feet. Watch how the wind is blowing from the bench. When the judges ask persistent questions that seem to indicate that they do not agree with your position and their questions are really not designed to elicit further information, it is time to shift gears. You may wish to provide a transition by saying, "If the court please, we have stated our position, and I believe that Your Honors understand our argument. Permit me now to address the second point."

Be careful about making concessions. If in the preparation of your argument you believe that it may be appropriate to make concessions, then do it. Do not make careless concessions at oral argument on the spur of the moment. They may come back to haunt you. Therefore, as noted in the judges' comments from Chapter Sixteen, an important part of your preparation should be deciding what you can concede.

When two of the judges engage in private conversation during your presentation, do not stop. Address your argument to the other judge or judges. In any event, never stop talking. The judge or judges who are paying attention to you will resent that you have interrupted your delivery to them.

It is a normal reaction to try more vigorously to persuade in the face of a bench that is not buying your argument. If the point in controversy is the major premise on which your second and third arguments depend, you must hang tough. If, however, the point under attack is independent of other points in your argument, as soon as you get the storm signals from the bench, it is time to move on to another argument.

18.6   Visual Aids

Think very carefully before using visual aids at oral argument. When used properly, they can be very effective; when the props are technically insufficient, you run a serious risk. Because some judges come to the bench equipped with reading glasses only and do not have the eyesight to read at a distance, be certain that your visual aids are large enough to be examined or, as Fifth Circuit Judge James Dennis suggests, bring copies to give to the courtroom deputy to give to the judges to view at the bench

Judge Aldisert recounted one positive experience with visual aids in a Tenth Circuit argument. Involved was the interpretation of certain regulations of a federal agency. These regulations were set forth in the briefs and the judges were fairly familiar with them. Nevertheless, counsel had magnificent blown-up reproductions of the key sections of these regulations. Using a pointer, counsel very effectively led the judges through the important sections of the regulations suitably highlighted.

Yet there is a down side. Setting up visual aids invades your allotted time. Moreover, there are times when a page or two from the Appendix or Excerpts of the Record are more effective. Because you should not assume that every judge has a copy on the bench, have copies available for them to follow along with your argument. Do not proceed on the basis that the judges may look at the Appendix when they return to chambers. The tentative decision-making conference takes place at the end of the day's argument list, so make certain they have their copies while on the bench so they have them at conference. Your visual aids propped up in the courtroom do not follow the judges into the conference room.

Increasingly, it may be more effective to put any necessary visual charts or aids in the brief, which the judges almost certainly have with them on the bench. For example, in *Reed v. Town of Gilbert*,[7] a Supreme Court case involving a First Amendment challenge to a town's sign ordinance, the counsel representing the church challenging the sign ordinance included in his brief pictures of signs in the town accompanied by graphs and charts that allowed the justices to see clearly what size signs were permitted under the ordinance and the duration that the signs could be displayed.[8] The various graphics made the complicated ordinance easy to understand, and the counsel challenging the ordinance won unanimously before the Court.[9]

18.7   Arguing before a Cold Court

Where judges of an appellate court do not have the opportunity of examining briefs before oral argument, the court is known as a "cold" court. You must tailor your arguments accordingly.

Generally speaking, the court is cold because the sheer volume of appeals prevents pre-argument study of the briefs. Under these circumstances, you will be exposed to less questioning and given a shorter time to argue than in a hot court. For the most part, you should follow the same suggestions for preparation previously outlined in Chapters Sixteen and Seventeen. Your delivery must be tailored to a different audience.

Primarily, the appellant must open the argument with a one or two-minute orientation statement that should parallel the statement of the case discussed in Chapter Twelve:

- *What*: What is the general area of law implicated in the appeal? What are the issues, and what is the theme or gut issue? Expose the jugular, the focus of your attack.

- *Who*: Who won in the tribunal below? Who is talking the appeal?

- *When*: When was the alleged error committed? Is the appeal from an adverse verdict because of insufficiency of evidence? Is it alleged that error was committed in the pleadings, at pretrial, trial, or post-trial?

- *How*: How was the case resolved? Was the judgment entered as the result of summary judgment, a directed verdict, a jury verdict, or a nonjury award?

---

7. Reed v. Town of Gilbert, 135 S. Ct. 2218 (2015).

8. Brief for Petitioner, at 3, 11–12, Reed v. Town of Gilbert, 135 S. Ct. 2218 (2015) (No. 13-502). See Appendix C for the statement of the case from this brief.

9. *See Reed*, 135 S. Ct. at 2232.

- *Where*: Where does the appeal come from: a trial court, administrative agency, or intermediate appellate court?

Immediately thereafter, you state the material facts as succinctly and interestingly as possible. Do not waste time on any facts except those necessary to support the argument you will be making. Be prepared to answer questions at this time. Some of the judges immediately will want to pigeonhole your case into past decisions. Know the facts completely and do not let questioning lead you astray. Your factual recitation should follow the guidelines set out in Chapter Twelve.

You then identify the points you will argue in support of your main contention, making certain to advise the court that you are relying on your brief for other points. Having identified the issues you will argue, proceed immediately to explain the standard of review for each point.

Then proceed into your argument. Presume that you are before a hot court that has studied the precedents cited in the briefs. However, when you mention a case as precedent or you wish to distinguish a case upon which you know your adversary will rely, give a one-sentence description of its holding. State both the factual component and the legal consequence attached thereto. In a nutshell, you must paint a broader picture before a cold court.

18.8   How to Answer Questions

Oral argument is no longer the formal, uninterrupted presentation characteristic of appellate proceedings of yesteryear. Wisconsin Supreme Court Justice Shirley Abrahamson reports: "At one time oral argument in the Wisconsin Supreme Court was so quiet that you could hear the justices' arteries clogging."

In most appellate courts today, however, oral presentations consist primarily of a dialogue between the judges and the advocate. Answering questions from the judges is a vital part of modern advocacy. Answering them properly is critical to the modern art of persuasion.

To answer a question intelligently, you must first *listen* to the question. Judges recognize that some lawyers may be a little nervous, and understandably so. But judges also recognize that lawyers, just like people in private conversations, sometimes tend to "hear" only a part of the question asked. In appellate advocacy, it is important to listen to the entire question and to answer the entire question, not only a discrete part of it.

In listening to the question, be certain that you *understand* it before attempting an answer. This is especially true in federal appellate courts, where the judges deal with specialized subject matter and tend to speak in shorthand expressions. Less experienced lawyers may not be familiar with the jargon used. For example, the court may inquire, "Counsel, do the authorities you rely on come up in the context of a *Teague* matter?" What the court is really asking goes to the distinction between a direct appeal in a criminal case and an appeal on collateral review. If you do not understand the question, say so. You will not necessarily lose any points. Regardless of a possible penalty, never try to answer a question you do not understand.

Answer the question directly. Do not evade. If the question calls for a "yes" or "no" answer, respond with a "yes" or a "no." Then elaborate. You do not have time to beat around the bush, and you do not want to give the impression that you are stonewalling. Do not postpone the answer by saying, "I have not got to that point in my argument yet." The judge will respond, "Yes, you have."

This problem often arises where more than one lawyer is representing a single party. The practice of divided representation is appropriate to avoid conflicts of interest, but it is otherwise disfavored. To be sure, we understand that clients want their own lawyers to argue. We also understand the converse: Lawyers who have lived through the trial and have prepared a brief want a chance to get in at least five minutes of argument (and have their names in the Reporter showing that they argued the case). But, in cases of severely rationed time, judges want to get to the heart of what interests them and do not like to hear, "If the court please, my colleague is handling that part of the argument."

Your responses should be clear and concise. Judges know the time limitations you are under, and ordinarily the questions put are not designed for a lengthy response. One or two sentences usually will suffice.

Yet there are questions that demand a longer response and will take up substantial amounts of your limited time. In this situation, be cheerful, or at least pretend that you are. Do not create the impression that the mere putting of the question annoys you.

A number of years ago, a constitutional law professor appeared before Judge Aldisert, and he had brought along his entire class to witness his dazzling performance as the appellant's lawyer. Early in his presentation, Judge Aldisert interrupted and asked him to address the question of the court's jurisdiction in the appeal. The law professor sloughed Judge Aldisert off with a scowl, saying that there was no such issue in the case. A little while later, Judge Aldisert tried again, and the law professor responded with some annoyance, "I've already answered that question." When Judge Aldisert was rebuffed the third time, the presiding judge unloaded on him, "Counselor, answer the question and answer it right now. For your information, the question of jurisdiction has been in this case ever since the moment Judge Aldisert raised it ten minutes ago." The professor glared, and then stumbled, and stumbled some more. The opinion was assigned to Judge Aldisert, and the court dismissed the appeal for lack of jurisdiction.

When the questions put by the court are relevant—and most of the time they are, especially when more than one judge pursues a particular line of inquiry—it is a clear signal that this is the direction in which the judges are moving. Throw away your planned argument and proceed in the direction of the questions. This probably is the issue the judges will talk about in conference.

It may be that one of the judges goes off on a tangent that is from any reasonable perspective completely irrelevant. Unfortunately for the advocate, the questions are relevant to one of the judges you want to convince. Never indicate by word or expression your sense that the path you are being sent down is a rabbit trail. We will discuss later how to handle questions from the judge who, by persistent irrelevant questions, appears to have gone off on an intellectual frolic. If you are fully prepared on the subject matter of the case, you will know what questions are totally off base.

What do you do when you are asked a point-blank question about a case that you do not know, notwithstanding thorough preparation? Do not bluff. Be frank with the court. Judge Aldisert suggested stating, "If Your Honor will refresh my recollection of the holding, I would appreciate it." Another approach would avoid calling on the judge to educate you, but simply to admit your unfamiliarity. You might ask for permission to respond in writing within a few days after the argument. You might say, "Your Honor, I'm sorry that I must have overlooked that case. May I please have the opportunity of filing a supplemental brief discussing it within forty-eight hours?" It would be the most hard-hearted judge who would refuse such a request. Counsel should not overlook the opportunity of seeking to file a post-argument supplemental brief where a judge's question plowed novel ground. But to be effective, promise to have the supplement filed in a matter of days, not weeks.

Be careful about making on-the-fly concessions in response to unanticipated questions. When you go through the questions check list contained in section 16.7 in preparation for oral argument, you may decide that you are willing to concede some points. This decision can serve two important goals. First, you may wish to clear away the underbrush of questionable points that may possibly detract from the jugular point. It is better to prune than to be subjected to time-consuming interrogation on minor points. Second, it is one thing to plan a concession after calm and careful reflection in the environment of your office; it is quite another thing to concede hastily in open court while under pressure from the bench.

To concede or not to concede a point at oral argument depends upon the extent of your advance preparation. You should know what will hurt or help you. Without sufficient preparation, you may be faced with a dilemma. On this one hand you do not want to concede something that may come back to haunt you, but on the other hand you do not want the judges to conclude that you are stonewalling.

But there is a difference between factual and legal concessions. If the record facts are against you, concede their existence but hasten to argue that this concession does not destroy your case. Be very careful, however, of legal concessions. If on the way home from the courthouse, you realize that you have made an improvident concession on a point of some significance, all is not lost. It is appropriate to immediately file a supplemental brief by letter that refers to the question and your response and clarifies it. Be certain to serve your adversary with a copy. There is no guarantee that all judges would accept it, but it is worth the effort.

Often, the unfortunate situation develops where a very argumentative judge will try to force you to make a concession that you are not prepared to make. Handle this with great diplomacy, but with firmness. Be attentive, but do not be intimidated:

> Your Honor, I regret that I cannot improve on the answer I previously gave the court on that point. With great respect, Your Honor, we see that issue in a very different light. In my view, I believe . . . .

18.8.1 Types of Questions: User-Friendly and Otherwise

Many lawyers are instinctively suspicious of questions from the bench, and they answer so cautiously that they sound evasive. When this happens, judges are often inclined to say, "Look here, all the questions put to you are not designed to trap you. Please listen to the question before attempting an answer." Too many lawyers operate under the impression that bench questions are all cross-examination. Actually, there are several discrete categories.

The most important question is where a judge sweeps away all the clutter and zeroes in on the basic issue in the case. It is the question that sums up the case in a single sentence. If you have prepared thoroughly, you should expect this, notwithstanding the structure of your brief or your game plan at argument. When this question comes thundering down, you can run but you cannot hide. It will reappear in the opening sentence or paragraph of the opinion: "The major question for decision in this appeal is whether . . . ." Be ready for it. If you are not, then you are not ready to give the oral argument.

Many questions are designed to clarify something in the record. Some judges vote for oral argument in a case because they need help from counsel in getting to this information. Thus the question will proceed, "Counsel, on page so-and-so of the brief you refer to such-and-such evidence in the record. Will you please tell us where we can locate it?" Often, when this factual predicate is established, it will serve as the springboard to other questions. If you cannot answer these questions, you are unprepared for argument. You should know the record like the back of your hand—even if you were not counsel below.

Many questions relate to the standard of review. Often, counsel will argue the evidence presented at trial instead of the facts as found by the fact-finder. This provokes the questions: "What did the fact-finder find? If the jury found it, can we touch it in view of the Seventh Amendment? If found by the judge, is it clearly erroneous? If found by the agency, was there substantial evidence in the record as a whole to support it?"

Often, we get ambiguous standards of review in the briefs. Oral argument provides the opportunity to focus on the correct standard. In many cases, the standard of review determines the outcome of the appeal. Again, you should be able to answer these questions. These questions should have been mooted in the days leading up to the argument.

Then there are the "quiz" questions, which are utilized by individual judges for at least three objectives: Socratic or debating purposes, for internal judicial advocacy, and to communicate outright hostility to the lawyer's position. Judges use the Socratic method to test the validity of the logic employed and to determine by means of hypotheticals where a proposed rule will take the court. Lawyers must expect that the logic of the argument will be put to the test. They must be prepared to defend their reasoning, both in form and content.

Be prepared for the hypothetical. Do not antagonize the court by saying, "Well, those facts are not before the court here. That is a different case." The judges know that. Counsel must understand that there is a limit to every principle, as immutable in the law as the principle may be; that there comes a point when the extension of a legitimate principle brings it into conflict with another, equally legitimate, and the court must decide where along the line the axe must fall. Accordingly, counsel should not try to move the application of a principle too far or too fast. Know where you would draw that line as counsel and communicate that to the panel when answering hypotheticals.

In a multi-judge appellate court, judges do not usually discuss cases in advance. In the United States Courts of Appeals and state appellate courts, judges often do not live in the same city. They meet for the first time at oral argument, and often questions are put to counsel by a judge solely to test the jural waters. When this occurs, the lawyer is merely a conduit. He is simply the medium by which the questioning judge may disclose to the other judges some inclination on the case.

The most difficult question-and-answer colloquy for the lawyer occurs when a judge is blatantly hostile to counsel's stated position. Often, the hostile judge becomes the proverbial dog on a bone, who will not let go or let up. This is no time for the lawyer to become distraught. The hostility is often a sign that the judge is in the minority, and thus the unrelenting attack is motivated by the frustration that impotency brings. When the lawyer realizes that the judge is trying to achieve a capitulation, the lawyer should respond with courteous, but confident arguments explaining why capitulation would not be appropriate. When the judge says, "Counsel, that argument is simply ridiculous," the response could be, "Your Honor, I respectfully disagree, and I have offered legitimate reasons why it is not. My hope is only that Your Honor, on reflection, will change your mind."

18.8.2 How to Disengage from Persistent Questioning by a Single Judge

18.8.2.1 In General

There is a forensic dilemma in oral argument: when faced with a continuous barrage of questions from a single judge, how can you please the court by answering and yet diplomatically return to the argument you are there to make? This calls for the highest advocacy and impromptu skills.

One method is to announce that you have multiple responses to the question, one of which returns you to your planned format: "If the court please, I have two responses to make to that question." Then proceed to make a direct response to the question and immediately state, "For my second response to the court's question I would add . . ." and then slip in your "indirect, by way of analogy response," which tracks your planned presentation. This sometimes helps prevent interruption until you briefly give your two answers. At worst, it will give you a transition back to your planned presentation. Such a segue, though, must be a plausible route back to your desired argument and not an obvious pretext. A good advocate simply needs to respond to the situation as it presents itself.

Keep in mind that the entire purpose of argument is *to persuade*. You do not want to antagonize a judge by calling a question irrelevant. In fact, you should err on the side of assuming anything that a judge asks you is relevant. We are referring here to the extreme situation where it is crystal clear that a question is off-base. If pivoting in your answer does not work, you can try a neutral answer: "If the court please, in my view of the case we have not stressed that particular point, and this is why we have not . . . ."

A very serious situation arises where a single judge takes over the questioning on matters that you feel are irrelevant, and the questioning is so persistent and continuous that you may be totally precluded from making your argument. That may be the most difficult scenario facing the oral advocate. We have asked current and former federal and state judges for their advice.

18.8.2.2 Advice from Judges

How does the lawyer who is being bombarded by a series of questions from a judge that the lawyer believes to be completely off-base—respectfully answer, yet return to the issues that the lawyers and ostensibly the other two judges, deem relevant? The judges (and former judges) provide a few options below.

Michael Boudin *Senior Judge, First Circuit*	I used several different techniques when I was in practice but the one that seemed to me to work best was to give a succinct answer to the judge and say firmly something like: "That is about all I can say in response to your question, and in the few minutes I have left, I had better address the remaining two issues in this case." Most of the other alternatives, I found, were too mild to produce results or too strong to be stomached save by a very good-humored judge.
Dennis Jacobs *Judge, Second Circuit*	Prepare for argument by thinking about how many different ways you can win and, if a judge is rejecting one of your arguments, back away by explaining how you win anyway, without (however) conceding the point. And do not panic, because one judge on a panel may very well turn out to be just one judge.

John M. Walker, Jr.
Senior Judge, Second Circuit

Say, "I want to answer your question but then turn to the other critical points, (x) and (y), raised by this appeal." Then answer the question briefly and move rapidly to (x) and (y). Then hope that this maneuver works.

Thomas L. Ambro
Judge, Third Circuit

Dealing with judges who dominate questions—and, worse, do not wait for full responses before interrupting—is, no doubt, difficult. The first thing to do is remain calm and respectful. Suggestions include asking the court if you may have the time to develop what you believe are other issues that will aid in deciding the case. Also, in answering a question, do so directly but note that the direct answer comes appended with an explanation. In giving that explanation, weave into it your theme or themes.

Anthony J. Scirica
Senior Judge, Third Circuit

Be patient. In most cases, there will be a break that will enable you to return to your argument. If time has run, ask the court for a few minutes to present your most compelling argument. Usually, one judge on the panel will respond favorably.

Albert Diaz
Judge, Fourth Circuit

If the judge is asking a question, then it's relevant. The advocate should do his best to respond and trust that the other members of the panel will join the fray if necessary. In any event, the advocate should not be banking on a twenty-minute argument as his/her one best shot to persuade; if the brief has not accomplished that, there is little the oral argument will do to move the ball.

Gregg J. Costa
Judge, Fifth Circuit

Counsel should always answer a judge's questions even in this scenario (the fact that the questioner is one of three judges deciding the case makes the question relevant), but after doing so pivot to the issues the attorney things are determinative.

Jennifer Walker Elrod
Judge, Fifth Circuit

In general, it is the duty of the presiding judge, not the lawyer, to handle this situation. A lawyer may have to say, "I can see that I am not going to persuade you, Judge X. Turning to Judge Y's question . . . ."

Edith H. Jones
Judge, Fifth Circuit

When an attorney faces relentless questioning by a judge, I think the only thing to do is to try to answer questions and politely say, "and here's my main point," or something like that, until another judge tries to bail him/her out.

Carolyn Dineen King
Senior Judge, Fifth Circuit

The lawyer answers briefly and then says, respectfully, that he or she would like to make one or two additional points. The lawyer then returns to his or her argument.

Edward C. Prado
Judge, Fifth Circuit

"Your Honor, even if you are correct, there is still the issue of . . . ." Find a way to politely get back to the issues you want to talk about.

Jerry E. Smith
Judge, Fifth Circuit

Best just to put up with it and not act annoyed.

John M. Rogers
Judge, Sixth Circuit

Answer as best you can, and figure out how to turn your answers to your central point.

David F. Hamilton
Judge, Seventh Circuit

After two or three fruitless attempts to answer, it might be best for counsel to tell the judge in the rut that you might just not be able to persuade him/her on that point, but that there are some other issues you hope to address. As a member of the panel in such situations, I usually try to apply a rule of three: if a colleague has asked the same question three times without satisfaction, further progress is not likely. At that point, I feel I can change the subject.

Ilana Diamond Rovner
Judge, Seventh Circuit

A judge's questions are rarely irrelevant. If the questions seem irrelevant, the lawyer should try to understand why the judge is asking them. If the lawyer is truly at a loss to understand the judge's focus, it is acceptable to ask the judge what concern is driving the question. Judges ask questions for many reasons. Sometimes the judge simply needs the answer or is concerned about the effect of this ruling on other cases. Sometimes the judge knows the answer and is using the question to persuade a fellow judge about some aspect of the case. If the other judges believe that the other issues are more important, they will redirect the argument. If they are not redirecting the argument, the chances are good that they find their colleague's questions relevant and the lawyer should address them.

Carlos T. Bea
Judge, Ninth Circuit

That is a very delicate situation. After answering the extraneous questions, he should say "I hope that I have answered Judge ____, and I would like to invite the panel's attention to some points which I think determine this case . . . and I might even ask you to indulge me with a couple of minutes extra."

Richard R. Clifton
Judge, Ninth Circuit

It's a tough situation, but you must respond to each question in a direct manner, including within your response why you think the subject is irrelevant. Make sure you indicate no disrespect to the difficult judge. Take comfort in knowing that the other judges have been in the situation many more times than you have. If the questions should be ignored or deserve disrespect, it's far better for you that it comes from the other judges after argument.

Dorothy W. Nelson
Senior Judge, Ninth Circuit

The presiding judge should control this. The attorney should not ask the judges to get to the "relevant" issues. The attorney might ask the presiding judge for a little time to address the issue he/she thinks important.

Mary M. Schroeder
Senior Judge, Ninth Circuit

Briefly summarize the issue the judges' questions are concerned with, briefly state your position on that issue and then direct the court's attention to the "even more important issue" you wish to discuss.

Harris L. Hartz
Judge, Tenth Circuit

The presiding judge should be the one to prevent this from happening, but occasionally it is the presiding judge who is the problem. The only device that might work is to give one of the other judges an opportunity to help. Perhaps the attorney could other judges an opportunity to help. Perhaps the attorney could respond to the umpteenth question by saying, "Your Honor, even if you are not persuaded on that point, we have alternative grounds for reversal," and then another member of the panel could butt in with, "Yes, I would like to hear what you have to say about the preclusion issue."

Carolyn B. McHugh
Judge, Tenth Circuit

If the other judges are concerned, one or both of them will intervene. In the interim, the lawyer should politely answer what is asked, but should feel free to explain why the issue the dominate judge is fixated on does not matter in this case. And it is also appropriate to respectfully attempt to change the subject or to ask to reserve time for rebuttal.

Deanell Reece Tacha
Former Judge, Tenth Circuit

I counsel lawyers and students to have two or three central points that they simply must make in order to make sure that the judges understand their theory of the case. This limited number of points should be etched indelibly in the brain of the lawyer so that no matter how fast and furious the questioning is or how flustered the lawyer gets, the points will naturally be part of the responses to questions or the next point made after questions. I think perhaps the most useful advice that can be given to counsel is to view the oral argument as a conversation with the bench and treat it as the opportunity to organize a set of questions. In other words, the judge's questions will necessarily occupy a significant portion of the argument, but the organization and emphasis on specific points needs to be provided by the lawyer. The opportunity to provide this organization around a set of questions that may, at times, seem absolutely random is the challenge facing every oral advocate. It is, however, a challenge that must be met in order to present an effective and persuasive argument.

Robin S. Rosenbaum
Judge, Eleventh Circuit

That's a tough situation. Sometimes a judge may ask questions concerning one particular issue because that's the only issue that troubles the judge, so steering the judge away from that issue without satisfactorily responding to the judge's questioning can be a strategic error. Attorneys should listen carefully to the questions and be sure that that is not the situation before attempting to turn the argument away from such an issue. Once a lawyer satisfies herself that the issue truly is irrelevant, the attorney should consider answering the question as succinctly as possible and then immediately stating something to the effect of, "Returning to the issue of . . . ," or "Another issue that is critically important to this case involves . . . ," or "If it pleases the court, may I briefly address the issue of . . . before concluding," before launching into the other issue.

Douglas H. Ginsburg
Senior Judge, D.C. Circuit

A lawyer cannot fail to answer a question posed by a judge. Nevertheless, in order to avoid getting too far off message, a lawyer should answer the question as succinctly and briefly as possible. Once an answer as been provided, the lawyer should immediately go back to his argument and continue with points he would like to address. While the judge may ask another question requiring an answer, the lawyer once again has to answer quickly and then change the topic

Patricia M. Wald
Chief Judge Emeritus, D.C. Circuit

The only advice I can give is to ask at the end for a minute or two to sum up the key points you didn't get to make. Often the other judges will be sympathetic to your plight and let you have it. And, of course, you may never prophesy how a close case will come out by the way the judges act at argument. After all, that one week a month in court is the only recreation an appellate judge gets from the paperwork and she will likely act up, play devil's advocate, lead you down primrose paths, and pounce at the dead end. Later in conference she will say she was having some fun, testing the waters, and seeing how far you would actually go on a point.

Haldane Robert Mayer
Senior Judge, Federal Circuit

If faced with a "hot court," before deciding that a judge is off on a frolic of his own, carefully analyze the questions that are being posed. A judge's frolic may suggest a lack of understanding of the issues, or perhaps the judge views the case from a perspective that you had not considered. In the early stages of preparing your appeal, write and rewrite until each issue and answer can be expressed in one succinct sentence. When a judge begins to go astray, answer the questions as succinctly as possible, always returning to one of your main points.

Rita B. Garman
Justice, Illinois Supreme Court

If a judge feels that an issue is relevant, it is relevant—at least with respect to his or her analysis of the case. So answer the questions respectfully, if briefly, and try to return to the theme of your planned argument. If the other judges feel that the "domineering" judge is steering the discussion away from more important issues, they will not hesitate to intervene.

Michael G. Heavican
Chief Justice, Nebraska Supreme Court

First off, if a judge is asking, it might not be as irrelevant as you think. Otherwise, answer the question the best you can, in a respectful way, then bring the argument back where you want it, and hope the rest of the court goes with you.

Thomas G. Saylor
Chief Justice, Supreme Court of Pennsylvania

Attorneys in this situation should patiently try to steer the discussion back on course, while perhaps hoping for some assistance from a different corner of the bench.

Sharon Keller
Presiding Judge, Texas Court of Criminal Appeals

That can be a challenge. An attorney can say, "Respectfully, Your Honor, that's the best answer I can give," and try to move back to the argument. If a judge really doesn't seem to understand that he is off-base, the attorney can say, "Judge, respectfully, that's not an issue in this case." If a judge is just picking on the attorney, he can try, "Judge, we'll just have to disagree." Sometimes the attorney can say, "Judge, I want to answer that question, but I would like to get back to Judge So-and-So's question first, if I may."

Nathan L. Hecht
Chief Justice, Supreme Court of Texas

First, remember that the other judges deal with each other all the time, know who tends to dominate oral argument, and often sympathize with the lawyer.

Second, always be diplomatic. Even the slightest expression of irritation or frustration is likely to draw disapproval from all the judges. It's like, I can criticize my brother, but you can't.

Third, having begun by stating that you want to make three points, offer to return to them. Or offer to answer any questions other judges have.

18.9   The Appellee's Argument

Appellees' lawyers are always faced with two presentations: the one they prepare and the one they deliver. In preparing, you concentrate on those issues that will follow ruling case law of the appellate tribunal and will most effectively defend the action taken by the trial or intermediate court. Remember that the appellee simply defends, while the appellant must carry the burden of persuading the appellate court that the court below erred.

As stated in section 14.11, in the appellee's brief you *confirm* your view of the applicable law and *refute* the legal argument offered by the adversary. By the time oral argument rolls around, you have had the advantage of reading the appellant's reply brief (if one has been filed), and the preparation of your oral argument should include any new matter presented there. But your preparation should consist essentially of a mastery of all relevant law pertaining to the subject matter. You should not be content to rely on your brief. Why? Because the judges will not. The questions they will ask you and your adversary will probably range far beyond the contours of the briefs.

As you prepare, you will try to anticipate the points your adversary will argue. From experience in the lower courts and from the tenor of the appellant's brief, you already know the main thrust of your opponent's theory. Be prepared to meet it head-on.

Appellee's counsel should prepare a written outline of a possible argument, in broad terms covering points likely to be raised by the appellant. Preparing thoroughly and constructing a general outline are necessary; preparing a canned speech is not. Bring the outline to oral argument, and prepare your plan of attack by annotating the outline *during* the appellant's presentation. Use a highlighter to identify the portions of your outline actually argued by the appellant. You will not have to divert your attention and dissipate your energies by writing feverishly during your opponent's performance. Your annotations should also reflect the dialogue between the judges and appellant's lawyer, which is even more important than the lawyer's presentation.

You must monitor all questions from the bench. This is critical because, first, the questions from the bench disclose the points that are troubling the court; they provide the strongest signal of the direction your answering argument *must* take. Second, the questions often reveal that the judges already know and understand, and possibly agree with, your strongest points; in this case, you need not belabor these points when you get up to speak. Often, all you need say is, "As to point *A*, from the questions put to opposing counsel, it appears that the court understands our position. If the court has any additional questions to ask me on it, I will be pleased to oblige. If not, I will move to point *B*." Stick to your annotated outline. This guarantees that you will cover precisely the points raised by your adversary.

We have indicated that the appellant should begin with its strongest point. How should the appellee open? It depends. If the court's questions indicate an interest in the last point addressed by the appellant, it is probably advisable to continue the dialogue on that point. Because the issue is fresh in the judges' minds, leading off with it may put that issue to bed at the earliest opportunity. Alternatively, if the appellant has made a concession that devastates his position, you should respectfully address that issue first.

At the very minimum, the appellee must weave into the argument the matters raised by the judges' questions. Frequently, it is helpful to turn to specific questions put to your adversary, and then provide corrected, or at least amplified, responses.

Statistics set forth in Chapter One disclose that the odds of prevailing on appeal are with the appellee. Although court rules give the appellee argument time equal to that of the appellant, in most cases the appellee does not need all the allotted time. The good appellee lawyers can sense when the court understands their arguments; indeed, they can often sense this during their adversaries' presentations. Under these circumstances, it is not necessary to pad the presentation to fill up the time allotted. Make your points, and then ask, "If the court please, I believe that the court understands our position. May I inquire if the court has any further questions to put to me?" If there are none, sit down.

"Never" is a very strong word, but we will use it here: If you have addressed your major points, *never* fill in the remaining time with answers to arguments contained in the appellant's brief but not presented in oral argument. If a point was not important enough for the appellant to argue, it is not important enough for you to answer. If the court desires you to respond to issues submitted on the appellant's brief, the judges will ask you to do so. If not, do not volunteer. Quit while you are ahead. The appellee's addressing matters the appellant did not raise in its opening argument also broadens the arguments that can be addressed in rebuttal. There is no reason to give an appellant new lines of challenge, as he may have overlooked a favorable one.

Paul Freund, for five decades the great Harvard constitutional law scholar, formerly served as a deputy United States Solicitor General. Once when he was arguing a case before the Supreme Court, the justices brought out in their questioning of the petitioner everything he had planned to say. Freund walked to the podium and said, "May it please the court, there is a typographical error on page 10 of our brief." He made the correction and then said, "If there are no questions, the government will rely on its brief." The court had no questions and government prevailed in a unanimous decision. For years afterwards, Justice Felix Frankfurter often would refer to Freund's performance and say: "Since I have been on the Court, I have heard learned arguments. I have heard powerful arguments. I have heard eloquent arguments. But I have only heard one *perfect* argument."[10]

18.10   The Rebuttal

As appellant you should *always* reserve some time for rebuttal, even if later it appears that you will not need it. The very act of reserving rebuttal time is an insurance policy to protect you against possible extravagant or unsubstantiated statements from the appellee. Protect yourself with the opportunity of having the last word to expose an exorbitant utterance. This alerts the appellee in advance that you are hanging back to enter the ring again if necessary. Whether you will also depends on what is said by your adversary, but the fact that you have reserved time is in itself a strategic ploy. The appellee knows that you may have the last word.

---

10. *The Talk of the Town*, THE NEW YORKER, Feb. 24, 1992, at 27 [emphasis original].

Strategy aside, keep in mind that unless you are competing in a moot court competition rebuttal should be used sparingly. It is the opportunity to respond to the appellee's presentation, not to rehash your argument in chief. Generally speaking, appellate judges seem to be impatient with rebuttal speeches. To be effective, the argument should be very concise—"snappy" is the word some experienced lawyers use. Select only one or two major emphases, and cite the authority that most effectively rebuts any new dimension added to the case by your opponent and not already covered by you.

Many judges consider rebuttal at oral argument the same as redirect examination of a witness at trial. You are limited to what was brought up in cross-examination. This is not the time to bore the judges with a repetition of what was said in your argument in chief. Its purpose is to respond to new matter—both facts and law—presented by the appellee.

Unless there has been some misrepresentation that deserves rejoinder and you detect that the appellee's argument did not impress the judges, stand up with confidence and state, "Unless the court has questions, we waive rebuttal." If you misjudged the court, you may get questions. So be careful not to be overconfident when analyzing the appellee's argument.

18.11 Summing Up

All the foregoing represents contemporary advice. Yet as early as 1851, the famed constitutional scholar and prolific legal writer, Joseph Story, Justice of the United States Supreme Court and Dane Professor of Law at Harvard, encapsulated all of this in rhyme:

> You wish the Court to hear, and listen too?
>
> Then speak with point, be brief, be close, be true.
>
> Cite well your cases; let them be in point;
>
> Not learned rubbish, dark, and out of joint;
>
> And be your reasoning clear, and closely made,
>
> Free from false taste, and verbiage, and parade.
>
> Stuff not your speech with every sort of law,
>
> Give us the grain, and throw away the straw.
>
> . . . .
>
> Whoe'er in law desires to win his cause,
>
> Must speak with point, not measure our "wise saws,"
>
> Must make his learning apt, his reasoning clear,

Pregnant in manner, but in style severe;

But never drawl, nor spin the thread so fine,

That all becomes an evanescent line.[11]

18.12 Advice from Current and Former State Court Justices

Charles E. Jones
Former Chief Justice, Arizona Supreme Court

State the strongest and best arguments first. Try to anticipate the difficult questions and provide answers. The latter point is also valid in preparing for oral argument.

Sabrina McKenna
Associate Justice, Supreme Court of Hawai'i

Be prepared. Listen to questions.

Rita B. Garman
Justice, Illinois Supreme Court

Oral advocates need to slow down and speak more clearly. This is not a contest to see how many words you can fit in to the time allotted. It is an opportunity to engage in a conversation with the court.

Bill Cunningham
Justice, Supreme Court of Kentucky

Be courteous and polite to the opposing lawyer. Don't be sarcastic or belittling of the opponent's case or argument. Concede weak points. You don't have long. Even less time with questions. Don't dwell too much on the facts at the beginning. The judges will have acquainted themselves with the facts. Go straight to your strongest point off the bat. "I know each of you are familiar with the facts in this case, so I'd like to move immediately to our main issue."

Leigh Ingalls Saufley
Chief Justice, Maine Supreme Judicial Court

Do not waste time reciting the facts or procedural history as an introduction to argument. The court has always read the briefs and bench memo before oral argument begins, and repetition only detracts from the amount of time you will have to address the important issues of the case. Begin your argument by going right to the heart of your strongest point, and never read from your brief. Oral argument should be a dynamic flow of questions and answers getting to the heart of the concept. You will not persuade the court by rereading matters that have already been read. Never respond to a question from a justice with, "I'll get back to that." Be sufficiently familiar with all issues in your case so that you can flexibly respond to questions on different issues in a short period of time.

---

11. Joseph Story, *in* 2 Life and Letters of Joseph Story 89–90 (William W. Story ed. 1851).

Michael G. Heavican
Chief Justice, Nebraska Supreme Court

[What are the characteristics of a good oral argument?] (1) Listening to the questions asked. (2) [Having the a]bility to identify what a court actually cares about (obviously this can sometimes be difficult). (3) Making concessions when necessary. (4) Knowing standard of review and how it applies in the case being argued.

Patricio M. Serna
Former Chief Justice, Supreme Court of New Mexico

Clarify and explain rather than reiterate material in the briefs. Focus on the strongest arguments from the briefs and account for time to answer questions in allocating time between arguments. Be familiar with the facts so the argument is not distracted by counsel rifling through the record.

Thomas G. Saylor
Chief Justice, Supreme Court of Pennsylvania

I see many good arguments, but those that are not so good often reflect a lack of preparation, focus, and/or sensitivity to concerns being raised from the bench.

Frank J. Williams
Former Chief Justice, Rhode Island Supreme Court

State the standard of review during argument and confine argument to the applicable standard. If you don't know the answer to a question, say so directly and move on to the next point. Do not give detailed background of the case. Assume the justices are familiar with the facts and begin and limit your discussion to the most important issues.

David Gilbertson
Chief Justice, South Dakota Supreme Court

During oral argument, answer questions from the bench directly and do not try to mislead the court. If you have a weak point in your case, admit it because it is probably already apparent to the court and your opponent will really work you over on rebuttal if you try to slide by without informing the court. Oral argument before an appellate court is not a jury argument. Leave the theatrics at home.

Sharon Keller
Presiding Judge, Texas Court of Criminal Appeals

During oral argument, lawyers should tell the court where they are going by briefly summarizing the points to be made. Argument should focus on the points that are critical to their case and avoid side issues. Lawyers should refrain from making jury arguments and stick to the legal issue.

Nathan L. Hecht
Chief Justice, Supreme Court of Texas

An almost indispensable approach is to open by stating the two, three, or at most four points the lawyer wants to make.

One of the most important things missing in appellate advocacy is the opportunity for direct confrontation. A lawyer will always want to point out the things the other side cannot answer. But it is better to suggest to the court that a question to the other side about a point will reveal that there is no answer. Judges do this on their own, of course, but an effective advocate will invite it.

Gerry L. Alexander
Former Chief Justice,
Washington Supreme Court

On oral argument, any statement of the facts should be brief. Counsel should assume that the judges are familiar with the facts by virtue of reading the briefs. Counsel should also let us know early in his or her argument what relief they seek for their client. A strong ending is important. Counsel should not end like many do with, "If there are no further questions, I will stop now."

Shirley S. Abrahamson
Justice, Wisconsin Supreme Court

Have clearly in mind the key points you want to make. Make them in the first few minutes and keep coming back to them. Do not plan on restating every argument set out in your brief. Focus on your best points. Start with your strongest argument, because if the court has many questions you may not get beyond your first point. Read articles on oral argument and brief writing. They tend to be very repetitive, because the advice given is good. If you cannot answer a question, say so. If you want to take a shot at it, say, "My immediate reaction is . . . ." If the question raises an important point that neither party considered, ask permission to address the issue in a letter to the court and opposing counsel within three days of the oral argument.

18.13   Advice from Circuit Court Judges

Bruce M. Selya
Senior Judge, First Circuit

[D]evelop your own style and . . . be direct and forthright.

Michael Boudin
Senior Judge, First Circuit

In oral argument, I have only one critical piece of advice: take up a yellow pad with a one-page outline, if you must, and nothing more, and if possible, take nothing at all (the idea is to have an organized conversation with the judges rather than to make a speech).

Dennis Jacobs
Judge, Second Circuit

Everyone knows: listen to the questions. Less appreciated: know when you are being offered a softball, especially after another judge has done a grilling. Use your own personality, whatever it is, to establish an honest and genuine presence, and do not model yourself on others or on anybody's notion of oratory.

Thomas L. Ambro
Judge, Third Circuit

Be credible. To do so (and thus be persuasive) you must tell the truth, concede weaknesses, and craft counters to them that make sense.

Kent A. Jordan
Judge, Third Circuit

The best advocates are able and willing to directly answer questions and still steer the argument to the strong points of their case.

Albert Diaz
Judge, Fourth Circuit

Be honest with the court. Not every lawyer can rise to the heights of those universally considered to be top-flight advocates, but there is no reason why a lawyer can't be the equal of those advocates when it comes to candor with the court.

Gregg J. Costa
Judge, Fifth Circuit

The brief is the lawyer's opportunity to provide her view of the case; oral argument should be about responding to the judge's concerns. The best oral arguments are not arguments at all; they are conversations between counsel and the judges about how the law should apply to the case.

James L. Dennis
Judge, Fifth Circuit

[In response to biggest critiques of oral argument]

A. Not knowing what is in the record and saying, "Well, I was not the trial counsel," as if that explains their lack of familiarity with the record. Counsel should always know the record inside and out and top to bottom.

B. Not answering the question the judge asks, or saying they will address it later. Sometimes counsel do not answer . . . or do not understand the question. If they do not understand, they should say so and see if they can get a better handle on what issue is troubling the judge. As for saying they will get to the question later, there is always the danger that they will forget or will run out of time.

C. Arguing with the judge who asked the question.

D. Making disparaging comments about other counsel.

E. Not watching their time and then rushing to finish, or conversely, if there are no or few questions and counsel has finished argument, knowing when to say no more and sit down.

F. Having ineffective charts, diagrams, etc., which the judges cannot see and which often prompt counsel to walk away from the podium to point to something, and the judges cannot hear what counsel is saying. If counsel needs to use such items, be sure there is a smaller version given to the courtroom deputy so she can give each judge a copy to look at while on the bench.

Jennifer Walker Elrod
Judge, Fifth Circuit

In general, I think argument is helpful and the lawyers do a good job. Lawyers are better if they don't "fight the hypos" and instead try to thoughtfully go through them with the court. Lawyers are better if they have thought through what points they need to win to win their case and what points they should concede to enhance their credibility with the court. Lawyers are worst when they are arguing and even yelling at the court.

Edith H. Jones
Judge, Fifth Circuit

An oral argument, being much shorter than a brief, has to focus and condensethe facts and issues. The points should be stated at the outset, then time allotted to each in proportion to its importance. The oralist has to know which cases are his best or worst and explain (or distinguish) them. Likewise, he must be candid about adverse facts or standards of review. A focus on precise statements in the record, like jury instructions or cross-examination, etc., strengthens the presentation. Finally, in technical areas of law or fact, the oralist has to find a way to convey the concepts clearly, i.e., without using regulatory or scientific jargon and citing reams of numbers and letters.

Carolyn Dineen King
Senior Judge, Fifth Circuit

Address the most important issue first; you may never get to the others. Be absolutely candid and honest with the court. Focus only on those facts or procedural history, if any, that are critical to the outcome—don't get into a long recital on these items; the court is familiar with them.

Thomas M. Reavley
Senior Judge, Fifth Circuit

Write and speak so the judges will hear and understand— who will be glad.

Jerry E. Smith
Judge, Fifth Circuit

The brief has to cover all the important issues. The argument is a summary. The lawyer should treat argument as though he were sitting at a conference table with the judges and were saying, in effect (though certainly not actually), "OK, folks, you've read the briefs; now let me tell you what this case is really all about."

John M. Rogers
Judge, Sixth Circuit

The real value of oral argument from the perspective of the advocate is to do one of two things: to seal the deal with respect to a judge who is leaning your way, or to create doubt with respect to a judge who is leaning against you. To do this, the advocate needs to get a feel of which way the judges are leaning. This is done (pretty much only) by eliciting questions. Effective advocacy, accordingly, elicits questions—by body language, by eye contact, by appropriate pauses, by genuinely wanting questions, and by eagerness to engage when questions are asked. The effectiveness of oral argument is directly related to the number of questions. Then answer them—clearly and in a way that supports your key point(s).

---

12. Myron H. Bright, *The Ten Commandments of Oral Argument*, 67 A.B.A. J. 1136, 1139 (1981).

Ilana Diamond Rovner
Judge, Seventh Circuit

Be aware of the judges' perspectives. We have oral argument so that we may ask questions, and our questions relate not just to the case in front of us but to the future cases that will be affected by our ruling. A good oral advocate always answers the questions without treating them as irritating interruptions and with some awareness that we must take the long view on precedent.

Myron H. Bright
Senior Judge, Eighth Circuit

Know your customer, the court.

A.B.P.—always be prepared.

Go for the jugular.

Questions, questions, good and bad. Answer directly, then return to your main theme.

Be flexible and innovative.

One lawyer is better than two.

Look up, speak up.

Don't snatch defeat from the jaws of victory.

Believe in your case and be natural.

Above all, don't kid yourself. Oral argument is important; indeed, it may be crucial.[12]

Carlos Bea
Judge, Ninth Circuit

Confidence at the podium is the most important element of style. Hurried presentation, in the hopes of getting everything thought said is a losing tactic. Confidence can be bred by a thorough knowledge of the case and the law applicable, so that extraneous matters do not have to be mentioned.

Richard R. Clifton
Judge, Ninth Circuit

Too many arguments seek to recap the briefs. Judges view oral argument as time that belongs to the judges. Lawyers have control over the briefs they write. Judges have control of oral argument. Respond to questions. Even before questions are asked, lawyers should identify what the judges will want to hear about and focus on those subjects.

Andrew J. Kleinfeld
Senior Judge, Ninth Circuit

The best oral advocates listen to the judge's questions and provide useful answers. The lawyer is a teacher, not a con artist. Clarity and candor work the best.

Dorothy W. Nelson
Senior Judge, Ninth Circuit

Listen to judges' questions and answer them without going astray. Know your case so well, you can look at the judges at the beginning and tell them what you are seeking and why.

N. Randy Smith
Judge, Ninth Circuit

[On the characteristics of a good oral argument]

a) Be clear, candid, and truthful with the court.

b) Keep the judge's perspective in mind.

c) Know and use the record

d) Appreciate questions from the bench; have a conversation with the judges; address the problems in your case.

e) Simplify the case. Concede as much as you can and still prevail. Focus on the dispositive point in the case on which it should turn.

f) Be sincere and professional

g) Be aware of the standard of review

h) Know what relief you want

i) Know when to sit down

Harris L. Hartz
Judge, Tenth Circuit

[In response to biggest critiques of oral argument]

A) Attorneys do not answer the question. I sometimes have to ask the question three times and then give up. Answering questions is the most important part of oral argument. If an attorney does not take advantage of the opportunity to disabuse the judge of a misconception, the game may be over.

B) Attorneys do not listen to the opposing party's argument and the court's questions. I notice that good advocates for appellees often realize they have won and simply state that they are available for any questions from the court.

C) Attorneys do not know when to concede and when not to. By not conceding a point, counsel often lose the opportunity to make a strong back-up argument. On the other hand, some are so intent on being agreeable that they concede a point until another judge asks whether the attorney really meant to give away the case.

D) Attorneys sometimes treat the appellate panel as a jury and try to reargue the facts. I do not ever recall that being effective.

Carolyn B. McHugh
Judge, Tenth Circuit

The panel has already read your brief and is familiar with the facts. Do not waste any time repeating the facts or restating everything in your brief. You only have fifteen minutes, so you must hit the high points. If the standard of review is helpful to you, state the issue accordingly: the district court did not abuse its broad discretion in excluding Dr. Smith's testimony as unreliable. Use the record and controlling authority to illustrate your points, but avoid long quotes from either. That may be appropriate in a brief, but it does not work at oral argument.

Treat rebuttal differently than your opening argument. Rebuttal should be staccato: quick punches in response to the opposition argument. Hit your points, ask for the relief you are seeking, and sit down.

Robin S. Rosenbaum
Judge, Eleventh Circuit

Some attorneys seem to view oral argument as an exercise that they must just survive instead of as perhaps the last opportunity to win the case. That's unfortunate. Instead of dodging questions, or just trying to get through them, lawyers should embrace questions and answer them head-on. When a judge says she has a problem with a particular part of a case, that's code for telling the lawyer that her client may well lose unless the lawyer can explain why what the judge perceives to be a fatal problem is not really a problem. Dodging a question like that is the same thing as telling the judge that she's right, and the client should lose. It is a total waste of the opportunity that oral argument presents.

Douglas H. Ginsburg
Senior Judge, D.C. Circuit

Do not argue with a judge in response to a judge's question. Do not simply repeat in oral argument what is in the briefs. Get your important points across as succinctly and quickly as possible.

Patricia M. Wald
Chief Judge Emeritus, D.C. Circuit

Apart from an acceptance of the "life is not fair" motif to oral argument, probably the most important thing for an appellate lawyer is to "know the record." It is not good enough that the paralegal or the associate who drafted the brief knows the record inside and out; the lawyer who argues the case must. I concur with Chief Justice Rehnquist's lament about oral advocates who depend too heavily on their subordinates in writing the brief, and who cannot answer questions about the basic case or the record. The more arcane the subject matter, the more intimate with the record the advocate needs to be. All the questions of fact and expert opinion that the brief may have raised in the judges' minds will surface at argument, and nothing frustrates a bench more than a lawyer who does not know the answers. Your credibility as a legal maven spurts as soon as you show familiarity with the facts of the underlying dispute. When a lawyer cannot smoothly answer a question securely rooted in his knowledge of the record, the specter of a remand for inadequate explanation by the agency comes quickly to the fore. If you watch, we don't ask you so many questions about the meaning of precedent as we do about the underlying dispute in the case: What is it really all about? Why does one party care so much about a few words in an agency rule? Of course counsel can always offer to submit record cites after argument, but inability to locate them onsite definitely detracts from the image of her being in complete control of the case.

Haldane Robert Mayer
Senior Judge, Federal Circuit

Argue the law—the appellate court's primary function is to insure that the lower court has not committed reversible legal error. Given the standard of review, if the lawyer is arguing facts, he is fighting an uphill battle. Do not use exhibits—exhibits waste time, are distracting, and draw attention away from the advocate. However, if a lawyer insists on using exhibits, he should take care not to argue the facts. Advance the ball—the judges have read your briefs, do not stand at the podium and rehash them. Use the time to answer the court's questions and address your opponent's arguments.

Part Five

Checklists

Chapter Nineteen

Two Important Checklists: Brief Writing and Oral Argumentation Preparation

19.1   Brief Writing Checklist

The following may serve as a handy checklist in preparing an appellate brief. As you finish each step, indicate its completion with a checkmark.

A)   Follow a planned sequence of preparation.

1) *File a timely notice of appeal.* Examine the applicable statute or court rule.

2) *Learn the court rules.* Familiarize yourself with all rules relating to contents and filing of briefs. This includes reviewing any local rules or internal operating procedures.

3) *Ensure that the appellate court has jurisdiction.* Is the appeal from a final judgment or order of the trial tribunal? Have all the parties' claims been adjudicated? If it is not a final judgment, does the appeal qualify as an interlocutory appeal under the relevant statute or rule? If you are in federal court, did the district court have subject matter jurisdiction?

4) *Prepare a written statement of jurisdiction and timeliness of filing the appeal.* Save this for inclusion in the brief.

5) *Order the record if it is not available electronically.* Do not delay. You are faced with a tight briefing schedule. The clerk of court will not excuse a late brief because you have not ordered a timely transcript of the record.

6) *Know the record cold.* You must be totally familiar with the record before beginning your research and certainly before you start writing the brief.

7) *Make an informal list of issues.* Make an inventory of all possible points. Do not spend time phrasing the issues. This should be a gross listing of unrefined possibilities.

8) *Investigate issue preservation.* Locate in the record where the issue has been preserved for review. Appellate determination of reversible error is based on the presence of three interrelated circumstances:

 a) special rulings, acts, or omissions by the trial tribunal constituting trial error,

 b) which follow an objection by counsel or the grant or denial of an oral or written motion or submission,

 c) accompanied by a proper and appropriate course of action recommended by the appellant which was rejected by the tribunal.

 If the issue has not been preserved at trial, consider the possibility of plain error if your jurisdiction permits.

9) *Begin legal research.* Use the system you find most effective—electronic annotations, spreadsheets or other electronic tools, yellow pad notes, file cards, or photocopies of leading cases. Highlight important passages and possible direct quotes for inclusion in the brief. Make lots of notes. Do not trust your memory. You do not want to let a good case get away because your memory failed. Do not start to write the brief. You are not ready yet.

10) *Weed out the issues (points) that will not persuade.* You have not written one word of your brief yet, but this process may be the most important part of brief "writing." What you exclude is as important as what you include. Avoid the shotgun approach. Choose only those arguments that have a chance of prevailing. Do not fall in love with a pet issue. Look at each potential issue from the judge's viewpoint. The "finalists" on your list must meet this test: *the issue more probably than not will attract the interest and serious consideration of the judges.*

11) *Limit your issues to three (possibly four) points.* Keep in mind the advice of all the judges in this book. Limit your discussion to a very small number of issues. When it comes to appellate advocacy, more is not better.

12) *Refine and intensify your legal research to focus on the chosen issues.* It is time to go back to the books again to determine whether additional research will be necessary.

13) *Draft the standard of review.* Prepare a draft of the standard of review for each issue selected, including appropriate supporting authorities.

14) *If electronic filing is available—or required—in your jurisdiction, complete any necessary steps to obtain a login that will allow you to file your brief.* Carefully review any rules regarding electronic filing, including document size and filing and service deadlines. Also check to see if any paper copies are required.

B) Draft the appellant's (or petitioner's) brief.

1) *Allow adequate time in your schedule.* Ideas need time to percolate. Crucial cases get overruled or reversed during the briefing process. Colleagues let you down on offers of vital help. Illness or emergency matters upset your schedule. All of your research is in the computer, and it crashes. If you arrange to have your brief ready for filing two or three days early, none of these events need concern you.

2) *Write the issues.* Rephrase with care the issues that you have selected for inclusion in your brief. Write each issue in the form of a simple declarative sentence or interrogatory to serve as the topic sentence of the point heading in the argument portion of your brief. The argument headings (points or issues) and their subparts must be full enough and clear enough for the judges to follow and convincing enough for the court to accept.

3) *Express each issue as narrowly as possible to achieve your objective.* Be satisfied to have the court affirm or reverse. Do not insist that the court promulgate a holding broader than necessary.

4) *Look for a single dispositive issue.* Will the resolution of a single issue determine the outcome of the appeal? If yes, say so. That is the first issue to list. Indicate that other issues are alternatives only.

5) *Select the theme or equitable heart of the argument from your selected issues.* The theme should be the strongest point in your brief and the first one stated. *Your strongest point is that argument, objectively considered, based on precedent and the court's previously stated policy concerns, most calculated to persuade the court to your point of view.*

   a) Look back to this theme as you write. (You may, of course, have more than one theme.) It will help bring order and focus to your writing, as well as unity, logic, and concision, but keep in mind that the organizing theme may need revision and refinement as the writing progresses.

   b) In writing your theme, you must identify the flashpoint of controversy and discuss only what is essential to that point in the brief.

6) *Organize the brief.* Make an outline of your argument. It must include all the points selected and should serve as the framework of the argument portion of your brief. Remember these words of Henry M. Hart, Jr.: "Briefs on the merits need not only tell their story to one who takes the time to read all the way through them, but ought to be so organized that they can be used, like a book of reference, for quick illumination on any point of concern."

7) *Write your argument, point by point.*

    a) Present a systematic discussion of the issues. Argument headings and subheadings must flow logically.

    b) Keep your argument focused on your theme and the flashpoint of controversy in your brief.

        i) If the law and its application are clear, your discussion should be short and to the point.

        ii) If the law is certain and the application alone is doubtful, explain how the law applies to the facts. Do not waste the judges' time justifying the choice of law.

        iii) If neither the rule of law nor its application is clear, discuss:

           • the choice, interpretation, and application of the legal precept, or

           • the interpretation and application of the legal precept.

    c) Do not overwrite. Do not belabor or state the obvious. Keep it brief!

    d) Write persuasively. Keep the standard of review in mind and incorporate it into your headings and discussion.

    e) Follow the canons of logic.

        i) Is the choice of a major premise supported by applicable law?

        ii) Are you observing the rules of inductive and deductive reasoning? If analogizing, do you emphasize the resemblances and differences in the facts of the compared cases?

        iii) Avoid formal and informal fallacies in your argument.

        iv) Does each thought follow from the previous one?

        v) Is each thought explained or illuminated by the statements that follow?

        vi) Are unobvious conclusions supported by citation or argument?

8) *Analyze the lower court's opinion.* The appellant must respond to every important authority relied upon by the lower court. If the flashpoint of controversy is the choice of a controlling legal precept, explain the reasons why your choice presents the better view. If the controversy is over interpretation, do the same. If the issue involves application of settled law to facts, explain factual resemblances and differences in the compared cases.

9) *Write the summary of your argument.* Encapsulate the theme of the argument and explain the substance of your brief. View this as "preview" of what is to come that can also serve as a refresher before argument.

10) *Write the statement of the case.* State briefly the nature of the case, the course of the proceedings and its disposition in the court below. Tell the appellate court "how you got here."

11) *Write the statement of facts.* Prepare a selective, economical, succinct exposition of the facts so that the reader can understand what follows.

   a) Do not begin writing until you have decided what issues you will raise. *Never, never* write the facts first.

   b) Master the record to glean the facts that support your issues and arguments.

   c) Tailor the narrative so that it fits the issues raised. Write as tersely as you can.

   d) Be accurate. Do not steal the facts. Set forth the findings in light of the verdict winner. You must follow the fact-finding of the lower court, even when they were contested.

   e) Even while you are candid as to what the lower court found, also be clear as to what fact-finding you are arguing was in error, and what the correct facts are, giving record references.

   f) Within the bounds of accuracy, however, state your facts in such a way that the judges will receive a favorable, lasting impression from your account of the facts.

   g) Unless the fact was uncontroverted, cite to the appendix or record for every assertion in the statement.

   h) Remember: be clear. It is not unconstitutional to be interesting. What you write must compete for attention in a mountain of other communications. Try to make it rise above the surrounding peaks.

12) *Spell out the conclusion.* Tell the court exactly what relief you want—that is, reverse the judgment, affirm, or vacate and remand with a specific direction.

13) *Create the front cover.* Check the rules. Ascertain what information front covers should contain.

   a) *Cover color.* Check the rules. The United States Courts of Appeals require that the cover of the appellant's brief be blue; appellee's brief, red; and the intervenor or amicus brief, green.

b) *Multiple parties.* When there are multiple appellants or appellees, identify the name of the party on the cover—for example, "Brief of the Appellant Harvey M. Tillman."

14) *Compile a table of contents.* After the brief is in final form, prepare a detailed table of contents with accurate page references.

15) *And the table of authorities.* Begin preparing the table of authorities with plenty of time to spare. Do not wait until the last minute to start it. After the brief is in final form, check the page references for accuracy and completeness. Avoid typos. Proofread carefully.

C) Use authorities properly.

1) *Be accurate.* Do not miscite. Do not "trample on graves"—do not represent that a case stands for something that it does not.

2) *Distinguish between binding precedent (mandatory authority) and persuasive authority.* It will be precedential only if the court opinion is from the highest court in your jurisdiction, but even some of those opinions may not be binding according to local practice, such as if the opinion is not published in the official reporter; if it is unpublished, or from another court, it is merely persuasive.

3) *Follow the* Bluebook *citation style (or applicable citation form in your jurisdiction).* Always identify the circuit when citing a court of appeals case. Give the year for every citation.

4) *Rely on primary authorities.* Cases and statutes are primary authorities. Secondary sources include *Corpus Juris Secundum, American Jurisprudence,* and other legal treatises. These are properly cited as "*see* cases collected in . . . ." A citation to a restatement is persuasive, but unless it has been adopted by the jurisdiction, it is not a primary authority.

5) *Do not overwrite when discussing a cited case.* You usually cite a case for its facts, its reasoning, or its holding. Seldom do you cite for all three purposes. Always consider *why* you are citing it. If you limit the discussion to this purpose, you will not unduly pad the discussion. If appropriate, use a parenthetical to provide a paraphrase or direct quote.

6) *Do not use string citations.* Do not overcite if the most recent case says it all. But it is proper to use *multiple* citations to demonstrate that many courts follow a particular legal precept or that the question is not settled.

7) *Cite check your brief.* Bring all citations up to date. Set up email citation alerts for cases so that your research can be updated up to the point of oral argument. Do not end up with egg on your face when you subsequently

learn that your major authority has been overruled. Ascertain the most recent holdings. Do not show up at oral argument with supplementary citation lists that furnish the court with cases handed down months or years before the brief was written. These cases belong in your brief.

8) *Use pinpoint citations.* When referring to a particular statement in a cited case, furnish the court with the page number where the statement appears.

9) *Cite adverse holdings in your jurisdiction.* Canons of ethics typically require lawyers to advise the court of controlling authorities adverse to their position.

10) *Respond to the unfavorable controlling case.* Do not "lie down." You should attempt to distinguish a case cited in the trial court's opinion or in your opponent's brief that seems to be on all fours against you. Do the best you can. Do not wait for oral argument to have a judge ask you about it the moment you open your mouth. If the case is against you, try to distinguish it. If you cannot, show why it should not be followed. Know what you are doing, and let the court know, too.

D) Prepare the appendix, excerpt of record, clerk's transcript, or reproduced record.

1) *Know the court rules.* Determine precisely what the court rules require, because that's what the judges will expect. This is especially true in United States Courts of Appeals, where each circuit has its own idiosyncrasies.

2) *Prepare an adequate appendix.* When in doubt, include, rather than exclude, material. The appendix or excerpt of record is designed for one purpose: to authenticate statements contained in your brief. The court may have a rule as to what must be in the appendix. If so, follow it. Usually, the appendix will include trial court docket entries, the lower court's opinion, evidence adduced at trial, and relevant portions of pleadings, jury charge or findings, and pre-trial and post-trial motions. If a portion of the record helps you authenticate a passage in your brief, be certain that it reaches the judges in their chambers; do not expect the judges to search through the files in the clerk's office. If the material is important enough to be cited in your brief, it is important enough to be included in the appendix and sent to all judges who will be reading the briefs.

3) *Use discretion in including materials.* Do not clutter the appendix with materials unnecessary to authenticate statements made in the brief. It is seldom necessary to furnish the entire trial testimony unless a serious

question of sufficiency of evidence is presented. Even then, do not clutter the record excerpts if the court has easy access to the entire record.

4) *Paginate the appendix.* Regardless of what the letter of the court rule provides, paginate every page of an appendix or excerpt of record. Tabs or electronic bookmarks are generally insufficient. Remember that you are always fighting time; make it as easy as possible for the judges.

5) *Compile a table of contents.* Be certain to have a complete table of contents in your appendix or excerpt of record. If more than one trial court opinion appears in a proceeding, describe the subject matter and date of each opinion in the table. When reproducing a portion of testimony, be sure to identify the date, the witness, and the lawyers. In preparing the table, err on the side of detailed description rather than abridgment.

6) *Submit clean photocopies.* Appendix items are not very helpful if the judges cannot read them. Do not supply fifth-generation photocopies of the originals. Use *photographic* prints of pictures, not *photocopies.* Color photos always impress. Where handwriting appears in the appendix, attach a scrupulously accurate, legible, typewritten version to it.

7) *Create the front cover.* Check rules to determine what the front cover should contain. Usually, the front cover of an appendix, if separately printed, is white.

E) Writing the appellee's (or respondent's) brief.

1) *Remember: you defend.* Your opponent has the burden. Show that the burden has not been met and that the lower court was correct. Use the standard of review to your benefit.

2) *Follow the same basic procedure as suggested for the appellant.* Using the procedure outlined in Section *B* above, prepare a proper statement of issues, summary of the argument, enunciation of theme or focus, and point-by-point discussion. You may accept the appellant's statement of facts *in toto* or in part. Follow the same approach for preparing the front cover, table of contents, table of authorities, and conclusion.

3) *Confirm and refute.* In the style of the Greco-Roman rhetoricians, your argument must be a combination of *confutatio,* refuting your opponent's argument, and *confirmatio,* confirming the result reached by the court below.

4) *Analyze the trial court rationale.* Evaluate the reasons given by the trial court for its decision. You may either adopt them or offer alternative reasons to affirm.

5) *Review the statement of facts.* If you agree with your opponent's statement, say so (even if you are not happy with the literary style or length). If you disagree, accept it with some modifications of your own or present your own statement.

6) *Look for any controlling cases omitted by your opponent.* This is your big gun. Use it to blow your opponent away, but avoid *ad hominem* accusations.

7) *Answer every case or authority.* As a rule of thumb, respond to every authority cited by the appellant, although the response need not be unduly prolix. Where the appellant has used irrelevant citations to pad the brief, use a footnote to dispose of them. Where the flashpoint of controversy is choice of law, give reasons to accept your choice; where the controversy is over interpretation, do the same. Where the issue involves an application of settled precept to facts, use canons of analogy to show factual resemblances or differences in the compared cases. Follow the suggestions for proper use of authorities set forth in Section *C* above.

8) *Identify formal or material fallacies.* Do not just say, "The appellant's reasoning is flawed." Note precisely what rule of syllogistic logic is being violated or which material fallacy is present.

9) *Defend any controlling case.* When you (and ostensibly, the lower court) insist that a certain case controls explain why.

F) Preparing the reply brief.

1) *Think carefully about the need for a reply brief.* In earlier editions of this book, Judge Aldisert stated that reply briefs should not be filed unless absolutely necessary. Other judges have the opposite view, meaning, a reply brief should be filed unless there is clearly nothing further that needs to be said in response to the appellee's brief. What is particularly harmful is to leave unrebutted some meaningful point in the appellee's brief, including case law or possible mischaracterization of the facts. There are judges who believe that failure to file a reply brief responding to some new point in the appellee's brief constitutes a waiver due to failure to argue a point.

2) *Use the reply brief properly.* A reply brief is primarily necessary to a) rebut cases cited by the appellee that are not covered in the opening brief, b) expose an irrelevant argument, or c) correct misstatements of fact. It may be used also to furnish the court with a discussion of relevant cases handed down since the opening brief was filed and which serve as proper rebuttal.

19.2 Oral Argument Preparation Checklist

The following may serve as a handy checklist in preparing for oral argument before an appellate court. As you finish each step, indicate its completion with a checkmark.

A) Follow a planned sequence of preparation.

1) *Know the court rules.* Some courts have specific rules governing oral argument. For example, know if the court rules require you to request and justify oral argument in your brief.

2) *Reread your brief carefully.* Master it. Make notes regarding a) the themes, b) key facts in the case, and c) key authorities.

3) *Reread the entire appendix (or excerpts of record).* Read this from cover to cover and make notes. Paper-clip key pages on the top; tabs bend easily and fall off. For quick reference during argument, mark on the front cover of each appendix volume the key materials you may need during the argument. Use a felt-tip pen to note clearly the page numbers of, and a brief phrase describing, all key record citations. Do this even if a digest of key appendix references is available.

4) *Reread the adversary's brief(s).* Note the key points. Look for the weaknesses in your own case that the adversary has identified, and be prepared to respond to questions from the court about them.

5) *Reread the lower court opinion(s).* Appellant's counsel should reread and make notes concerning the opinion below. Can you identify any misstatements of fact or law? Errors of logic? How do any analogies stand up? Are cases miscited? Have appellate cases been decided subsequently that should change the result? What are the policy implications if the approach of the court below is upheld? How sound are the reasons supporting the opinion?

6) *Reread key cases.* Read thoroughly and understand the key cases upon which both sides rely. Be prepared for interrogation by the judges on the facts, reasoning, and holdings. You may find it useful to listen to archived oral argument from these cases if it is available.

7) *Select your now-or-never points.* Select those points upon which you must prevail to win the appeal. Try to limit your argument to two points, and no more than three, even if given a full thirty minutes of argument. (You may be allotted as little as fifteen minutes.) Be prepared to accept a narrower ruling than the one you advocate if that holding will achieve the results requested.

8) *Know what you can concede.* Think carefully about your case and determine what points you can concede at oral argument without undermining the heart of your appeal.

9) *Be prepared on other points.* Because the judges or your adversary may be interested in other points set forth in the brief, be prepared to discuss them as well.

10) *Plan a presentation taking one-third of allotted time.* Unless you are appearing before a court that you know asks very few questions (a cold bench), expect that questioning will consume at least two-thirds of the allotted time. In case the court does, in fact, consume that much time, prepare a "fail-safe" presentation that permits you to deliver your points in the other third of the allotted time. In addition, when the judges' questions require the advocate to spend most of the time addressing just part of the appeal, be ready to argue in a very summary fashion the remaining important issues.

11) *Start your outline.* Prepare an outline based on your notes. Use those techniques with which you are comfortable. Many experienced lawyers use a plain sheet of 8½x11-inch white paper for each point of the argument. Others use index cards, but here you run the risk of the cards getting out of order or falling out of your file folder on the way to the lectern. The outline should be concise, but as long as necessary to include for each point, key themes, leading authorities and record citations to the briefs and appendix. Use a very short, key-word approach. This is an *outline* to assist in preparation, not a *script* to be placed on the lectern. Some hints:

   a) The purpose of this outline is to distill the essence of the case, not for use at the oral argument.

   b) Wide margins should be left for revisions and notes.

   c) Put the outline in a looseleaf notebook (or file folder), along with excerpts from a few key authorities and important pages from the appendix.

   d) For every case cited in the briefs, place in the notebook the names of the judges who sat on the panel. You may be appearing before a judge who wrote the opinion or who served on the panel.

12) *Refine your outline.* On the day before the oral argument, reduce the outline as much as possible, preferably to one page. Although the notebook and full outline will be available at oral argument should your mind go blank, try not to look at anything other than this final outline during argument. You must demonstrate courtroom presence. It is eyeball-to-eyeball time. Do not even give the appearance of reading your argument. The final outline serves only as a roadmap of points to be made when sidetracked by questions. By the day of argument, you must know your case well enough to talk about it, not just read notes.

13) *Final research.* Keep your eyes on the email citation alerts that you set up to check the currency of the cases you used in your brief.

14) *Anticipate questions.* Think of questions the court may throw at you. Your adversary's brief will suggest most, but not all, of them.

15) *Watch or listen to arguments online.* Check to see if the court has live streaming or archived video or audio of oral arguments. Spend some time watching or listening to arguments to get a feel for the judges and the types of questions they ask.

B) **Preparing when you are the appellee.**

1) *Follow the preparation steps for the appellant outlined in Section A above.* Do the detailed study and preparation required for the appellant, making appropriate adjustments.

2) *Determine your own scope of presentation.* To a large extent the appellee responds to the appellant, but your adversary should not determine the scope of your presentation. Make whatever points are necessary, even if the appellant chooses not to mention them. If the point is crucial, do not rely on your brief alone.

3) *Prepare your outline.* Always prepare an outline of key points. Do not trust your memory. Leave space in the outline to fill in rebuttal points during appellant's argument.

C) **Rehearse at the office.**

1) *Conduct a mandatory office moot court.* If the case is important enough to appeal, it is important enough to rehearse the oral argument in your office. Enlist partners and associates (preferably those who are somewhat detached) to read the briefs and to assume the roles of judges and your adversary. Have them pepper you with questions. Rehearsing your argument is as important as any other billable hour. If you are a sole practitioner, enlist lawyer friends. If enough money is in the case, bring in some top-flight appellate lawyers or retired appellate judges to sit on the moot court.

D) **Reconnoiter the court and the courtroom.**

1) *Discover who will hear your case.* Unless it is a full court (en banc), learn the names of the judges before whom you will appear. Many United States Courts of Appeals identify the panel a week before the argument. If your court does not, send someone to the court every day during the week before the argument to see who is on the panel. If a trial judge or judge from another court is sitting, use WestlawNext or Lexis Advance to determine whether that judge has written any opinions on the points involved in your appeal.

2) *Case the joint.* Familiarize yourself with the courtroom. Try to get to the court a day in advance to witness the judges in action. Find out where lawyers must report, how to reserve time for rebuttal, the arrangement of counsel tables, the size of the lectern for placement of materials, and how the court controls the length of argument. Get a feel for the acoustics. You do not want to shout at the judges, but you want to ensure that they can hear you.

APPENDICES

Appendix A

Standards of Review

A.1 Some Good Ones

This court applies the clearly erroneous standard, Fed. R. Civ. P. 52(a), to a review of facts found by a judge. "It is the responsibility of an appellate court to accept the ultimate factual determination of the fact-finder unless that determination either (1) is completely devoid of minimum evidentiary support displaying some hue of credibility, or bears no rational relationship to the supportive evidentiary data. Unless the reviewing court establishes the existence of either of these factors, it may not alter the facts found by the trial court." *Krasnov v. Dinan*, 465 F.2d 1298, 1302–03 (3d Cir. 1972).

Comment: Here, the standard was not only stated but also defined (although the quote is quite long). After checking the citation, the judge could lift this verbatim for inclusion in an opinion. Giving a citation is critical because it not only authenticates the statement but also assists the court in pre- and post-decision research. This standard is also persuasive for an appellee—showing the difficulty the court faces in overturning factual findings.

This court's review of the grant of summary judgment is plenary. *Little v. MGIC Indemnity Corp.*, 836 F.2d 789, 792 (3d Cir. 1987). This court, like the district court, should consider only facts of record. *Harold Friedman, Inc. v. Thorofare Markets, Inc.*, 587 F.2d 127, 131 (3d Cir. 1978). Arguments of counsel alleging facts not supported by the record must be rejected. *Ness v. Marshall*, 660 F.2d 517, 519 (3d Cir. 1981).

This court should affirm if summary judgment could have been entered on any ground raised below. "A prevailing party can support a district court judgment on any ground, including ones overlooked or rejected by the trial court." *Cospito v. Heckler*, 742 F.2d 72, 78 n.8 (3d Cir. 1984), *cert. denied*, 471 U.S. 1131 (1985) (*quoting Washington Steel Corp. v. TW Corp.*, 602 F.2d 594, 600 (3d Cir. 1979)).

The standard of review over a district court's denial of qualified immunity is plenary. *Brown v. United States*, 851 F.2d 615, 617 (3d Cir. 1988); *Hynson v. City of Chester*, 827 F.2d 932, 934 (3d Cir. 1987), *cert. denied*, 108 S.Ct. 702 (1988).

This court reviews admission of evidence under Rule 404(b), Federal Rules of Evidence, under the abuse of discretion standard. *United States v. Lewis*, 837 F.2d 415, 418–19 (9th Cir. 1988). If the court concludes that the trial court abused its discretion in admitting the evidence, the conviction must be reversed unless the error was harmless. *United States v. Hodges*, 770 F.2d 1475, 1480 (9th Cir. 1984). The error was harmless if it is more probable than not that the erroneous admission of evidence did not affect the jury's verdict. *Id.*

Comment: This example is good, but it could be more persuasive. It is hard to tell if this brief is from an appellee or appellant brief. For example, the brief writer could have defined "abuse of discretion" better or provided more insight into what constitutes harmless error.

The district court's judgments dismissing *Fleming* and *Diamond* present this court with purely legal issues for review in that they are based solely on the district court's authority to issue process under RICO and the Federal Rules of Civil Procedure. The error of the district court, being solely one of law, is subject to *de novo* review. *Pullman-Standard v. Swint*, 456 U.S. 273 (1982).

Comment: This is a little wordy.

Federal Rule of Civil Procedure 23 sets forth several requirements for class certification. In particular, under Rule 23(b)(3), "a plaintiff must . . . show that the common issues predominate" over individualized issues. *Sandwich Chef of Texas, Inc. v. Reliance Nat'l Indem. Ins. Co.*, 319 F.3d 205, 218 (5th Cir. 2003). "The party seeking certification bears the burden of proof." *Id.*

This Court generally "review[s] the district court's class certification decision for abuse of discretion." But "[a] district court by definition abuses its discretion when it makes an error of law." *Id.* (quotations omitted).

Thus, "[w]hen a district court certifies a case as a class action, despite the fact that the predominance requirement cannot be met, it errs as a matter of law." *Id.* at 219 (citations omitted). *See also id.* ("If the court erred in these [predominance] holdings, its class certification decision was necessarily an abuse of discretion and must be reversed."); *Patterson v. Mobil Oil Corp.*, 241 F.3d 417, 419 (5th Cir. 2001) ("the district court erred as a matter of law in certifying this class because the predominance requirement could not be met") (citations omitted).[1]

"The class certification determination rests within the sound discretion of the trial court." *Unger v. Amedisys, Inc.*, 401 F.3d 316, 320 (5th Cir. 2005). This Court reviews "class certification decisions for abuse of discretion in recognition of the essentially factual basis of the certification inquiry." *Regents*, 482 F.3d at 380. It "may not conduct an independent inquiry into the legal or factual merit of this case as though [it] were reviewing a motion under Federal Rule of Civil Procedure 12(b)(6) or 56." *Id.*

Defendants try to bootstrap a *de novo* standard by proposing that district courts necessarily err "as a matter of law" whenever their judgments as to the predominance of common questions are incorrect. *See* Br. 9-10. That would be a radical transformation of the standard of review. This Court has instead explained that a district court only necessarily abuses its discretion in the sense defendants advance when it "premises its legal analysis on an erroneous *understanding* of the governing law." *Unger*, 401 F.3d at 320 (emphasis added). Here, the district court premised its analysis on a precisely accurate understanding of the governing law, distinguishing between different types of fraud allegations that would and would not require individualized proof of reliance. *See id.* at 320-21 (emphasizing this distinction as the relevant inquiry); *infra* Part II. Defendants simply challenge the district court's predictive judgment that individualized reliance issues would not predominate under the theory it certified, and that "essentially factual" determination lies within the heartland of the district court's discretion.[2]

Comment: The preceding two examples are from the same case. Note how both the appellant and the appellee tried to frame the standard of review in a favorable manner. In addressing the standard of review, the Fifth Circuit said, en banc, "We review a district court's certification of a class for abuse of discretion, but if the court's error is a matter of law, the court necessarily abuses its discretion. Our review is deferential 'in recognition of the

---

1. Brief of Appellants at 9–10, Torres v. SGE Management, LLC, 805 F.3d 145 (5th Cir. 2015) (No. 14–20128), 2014 WL 3703146, at *9–10.
2. Brief of Appellees at 25–26, Torres v. SGE Management, LLC, 805 F.3d 145 (5th Cir. 2015) (No. 14–20128), 2014 WL 5302704, at *25–26.

essentially factual basis of the certification inquiry and of the district court's inherent power to manage and control pending litigation.'"[3]

This Court reviews *de novo* the district court's decision as to standing and ripeness. *Nat'l Wrestling Coaches Ass'n v. Dep't of Educ.*, 366 F.3d 930, 937 (D.C. Cir. 2004) (standing); *Nat'l Ass'n of Home Bldrs. v. U.S. Army Corps of Eng'rs*, 440 F.3d 459, 461 (D.C. Cir. 2006)(ripeness). Because the district court "disposed of appellants' complaint on a motion to dismiss," this Court "must assume that general factual allegations in the complaint embrace those specific facts that are necessary to support the claim." *Nat'l Wrestling Coaches*, 366 F.3d at 938. And if one plaintiff's standing can be shown for each claim, the Court needs not consider the other plaintiffs' standing to bring that claim. *Mountain States Legal Found. v. Glickman*, 92 F.3d 1228, 1232 (D.C. Cir. 1996).

The States are entitled to "special solicitude" with respect to their standing to sue in defense of their own sovereign and quasi-sovereign interests. *Massachusetts v. EPA*, 549 U.S. 497, 520 (2007). But in this case no "special solicitude" is needed, because the allegations set forth in the Complaint already satisfy "the most demanding standards of the adversarial process." *Id.* at 521.[4]

Comment: Notice again the persuasive language used in explaining the standard of review.

A.2 Some Not-so-Good Ones

Standard of Review: Abuse of discretion.

Comment: Even if correct, this is no help to the court, because it is unsupported by the proper authorities. It also does not explain what constitutes abuse of discretion in this particular instance.

The standard of review for issues numbers 1 through 4 and 6 is whether the district court erred as a matter of law. This court has plenary review over issue number 5.

Comment: What is the difference between review of an error of law and plenary review? None, of course. Moreover, this is an example of "Let's give the court a little workout here." The brief writer provides no information here as to the substance of each

---

3. Torres v. SGE Management, LLC, 838 F.3d 629, 635 (5th Cir. 2016) (footnotes omitted).

4. Opening Brief for the State Appellants at 15–16, State Nat'l Bank of Big Spring v. Lew, 795 F.3d 48 (D.C. Cir. 2015) (Nos. 13–5247, 13–5248), 2014 WL 546549, at *15–16.

issue. The judge is forced to flip back and forth in the brief to figure out the content of the issues. Furthermore, six issues are a lot to raise on appeal, as discussed in Chapter Six.

ARGUMENT AND CITATIONS OF AUTHORITY ISSUE I 8

ISSUE II 12

* * *

(iii) Statement of the standard or scope of review

ISSUE I

This court has held that a sentencing court's determination with respect to a defendant's acceptance of responsibility is entitled to great deference on review and should not be disturbed unless it is without foundation. *United States v. Spraggins*, 868 F.2d 1541, 1543 (11th Cir. 1989); *United States v. Davis*, 878 F.2d 1299 (11th Cir. 1989). Moreover, the court of appeals shall accept the findings of fact unless they are clearly erroneous. 18 U.S.C. 3742.

ISSUE II

This involves a question of fact. Questions of fact are judged under the clearly erroneous standard. 18 U.S.C. 3742.

Comment: This is excerpted from a brief filed not by a store-front lawyer but by a U.S. Attorney's office located in the Eleventh Circuit. The form of the brief leaves much to be desired. Note the statement of issues: "Issue I" and "Issue II." How does this help the judge? The standards of review are set forth on pages 5 and 6, but the statement of Issue I does not appear until page 8, and the statement of Issue II is on page 12. The statutory references should have been pinpointed to section 3742(d); the section contains five subsections with many subparts. Nor does the citation follow the *Bluebook*. It should properly have read: 18 U.S.C. § 3742(d) and included a year.

This court reviews findings of fact under the clearly erroneous standard. *In re Teichman*, 774 F.2d 1395, 1397 (9th Cir. 1985). When a case is submitted wholly on documents, less deference is accorded to the district court's findings of fact. *Bulls Corner Restaurant, Inc. v. Director of Federal Emergency Management Agency*, 759 F.2d 500, 502 (5th Cir. 1985).

Comment: This brief was filed in the 1990s. Note the reference to a 1985 case suggesting the distinction between written and oral evidence, a distinction that was wiped out by an amendment to Rule 52(a) effective August 1, 1985.

APPENDIX B

ISSUE STATEMENTS AND POINT HEADINGS

B.1 Examples of Traditional Issue Statements

An easy way to look at examples here is to compare how counsel framed the issues with what the court actually determined them to be. Usually the court is correct; in any event, it has the last word. Consider these examples from actual briefs and subsequent opinions. Note the large number beginning with "whether." In your mind, restate the issue in a simple declaratory sentence or interrogatory favoring you.

Issue Formulation: Appellant/Petitioner, Appellee/Respondent, and Court

Petitioner: After a law enforcement officer has completed a stop for a traffic infraction, does the continued detention of the driver to conduct a dog sniff, without probable cause or reasonable suspicion to believe that the vehicle contains contraband, violate the Fourth Amendment's prohibition against unreasonable seizures?[1]

Respondent: Whether, in the context of a traffic stop, a police officer may conduct a dog sniff of a vehicle after issuing a written traffic warning, where the traffic stop was not unreasonably prolonged.[2]

Court: This case presents the question whether the Fourth Amendment tolerates a dog sniff conducted after completion of a traffic stop. We hold that a police stop exceeding the time needed to handle the matter for which the stop was made violates the Constitution's shield against unreasonable seizures.[3]

Comment: The petitioner issue presented is excellent. It clearly explains who the relevant parties are and what the relevant legal issue. The Court latched on to the "completion" language in the opinion. The Government's issue presented is also good, except that it uses the "whether" format.

---

1. Brief for Petitioner at i, Rodriguez v. United States, 135 S. Ct. 1609 (2015) (No. 13–9972), 2014 WL 6466938, at *i.

2. Brief for the United States at I, Rodriguez v. United States, 135 S. Ct. 1609 (2015) (No. 13–9972), 2014 WL 7205515, at *I.

3. Rodriguez v. United States, 135 S. Ct. 1609, 1612 (2015).

Petitioner: Once a co-tenant has expressly told police officers that they may not enter his home, does the Fourth Amendment allow the officers to obtain valid consent to do so by removing the objecting tenant from the scene against his will and then seeking permission from the other tenant shortly thereafter?[4]

Respondent: Whether petitioner's objection to police entry into his shared apartment barred the police from later conducting a warrantless search of the apartment based on the consent of his cotenant obtained after petitioner had been removed from the premises for a domestic violence investigation and then lawfully arrested for a prior robbery.[5]

Court: Our cases firmly establish that police officers may search jointly occupied premises if one of the occupants consents. In *Georgia v. Randolph*, we recognized a narrow exception to this rule, holding that the consent of one occupant is insufficient when another occupant is present and objects to the search. In this case, we consider whether *Randolph* applies if the objecting occupant is absent when another occupant consents. Our opinion in *Randolph* took great pains to emphasize that its holding was limited to situations in which the objecting occupant is physically present. We therefore refuse to extend *Randolph* to the very different situation in this case, where consent was provided by an abused woman well after her male partner had been removed from the apartment they shared.[6]

Comment: Both issues presented are excellent (although the Government uses the "whether" format). Note how the Court picked up on the fact that this was a domestic violence incident, important factual information included in the Government's issue presented.

Petitioner:

1. Whether a non-custodial parent can invoke the Indian Child Welfare Act of 1978 (ICWA), 25 U.S.C. §§ 1901-63, to block an adoption voluntarily and lawfully initiated by a non-Indian parent under state law.

---

4. Brief for Petitioner at i, Fernandez v. California, 134 S. Ct. 1126 (2014) (No. 12–7822), 2013 WL 3972445, at *i.

5. Respondent's Brief on the Merits at i, Fernandez v. California, 134 S. Ct. 1126 (2014) (No. 12–7822), 2013 WL 5400266, at *i.

6. Fernandez v. California, 134 S. Ct. 1126, 1129–30 (2014) (footnotes and citations omitted).

2. Whether ICWA defines "parent" in 25 U.S.C. § 1903(9) to include an unwed biological father who has not complied with state law rules to attain legal status as a parent.[7]

Respondent:

1. Whether an Indian child's biological father who has expressly acknowledged that he is the child's father and has established that he is the father through DNA testing is the child's "parent" within the meaning of the Indian Child Welfare Act of 1978, 25 U.S.C. §§ 1901-1963.

2. Whether the ICWA governs state proceedings to determine the custody of a minor who all parties concede to be an "Indian child" within the meaning of the Act.[8]

Court: Contrary to the State Supreme Court's ruling, we hold that 25 U. S. C. §1912(f)—which bars involuntary termination of a parent's rights in the absence of a heightened showing that serious harm to the Indian child is likely to result from the parent's "continued custody" of the child—does not apply when, as here, the relevant parent never had custody of the child. We further hold that §1912(d)— which conditions involuntary termination of parental rights with respect to an Indian child on a showing that remedial efforts have been made to prevent the "breakup of the Indian family"—is inapplicable when, as here, the parent abandoned the Indian child before birth and never had custody of the child. Finally, we clarify that §1915(a), which provides placement preferences for the adoption of Indian children, does not bar a non-Indian family like Adoptive Couple from adopting an Indian child when no other eligible candidates have sought to adopt the child.[9]

Comment: Both parties, unfortunately, used the "whether" format and included unnecessary citations and acronyms. But, the parties wrote the questions persuasively and included important facts that were persuasive to their case.

---

7. Brief for Petitioners at i, Adoptive Couple v. Baby Girl, 133 S. Ct. 2552 (2013) (No. 12–399), 2013 WL 633597, at *i.

8. Brief for Respondent Birth Father at i, Adoptive Couple v. Baby Girl, 133 S. Ct. 2552 (2013) (No. 12–399), 2013 WL 1191183, at *i.

9. Adoptive Couple v. Baby Girl, 133 S. Ct. 2552, 2557 (2013).

Appellant:

1. Whether the district court erred in failing to apply the proper standard relating to constructive discharge, and in injecting a "notice" requirement into that doctrine?

2. Whether the district court was clearly erroneous in holding that appellant was required to give additional notice to the president of the employer-corporation prior to resigning?

Appellee:

1. Whether the district court was clearly erroneous in finding that the employee's claim for gender discrimination by constructive discharge could not be sustained since the employee prematurely and precipitately resigned without informing her employer of the purportedly intolerable working conditions prior to her resignation?

2. Whether the district court was clearly erroneous in finding that the employee's resignation was premature and precipitate since she voluntarily chose to resign rather than inform her employer of the purportedly intolerable working conditions?

Court: In the primary appeal at No. 89-3727 we must determine whether the district court erred as a matter of law in injecting a notice requirement into the doctrine of constructive discharge under Title VII of the Civil Rights Act of 1964, as amended, 42 U.S.C. §§ 2000e–2000h(6). Subsumed in this problem are two somewhat related but distinct subordinate inquiries: whether the existence of notice *vel non* is a question of fact, and if so, was the court clearly erroneous in finding no notice (a) on the basis of imputed notice to the employer based on actions of and notice to the employer, or (b) on the basis of inferred notice to the employer given the small size of the business enterprise and repeated unsuccessful efforts by the employee to reach the employer to complain about acts of gender discrimination.

Comment: The appellant's issues presented leaves out important, persuasive information that the court mentions in the opinion and that the appellee even brings up. From reading the appellant's issues you would not know that the case involved gender discrimination.

Appellant:

1. Are there genuine issues of material fact as to the question of whether a contract was formed, or whether an enforceable contract was breached?

2. Did the district court err in granting defendant's motion for summary judgment?

Appellee:

1. Whether the entry of summary judgment by the lower court in favor of the appellee and against the appellant as to all claims asserted by the appellant was proper based upon the record presented to the court by the parties.

2. In defending the summary judgment motion in the court below, whether Automotive Management Systems, Incorporated failed to make a showing sufficient to establish the existence of an element essential to its case and on which it would bear the burden of proof at trial.

Court: Presented for decision is a rather straightforward issue of contract law requiring us to decide whether there was an acceptance of an offer to sublease space in a shopping mall.

Comment: The parties make this case much harder than it needed to be!

———————————

Appellant:

1. Whether the trial court erred in its conclusion of law that all defendants were part of a partnership under Pennsylvania law.

2. Whether the trial court erred as a matter of law in applying 59 Pa. C.S.A. § 328, holding all defendants, in the alternative, to be partners by estoppel in the absence of evidence that Rose Fantasia consented to representation as a partner and in the absence of evidence that plaintiff relied on representation that any appellant was a partner.

3. Whether the court erred in concluding that transfers of residential real estate between family members constitute wrongful acts of partners within the meaning of 59 Pa. C.S.A. § 325.

4. Whether the trial court erred in failing to apply the Statute of Frauds, 33 P.S. § 3.

5. Whether the trial court erred in failing to apply the Statute of Frauds of the Uniform Commercial Code, 13 Pa. C.S.A. § 2201.

6. Whether the trial court erred in failing to interpret the written credit application as a guaranty according to the expressed understanding of the parties.

7. Whether the trial court erred in failing to consider the defenses of fraud, or alternatively, mutual mistake in its interpretation of the credit application.

8. Whether the entry of judgment against Rose Fantasia in favor of Jeff Pozsonyi violates the due process clause of the Fifth Amendment of the United States Constitution, since Jeffrey Pozsonyi did not file any pleading against Rose Fantasia.

9. Whether the imposition of prejudgment interest in favor of Jeff Pozsonyi is inequitable.

10. Whether fact findings of the trial court are clearly erroneous.

Appellee:

I. Did the United States District Court err in its determination that appellee had established by a preponderance of the evidence presented at trial that appellants along with Amalia Fantasia and Fantasia Enterprises, Inc., were jointly and severally liable for the debt owed to appellee in the sum of $41,808.12.

(Appellee contends the answer is no.)

(Appellants contend the answer is yes.)

II. Did the United States District Court abuse its discretion in denying appellants' motion to alter or amend the judgment, or alternatively, to grant a new trial?

(Appellee contends the answer is no.)

(Appellants contend the answer is yes.)

Court: The major question for decision is whether findings of fact made by the district court in a nonjury trial were clearly erroneous.

Comment: Do you get the feeling that the appellant lost the case the moment ten contentions were presented on appeal?

———————————

Appellant:

I. Appellant was convicted of offenses for which she was not charged by the grand jury, thus violating her right to due process as to counts 2 to 24.

II. The statement by the district court that it would give a requested instruction, but then did not, violated Rule 30 and appellant was prejudiced.

National Institute for Trial Advocacy

III. As a matter of law the appellant as an officer of a corporation cannot legally conspire with herself as an individual, and the possibility of conviction on an impermissible legal theory requires reversal. Alternatively, the court erred in not giving the instruction requested by the defense (see preceding argument).

IV. Neither the mail fraud nor the wire fraud statute (18 U.S.C. §1341 and §1343) allows conviction where the person defrauded is not the person from whom the money or property is obtained.

V. The failure of the instructions to require the jury to find that the alleged mailings, wire communications, and falsities occurred on the dates alleged in the indictment requires reversal.

VI. The district court's failure to make a determination as to appellant's objection to the pre-sentence report is a violation of Rule 32 and requires remand for resentencing.

Appellee:

A. The instruction regarding the substantive offenses and the conviction of the substantive offenses were proper either because defendant directly participated, or because defendant was vicariously responsible for the acts of co-conspirators.

B. The court properly complied with Fed. R. Crim P. 30 and the defendant failed to properly object to the purported violation and such purported violation did not constitute plain error nor was the defendant prejudiced by it.

C. The remote possibility that the jury could have concluded that the defendant, as an officer of the corporation, conspired with herself does not require reversal.

D. The instruction concerning corporate responsibility was accurate and the defendant was not prejudiced by it.

E. The mail fraud and wire fraud convictions were proper in light of *McNally v. United States*, 483 U.S. 350 (1987).

F. The instructions accurately set forth the law regarding the requirement that the jury find that the crimes occurred on certain dates.

G. A hearing was held on defendant's objections to the presentence report and the court made findings regarding those objections.

Court:

The appellant presents many contentions on appeal, but her major argument is that the government made a basic change in its theory during trial to prove her culpability on the substantive counts. She argues that although she was prepared to defend the allegation that she directly participated in these offenses, she was not prepared when the government proceeded to rely also on the vicarious liability theory approved in *Pinkerton v. United States*, 328 U.S. 640 (1945), *reh'g denied*, 328 U.S. 818 (1946). *Pinkerton* teaches that a party to a conspiracy may be held responsible for a substantive offense committed by a co-conspirator in furtherance of the conspiracy even if that party did not participate in the substantive offense or have knowledge of it.

The appellant also argues that the trial court erred in its instructions to the jury, to wit: in instructing that she could be held culpable under the *Pinkerton* theory; in failing to deliver a requested instruction that she could not conspire with herself; in improperly describing corporate responsibility; and in failing to instruct that the jury must find that the crimes occurred on the exact dates alleged in the indictment. Additionally, she argues that the holding of *McNally v. United States*, 483 U.S. 350 (1987), precludes a mail or wire fraud conviction in her case and that the court violated the hearing requirements relating to presentence investigation matters as required by Fed. R. Crim. P. 32.

Comment: Until you read the excerpt from the court's opinion, did you have any idea of the appellant's major argument?

B.2 Examples of "Deep" Issue Statements

Here are a few examples of the "deep issue" formulation that provides a bit of background leading up to the issue presented.

Petitioner:

The Department of Homeland Security has long engaged in "a regular practice * * * known as 'deferred action,'" in which the Secretary "exercis[es] [his] discretion" to forbear, "for humanitarian reasons or simply for [his] own convenience," from removing particular aliens from the United States. *Reno v. American-Arab Anti-Discrimination Comm.*, 525 U.S. 471, 483-484 (1999). On November 20, 2014, the Secretary issued a memorandum (Guidance) directing his subordinates to establish a process for considering deferred action for certain aliens who have lived in the United States for at least five years and either came here as children or already have children who are U.S. citizens or permanent residents.

The questions presented are:

1. Whether a State that voluntarily provides a subsidy to all aliens with deferred action has Article III standing and a justiciable cause of action under the Administrative Procedure Act (APA), 5 U.S.C. 500 et seq., to challenge the Guidance because it will lead to more aliens having deferred action.

2. Whether the Guidance is arbitrary and capricious or otherwise not in accordance with law.

3. Whether the Guidance is invalid because it did not go through the APA's notice-and-comment rulemaking procedures.

4. Whether the Guidance violates the Take Care Clause of the Constitution, Art. II, § 3.[10]

Respondent:

The Executive Branch unilaterally created a program that would deem four million unlawfully present aliens to be "lawfully present" and eligible for a host of benefits including work authorization. Pet. App. 413a. This program, called DAPA, goes far beyond forbearing from removal or enforcement discretion.

The district court entered a preliminary injunction of DAPA under the Administrative Procedure Act. The court of appeals affirmed. Both courts explained that the injunction does not require the Executive to remove any alien and does not impair the Executive's ability to prioritize aliens for removal. In fact, on the same day it announced DAPA, the Executive issued a separate memorandum defining categories of aliens prioritized for removal. This lawsuit has never challenged that separate memorandum. The questions presented are:

1.a. Whether at least one plaintiff State has a personal stake in this controversy sufficient for standing, when record evidence confirms that DAPA will cause States to incur millions of dollars in injuries.

1.b. Whether DAPA—which affirmatively grants lawful presence and work-authorization eligibility—is reviewable agency action under the APA.

---

10. Brief for the Petitioners at I, United States v. Texas, 136 S. Ct. 2271 (2016) (No. 15–674), 2016 WL 836758, at *I.

2. Whether DAPA violates immigration and related benefits statutes, when Congress has created detailed criteria for which aliens may be lawfully present, work, and receive benefits in this country.

3. Whether DAPA—one of the largest changes in immigration policy in our Nation's history—is subject to the APA's notice-and-comment requirement.

4. Whether the Guidance violates the Take Care Clause of the Constitution, Art. II, § 3.[11]

Comment: The issues raised in *United States v. Texas* were several and complex, including the justiciability issue of standing. Still, both parties far exceeded the length recommended by Garner. While the issue statements are persuasive, cutting out citations and some of the procedural history could shorten the statements.

Respondents:

Under federal law, health insurers and employer-sponsored group health plans generally must cover certain preventive health services, including contraceptive services prescribed for women by their doctors. Petitioners object to providing contraceptive coverage on religious grounds but are eligible for a regulatory accommodation that would allow them to opt out of the contraceptive-coverage requirement. Petitioners contend, however, that the accommodation itself violates the Religious Freedom Restoration Act of 1993 (RFRA), 42 U.S.C. 2000bb et seq., because the government will require or encourage third parties to provide petitioners' employees and students with separate contraceptive coverage if petitioners opt out. The question presented is:

Whether RFRA entitles petitioners not only to opt out of providing contraceptive coverage themselves, but also to prevent the government from arranging for third parties to provide separate coverage to the affected women.[12]

Comment: This deep issue formulation is 134 words long. It persuasively explains a complicated issue to the Court.

---

11. Brief for the State Respondents at I, United States v. Texas, 136 S. Ct. 2271 (2016) (No. 15–674), 2016 WL 1213267, at *I.

12. Brief for the Respondents at I, Zubik v. Burwell, 136 S. Ct. 1557 (2016) (Nos. 14–1418, 14–1453, 14–1505, 15–35, 15–105, 15–119, 15–191), 2016 WL 537623, at *I.

Petitioners:

Section 36B of the Internal Revenue Code, which was enacted as part of the Patient Protection and Affordable Care Act ("ACA"), authorizes federal tax-credit subsidies for health insurance coverage that is purchased through an "Exchange established by the State under section 1311" of the ACA.

The question presented is whether the Internal Revenue Service ("IRS") may permissibly promulgate regulations to extend tax-credit subsidies to coverage purchased through Exchanges established by the federal government under section 1321 of the ACA.[13]

Respondents:

Whether the Treasury Department permissibly interprets 26 U.S.C. 36B to make the Affordable Care Act's federal premium tax credits available to eligible taxpayers through the Exchanges in every State.[14]

Comment: In seventy-nine words, the Petitioner explains the heart of the case, which was one of statutory interpretation. The Respondents' issue presented could have benefitted from more information.

Respondent:

In accordance with longstanding policy, the President, through the actions of the Secretary of State, has recognized no state as having sovereignty over the city of Jerusalem, and has instead left this highly sensitive issue to be resolved through negotiations by the foreign parties to that dispute. In order to implement that policy, the Secretary of State lists "Jerusalem" instead of "Israel" as the birthplace in passports, and in consular reports of births abroad, of U.S. citizens born in that city. In 2002, Congress enacted the Foreign Relations Authorization Act, Fiscal Year 2003, Pub. L. No. 107-228, 116 Stat. 1350, Section 214(d) of which states that "[f]or purposes of the registration of birth, certification of nationality, or issuance of a passport of a United States citizen born in the city of Jerusalem, the Secretary [of State] shall, upon the request of the citizen or the citizen's legal guardian, record the place of birth as Israel." 116 Stat. 1366. The question presented is:

---

13. Brief for Petitioners at i, King v. Burwell, 135 S. Ct. 2480 (2015) (No. 14–114), 2014 WL 7386999, at *i.

14. Brief for the Respondents at I, King v. Burwell, 135 S. Ct. 2480 (2015) (No. 14–114), 2015 WL 349885, at *I.

Whether Section 214(d) impermissibly infringes the President's power to recognize foreign sovereigns.[15]

Comment: The deep issue formulation allows the separation of powers issue to be set up clearly. This issue presented would have been better if the citations had been omitted, the "whether" formulation not used, and the first paragraph broken up into two paragraphs.

B.3   Examples of Point Headings

Petitioner:

II. Applying The Challenged Regulations To Petitioners Does Not Satisfy RFRA's Strict Scrutiny Test

    A. The Government Has Not Established that Requiring Petitioners To Comply with the Contraceptive Mandate Furthers a Compelling Interest

        1. The government's compelling interest arguments are defeated by the pervasive non-religious exemptions to the mandate

        2. The government's arguments are independently undermined by the religious exemptions that it has granted

        3. The government's arguments fare even worse as to employers in the Little Sisters' situation

    B. The Government Has Not Established that Requiring Petitioners To Comply Via the Regulatory Mechanism Is the Least Restrictive Means of Furthering the Interests It Asserts[16]

Respondent:

II. The accommodation is the least-restrictive means of furthering the government's compelling interest in providing women with full and equal health coverage

    A. The regulations further the government's compelling interest in ensuring that women receive full and equal health coverage, including contraceptive coverage

---

15. Brief for the Respondent at I, Zivotofsky ex rel. Zivotofsky v. Kerry, 135 S. Ct. 2076 (2015) (No. 13-628), 2014 WL 4726506, at *I.

16. Brief for Petitioners in Nos. 15-35, 15-105, 15-119, & 15-191, at vi–vii, Zubik v. Burwell, 136 S. Ct. 1557 (2016) (Nos. 14–1418, 14–1453, 14–1505, 15–35, 15–105, 15–119, 15–191), 2016 WL 93989, at *vi–vii.

1. The government has a compelling interest in ensuring that women's health coverage includes contraceptive coverage

2. The Affordable Care Act's provisions governing grandfathered plans and small employers do not undermine the compelling nature of the government's interest

3. The regulatory exemption for houses of worship does not undermine the compelling nature of the government's interest

B. The accommodation is the least restrictive means of ensuring that women receive full and equal health coverage, including contraceptive coverage

   1. The government's interest in securing full and equal health coverage for women requires the provision of contraceptive coverage without financial, administrative, or logistical burdens

   2. Petitioners' proposals do not qualify as less-restrictive alternatives

   3. Petitioners do not endorse an alternative notice procedure, which is in any event not a valid less-restrictive means[17]

Comment: Both parties effectively weaved in facts and legal standards to allow their table of contents to read like an outline of the argument. A judge reviewing these tables would be able to quickly recall the arguments in the briefs. Notice how the Government as Respondent leads with the affirmative points before rebutting the Petitioners' arguments.

———————

Respondent:

I. PETITIONER'S ARGUMENTS ARE BASED ON POLICY, NOT LAW

A. All Three Branches Of The Government Have Historically Rejected Petitioner's Reading Of The PDA

B. Other Federal And State Statutes May Address The Policy Concerns Petitioner Advances Here

C. UPS Has Elected As A Matter Of Corporate Discretion To Provide More Expansive Accommodations

———————

17. Brief for the Respondents at III–IV, Zubik v. Burwell, 136 S. Ct. 1557 (2016) (Nos. 14–1418, 14–1453, 14–1505, 15–35, 15–105, 15–119, 15–191), 2016 WL 537623, at *III–IV.

II. THE PDA DOES NOT PRECLUDE EMPLOYERS FROM AWARDING OR WITHHOLDING BENEFITS PURSUANT TO NEUTRAL CRITERIA

A. Text

B. History

C. Structure

III. PETITIONER FAILED TO RAISE A GENUINE ISSUE OF MATERIAL FACT WITH RESPECT TO HER DISPARATE-TREATMENT CLAIM[18]

Comment: Although some of these point headings are good, the ones under Roman numeral II are unhelpful. They do not remind the judge at all what the statutory construction arguments are, other than that they involve textual, historical, and structural arguments.

Respondent:

I. The Constitution grants the President exclusive power to recognize foreign states and their territorial boundaries

    A. The Constitution assigns exclusively to the Executive the authority to recognize foreign states and governments, including their territorial boundaries

        1. Article II of the Constitution assigns the recognition power to the President

            a. The Reception Clause confers recognition power on the President

            b. The President's other foreign-affairs powers reinforce his recognition power

            c. The Founding generation understood the Executive's recognition power to include the exclusive authority to decide whether recognition is appropriate

        2. Structural and functional considerations confirm that the President's recognition power is exclusive

    B. Historical practice confirms that the Executive Branch has sole authority regarding recognition

---

18. Brief for Respondent at iii, Young v. United Parcel Service, Inc., 135 S. Ct. 1338 (2015) (No. 12–1226), 2014 WL 5464086, at *iii.

1. The Executive has consistently asserted sole authority over recognition, including recognition of territorial boundaries

2. Congress has acquiesced in the President's sole recognition power

3. Petitioner's attempt to demonstrate that Congress has exercised recognition power is unavailing

C. This Court and individual Justices have repeatedly stated that the Constitution assigns recognition authority to the President alone

II. Section 214(d) unconstitutionally interferes with the President's exclusive recognition power

A. The Executive has constitutional authority to determine the content of passports as it relates to recognition

1. The Executive possesses constitutional authority over passports as instruments of diplomacy

2. Any passport legislation must be in furtherance of Congress's enumerated powers, and may not interfere with the Executive's recognition determinations

B. Section 214(d) unconstitutionally forces the Executive to communicate to foreign sovereigns that the United States views Israel as exercising sovereignty over Jerusalem

1. The place-of-birth designation on passports and reports of birth abroad implements the Executive's recognition policy

2. Section 214(d) unconstitutionally interferes with the Executive's core recognition power[19]

Comment: This is a complex set of point headings that gets down to outline levels that most arguments do not reach. Nonetheless, a person reading this table gets a solid understanding of the arguments that the Government presented in the case.

---

19. Brief for the Respondent at III–IV, Zivotofsky ex rel. Zivotofsky v. Kerry, 135 S. Ct. 2076 (2015) (No. 13-628), 2014 WL 4726506, at *III–IV.

Appendix C

The Brief: Statement of the Case

C.1   Examples of Statements of Facts

What follows is a sampling of statements of facts. Are they clear? Readable? Could they have been shortened?

The Tucson Airport Authority (hereinafter "TAA") is a nonprofit Arizona corporation which operates the Tucson International Airport pursuant to A.R.S. §§ 2–311 and 2–312. The Airport exists for the purpose of movement of arriving and departing airline passengers, and all the streets surrounding the airport are private, nondedicated roadways constructed, maintained and operated exclusively with revenues derived from the use of Airport facilities without benefit of local tax dollars or highway user funds.

The TAA does not collect "taxes," nor does it get "tax" dollars from the City of Tucson. It collects revenue from users of the Airport. All its users, including but not limited to the airlines, car rental agencies and facilities, the telephone company, banks with twenty-four-hour teller machines on the property, shoeshine establishments, gift shops, taxis, limousines, off-airport bus services, parking space users, insurance companies vending insurance policies through vending machines, concessionaires vending food and beverages from vending machines, restaurants, gift shops selling books and newspapers and other items, users of advertising space on the walls at the airport, pay rent or fees to the TAA. The rents and fees are calculated upon one or more negotiated formulae. These formulae may include total space occupied, total revenue generated per month, number of passengers using the airport, result of competitive bidding, and others.

The TAA Board of Directors authorized the collection of rental fees from newsracks by the Airport staff. The rental suggested for the newsracks at that time was an amount of $23.69 per month per newsrack, which reflects a space improvement charge and cost of custodial services, or 15 percent of gross sales, whichever is higher. Rental is routinely charged by other airports across the country and paid by newspaper publishers who vend newspapers through newsracks at airports. For example, *USA Today* pays $209 per rack, per year to the Denver airport, $60 per rack, per year to the Salt Lake City airport, $316 per rack, per year to the Dayton airport, and $1,165 per rack, per year to the Detroit airport.

Phoenix Newspapers, Inc. (hereinafter "PNI") is an Arizona corporation and publisher of an Arizona newspaper, and is vending newspapers through vending machines at the Airport. It delivers newspapers through a network of distributors and has very limited home deliveries in the Tucson area. In Tucson, the bulk of PNI's newspapers are distributed through gift shops, grocery stores, and convenience markets like Circle K and 7-Eleven. These various distributors, including the concessionaires at the Airport, get the daily papers from PNI at wholesale, or twenty cents each for dailies, and 53 cents each for Sunday papers. The distributors in turn sell those newspapers to the retailers at 29 cents each for dailies, and 89 cents for the Sunday papers, thereby making a profit of 9 cents each for the weekly papers and 36 cents each for the Sunday papers. The retailers in turn sell the dailies for 35 cents and the Sunday papers for one dollar, thereby making a 6-cent profit on the dailies and an 11-cent profit on the Sunday paper.

When the newspapers are sold through the newsracks instead of through gift shops, grocery stores, and convenience markets, the profit margin for the distributor goes up to 15 cents for the dailies and to 47 cents for the Sunday paper. This helps the newspapers meet the minimum $300 per month guaranteed to their distributors. It also directly competes with income derived from TAA from sale of newspapers sold through the newsstands. PNI does not sell newspapers through newsracks in front of or nearby convenience stores, gift shops, and grocery stores so that it does not compete.

Comment: This statement is wordy and unfocused. At this point, it is not entirely clear what the case is about or who the relevant parties are in the case.

The petitioner's conviction stems from her involvement with a narcotics distributor. The evidence at trial showed that from 1980 to 1986, the distributor controlled a large narcotics operation in Chicago, Illinois. He purchased cocaine and heroin from importers and (with the help of others) distributed it through several gambling establishments and lounges that he owned or controlled. He used the profits to purchase real and personal property, which he frequently placed in the names of other persons, including the petitioner and another codefendant.

In 1988, a grand jury returned a twenty-three-count indictment against the petitioner and others arising from the distributor's drug operation and his attempts to conceal assets and income. The indictment charged the distributor with managing a continuing criminal enterprise, and it charged the others with conspiracy to violate, and violation of, various narcotics statutes and related laws. Most pertinent to this case, Count 20 of the indictment alleged that the distributor, the petitioner and another codefendant joined in a conspiracy to defraud the federal government, in violation of 18 U.S.C. § 371. Count 20 identified two objects of the conspiracy: (1) impairment of the efforts of the Internal Revenue Service to ascertain income taxes (the IRS object); and (2) impairment of the efforts of the Drug Enforcement Administration to ascertain forfeitable assets (the DEA object).

The evidence relevant to Count 20 showed that the distributor held and controlled assets in the names of both the petitioner and the other codefendant. He arranged for the codefendant to become (without capital contribution) the majority shareholder of Blacom Corporation, a company that he used to control various properties he acquired through his drug operation. He also placed real estate and a Mercedes Benz automobile that he used in the codefendant's name. Following the same modus operandi, he purchased a tavern and an adjoining building in the petitioner's name. The petitioner filed tax returns claiming the tavern as her own in order to conceal the distributor's ownership of the business and his underreporting of income. The distributor also purchased a $35,000 Jaguar automobile in the petitioner's name, and structured the payments on the car to evade federal reporting requirements for cash payments in excess of $10,000.

During the trial, the petitioner unsuccessfully moved for a severance, arguing that the government had failed to prove that she knew the distributor was a drug dealer or that she was aware of the DEA object of the conspiracy. At the close of trial, the petitioner proposed jury instructions that would have required the jury to find that she knew the object of the conspiracy was to impede the IRS in ascertaining the distributor's taxes. She also asked the court to require the jury to identify, through special interrogatories, whether the petitioner had knowledge of the IRS and DEA objects of the conspiracy. The court denied both the proposed jury instructions and the request for special interrogatories. The jury returned a general verdict of guilty against the defendants on Count 20.

Comment: This statement of the facts is more focused. The identity of the parties, however, is confusing. It would be better if the writer used the petitioner's name rather than the status designation.

A. Timothy Lee Hurst's Crime

On the morning of May 2, 1998, there was a murder and robbery at a Popeye's Fried Chicken restaurant in Pensacola. JA27. Cynthia Harrison, a young assistant manager, was scheduled to begin work at eight that morning. JA27. Around 10:30, other employees entered the restaurant and found the restaurant's safe unlocked and open, its contents ($375 and the previous day's receipts) missing. JA28- 3 29. They also found Ms. Harrison, dead on the floor inside the freezer. JA28-29.

Black electrical tape bound Ms. Harrison's hands and covered her mouth. JA29. She had suffered "at least sixty slash and stab wounds," including on her face, neck, back, and arms. JA129. The wounds, which were consistent with those a box cutter would inflict, included some so deep that they "cut through the tissue into the underlying bone." JA29. Although it appeared someone had tried to clean the scene, a "significant amount" of Ms. Harrison's blood remained on the floor, JA129, and blood on her pant knees indicated she had been kneeling in it, JA29. Her blood was also on a box cutter that lay nearby. JA129.

Other than Ms. Harrison, the only employee scheduled to work at eight that morning was Hurst. JA27-28. Evidence at trial showed that Ms. Harrison and Hurst were alone in the restaurant at the time of the murder. JA27-28. Evidence also showed that the box cutter at the scene was like one Hurst displayed a few days earlier but not the type used at Popeye's. JA29. And evidence showed that the electrical tape that bound Ms. Harrison was similar to tape later found in Hurst's car. JA29.

According to Hurst's friend Michael Williams, Hurst had previously talked about robbing Popeye's and subsequently admitted murdering Ms. Harrison with a box cutter. JA130. A second friend, Lee-Lee Smith, similarly testified that Hurst admitted the murder and robbery. JA130; see also JA597-99. According to Smith, Hurst came to Smith's house that morning and asked Smith to keep a container filled 4 with the robbery's proceeds. JA30. Smith further testified that he washed Hurst's bloody pants and threw away Hurst's shoes and bloodstained socks. JA30. Police later recovered the shoes and other evidence (including Ms. Harrison's driver's license and coin purse, a bank bag marked with "Popeye's" and Ms. Harrison's name, and a bank deposit slip bearing Hurst's fingerprints) from a trash can at Smith's house. JA30-31.

Authorities promptly apprehended Hurst and charged him with murder. From the beginning, Hurst denied that he ever made it to work that morning, explaining that car troubles kept him away. JA31. He provided a statement to police, recounting his supposed activities that day and insisting that he was not at Popeye's when Ms. Harrison was murdered. JA31. Hurst was convicted of murder and twice sentenced to death. JA289, 297.[1]

Comment: This statement is very interesting, but not overly sensational, despite the facts. Notice how the brief writer uses headings to break up the statement of facts. A second section, which provides an overview of Florida's death penalty sentencing framework, is omitted from this excerpt. Notice also the frequent citations to the joint appendix.

A. Factual Background

Just after midnight on March 27, 2012, petitioner Dennys Rodriguez and his passenger, Scott Pollman, were driving westward from Omaha, Nebraska, to Norfolk, Nebraska, on Nebraska State Highway 275. J.A. 17-18, 20, 24. About twenty miles into their trip, just outside the small community of Valley, Nebraska, Mr. Rodriguez drove past Officer Morgan Struble of the Valley Police Department. J.A. 35, 39. Officer Struble was positioned in a turnaround median watching for "speeders and intoxicated drivers and so on." J.A. 36. Although Mr. Rodriguez was not speeding or driving erratically, Officer Struble immediately pulled onto the highway and began traveling westbound behind Mr. Rodriguez's Mercury Mountaineer. J.A. 19, 44.

Officer Struble pursued Mr. Rodriguez's vehicle until he was approximately three to four car-lengths behind, with Mr. Rodriguez traveling in the right lane of the four-lane divided highway and Officer Struble staying in the left lane. J.A. 44-45. From this vantage point, Officer Struble saw the passenger-side tires of Mr. Rodriguez's vehicle cross for about two seconds over the line separating the right lane of traffic from the shoulder of the highway. J.A. 46. Mr. Rodriguez then

---

1. Brief for Respondent at 2–4, Hurst v. Florida, 136 S. Ct. 616 (2016) (No. 14–7505), 2015 WL 4607695, at *2–4.

quickly corrected back into his lane of traffic. J.A. 48-49. Officer Struble decided to stop Mr. Rodriguez for driving on the shoulder of the road. J.A. 44. He pulled over Mr. Rodriguez's vehicle at approximately 12:06 a.m. J.A. 26.

As Officer Struble approached Mr. Rodriguez's Mountaineer from the passenger's side, he noticed a strong odor of air freshener. J.A. 20. At the vehicle, he spoke first with Mr. Rodriguez, obtained Mr. Rodriguez's license, registration, and proof of insurance, and asked why he had driven onto the shoulder. J.A. 22, 50. Mr. Rodriguez said he had swerved to avoid a pothole and was agitated when Officer Struble informed him that momentarily crossing onto the shoulder was a traffic violation. *Id.* While Officer Struble was speaking with Mr. Rodriguez from the passenger side of the vehicle, he noticed that the passenger, Mr. Pollman, seemed nervous. J.A. 21. Mr. Pollman pulled his cap low over his eyes, smoked a cigarette, and did not look at Officer Struble. *Id.*

Officer Struble asked Mr. Rodriguez to step out of the vehicle. J.A. 23. Mr. Rodriguez complied and met Officer Struble at the back of the Mountaineer. *Id.* Officer Struble then asked Mr. Rodriguez to accompany him to his patrol car so that the officer could complete some paperwork. *Id.* Mr. Rodriguez asked if he was obligated to do so. *Id.* When Officer Struble said "no," Mr. Rodriguez demurred, saying he would rather just sit in his own vehicle. Id. Officer Struble was taken aback by Mr. Rodriguez's response. J.A. 52-54. Although he had never before had anyone refuse to come back to his patrol car, he claimed that, "in [his] experience," doing so was a "subconscious behavior that people concealing contraband will exhibit." J.A. 53.

Officer Struble returned to his cruiser and called in a request for a records check on Mr. Rodriguez. J.A. 23. He then returned to Mr. Rodriguez's vehicle to talk with Mr. Pollman. J.A. 24. Officer Struble asked Mr. Pollman for his identification and then began inquiring about "where he was coming from and where they were going." *Id.* Mr. Pollman explained that he and Mr. Rodriguez had made the two-hour trip from Norfolk to Omaha to investigate the possibility of purchasing an older-model Ford Mustang. J.A. 60-61. They had decided against buying the car when the owner could not produce the title. *Id.* Officer Struble asked whether they had viewed any pictures of the Ford Mustang before driving to Omaha to see the car in person, and Mr. Pollman replied that they had not. J.A. 25.

Officer Struble had specifically noted Mr. Pollman's nervousness during the officer's first exchange with Mr. Rodriguez at the vehicle. J.A. 21. When he was speaking to Mr. Pollman directly, however, Officer Struble did not testify that he observed any signs of nervousness. Nonetheless, Officer Struble found the plan to purchase the car strange because Officer Struble himself would not have made such a drive without first seeing photos of the vehicle he was thinking about purchasing. J.A. 25-26. He also found their decision to drive from Norfolk to Omaha late on a Tuesday night "abnormal." J.A. 26. It was "common knowledge," he said, that people do not drive a long distance to look at a vehicle and come back at midnight. J.A. 60. But, during the traffic stop, Officer Struble did not ask how long Mr. Pollman and Mr. Rodriguez had been in Omaha, when they had actually looked at the Mustang, or whether they had attended to any other business before or after looking at the car. J.A. 61-63.

After obtaining Mr. Pollman's driver's license, Officer Struble again returned to his cruiser. It was 12:19 a.m.—about thirteen minutes into the traffic stop. J.A. 26-27. Officer Struble had a drug-detection dog in his car, and decided that he was "going to walk [his] dog around the vehicle regardless whether [Mr. Rodriguez] gave [him] permission or not." J.A. 71. However, Officer Struble wanted a second officer to act as a backup because there were two persons involved in the stop. J.A. 71-72. Officer Struble requested a records check on Mr. Pollman's license and then contacted a second officer. Officer Struble then began writing a warning ticket for Mr. Rodriguez. J.A. 26-27.

Officer Struble returned to Mr. Rodriguez's vehicle for a third time, where he returned all of the documents he had collected to Mr. Rodriguez and Mr. Pollman. J.A. 27. Officer Struble then issued a written warning to Mr. Rodriguez for driving on the shoulder of the road. J.A. 76. Officer Struble completed the warning at 12:25 a.m. and said he gave it to Mr. Rodriguez no more than a minute or two later. J.A. 27-28.

By the time Officer Struble had returned Mr. Rodriguez's documents and issued the warning, Officer Struble had "[taken] care of all the business" of the traffic stop. J.A. 70. In his words, he had "got[ten] all the reason for the stop out of the way." *Id.* Nevertheless, because of his plan to conduct the sniff regardless of what else happened, Officer Struble did not allow Mr. Rodriguez to leave. Instead, Officer Struble asked Mr. Rodriguez if "he had an issue with [Officer Struble] walking [his] police service dog around the outside of [the] vehicle." J.A. 29, 72-73. When Mr. Rodriguez replied that he did, in fact, have an issue with that, Officer Struble directed Mr. Rodriguez to turn off the ignition, get out of his vehicle, and stand in front of the cruiser until the second officer arrived. J.A. 29-30. Officer Struble acknowledged that at this point Mr. Rodriguez "was not free to leave." J.A. 69-70.

Officer Struble's backup officer, Deputy Duchelus of the Douglas County Sheriff's Office, arrived at 12:33 a.m. J.A. 32, 98. About one minute later, or approximately seven to eight minutes after Officer Struble had issued the warning for driving on the shoulder, Officer Struble walked his dog around Mr. Rodriguez's Mountaineer. The dog alerted. J.A. 32-33. During a search of the vehicle, officers discovered a bag of methamphetamine. J.A. 34. Mr. Rodriguez was later charged with possession with intent to distribute 50 grams or more of methamphetamine in violation of 21 U.S.C. § 841(a)(1) and (b)(1). J.A. 116.[2]

Comment: From reading this statement, you should be able to ascertain that it comes from the petitioner's brief. The brief writer persuasively wove the facts in a way that made the stop and dog sniff appear to go too far, even though drugs were ultimately found by law enforcement. This was largely accomplished through direct quotes from the officer. Notice again the frequency of citation in the statement.

Petitioner John Yates was convicted under 18 U.S.C. § 1519 for directing his crewmen to throw undersized fish back into the sea, after receiving a civil citation and being told to bring the fish to dock to be destroyed. Section 1519, commonly known as the anti-shredding provision of the Sarbanes-Oxley Act of 2002, criminalizes the destruction, alteration, or falsification of "any record, document, *or tangible object,*" with the intent to obstruct or influence the proper administration of any federal matter. 18 U.S.C. § 1519 (emphasis added). Concluding that a fish is a "tangible object," the court below affirmed Mr. Yates's conviction. Mr. Yates seeks reversal of that decision as it is contrary to this Court's precedents, which require that the phrase be interpreted in the context of its surrounding terms and the statutory scheme.

1. The Sarbanes-Oxley Act was enacted in the wake of the Enron Corporation debacle. *See Lawson v. FMR LLC*, 134 S. Ct. 1158, 1161-62 (2014). Before its collapse, Enron was considered the nation's seventh largest corporation based on its reported revenues. *See United States v. Arthur Andersen LLP*, No. 02- 121, 2002 WL 32153945, at ¶ 2 (S.D. Tex. Mar. 14, 2002) (indictment). Enron's financial prosperity, however, was largely a ruse perpetrated by Enron and its auditor, Arthur Andersen, which assisted Enron in defrauding its

---

2. Brief for Petitioner at 2–6, Rodriguez v. United States, 135 S. Ct. 1609 (2015) (No. 13–9972), 2014 WL 6466938, at *2–6.

investors and reaping millions of dollars for certain insiders. *Id.* at ¶ 8. Anticipating an imminent investigation, Enron and Arthur Andersen devised and orchestrated a plan to purge Enron's corporate records under the guise of enforcing Enron's document retention policy. *Id.* at ¶¶ 5, 9-11. The purge was not limited to the tons of paper records and documents that were shredded; it extended to the computer hard drives and the email system that preserved any documentation relating to Enron. *Id.* at ¶ 10; *see also Arthur Andersen LLP v. United States*, 544 U.S. 696, 698-702 (2005).

Federal obstruction of justice statutes in effect at the time did not criminalize the destruction of documents *prior* to the onset of an official federal investigation. *See generally* 18 U.S.C. §§ 152(8), 1503, 1512(a), (b) (2000). Then-existing laws thus proved to be inadequate to hold Arthur Andersen criminally responsible for its involvement in the document-shredding scandal. *See Arthur Andersen LLP*, 544 U.S. at 702, 706-08. Hence, Congress passed the Sarbanes-Oxley Act to "prevent and punish corporate and criminal fraud, protect the victims of such fraud, preserve evidence of such fraud, and hold wrongdoers accountable for their actions." *Lawson*, 134 S. Ct. at 1162 (quoting S. Rep. No. 107-146 at 2 (2002)); *see also id.* at 1161 ("To safeguard investors in public companies and restore trust in the financial markets following the collapse of Enron Corporation, Congress enacted the Sarbanes-Oxley Act of 2002, 116 Stat. 745.").

2. Mr. Yates, a commercial fisherman, was employed as the captain of the *Miss Katie*. JA 25, 96, 125. On August 23, 2007, when the *Miss Katie* was six days into a commercial harvest of red grouper in the Gulf of Mexico, a Florida Fish and Wildlife Conservation Commission officer boarded the boat to conduct a routine inspection in federal waters. JA 22-25, 125. The officer was federally deputized to enforce size limits for fish by the National Marine Fisheries Service, which is a division of the National Oceanic and Atmospheric Administration under the Department of Commerce. JA 13, 61.

In 2007, federal law required that harvested red grouper be at least 20 inches in length. JA 31, 109, 125 & n.2; 50 C.F.R. § 622.37(d)(2)(ii) (2007). While aboard the *Miss Katie*, the FWC officer noticed three red grouper that appeared to be smaller than 20 inches. JA 23-24, 125. After visually inspecting the grouper harvested by the *Miss Katie's* crew and finding some were "obviously well oversize," the officer measured the grouper that appeared to him to be less than 20 inches long. JA 26-27, 126.

Federal law requires that fish be measured with their mouth open, their mouth closed, their tail pinched, and their tail not pinched, whichever combination yields the "greatest overall measurement." JA 58-59, 109, 125-26 n.2; *see also* 50 C.F.R. § 622.2 (2007). The officer, however, opted only to measure the fish with their mouth closed and their tail pinched. JA 30, 59, 126. Using that method, he determined that 72 grouper measured between 18- 3/4 and 19-3/4 inches. JA 31, 82-84, 126.

Harvesting undersized fish is not a crime; rather, it is a civil violation punishable by a fine or fishing license suspension. *See* 16 U.S.C. §§ 1857(1) (A), (G), 1858(a), (g), 1859(a) (2006). The officer thus issued Mr. Yates a civil citation for harvesting 72 undersized grouper. JA 41, 81, 126. The undersized fish were placed in crates in the *Miss Katie*'s fish box. JA 41. The officer told Mr. Yates to leave them there and return to dock, where the fish would be seized and destroyed. JA 44, 126.

Two days after the *Miss Katie* returned to dock, the officer re-measured the fish in the same manner as he had at sea. JA 46-51, 100, 125-26 & n.2, 127. This time, he determined that 69 (rather than 72) fish measured less than 20 inches. JA 53-54, 126-27. He also found that the majority of the fish at dock measured close to 20 inches long; whereas, a majority at sea measured closer to 19 to 19-1/2 inches. JA 53- 55, 127.

The officer, although he had never previously remeasured fish at dock, surmised that the discrepancies in his measurements meant that the fish he measured at dock were not the same fish he had measured at sea. JA 53-56, 127. His suspicions were later supported by one of the *Miss Katie*'s crewmen, who told federal agents that Mr. Yates had directed the crew to throw the undersized fish overboard and to replace them with fish of legal size. JA 69-70, 127.[3]

Comment: The opening paragraph clearly and concisely explains the parties to the case and the nature of the dispute in terms that are fair but persuasive to the petitioner. The statement also does a good job explaining the history of the statutory provision at issue, which again leans in the petitioner's favor.

---

1. Petitioners' Church Invitation Signs

Petitioner Clyde Reed is the Pastor of Good News Community Church. Pet. App. 54a. Good News exists to bring together like-minded Chris-

---

3. Brief of Petitioner at 2–5, Yates v. United States, 135 S. Ct. 1074 (2015) (No. 13–7451), 2014 WL 2965254, at *2–5 (footnotes omitted).

tians who desire to propagate the Christian faith. App. 98-99 ¶ 14. The Church holds services on Sundays, where attendees worship and fellowship together, learn biblical lessons, sing religious songs, pray for their community, and encourage others whenever possible. Id. at 99, 104 ¶¶ 15, 42.

Good News' religious convictions mandate that it reach as many people as possible with its religious message. App. 104 ¶ 45. It follows the Great Commission, which is Jesus' command that Christians "go and make disciples of all nations, baptizing them in the name of the Father and of the Son and of the Holy Spirit, and teaching them to obey everything I have commanded you." Pet. App. 4a-5a; App. 104 ¶¶ 43-44. Good News follows this "directive by displaying signs announcing their services as an invitation for those in the community to attend." App. 104 ¶ 47; Pet. App. 5a.

The district court correctly ruled that Good News' "signs communicate a religious message" and that they therefore "fall within the category of protected speech." Pet. App. 128a & n.3. Gilbert also admitted that "[Good News'] signs are speech that is protected by the First Amendment." App. 111 ¶ 84; App. 151 ¶ 84. Petitioners' signs typically state the Church's name and the phrase "Your Community Church," provide the Church's website address, phone number, location, and service time, and provide directions. Pet. App. 88a; App. 165.

The Church is very small, averaging between 25-30 adults and 4-10 children per week, Pet. App. 54a, has limited financial means, App. 105 ¶ 50, and has met at various temporary facilities throughout this litigation. At the time Good News filed this case, it met at an elementary school in Gilbert. Pet. App. 87a. In 2008, it moved to a high school just across the Gilbert border in Chandler, Arizona. Id. n.1; ER 495 at 6:8-9:10. It currently meets at a senior living center in Gilbert. See Good News' website, http://www.goodnewspres.com/location.htm ("We worship at Sunrise Senior Living . . . 580 S. Gilbert Road / Gilbert, AZ 85296").

Good News' signs are an essential means by which it invites the public to its services. Pet. App. 54a; App. 105 ¶¶ 50-51. They are inexpensive, require little manpower, and play a critical role in ensuring people know where to find a Church that periodically moves. Id. Pastor Reed finds the church invitation signs "very, very effective" based on his "experience over ten years" using them in Gilbert. ER 505 at 47:17-22.

2. Gilbert's Content-Based Sign Code

Gilbert's Code defines "Sign" as "[a] communication device, structure, or fixture that incorporates graphics, symbols, written copy, and/or lighting," App. 58, and "Temporary Sign" as a "sign not permanently attached to the ground, a wall or building, and not designed or intended for permanent display," *id.* at 70. The Code mandates a permit for all signs, but then exempts certain signs from this requirement. *Id.* at 27-30.

Several of these exemptions define the exempted signs based on content. *Id.* It is through these content-based categories of signs that Gilbert regulates a sign's size, duration, number, location, whether it must relate to an event occurring within the town, and whether it requires a permit. *Id.* at 31-32, 38-39, 84, 89.

Among the Code's relevant categories, and their definitions, both of which are content-based, are the following:

- Political Sign - § 4.402(I): "A temporary sign which supports candidates for office or urges action on any other matter on the ballot of primary, general and special elections relating to any national, state or local election." App. 68.

- Ideological Sign - § 4.402(J): "[A] sign communicating a message or ideas for non-commercial purposes that is not a Construction Sign, Directional Sign, Temporary Directional Sign Relating to a Qualifying Event, Political Sign, Garage Sale Sign, or a sign owned or required by a governmental agency." App. 66–67 (italics omitted).

- Qualifying Event Sign - § 4.402(P): "[A] temporary sign intended to direct pedestrians, motorists, and other passersby to a 'qualifying event.' A 'qualifying event' is any assembly, gathering, activity, or meeting sponsored, arranged, or promoted by a religious, charitable, community service, educational, or other similar non-profit organization." App. 70 (italics omitted).

- Homeowners Association ("HOA") Facilities Temporary Sign - § 4.406(C)(4): "Banners and Directional Signs . . . that display information concerning seasonal or temporary events occurring in the development." App. 54.

- Real Estate Sign - § 4.405(B)(2): "A temporary sign advertising the sale, transfer, lease, or exchange of real property." App. 69.

Since the very outset of this case, Gilbert has classified Petitioners' signs promoting their church services as temporary, Qualifying Event

Signs and applied §4.402(P) of the Sign Code. App. 123 (Notice of Code violation); Pet. App. 117a.

The Code applies different size limitations according to the content-based category into which a sign is placed. The following diagram, which is drawn to scale, depicts this differential treatment:

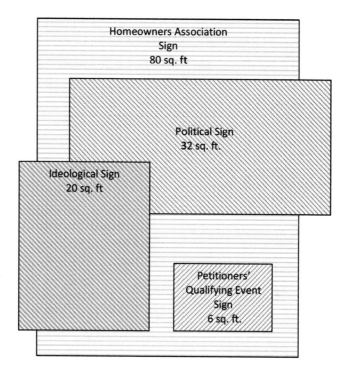

App. 31-32, 38, 54.

The Code also applies different duration limits according to the content-based category into which officials place a sign. Consider the following diagram, which demonstrates the Code's application to five signs that relate to Saturday events that begin at 8:00 a.m., each lasting 12 hours: (1) an ideological sign commenting on any of the events, (2) a polling station open for an election with a primary, (3) an HOA's community festival, (4) a weekend real estate sale, and (5) a religious event hosted by a church:

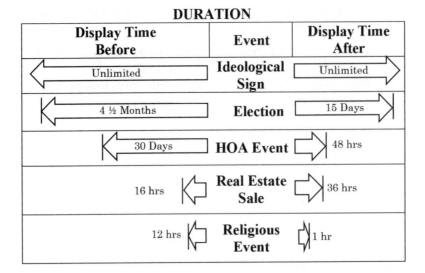

App. 32, 38, 52, 54-55, 84, 93.

The Code also regulates location, whether a sign must relate to a Gilbert event, number, and permit requirements based on a sign's content. The following table sets out this differential treatment:

	Right of Way	Gilbert Event Only	Number	Permit
Political	Yes	No	Unlimited	No
Ideological	Yes	No	Unlimited	No
Qualifying Event	Yes, but Gilbert events only	Yes	Four per property	No
HOA	Yes	Yes (indirectly)	Up to 80 sq. ft. total	Yes
Real Estate	Yes	Yes (indirectly)	15	Yes

App. 31-32, 38-39, 52-55, 84, 89.

Gilbert asserts two interests to justify its differential treatment of temporary signs based on the content-based category into which officials place them: "safety and aesthetics." App. 100 ¶ 24; App. 139 ¶ 24.

There are severe repercussions for violating Gilbert's Code. The penalties "range from a notice of violation to substantial fines and time in jail." ER 169 ¶ 28; ER 156 ¶ 28. See also ER 305 at 20:12- 21:1 (confirming penalties of fines and possible jail time).

3. Gilbert's Content-Based Regulation of Signs Has Persisted Throughout this Litigation

Gilbert's content-based regulation of Good News' church invitation signs began in 2005 and continues unabated. At that time, Good News placed its signs early on Saturday and removed them several hours after services on Sunday. App. 105 ¶ 54.

In July and September 2005, Gilbert enforced its Code against Good News' signs, both times citing the Church for exceeding the time limit for displaying its signs pursuant to § 4.402(P). Pet. App. 117a; App. 123-26. Gilbert officials confiscated one of Good News' signs, which Pastor Reed had to retrieve from the town offices. ER 514 at 82:24-83:11. After these enforcement actions, Good News reduced the number and duration of its signs to avoid further enforcement. App. 106 ¶ 58.

Because placing more signs for longer periods of time would allow Good News to invite more people to church, App. 106 ¶ 59, Pastor Reed contacted Gilbert's "Code Compliance Department to try to reach some sort of accommodation" in February 2007. Pet. App. 117a. But the "Code Compliance Manager told Good News 'that there is no leniency under the Code, and that the Church would be cited if it was determined that it had violated any of the applicable provisions in the Code.'" *Id.* at 90a.

Good News filed suit one month later, App. 1, challenging the Code, *inter alia*, as a content-based regulation of speech both "on its face and as applied" to the Church's signs. Verified Complaint 8 ¶ 67, Case No. 2:07-cv-00522-SRB, Doc. 1. At that time, § 4.402(P) of the Code applied solely to "Religious Assembly Temporary Directional Signs." *Id.* at 3-4 ¶ 21. But, it contained the same content-based categories (*i.e.*, Political Signs, Ideological Signs, HOA Signs, etc.) that exist on the face of the Code today. *Id.* ¶¶ 18-24. Also like the present Code, it treated signs placed in those categories far better in relation to their size, duration, location, and number, than Good News' church invitation signs. *Id.*

Shortly after this suit was filed, Gilbert stipulated to a preliminary injunction against § 4.402(P) and set out to amend its Code. App. 1-2. It passed an amendment in January 2008, App. 73-79, which left intact each content-based aspect of the Code Good News initially challenged. In sum, the amendment (1) slightly increased the height of Good News' signs to 6 feet but retained their 6 square foot area requirement, App. 76; (2) slightly increased the 15 duration limit on Good News' signs from 2 to 12 hours before an event, *id.*; and

(3) changed § 4.402(P)'s name from "Religious Assembly Temporary Directional Signs" to "Temporary Directional Signs Relating To A Qualifying Event" and added a new definition to the Code's Glossary (which is set out above) for the latter signs. Id. at 75, 77-78. This change subjected some additional nonprofit groups' signs advertising meetings, events, and activities to § 4.402(P)'s onerous restrictions. *Id.*

Gilbert amended the Code yet again in 2011, while the case was on appeal to the Ninth Circuit. App. 80-94. This amendment not only left intact all of the content-based restrictions Good News initially challenged, but expanded upon them by exchanging the ban on Qualifying Event Signs being placed in the right of way for a requirement that they relate to events in Gilbert. App. 89. The "Gilbert-events-only" requirement only applies to Qualifying Event Signs. Thus, a church cannot place signs in rights-of-way advertising events occurring outside of Gilbert, but political and ideological signs that do not relate to Gilbert events may be placed freely within rights-of-way. App. 31-32. Gilbert conceded, for example, that Political Signs have no in-town "situs," Defs.' Ans. Br. 31, 9th Cir. Case No. 11-15588, Doc. 13, yet they are liberally permitted in rights-of-way.

Further, it is plain that Gilbert again targeted Good News with the Gilbert-events-only limitation. The Church had moved its services (several years before) a few blocks across the Gilbert border to a school located in Chandler, Arizona. Pet. App. 87a n.1. Thus, even though Gilbert removed the bar on 16 placing Qualifying Event Signs in rights-of-way, the Gilbert-events-only limitation prohibited Good News from placing *any* signs there. *Id.* at 20a (finding that the Gilbert-events-only requirement "bars Good News from erecting any [church] signs at all.").3 This bar lasted from the time the 2011 amendment took effect until the Church's November 2013 move back to Gilbert. App. 89. Although the church currently meets in temporary facilities in Gilbert, there is a strong likelihood in the near future that it will move its meeting location just across Gilbert's border and be barred once again from placing signs in Gilbert.[4]

Comment: This statement of facts shows how visual aids can be used effectively to explain a complicated ordinance. If the brief writer had simply listed the sizes, it would be easy for the reader's eyes to just skim over the numbers. The charts, however, are hard to miss and grab the attention.

---

4. Brief for Petitioners at 7–16, Reed v. Town of Gilbert, 135 S. Ct. 2218 (2015) (No. 13–502), 2014 WL 4631957, at *7–16 (footnotes omitted).

National Institute for Trial Advocacy

C.2 Procedural History after Statement of Facts

1. The adoption proceeding was tried before a South Carolina family court in September 2011, at which point Baby Girl had been living with her Adoptive Parents for two years. Pet. App. 10a. The child's guardian *ad litem* recommended that the adoption be approved in the best interests of the child. JA 132. Mother urged the court to finalize the adoption. Trial Tr. 258.

The family court applied ICWA [Indian Child Welfare Act], denied the adoption petition, and ordered that custody of Baby Girl be transferred to Father. Pet. App. 130a. The court acknowledged that application of state law would have led to the approval of the adoption and the termination of Father's parental rights. *Id.* 120a-121a. The family court ordered Adoptive Parents to surrender their daughter to Father on December 28, 2011. *Id.* 130a. Days after Christmas, and after living as a family for twenty-seven months, Adoptive Parents handed Baby Girl over to Father. *Id.* 11a.

2. A divided panel of the South Carolina Supreme Court affirmed. *Id.* 1a-40a.

The majority held that Father was a "parent" under Section 1903(9) who could invoke the Act's substantive provisions. *Id.* 22a. The majority acknowledged that "[u]nder state law, Father's consent to the adoption would not have been required." *Id.* 21a-22a n.19. The court held that the biological father's "lack of interest in or support for Baby Girl during the pregnancy and first four months of her life as a basis for terminat[ing] his rights as a parent is not a valid consideration under the ICWA." *Id.* 32a n.26.

The majority also rejected the "existing Indian family doctrine," which some state courts have held prevents ICWA from interfering with the voluntary adoption of an Indian child born out of wedlock under the sole custody of a non-Indian parent. *Id.* 17a-18a n.17. The majority further held that Adoptive Parents did not satisfy the Act's requirement to show that "active efforts have been made to provide [to Father] remedial services and rehabilitative programs designed to prevent the breakup of the Indian family and that these efforts have provided unsuccessful," 25 U.S.C. § 1912(d). Pet. App. 26a-27a. The court explained that Adoptive Parents could have taken measures "for example, by attempting to stimulate Father's desire to be a parent or to provide necessary education regarding the role of a parent." *Id.* 26a.

The majority further held that the adoption could not proceed consistent with Section 1912(f)'s requirement to show that Father's "continued custody" would be seriously detrimental to Baby Girl. The court reasoned that Adoptive Parents had not shown that Father's "prospective legal and physical custody" would seriously damage the child. *Id.* 28a-33a. The court finally observed that placement with Adoptive Parents, who are not Indian, did not comport with ICWA's "hierarchy of preferences" for adoptive placement with the child's extended family, the child's Tribe, or other Indian families absent good cause. *Id.* 37a-39a.

Two justices dissented and would have "require[d] the immediate return of Baby Girl to [Adoptive Parents]." *Id.* 100a. [5]

Comments: An excellent summary of a complicated area of the law. Notice the use of descriptors—Father, Mother, Baby Girl—rather than the terms petitioner and respondent. The brief also contains a good description of the state supreme court's holding. Because this is the Adoptive Couple's brief, who were petitioners in the case, it would have been nice if they had included some of the reasoning of the dissenting justices.

---

3. In 2010, Mr. Yates was indicted for violating 18 U.S.C. § 2232(a), by throwing undersized fish overboard to prevent the government from taking the fish into its custody, and with violating 18 U.S.C. § 1001(a)(2), by falsely stating to federal agents that all the undersized fish the officer measured at sea were aboard the *Miss Katie* at dock. JA 6-8. Additionally, he was charged with violating the anti-shredding provision of the Sarbanes-Oxley Act, 18 U.S.C. § 1519, by destroying, concealing, and covering up "undersized fish with the intent to impede, obstruct, and influence the investigation and proper administration of the catching of red grouper under the legal minimum size limit." JA 7.

During his jury trial, Mr. Yates moved for a judgment of acquittal at the conclusion of the government's case-in-chief and of all evidence. He argued that when "tangible object" is read in the context of § 1519, the phrase means things akin to records and documents, in which "notations" can be made, such as "computer hard drives, logbooks, [and] things of that nature." JA 90-92.

The district court initially questioned whether fish fell within the meaning of "tangible object" for purposes of § 1519. Referencing the canon of statutory construction that a series of words must be inter-

---

5. Brief for Petitioner at 12–14, Adoptive Couple v. Baby Girl, 133 S. Ct. 2552 (2013) (No. 12–399), http://sblog.s3.amazonaws.com/wp-content/uploads/2013/02/12-399-pet-brief.pdf (last visited Mar. 20, 2017).

preted consistently, the court stated, "So if you're talking about documents, and records, tangible objects are tangible objects in the nature of a document or a record, as opposed to a fish." JA 93. The court expounded, "if you look at the title for at least a clue as to what congress meant, it talks about destruction, alteration, or falsification of records in federal investigations. It might be a stretch to say throwing away a fish is a falsification of a record." JA 95.

After taking the matter under advisement, the district court entered a written order that did not mention these concerns. Instead, the court denied the motion, relying on "the nature of the matters within the jurisdiction of the government agency involved in this case, and the broad language of § 1519," to conclude that "a reasonable jury could determine that a person who throws or causes to be thrown fish overboard in the circumstances of this case is in violation of § 1519." JA 116-17.

The jury acquitted Mr. Yates on the false-statement count, but convicted him on the other two counts. JA 6-8, 118-19. The district court sentenced Mr. Yates to 30 days' imprisonment, to be followed by three years' supervised release. JA 119-20.

4. The Eleventh Circuit Court of Appeals affirmed Mr. Yates's conviction for violating § 1519. JA 134. The appellate court began by quoting case law stating that the plain meaning of a statute controls and that undefined words are given their ordinary or natural meaning. JA 132. "In keeping with those principles," the court summarily concluded, "'tangible object,' as § 1519 uses that term, unambiguously applies to fish." JA 132 (citing Black's Law Dictionary 1592 (9th ed. 2009) (defining "tangible" as "[h]aving or possessing physical form")). The court added, "Because the statute is unambiguous, we also conclude the rule of lenity does not apply here." JA 132.[6]

Comments: Even without reading the factual statement, you can grasp the nature of the dispute in the case, despite the complex statutory scheme involved. Notice the use of case quotes that support Mr. Yates's position before the Supreme Court.

Plaintiffs, respondents here, represent a majority of the States in the Union. This lawsuit alleges that DAPA violates the Administrative Procedure Act, 5 U.S.C. §§ 553, 706 (APA), and the Constitution's Take Care Clause, art. II, § 3. J.A. 34-37. Plaintiffs moved for a pre-

---

6. Brief of Petitioner at 6–7, Yates v. United States, 135 S. Ct. 1074 (2015) (No. 13–7451), 2014 WL 2965254, at *6–7.

liminary injunction, R.137-82, and submitted over 1,000 pages of evidence including numerous declarations, R.1247-2307. After a hearing, R.5120-257, the district court issued a detailed opinion preliminarily enjoining DAPA, Pet. App. 244a- 406a. Defendants appealed and moved for a stay pending appeal, which the district court denied. Texas v. United States, No. 1:14-cv-00254, 2015 WL 1540022, at *8 (S.D. Tex. Apr. 7, 2015). The Fifth Circuit denied defendants' stay motion in a lengthy opinion, after over two hours of oral argument. Pet. App. 156a-210a. Judge Higginson dissented. Pet. App. 211a-43a. Defendants did not file a stay application in this Court.

After regular briefing, two rounds of supplemental briefing, and two more hours of oral argument, the Fifth Circuit affirmed the district court's preliminary injunction of DAPA. Pet. App. 1a-90a. The court held that plaintiffs have standing, Pet. App. 20a-36a, and DAPA is reviewable, Pet. App. 36a-53a. On the merits, the court found DAPA unlawful both procedurally (as promulgated without notice and comment) and substantively (as foreclosed by immigration statutes). Pet. App. 53a-86a. The court further agreed that plaintiffs satisfied the equitable requirements for a preliminary injunction. Pet. App. 86a-90a. Judge King dissented. Pet. App. 91a-155a. The Fifth Circuit also allowed three prospective DAPA applicants, proceeding under pseudonyms, to intervene. J.A. 5.[7]

Comment: This brief procedural history concisely tells the history of the case. Given that the plaintiffs were respondents and the defendants petitioners, it would have been better to just use the terms "States" and "United States" or "federal government." The procedural history could have also elaborated on the substance of the district court's order.

On automatic appeal to the Supreme Court of Florida, *see* Fla. Stat. § 921.141(4), Hurst challenged his sentence on several grounds. Among other things, Hurst argued that, in light of *Ring v. Arizona*, 536 U.S. 584 (2002), "constitutional error occurred in his case because the advisory jury in the penalty phase was not required to find specific facts as to the aggravating factors, and [because] the jury was not required to make a unanimous recommendation as to the sentence." JA307.

The Florida Supreme Court rejected Hurst's arguments and affirmed the death sentence. The court observed that, before *Ring*, this Court had upheld Florida's capital sentencing scheme in *Hildwin v. Florida*

---

7. Brief for the State Respondents at 13–14, United States v. Texas, 136 S. Ct. 2271 (2016) (No. 15–674), 2016 WL 1213267, at *13–14.

on the ground that "'[t]he Sixth Amendment does not require that the specific findings authorizing the imposition of the sentence of death be made by the jury.'" JA309 (quoting 490 U.S. 638, 640-641 (1989)). Florida courts had subsequently held that "*Ring* does not require the jury to make specific findings of the aggravators or to make a unanimous jury recommendation as to sentence." JA307. The Florida Supreme Court "decline[d] to revisit those decisions in [Hurst's] case." JA308. The court concluded that *Hildwin* remains good law because this Court "has never expressly overruled" it and because "Florida's sentencing procedures do provide for jury input about the existence of aggravating factors prior to sentencing—a process that was completely lacking in the Arizona statute struck down in Ring." JA309-310.

Justice Pariente dissented on the ground that "there was no unanimous jury finding of either of the two aggravating circumstances found by the trial judge." JA314. Justice Pariente observed that a defendant convicted of first-degree murder is not eligible for a death sentence in Florida unless additional findings of fact are made regarding aggravators and mitigators. JA316. And under *Ring*, all facts necessary for imposition of a sentence must be found by a jury. JA316-317. In Hurst's case, however, "the jury recommended death by the slimmest margin permitted under Florida law—a bare majority seven-to-five vote," and it was "actually possible that there was not even a majority of jurors who agreed that the same aggravator applied." JA315. In Justice Pariente's view, that outcome contravened *Ring, id.*, and raised "possible Eighth Amendment implications" in light of "Florida's outlier status" as the only State that does not require a unanimous jury finding of an aggravating circumstance before a death sentence may be imposed, JA319-320.[8]

Comment: This excerpt, from the petitioner's brief, does a nice job explaining the dissenting justice's opinion. But, there are several quotations from opinions or arguments raised by the petitioner that would be better (and clearer) if they were summarized.

---

8. Brief for Petitioner at 12–14, Hurst v. Florida, 136 S. Ct. 616 (2016) (No. 14–7505), 2015 WL 3523406, at *12–14 (footnotes omitted).

APPENDIX D

THE BRIEF: SUMMARY OF THE ARGUMENT

D.1 More Examples of Summaries of Arguments

Evaluate the following summaries of argument. They are not necessarily model summaries—some are good, some are rather pedestrian—but they do represent the summaries judges read in briefs today. Examine them through the judge's eyes and see if you can catch the "flavor" of the cases.

Check to see if the orientation sentence or paragraph is adequate. Does the opening qualify as a dominant argument of maximum potency? Does it describe the equitable heart of the contention? Does it give the theme of the argument? Do the various statements or points support the contention? Do they furnish the issues the court must confront? Do they have enough punch to convince? Should they have been shortened? Expanded? Did the summary present a neat balance between the questions presented and a synopsis of the argument to come?

Summaries from Opposing Briefs

Appellant:

Smith submits that the trial court erred in two respects. First, the Trial Court concluded that the mere fact that the filing used the unregistered trade name in and of itself rendered the Smith UCC-1 "seriously misleading" without regard to whether a reasonable searcher searching under the correct name would have found the UCC-1 filed by appellant. Second, the Trial Court gave undue emphasis to the fact that the UCC search under the correct name failed to disclose the Smith UCC-1 without determining whether a reasonable searcher searching under the correct name would have found the Smith UCC-1.

Smith submits that the court must disregard the fact that a governmental employee conducted the search. Instead, the test is whether a reasonable searcher searching under the debtor's name would have come upon the index card for the Smith UCC-1 and been prompted by the information on it to inquire further.

Under the uncontroverted facts here, Smith submits that the hypothetical searcher would have come upon the UCC-1 filed by it. Furthermore, the following information on that card would have prompted further inquiry: the ethnicity of the name "Stebow," the use of the same address as for the debtor and the signature of one of debtor's officers.

Smith further submits that the outcome of a search conducted through the New Jersey Secretary of State's office is not relevant to the inquiry as a matter of law and is further flawed because it is the product of a procedure that is contrary to state law.

Appellee:

The Trustee is vested with the right to avoid the lien asserted by Smith under the provisions of the Bankruptcy Code, 11 U.S.C. § 544(a), which provides that a trustee in bankruptcy is vested with the status and powers of a lien creditor who extends credit to a debtor at the commencement of a case and at such time receives in exchange a judicial lien to secure the loan whether or not such creditor exists. A trustee with this lien creditor status may avoid an unperfected interest. 11 U.S.C. § 544(b).

Smith had to perfect its lien on assets described in the UCC-1 Financing Statement with the Secretary of State of New Jersey, in compliance with N.J.S.A. §§ 12A:9-401(1), 12A:9-402, 12A: 403(1) (4), 12A:9-407, whereby the name of the debtor must be stated, with allowance for a minor error which is not seriously misleading. N.J.S.A. § 12A:9-402(5) (in effect in 1980, the subsection was changed in 1981 by the renumbering of subparagraph (5) to (8)). The trial court properly found that the error by Smith in naming the debtor in the UCC-1 to be Stebow Excavating Co., Inc., was not a minor error and was seriously misleading, whereby the lien was avoided as against the Trustee.

The trial Court's determination, which was affirmed by the District Court, was correct in refusing to attach any weight or effect to Smith's attack upon the procedure followed by the Secretary of State of New Jersey in responding to a request for search of a particular lien debtor. The filing of the financing statement or security agreement by the filing clerk after "indexing" on a card the pertinent information of the names of the parties, which financing instrument was available for inspection by the parties or creditors, was proper. The search was not extended by the employee of the State Department beyond the name of the debtor for whom a search was requested.

Comment: The first summary is wordy in using "Smith submits" three times. It lacks a theme, and it takes a bit of reading to understand what is happening. The second summary provides more detail, but the citations are distracting.

Miscellaneous Summaries

Alabama Code § 8-1-1 (a) expresses the public policy of the State of Alabama that contracts in restraint of trade are disfavored. Paragraph 11 of the employment agreement is a total restraint of trade as to the employee. The district court, in reaching this determination as to paragraph 11 followed its previous decision in *Hudson v. Nationwide*, CV-86-AR-1375-M. The facts of the case at bar are identical to the *Hudson* case and the language of the employment agreement is exactly the same.

Alabama case law holds that an employment contract which creates a total restraint of trade is void. Paragraph 11 of the employment agreement totally restrains Cornutt from selling insurance within a twenty-five-mile radius of his office in Gadsden, Alabama.

It is clear that the district court followed Alabama law in this case by following both prior Alabama decisions and its previous decision in the *Hudson* case.

Comment: This summary makes it clear what the issue in the case is, but the three paragraphs are repetitive. The information in the second paragraph regarding the substance of the restraint could be moved to the first paragraph and the remainder of the summary deleted.

This is an individual sex discrimination action under Title IX in which a District Court has made findings of fact based on the evidence presented at trial. The most significant of those findings are as follows:

> Plaintiff was dismissed from her high school's National Honor Society solely because the Faculty Council members sincerely believed that Plaintiff's conduct of engaging in premarital sex was inconsistent with the honorary society's standards of leadership and character and *not* because of Plaintiff's gender or pregnancy;

> Plaintiff failed to prove she was treated differently than any male NHS member who engaged in premarital sex;

> Even if Plaintiff had met her burden of proof on the question of liability, she was not entitled to relief.

None of these findings was clearly erroneous. To the contrary, they were supported by the overwhelming weight of the evidence.

Plaintiff uses various contrived theories in an effort to divert attention from the trial court's findings that she failed to prove unlawful discrimination and that she would not be entitled to relief even if she had proved her case. Plaintiff ignores and mischaracterizes the District Court's dispositive findings of fact, distorts the record and the applicable legal standards and invokes various constitutional arguments which have no application to this case.

These attempts must fail. In this appeal after trial on the merits, the Court of Appeals is bound to apply the clearly erroneous standard of review. Under that standard, the District Court's determination in Defendants' favor should be affirmed.

Comment: The final paragraph sets out the important standard that should be applied on appeal. That paragraph should be moved to the start of the summary.

This appeal presents the straightforward issue of whether the district court properly exercised its discretion by staying this case. It did. The stay order avoided the fundamental unfairness of forcing the Trust to choose between violating orders of the New York courts or having a default judgment entered against it in this case. It also fostered judicial efficiency and economy by allowing the district court and the parties to avoid the considerable time and expense of a trial while a class action, the settlement of which calls for the dismissal of the case below in favor of alternative dispute resolution, was proceeding in New York.

In their brief, the appellants attempt to divert the Court's focus from the discretion of the district court to various issues raised in the class action. In effect, appellants seek to appeal to this court issues which are appealable exclusively to the Second Circuit. Those issues are not properly before the court. Moreover, even were they somehow relevant to this appeal, the stay order still must be affirmed because appellants' arguments are without merit, as discussed below and in the New York court's exhaustive opinion certifying the class action and approving the settlement.

Comment: This summary is concise and has a nice, clear beginning, which sets out the standard for the appellate court to apply.

In the Copyright Act of 1976, Congress did not intend to grant a century of monopoly protection to cheerleader-uniform designs—or any garment designs for that matter. Quite the opposite, Congress first proposed and then deliberately excluded industrial-design protection in the Act, and it has declined every invitation to extend copyright protection to garment design, even for a period as short as three years.

When determining whether a design feature of a useful article like a garment can be copyrighted, courts must apply the separability analysis set forth in § 101 of the Copyright Act. At its most basic, that framework requires a court to identify all of the article's inherent, essential, or natural functions, then determine whether a design feature (1) can be recognized as a unit by itself, apart from the article's utilitarian aspects (the identified-separately requirement), and (2) can exist side by side with the useful article with both perceived as fully realized, separate works (the exist-independently requirement).

In a close case, a court should decline to provide copyright protection to a useful article's design features. This is consistent with Congress's choice not to extend the copyright monopoly to industrial design and protects the public interest.

But this is not a close case. The features of a cheerleader uniform do not satisfy the identified-separately requirement or the exist-independently requirement. Unsurprisingly, faithful application of the statutory test demonstrates that Varsity does not have a century-long copyright monopoly that prevents Star Athletica from competing in the cheerleader-uniform market.[1]

Comment: This summary does a nice job explaining a difficult issue in an interesting manner.

Enacted in the wake of the Enron document-shredding scandal, the anti-shredding provision of the Sarbanes-Oxley Act of 2002, 18 U.S.C. § 1519, criminalizes the destruction of "any record, document, or *tangible object*." For purposes of this provision, "tangible object" means a thing used to preserve information, such as a computer, server, or similar storage device.

This construction follows from this Court's precedents, which dictate that an undefined statutory phrase – such as "tangible object" here – be ascribed its ordinary or natural meaning in everyday usage. The ordinary or natural meaning of "tangible object" necessarily depends on the context in which the phrase is used. Indeed, the dictionary definitions of "tangible" and "object" are so general that the

---

1. Brief for the Petitioner at 22, Star Athletica, L.L.C. v. Varsity Brands, Inc., No. 15–866 (U.S. Jan. 7, 2016), 2016 WL 3923923, at *22.

phrase "tangible object" is chameleon-like, meaning different things in different contexts.

To ascertain the meaning of the phrase "tangible object" as used in § 1519, then, the phrase must be read in the context of its surrounding terms, "record" and "document." Those terms share a common meaning in everyday usage having to do with preserving information. It follows from the application of the canons *noscitur a sociis* and *ejusdem generis* that "tangible object" shares this common meaning. Aligned with the terms "record" and "document," "tangible object" is thus naturally read as meaning a thing used to preserve information, such as a computer, server, or similar storage device. This is also the most natural grammatical reading of "tangible object" when the phrase is read in conjunction with the immediately preceding series of parallel transitive verbs, most notably, "makes a false entry in."

Moreover, this common-sense and contextual interpretation of "tangible object" is bolstered by its placement in the larger context of the Sarbanes-Oxley Act, and by Congress's tacit approval of the United States Sentencing Commission's construction of the phrase "records, documents, or tangible objects," as meaning those things that preserve or store information. Further, the contextual interpretation of "tangible object" avoids absurd results and constitutional concerns that follow from a non-contextual construction. Finally, if after examining "tangible object" in the context of the statute and the statutory scheme any lingering doubt remains, this criminal statute's meaning must be resolved in Mr. Yates's favor.[2]

Comment: This is a concise summary on a complex topic. It could have been strengthened in paragraph 3 by contrasting storage devices with fish, the item Mr. Yates was charged with "shredding."

---

1. Florida's capital sentencing framework is fully consistent with *Ring v. Arizona*, 536 U.S. 584 (2002). *Ring* set forth a narrow and specific rule: other than the existence of a prior conviction, capital defendants are entitled to a jury determination of "any fact on which the legislature conditions an increase in their maximum punishment," including the existence of an aggravating circumstance. *Id.* at 589, 609. Florida's system, which divides sentencing responsibility between judge and jury, leaves the ultimate decision with the judge, but still

---

2. Brief of Petitioner at 8–9, Yates v. United States, 135 S. Ct. 1074 (2015) (No. 13–7451), 2014 WL 2965254, at *8–9.

provides for a jury determination of whether there is at least one aggravating circumstance—meaning the jury decides whether there are sufficient facts making the defendant eligible for the death penalty. *Ring* requires nothing more. *Ring* says nothing about who may decide whether a defendant eligible for the death penalty will actually receive the death penalty.

Once jury findings (or admissions) demonstrate at least one aggravating circumstance, the defendant is eligible for the death penalty. At that point, any additional court findings do not enhance the maximum penalty the defendant may receive, so they do not implicate *Ring*. The Court has long affirmed judges' broad sentencing discretion to impose sentences within the authorized range, even when judicial factfinding informs that discretion. By requiring the jury and the judge to find at least one aggravating circumstance (as opposed to the jury alone), Florida's hybrid system only provides additional protections. Additional protections do not violate *Ring*.

Nor does leaving the ultimate sentencing decision with the judge *violate* Ring. The Court has consistently recognized that the Constitution does not require jury sentencing. Even if jury sentencing were properly before the Court (this argument was neither presented in Hurst's certiorari petition nor preserved below), this Court should not overturn settled precedent upholding the hybrid judge-jury systems of Florida and other states.

2. Hurst conceded the presence of aggravating factors, and a jury found beyond a reasonable doubt that Hurst was eligible for the death penalty. Therefore, whatever one thinks of Hurst's challenges to Florida's system in the abstract (or in other scenarios), the sentence in Hurst's case is constitutional.

Hurst's concessions remove his case from *Ring's* scope, and Hurst's remaining challenges fail irrespective of *Ring*. The jury instructions (to which Hurst did not object) did not mislead; they accurately described the jury's role. And Hurst's jury unanimity argument fails because the Court has already recognized that jury unanimity does not "materially contribute" to the essential role of the jury, which is to interpose the commonsense judgment of a body of laymen between the accused and the accuser. In the specific context of Florida's capital sentencing, where the jury is a "cosentencer" with the judge, the jury fulfills that essential role.

Hurst received all that *Ring* requires. Florida's death sentencing scheme does not violate the Constitution in light of *Ring.*[3]

Comment: Another concise and effective summary with minimal citations. Notice the two different arguments—first that the challenged procedure is consistent with Supreme Court precedent, and second, that the Supreme Court precedent does not apply.

D.2   More Examples of Introductions

In 20 U.S.C. § 1415(*l*), Congress struck a balance between the Individuals with Disabilities Education Act (IDEA), 20 U.S.C. § 1400 *et seq.*, and other laws that protect the rights of children with disabilities. In the provision's first half, Congress established that the IDEA does not "limit" plaintiffs' substantive rights under any other laws; parents may protect their children using the full panoply of "rights, procedures, and remedies" that the Constitution, the Rehabilitation Act of 1973, 29 U.S.C. § 701 *et seq.*, and the Americans with Disabilities Act of 1990 (ADA), 42 U.S.C. § 12101 *et seq.*, afford. 20 U.S.C. § 1415(*l*). But Congress did not stop there. The second half of the provision imposes one important limitation: If parents wish to use these other laws to "seek[] relief that is also available under [the IDEA]," they must first attempt to obtain that relief through the IDEA's procedures. *Id.*

This case presents the question whether plaintiffs who seek relief that is in *substance* available under the IDEA can sidestep that limitation merely by demanding that relief in a *form* the IDEA does not provide. The answer is no. The statute's text is concerned with the actual "redress or benefit" a plaintiff seeks, not the form in which it is pled. Black's Law Dictionary 1317 (8th ed. 2004) (defining "relief"). In other cases where it has had to characterize the relief sought in a complaint, the Court has time and again looked to the substance rather than the form of the relief demanded to determine "on which side of the line a particular case falls." *Papasan v. Allain,* 478 U.S. 265, 278-279 (1986). Any other interpretation of section 1415(*l*) would render it a formalistic shell—inviting litigants to opt out of exhaustion simply by incanting the right legal formulation.

Under this straightforward application of the statute's terms, petitioners' complaint was properly dismissed for failure to exhaust. That complaint asks for monetary relief that could be obtained under the IDEA by replacing the word "damages" with the label "retroactive

---

3. Brief for Respondent at 12–14, Hurst v. Florida, 136 S. Ct. 616 (2016) (No. 14–7505), 2015 WL 4607695, at *12–14.

reimbursement" or "payment for compensatory education." And it asks for a declaratory judgment that would effectively determine that a particular accommodation should have been included in an Individualized Educational Program—the *core* type of relief that the IDEA is designed to provide. If section 1415(*l*) is more than just a rule of pleading etiquette, these claims seek "relief" the *3 IDEA makes "available," and petitioners are required to exhaust the IDEA's remedies before bringing them to court.[4]

Comment: This introduction explains the nature of the case without being overly argumentative. It would read easier if the citations were omitted and only included in the argument section.

Respondents Varsity Brands, Inc., and its affiliates sued Petitioner Star Athletica, L.L.C., for allegedly copying Varsity's cheerleader uniforms. A useful article—such as a chair, a dress, or a uniform—cannot be copyrighted. The Court granted the petition to determine when a useful article's design *features* are sufficiently separate from the article to warrant copyright protection.

As the Copyright Office has explained, "the copyright law is reasonably clear. Garments are useful articles, and *the designs of such garments are generally outside of the copyright law.* Parties who wish to modify this position must address their concerns to the Congress." Registrability of Costume Designs, 56 Fed. Reg. 56,530, 56,532 (Nov. 5, 1991) (emphasis added). Numerous commercial interests have attempted to do exactly that. But Congress has persistently declined all requests to extend the copyright laws to garment design. The most recent attempt, in 2012, would have granted such protection, but for only three years.

Varsity now asks this Court to ordain by judicial edict what these commercial interests have been unable to obtain from Congress— except the copyright protection Varsity seeks will last not three years, but for a century. Such a ruling would be a boon to companies like Varsity, who already hold a monopoly on their garment-market segment. But it would be deleterious to the public, which depends on the Copyright Act's exclusion of industrial design to keep useful articles like garments in the public domain. The Court should reverse the

---

4. Brief for Respondents at 1–3, Fry v. Napoleon Community Schools, No. 15–497 (U.S. Oct. 19, 2015), 2016 WL 5667526, at *1–3.

court of appeals and reinstate judgment as a matter of law for petitioner Star Athletica.[5]

Comment: Again, a persuasive framing of the case to introduce the parties and the controversy.

In 1879, Justice Field confronted a San Francisco ordinance requiring that the hair of inmates in the county jail be cut to a "uniform length of one inch from the scalp." *Ho Ah Kow v. Nunan*, 12 F. Cas. 252, 253 (Field, Circuit Justice, C.C.D. Cal. 1879). The ordinance burdened the "religious faith of the Chinese" because it required the queue—a long braid of hair—to be cut off. *Ibid.* Justice Field, writing for the court, held that the ordinance violated the Equal Protection Clause, because it "act[ed] with special severity upon Chinese prisoners, inflicting upon them suffering altogether disproportionate to what would be endured by other prisoners." *Id.* at 255. Indeed, it was as if the city had mandated that "all prisoners confined in the county jail should be fed on pork," even if they were Jewish. *Id.* at 255. It made no difference that the ordinance was written in "general terms" or that the prison officials had raised unjustified concerns of health and discipline. *Ibid.* Requiring an inmate to contradict his deeply held religious beliefs was "unworthy" of the United States. *Id.* at 256.

This case comes 135 years later, but the claims and defenses are substantially the same. The difference is that this case is easier: Petitioner seeks relief under a federal civil rights statute specifically designed to protect the religious exercise of prisoners, 42 U.S.C. § 2000cc *et seq.* (2006) (RLUIPA), and under a precedent that requires robust and individualized application of strict scrutiny, *Gonzales v. O Centro Espirita Beneficente Uniao do Vegetal*, 546 U.S. 418 (2006).

The state-imposed burden on petitioner's religious practice of keeping a beard is incontrovertible. Respondents say they can allow no exceptions to the nobeard rule because of security concerns. But that defense is not tenable when forty-four other state and federal prison systems with the same security interests allow the beards that Arkansas forbids. The defense is also untenable because the evidence offered to support it is too weak to satisfy RLUIPA's compelling interest test or to merit any deference. Like the health and discipline interests raised by

---

5. Brief for the Petitioner at 6, Star Athletica, L.L.C. v. Varsity Brands, Inc., No. 15-866 (U.S. Jan. 7, 2016), 2016 WL 3923923, at *6.

National Institute for Trial Advocacy

the defendants in *Ho Ah Kow*, these are post-hoc rationalizations for bureaucratic stubbornness, or worse.

In *Ho Ah Kow*, Justice Field believed that the ordinance was motivated by open hostility to the Chinese. Respondents' refusal to extend a religious exception to petitioner is almost as troubling because it indicates hostile indifference to the faiths of religious minorities. Just as San Francisco should not have knowingly inflicted on Ho Ah Kow "suffering altogether disproportionate to what would be endured by other prisoners" by cutting off his queue, *Ho Ah Kow*, 12 F. Cas. at 255, Arkansas should not knowingly inflict similarly disproportionate suffering on petitioner by prohibiting his religiously mandated beard.[6]

Comment: The comparison to the *Ho Ah Kow* case effectively sets the stage for the petitioners to argue the religious burden present in this case. It is persuasive, but not argumentative.

When Petitioner Dennys Rodriguez was pulled over on a Nebraska highway for momentarily driving on the shoulder of the road, he became one of more than seventeen million people "seized" each year for a traffic violation. Fourth Amendment seizures must be justified at their inception and limited in scope to the circumstances that warranted the intrusion in the first place. But the decision below proposes an exception to these principles for routine traffic stops. Under this exception, an officer who has stopped a driver for a minor traffic infraction may, without additional justification, continue to hold the driver for a "*de minimis*" amount of time after the stop is over based solely on the generalized possibility that the detention may lead to the discovery of contraband.

This Court should reject the "*de minimis*" exception because it authorizes a detention without individualized suspicion—an irreducible component of Fourth Amendment "reasonableness" whenever law enforcement pursues its general interest in crime control. In its place, this Court should recognize a bright-line rule that a traffic stop concludes when the tasks related to the reason for the stop are complete. Any further detention, however brief, is unconstitutional in the absence of individualized suspicion.[7]

---

6. Brief for the Petitioner at 3–5, Holt v. Hobbs, 135 S. Ct. 853 (2015) (No. 13–6827), 2014 WL 2200467, at *3–5.

7. Brief for Petitioner at 1–2, Rodriguez v. United States, 135 S. Ct. 1609 (2015) (No. 13–9972), 2014 WL 6466938, at *1–2 (footnote omitted).

Comment: The first paragraph does a nice job explaining the nature of the case, but the second paragraph seems more suited for a summary of the argument.

The Executive Branch unilaterally created a program—known as DAPA—that contravenes Congress's complex statutory framework for determining when an alien may lawfully enter, remain in, and work in the country. DAPA would deem over four million unlawfully present aliens as "lawfully present" and eligible for work authorization. Pet. App. 413a. And "lawful presence" is an immigration classification established by Congress that is necessary for valuable benefits, such as Medicare and Social Security.

The Executive does not dispute that DAPA would be one of the largest changes in immigration policy in our Nation's history. The President himself described DAPA as "an action to change the law." Pet. App. 384a. Yet the Executive claims it may effect this change without even conventional notice-and-comment procedure.

Far from interfering with the Executive's removal discretion, the preliminary injunction of DAPA does not require the Executive to remove any alien. And this lawsuit has never challenged the Executive's separate memorandum establishing three categories of aliens prioritized for removal. Pet. App. 420a-29a. This case is about an unprecedented, sweeping assertion of Executive power.

This case is not about the wisdom of particular immigration policies; legislators have disagreed on whether immigration statutes should be amended. But when Congress has established certain conduct as unlawful, the separation of powers does not permit the Executive to unilaterally declare that conduct lawful.[8]

Comment: Although this introduction may be considered by some to be too argumentative, separation of powers cases tend to present thorny issues. Here, the states challenging DAPA try to clarify, and in a sense narrow, the scope of their challenge in the introduction.

---

8. Brief for the State Respondents at 1, United States v. Texas, 136 S. Ct. 2271 (2016) (No. 15–674), 2016 WL 1213267, at *1.

TABLE OF AUTHORITIES

References are to chapters and footnotes.

Table of Authorities

National Institute for Trial Advocacy

D

E

F

H

I–J

National Institute for Trial Advocacy

M

N

National Institute for Trial Advocacy

O

P

Q–R

T

U–V

National Institute for Trial Advocacy

W–Z

INDEX

National Institute for Trial Advocacy

National Institute for Trial Advocacy